BEGINNING AT MOSES

A Guide to Finding Christ in the Old Testament

MICHAEL P. V. BARRETT

AMBASSADOR-EMERALD INTERNATIONAL
GREENVILLE, SOUTH CAROLINA • BELFAST, NORTHERN IRELAND

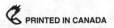 PRINTED IN CANADA

To my family—from the oldest to the youngest
And specially to Sandra Ann
Next to Christ, the best thing I've ever found

TABLE OF CONTENTS

FORWARD

"Did not our heart burn within us, while he talked with us by the way, and while he opened to us the scriptures?" These words, sadly, depict an adventure rarely experienced by Christians today. When Cleopas and his companion began their seven-mile journey from Jerusalem to Emmaus, they hardly seemed to be likely candidates for a life-changing encounter with the risen Messiah. Their journey, at the beginning, must have been drudgery. Their faith, that just a week before had seemed so vibrant, had become a confusing amalgamation of crushed hopes and nagging fears. They had heard that Jesus had instructed the Twelve that He would be killed and that He would rise again on the third day; they had heard that an angel had testified at His open sepulchre that He was alive, and they had verified that the tomb was empty; but none of this seemed real to them. In fact, so oppressive were their doubts and so sluggish their faith that they began their journey home on the very day of their Messiah's promised resurrection. It is no wonder that the Stranger, after hearing their mournful account of the evidence they had ignored, said, "O fools, and slow of heart to believe all that the prophets have spoken."

With these words, our Lord at once exposed a deep-seated problem and revealed a compelling need. The problem was dullness of heart; the need was for a Christ-centered study of the Old Testament Scriptures. Our Lord solved the problem and satisfied the need for the two Emmaus disciples by leading them step by step through the Scriptures and "expounding unto them…the things concerning himself."

In *Beginning at Moses*, Mike Barrett reverently follows the example of his Lord. He leads us back down the road to Emmaus and into the company of the Master, and reveals to us the sacred cord that lies at the heart of the Old Testament. In his formative years as a student of the Word, Mike discovered, as did the disciples of Emmaus, that "to see Christ is the key to unlocking the message of Scripture, including the Old Testament" (p. 14). Eventually, that truth so dominated his life and inflamed his soul that he became an attraction to others who were seeking the Savior–so much so that the elective classes he teaches in Old Testament began to fill up as soon as the doors for registration were opened.

I know of no one who is more diligent, more careful, and–above all–more reverent as a student of the Word than Mike Barrett. To many, the curse of Babel still hangs heavily over the prospect of the study of ancient languages. To Mike, Hebrew and Greek, which he has taught for years, have become faithful servants in his search for the Incarnate Word on the pages of the Written Word. It is this rare combination of consecrated scholarship and passionate devotion that makes *Beginning at Moses* a unique book. It is, in my estimation, a must for anyone who is serious about Bible study–or better yet–for anyone who is serious about his devotion to Christ.

A wise man once observed that the best books are not the ones you can't put down when you read them. The best books are the ones that so arrest your thoughts that periodically you find yourself laying them aside and looking deeply into you soul. On this basis, *Beginning at Moses* qualifies as a "best book" for those who would be wise.

Thurman Wisdom, Dean
School of Religion
Bob Jones University

ACKNOWLEDGMENTS

At the beginning of this project, the Lord gave me a word of promise that became my daily prayer in the early hours of the morning, as I would begin work on this book before the other obligations of the day required my attention. Along with David, I prayed, "Forsake me not, O Lord: O my God, be not far from me. Make haste to help me, O Lord my salvation" (Psalm 38:21-22). I wrote this verse on a "post-it" card and moved it daily in my Franklin Planner. This book stands as witness to God's gracious hearing and answering prayer. I begin by expressing my thanks to the Lord for His gracious and constant faithfulness.

Under God, I owe much to others and to two men particularly who have influenced my life beyond measure. Dr. Robert D. Bell, Chairman of the Seminary and Division of Graduate Studies at Bob Jones University, was my principal Old Testament and Hebrew professor. I esteem him most highly in the Lord, regard him as my mentor, and have enjoyed the privilege of being his colleague and friend for many years. His scholarship and love of Scripture has been an example. He taught me many things, not the least of which is the importance of thinking. Dr. Alan Cairns has been my minister for almost twenty years. His Christ-centered ministry has helped to shape and focus my ministry in ways I cannot begin to enumerate. He has, by example, inspired me to keep the heart in my teaching and preaching. It has been a privilege and honor to serve under him.

Special acknowledgment goes to Dr. Cairns for his prodding me to write and for his invaluable suggestions in reading the initial draft. Although his comments were at times uncharacteristically caustic, his insight was keen and his comments were most helpful. In many places, he protected me from myself, for which we can all be thankful. I thank him as well for his recommendation to Emerald House that made publication a reality.

Many others have helped to bring this work to completion. I express my thanks to Dr. Robert Taylor, Dean of the College of Arts and Science at Bob Jones University, for his evaluating the readability of the first draft. He is a good friend with whom I have enjoyed times of fellowship, Bible Study, and prayer. He actually volunteered his services: a kind gesture from a mathematician. Dr. Caren Silvester, a member of the English faculty at Bob Jones University, deserves many thanks for her work in checking my grammar and style. The precision of her work was outstanding. She made an invaluable contribution to this work. Thanks, too, to her husband, Sid, also of the English faculty, who read portions of the manuscript and offered suggestions. Good editors are priceless. I'm glad Hebrew does not use commas. I also thank my daughter-in-law, Mrs. Sharmin Barrett, for her tedious work in checking the accuracy of quotations and Bible citations. Were it not for my well-behaved grandchildren that work could not have been done. Thanks to my wife, Sandra, for proofreading the final draft. I am indebted to all these.

I must offer Sandra my most honoring salute. I tried my best to be quiet every morning at 4:15, but was seldom successful. I don't think I ever left for the office without her being up when I left to give me encouragement for the day. I'm pretty sure she went back to bed, but at least she was up when I left. She was always the first to read the chapters as they were completed and never failed to say, "Good job, Michael." Whether that is true or not is beside the point. She has been a constant source of support, not just during this project, but for well over half of my life. Thanks Sandra.

INTRODUCTION

The tension between doctrine and experience is the stuff of Christian life. What we believe and know for a fact to be true doesn't match up sometimes with what is happening in our lives. In other words, objective truth seems to conflict with subjective experience. Although we affirm that God is good and great and that all things work together for good for those who love God, we quickly despair at the first hint of trouble. Why are these things happening? We boldly affirm our belief that God answers prayer, yet we wonder and doubt when the heaven seems to be brass and we do not perceive any answer. We experience countless occasions when something happens that tries our faith and raises some doubt whether what we believe is really true. More often than not our experience becomes more credible than our doctrine: this creates the tension in our hearts. This tension extends even to the Scripture, which is the source of everything we believe and the rule of everything we are to do. We believe that the Bible is God's Word. We believe that it is a living Word that is "powerful, and sharper than any twoedged sword" (Heb. 4:12). But notwithstanding that confession of faith, Christians far too frequently read the Bible and get nothing from it. Apart from a few familiar stories or a few favorite verses, the majority of the Bible, even for believers, seems to be irrelevant. Few know anything of David's experience when he confessed God's Word to be more desired than gold and sweeter than honey and the honeycomb (Psalm 19:10). It is my prayer that this work will find the key that unlocks the true meaning of all Scripture and creates true joy in the hearts of all who read God's Word, both the Old and the New Testaments.

The Problem

This disconnection from the Scripture is nowhere more evident than in the Old Testament. For various reasons, the Old Testament is a closed book for many Christians today. In theory (or better, according to doctrine) this ought not to be, but if we hope to solve the problem of the Old Testament's relevance, we first have to admit there is a problem. There is something about the Old Testament that corresponds to Peter's assessment of Paul's epistles: "in which are some things hard to be understood" (II Peter 3:16). From Genesis to Malachi, the reader encounters hard sayings, obscure details, unfamil-

1

iar and enigmatic expressions, forgotten customs, family trees with unpronounceable names, and detailed laws that have no immediately discernible application or relevance to modern life. Much of the Old Testament *seems to have no apparent value or purpose*. Who has ever read Exodus without wondering why Moses gave such extremely detailed instructions concerning the building of the tabernacle and the dress of the priests (Exodus 25-31) only to repeat the same details after the tabernacle was built and the priests clothed (Exodus 35-40)? Why should we bother slogging through all those details when we have neither tabernacle nor priesthood? That is a lot of hard reading without a lot of blessing. Who has ever read Numbers 7 with its twelvefold repetition of the same exact list of gifts brought by the twelve princes of the tribes of Israel for the dedication of the altar without wondering why Moses did not simply say once that they all brought the same thing? Why should we bother wading through those detailed lists when we have no altar now and most of us have no idea where to get, among other things, a "silver bowl of seventy shekels, after the shekel of the sanctuary"? That is a lot of hard reading without a lot of blessing. It seems to have no value for Christian living.

Other passages *seem to be outdated*, both theologically and culturally. Leviticus is a good example. On the one hand, Hebrews makes it unmistakably clear that there is no place for animal sacrifices after the once-for-all sacrifice of the Lord Jesus Christ, and it issues severe warnings to those who would return to the Old Testament ceremony. Yet the book of Leviticus goes on and on in its details of the proper methods of sacrificing animals. In light of the New Testament revelation, it would seem that Leviticus is something to be avoided rather than obeyed. To obey the strict regulations of the Levitical sacrifices would mark us religiously as a strange cult and culturally as an offense to animal rights advocates. In addition to the outmoded sacrifices, Leviticus is filled with detailed laws that belong to a culture long dead. Not marring the corners of beards (19:27) and not wearing garments of mixed material (19:19) hardly seem relevant to modern culture, where most men are clean shaven and manufactured fabrics are seldom of a single material. In short, Leviticus, too, is a lot of hard reading without a lot of blessing. Why bother?

These examples illustrate the problem. Whereas in theory Christians affirm belief in the Old Testament, in practice their frustrations with the Old Testament drive them to more familiar and more obviously devotional texts. Familiar and devotional texts are good. But when believers ignore much of the Old Testament–the majority of the Bible–they miss the blessing of finding precious nuggets of truth that are just as vital for modern Christians as they were for Old Testament believers. Indeed, that God's Word is compared to silver and hidden treasures suggests that the prize is not always lying on the surface. Part of the problem in most Bible study is that unless the message is on the surface, the average reader moves on in his reading, kicking up dust, until he finds an obvious surface lesson. Shuffling along does not typically result in discovered treasures; sometimes we have to dig. Proverbs 2 says that if we will seek truth as silver and search for it as if for hidden treasure, we will not be disappointed, for the Lord promises to give wisdom, knowledge and understanding. Even the digging becomes profitable and enjoyable when we realize we are handling the very Word of God–the Word without which we cannot survive. From Genesis to Malachi to Revelation, the Word of God reveals changeless and eternal truth. Let us keep our Bibles open and not give up until we discover the truth, because we know that God is the rewarder of those who diligently seek Him. The Lord promises that when we seek Him we will find Him if we seek Him with all our heart (Jeremiah 29:13). That is the truth.

The Answer

Faith is always the answer to the tension between doctrine and experience. II Timothy 3:16, 17 is perhaps the most direct statement concerning the doctrine of Scripture: "*All Scripture is given by inspiration of God and is profitable for doctrine, for reproof, for correction, for instruction in righteousness: that the man of God may be perfect, throughly furnished unto all good works.*" The Bible is unique: its every word was "breathed out" by the Holy Spirit. Although the mechanics of this divine, supernatural, miraculous work defy explanation, the result of the process is that we have the inspired, authoritative, infallible Word of God. The implications of the doctrine of inspiration are far-reaching and important, but the salient point for our discussion here is that what God "breathed out" He "breathed out" on purpose. The words that we have are the very words God wanted us to have. The history that we have is the very history God wanted us to have. The laws that we have are the very laws God wanted us to have. The gospel that we

3

have is the very gospel God wanted us to have. Everything is exactly what the all-wise and all-good God wanted us to have. He gave every word on purpose, and Paul tells us that His purpose was to perfect and furnish us unto all good works. It is the purpose of God's Word to bring men to a right relationship with Him.

Here is where faith must operate to resolve the frequent tension. Faith is not a subjective exercise of positive thinking that tries to convince that something is true contrary to fact. On the contrary, faith is based on objective truth, and it has value only in proportion to the worth of the object of that faith. This is why faith must always supersede and subdue experience. Experience is entirely subjective and can never be the final and sole judge of anything. This certainly applies to our approach to the Scripture. Doctrine says that all the Scripture is inspired and profitable. Faith believes it to be true. If experience concludes it to be without purpose, irrelevant, outdated, or in some other way without profit, experience is wrong. Faith ought to stop us short every time we are tempted to skip through or over any part of God's holy Word just because we are not immediately blessed. Before giving up on the passage, we should ask ourselves this question: Why, of all the things that God possibly could have said, did He say this? By faith, we know why He said it—"that the man of God may be perfect, throughly furnished unto all good works." It remains for us to learn, understand, and apply what He said. The Scripture is the means by which God reveals, not conceals, the truth.

Yet even here we must be realistic. To assume that we will understand everything in Scripture with equal ease is to reduce the Bible to a document that is less than ordinary and to set ourselves up for more frustration when we do not immediately get the point. The statement of the Westminster divines is a good and comforting reminder:

> All things in Scripture are not alike plain in themselves, nor alike clear unto all: yet those things which are necessary to be known, believed, and observed for salvation, are so clearly propounded and opened in some place of Scripture or other, that not only the learned, but the unlearned, in a due use of the ordinary means, may attain unto a sufficient understanding of them. (*Westminster Confession of Faith*, Chapter I, section 7)

INTRODUCTION

God has made enough of His Word so crystal clear that only blind and blatant disbelief will not understand. He has made enough of His Word so deep that even the most faithful must depend on His enlightenment, rather than their intellect. There is no book like the Bible—clear enough to speak to the layman, yet challenging enough to keep the scholar humble. Neither layman nor scholar should ever tire of this special revelation. Both should endeavor to increase the sphere of knowledge necessary to understand more and more. And the beauty of the Bible is that there is always more to understand. There is always more blessing to enjoy. May God increase our faith in His profitable Word and open our eyes to behold wondrous things out of the law (Psalm 119:18). Faith is the answer to keep us from abandoning the Old Testament. Who knows—we may actually find some profitable doctrine, reproof, or correction in Leviticus or Chronicles! Faith assures us that even in those obscure books, God spoke on purpose.

Presuppositions

When we approach the Scriptures through faith we do so with a set of beliefs that we take for granted to be true. These presuppositions are essential and inevitable. It is absolutely impossible to come to the Bible with an open mind. Liberal scholars often claim they approach Scripture with an open mind in order to evaluate the Word of God and judge its accuracy. In reality they come with the presupposition that human reason is superior to divine revelation. That is not an open mind; it is a closed heart that evidences a mindset predisposed against God and truth. Man cannot stand as the judge of Scripture; Scripture stands as the judge of man. As believers, we must come with an open and receptive heart to receive and believe what God says. The mindset of a believer every time he opens the Bible must be the conviction that *whatever the Bible says is true.* We cannot trust our reason to determine what is true or false, right or wrong. By faith we believe in the inspiration of the Bible, and therefore we affirm its authority, infallibility, sufficiency, and effectiveness from cover to cover.

By *authority*, we mean that it is the absolute standard of truth (matters of faith) and the absolute rule for living (matters of practice). The *Westminster Larger Catechism* summarizes well: "The holy scriptures of the Old and New Testament are the word of God, the only rule of faith and obedience" (question 3).

By *infallibility*, we mean that the Bible is free from error. Truth is absolute, and all truth has its ultimate source in God, who is Truth and the revealer of truth. Infalliblity extends to every statement of Scripture, including matters of history and science as well as matters of theology. The Bible, therefore, is the standard by which all matters of theology, history, and science are to be judged.

By *sufficiency*, we mean that the Bible is all we need to direct us in how to know God and please Him. It is all that we need to direct us safely and surely through this life and to the life to come. The Psalmist declared that "the law of the Lord is perfect" (Psalm 19:7). The word law refers here to the whole body of God's revealed instruction, the whole of special revelation. The word *perfect* refers especially to its completeness or wholeness. In simple terms, God's Word is complete. According to His infinite wisdom and good purpose, God has revealed all that we need for the welfare of our souls. Therefore, the Psalmist concludes that this complete Word converts the soul. There is no need for humanly defined philosophy, psychology, opinion, or experience to supplement the Bible. It may sound trite, but it is true: if God said it, that settles it.

By *effectiveness*, we mean that there is an inherent power in God's Word to accomplish what it says. The Lord Himself declared, "So shall my word be that goeth forth out of my mouth: it shall not return unto me void, but it shall accomplish that which I please, and it shall prosper in the thing whereto I sent it" (Isaiah 55:11). The Word of God is the hammer that in judgment breaks rocks in pieces (Jeremiah 23:29); it is the means of grace whereby God communicates the message of the gospel that saves all who believe (Romans 10:17).

The bottom line is that every time we open the Scripture, we must do so with awe and reverence generated by the certain knowledge that the Bible is not an ordinary book but the very word of the eternal God, whose veracity is beyond question or doubt. The Bible is not what men define it to be; it is what God declares it to be. Men can believe that or deny that, but they cannot alter that. My premise that the Bible is the inspired, authoritative, infallible, sufficient, and effective Word of God will be the foundation for the entire thesis and development of thought in this book. My premise is that all truth has its source in God and, consequently, that His truth is universal and timeless. Although times change, truth is changeless. Although applications of truth can vary, truth is constant.

Procedures

Once we have established the proper presuppositions and mindset about the Scriptures, we must develop proper procedures for interpreting the Bible. Interpretation is simply the process whereby we determine what something means, whether we read it or hear it. It is something that we do all the time; it is an indispensable part of communication. We all know how important it is when speaking to others to be understood. We all can tell stories, tragic or comical, of some misunderstanding of language. Husbands and wives sometimes even argue because one reads something into what the other said that was really not intended. This really is an essential key in the interpretative process: we must be careful to figure out what the speaker or writer meant. When we start reading in meanings not intended, misunderstanding and possibly serious consequences can ensue. Those consequences will be more or less severe depending on the nature of the communication. It certainly makes sense that if we are seeking to interpret God's Word, we should exercise every caution to figure out what God meant.

Truth is not what we define it to be; it is what God has revealed and declared it to be. One of the issues in modern discussions about biblical hermeneutics (the science of interpretation) is whether attention should be given to authorial intent or reader response. Focusing on authorial intent recognizes that there is an objective and understandable message conveyed that ought to be discoverable by the normal process of interpretation. It leads to objective truth. Focusing on reader response implies that what the author meant is irrelevant and indiscernible, and that therefore what the reader sees becomes truth. It eliminates the possibility of absolute truth; truth is some floating abstraction that subjectively changes from reader to reader. The authority resides in the reader and not in the Word. My premise is that what God means is infinitely more important than how I feel about what He said. Truth is whatever the Bible says, not whatever man thinks the Bible says. It may be trite, but it is true: God means what He says, and He says what He means. The purpose of His Word is not to mislead but to lead men to truth. One of the objectives of this book

7

is to help establish some guidelines for discovering what God has revealed.

Throughout the book we will be considering specific aspects of interpretation, but it is necessary first to suggest some basic principles of procedure that will govern all methods of Bible interpretation.

1. *Begin every session of Bible study with prayer*. As the Psalmist prayed for God to open his eyes to behold the wondrous things of the law, so must we pray (Psalm 119:18). We must pray that the Holy Spirit will teach us truth. The Lord Jesus promised His disciples that the Spirit of truth would guide them into all truth (John 16:13). Not only do the specific implications of that promise relate to the inspiration of the New Testament, but it also has great significance for every believer who seeks to hear God in the inspired Word. In I Corinthians 2 the apostle Paul refers to the great truths of the gospel as those things God has revealed to us by His Spirit (2:10). He then says concerning these truths that they are what the Holy Spirit teaches by "comparing spiritual things with spiritual" (2:13). This could be rendered literally "expounding spiritual [truths] to spiritual [men]." This statement highlights two essential points. First, it is the ministry of the Holy Spirit to illumine and instruct believers in the things of God. The Holy Spirit is the ultimate and consummate teacher of every believer. Second, we must have regenerated hearts before we can understand anything God says. "The natural man receiveth not the things of the Spirit of God: for they are foolishness unto him: neither can he know them, because they are spiritually discerned. But he that is spiritual judgeth [discerns] all things" (I Corinthians 2:14, 15a). Understanding God's Word depends in great measure on knowing Him. It is the Spirit of God that regenerates sinners, turning them into spiritual men and thereby introducing them to the knowledge of God; it is the Spirit of God that leads saints into a more intimate knowledge of God through the Word. That is His job. As believers–whether preachers, seminary professors, or laymen–we must learn more and more to depend on the Holy Spirit.

2. *Spend time in the Bible*. This may be a strange point to make in setting up the proper procedures for Bible study, but far too fre-

quently Christians tend to substitute reading about the Bible for reading the Bible. While there is nothing wrong with reading commentaries or devotional books, there is simply no substitute for reading the Bible itself. Much of what the majority of Christians know about Scripture, about God, and about Christ is hearsay. The Bible seems strange to many simply because they are strangers to it. In my years as a seminary professor, I have frequently taken a survey of my students who are prospective ministers. One of the questions is "how many times have you read the Bible completely through?" Taking into account that some have been saved longer than others, it nonetheless shocks me how few times on average these ministers-in-training have read the Bible. Some invariably confess that they have never read it completely, and invariably it is the Old Testament that has suffered the neglect. If these are men who testify to the call of God to be "professional" students and preachers of the Scripture, how tragically low must be the average in the church-at-large. Needless to say, proper interpretation of the Bible depends on reading the Bible. Familiarity with the source always aids in accurate interpretation. My wife and I can understand each other's idiosyncrasies and subtleties of speech because we have listened to each other for years. Because we are together so much, we almost intuitively know what the other means. So it ought to be with God's Word. The more we read, the less strange the language is. The more we read, the more we understand. Knowledge of Bible content is an essential tool in interpretation. Read your Bible.

3. *Pay attention to the context.* Taking something out of context is one of the most common errors of interpretation. We all know what it's like to come into the middle of a conversation and jump to the wrong conclusion because we have heard only part of what was said. It is unfair to any writer or speaker to extract statements from here and there and thereby totally misrepresent the intended meaning. If fairness demands caution and care in everyday communication, how much more vital it is to interpret Scripture in its context. Sometimes the quest for "proof-texts" or the attraction to isolated favorite verses has resulted in interpretations and applications that are far distant from what the original author intended. Giving attention to the context is only being fair to

Scripture. If our desire is to discover what God means and not just to prove our point with "biblical" evidence, then we will make sure to keep verses in context. To ignore the context is to jeopardize the authority of the message or at least make it suspicious.

By context, we simply mean the location or environment in which the text occurs. It certainly includes the immediately surrounding verses, but it extends also to the larger context of the entire book and then ultimately to the whole context of divine revelation. It is like looking at a target, with the bull's eye in the center and the various rings extending from the center. The bull's eye is contained within the entire ring structure and has no significance as a bull's eye independent from the other rings. Obviously, to hit the bull's eye you must stay within all the rings. The point is that there is a unity of meaning in all of Scripture because all of Scripture, whether Old or New Testament and regardless of human author, has a single author, the Lord God Himself. God is invariably consistent and so never contradicts Himself. This consideration of the larger context is often called the analogy of Scripture, which simply means that Scripture must be interpreted in the light of Scripture. I Corinthians 14:32 may hint at this principle: "And the spirits of the prophets are subject to the prophets." The Bible is its own best commentary. The *Westminster Confession* summarizes well:

> The infallible rule of interpretation of Scripture is the Scripture itself: and therefore, when there is a question about the true and full sense of any Scripture, (which is not manifold, but one), it must be searched and known by other places that speak more clearly. (Chapter I, section 9)

Paying attention to context involves reading and knowing the content of the Bible. Read your Bible.

4. *Meditate on what you read.* The blessed man is he whose "delight is in the law of the Lord; and in his law doth he meditate day and night" (Psalm 1:2). This word meditate has the idea of being consumed or preoccupied with something. The blessed man just cannot get the law out of his mind. This clearly defines the difference between what the Bible means by meditating and what

the typical notion of the world is. Whereas worldly meditation seeks to empty the mind of everything, biblical meditation seeks to fill the mind with the Word of God. According to that biblical definition, there is precious little meditation in the average Christian's life. Far too frequently Christians read the Bible without thinking. The eyes fall mechanically over the ink for a designated number of pages without the mind's comprehending a thing. Devotions sadly consist of little more than a few verses before leaving home at the beginning of a busy day or a few verses before going to bed after a busy day. There is just so much to do, and we feel guilty if we are not busy doing. The amount of blessing we receive from the Bible and the degree to which we understand the Bible will be in proportion to how much time we meditate on what we have read. Very simply, meditating is thinking, and here is the proverbial rub. Thinking takes time; thinking is work. But thinking time is not wasted time. Many Christians get nothing from the Bible not because they are ignorant but because they are thoughtless. At the very least, this exhibits irreverence toward God's holy Word. Although our tendency when we read Scripture is to skip over the parts we don't understand immediately, it is important just to pause and think and ask the Teacher, the Holy Spirit, to explain. Don't give up too quickly. Remember that the purpose of Scripture is to reveal and not conceal the truth. Take the time to pray and think over the open Bible. Time is like money in that we don't have much of either to spend. But one way or another we seem to have money to spend on the things we really want, and we seem to have time to spend on the things that are most important to us. If we truly agree with the Psalmist that God's Word is more precious than gold, we will want to devote as much thinking time to it as we possibly can.

5. *Use the appropriate tools.* Regardless of how prayerfully, consistently, and thoughtfully we read the Scripture, there will still be statements difficult to understand. How much we understand about anything we read or hear depends on the extent of our experience and knowledge of that subject matter. Because of my total lack of mechanical skills and ignorance of engines, I could listen to a conversation about cars and not have a clue about what I was hearing. I don't know the jargon; I don't know the lo-

cation or function of much of what makes a car run. My ignorance does not affect the reality of those things or diminish their
importance. Thankfully, there are those who have the skill and
the knowledge of mechanics, and I am most happy to depend on
them for what is beyond my knowledge or experience. On rare
occasions I have ventured outside my sphere of knowledge only
to regret the mess I made. A hole in the wall under our bathroom
sink testifies to my botching a simple job that a plumber could
have done without such consequence in a matter of minutes.
There are times when we must rely on experts.

The same principle applies to the study of Scripture. Matters of
ancient culture, ancient history, and ancient languages are factors
in the overall interpretation of Scripture. These issues help us to
put the Bible in the real context in which it was originally given.
But not every Christian who desires to read and understand the
Bible has this helpful knowledge. There are experts, though, who
have studied these areas and who can provide counsel and help.
Rather than despair about your lack of knowledge, be thankful
and consider that this is part of God's order and purpose. Among
the gifts that God has given the church are pastors and teachers
"for the perfecting of the saints, for the work of the ministry, for
the edifying of the body of Christ" (Ephesians 4:11, 12). The
same principle was true in the Old Testament. The detailed regulations in Leviticus concerning what was clean or unclean illustrate the point. God gave the people instructions that He
expected them to understand and obey. They themselves had to
take the Word and discern what it meant and how it applied. But
there were some matters beyond the experience or knowledge of
the people. In those instances, God instructed them to go to the
priests, whose experience and knowledge could answer their questions. God held the people responsible for both what they discovered on their own and what they learned from the priest.

It is not my purpose here to suggest all the tools available for
Bible study. But certainly every serious student of the Word
should have a good concordance, a good Bible dictionary or ency-
clopedia, an atlas, and a book of systematic theology. And don't
hesitate to ask the minister that God has given you. My guess is
that any minister would be thrilled to learn that his people are

becoming curious and serious about learning as much of God's Word as possible. That would be evidence that the body is being edified and that saints are being perfected for the work of the ministry.

The Key to the Bible

When we interpret any book, it is wise to identify the main theme and purpose of the author. The overriding purpose of special revelation—for us the Scripture alone—is to guide men to a proper relationship with God. God's gracious salvation is the only way guilty sinners can experience that relationship, and God's gracious salvation is in and through and by His Son, the Lord Jesus Christ. The Lord Jesus Himself declared that He was "the way, the truth, and the life," the only way for men to come to God (John 14:6). It follows that if the purpose of Scripture is to guide men to the Lord and if the only way to the Lord is through the redemption of the Lord Jesus Christ, then the revelation of Christ should be the grand and predominant theme of the Scripture. Indeed, it is. All revealed truth in one way or another relates to and is ultimately defined by the central truth of the Messiah, the Christ, the anointed. Obviously, the New Testament develops that saving theme. The Gospels, with the narratives concerning His earthly ministry, introduce the performance of His saving work, the historic foundation of the gospel. Acts records the initial proclamation and dissemination of the message of His saving work. The Epistles explain and expound the nature of His person and work and the implications for personal and church life. The Revelation assures the consummation of all the glorious truths of His person and work. Understanding the message of the New Testament is impossible without reference to Christ.

Understanding the Old Testament is also impossible without reference to Christ. He is the key that unlocks all the mysteries of the Old Testament. This is not speculation; this is the teaching of the New Testament, both by direct statement and by example. When the resurrected Christ walked with the two disciples on the road to Emmaus, He expressed His concern that they were slow to believe what the prophets had written concerning His suffering and glory (Luke 24:25-26). Then "beginning at Moses and all the prophets...he expounded unto them in all the scriptures the things concerning himself" (Luke 24:27). Later in the company of all the disciples He declared that "all things must be fulfilled, which were written in the law of Moses, and in the prophets, and in the psalms, concerning me" and then "opened he their understanding, that they might understand the scriptures" (Luke 24:44, 45). His reference to Moses, the prophets, and the psalms was the Jewish designation for the entire Old Testament, similar to our referring to the New Testament as the Gospels and Epistles. In other words, Christ said that the entirety of the Old Testament spoke about Him. The Pentateuch, the first five books with all their religious rituals, prepares the way for the Perfect Priest to stand between God and men as the perfect sacrifice for sin. The Historical Books draw attention to the Perfect King, who would come to rule His people and subdue His enemies. The Prophets anticipate the Perfect Prophet, who represents and reveals the only true and living God to man. The Poetical Books put it all together with the Christ as the great theme for worship and praise. What an authoritative clue for interpretation this is! It means that if we read any book of the Old Testament without reference to what it teaches concerning Christ, we are missing the key element in that book. If we do not see Christ, it is not because He is not there.

Philip's encounter with the Ethiopian eunuch illustrates how finding Christ opens the understanding of the Old Testament message (Acts 8:27-39). When Philip was directed to the wilderness by the Spirit of God, he met the eunuch reading Isaiah 53 without a clue concerning its meaning. But "Philip opened his mouth, and began at the same scripture, and preached unto him Jesus" (Acts 8:35). With that explanation, the eunuch confessed, "I believe that Jesus Christ is the Son of God." Finding Christ opened his eyes. According to Paul in II Corinthians 3, it is finding Christ that always opens the eyes to the true meaning of the Old Testament Scripture. In this chapter Paul exposes those who were misunderstanding and misusing the Old Testament. Although some elements of Paul's discussion are open to interpretation, one thing is unmistakable: the abusers of Moses were reading the Old Testament with a veil covering their eyes, "which vail is done away in Christ" (II Corinthians 3:14). The implication is clear and far-reaching. *Seeing Christ is the key to unlocking the message of Scripture, including the Old Testament.* To miss seeing Christ either in the overall scheme of the Old Testament or in the individual books is to miss the central message and to jeopardize the proper understanding of the rest of the message. Whereas the New Testament centered on the historic Christ, the Old Testament centered on the coming Christ. But they center on the same Christ, from the beginning the only way, the only truth, the only life.

The Purpose and Plan

This brings us to the special issue of this book. If Christ is the central theme of the Scripture and the key that unlocks the meaning and message of the Old Testament, it is imperative that every reader of the Old Testament see the Lord Jesus. I am not suggesting that the person and work of the Messiah is the only issue or doctrine in the Old Testament, but I am suggesting that every other truth or command finds its ultimate reference in Him. To attempt to implement anything the Bible requires of us without reference to Jesus Christ is folly, whether it is Old Testament or New Testament truth. The relationship between Christ and Christian living, that is, implementing the gospel, is itself a large and significant study. But the first step in applying Christ in life is knowing what is true about Christ. What we know about Christ is not the figment of imagination; it is the subject and focus of divine revelation. And the Old Testament is a major part of that revelation. But saying Christ is there and finding Him there are two different things. For Christians to hear from their pastors or teachers that Christ is on "every page" of the Old Testament creates frustration when in the real world of their personal study they see nothing that resembles what they know about Christ. Many can adopt the words of the bride when she expressed her longing for her beloved: "I sought him whom my soul loveth: I sought him, but I found him not" (Song of Solomon 3:1). She then asks the question of the watchman: "Saw ye him whom my soul loveth?" (Song of Solomon 3:3). We can sympathize with her desire and her frustration. They parallel closely the desire and frustration of many who read their Old Testaments looking for their beloved Savior but not finding Him in what seems to be the darkness. The problem very often is simply not knowing how to look, where to look, or what to look for. I propose in this study *to define and illustrate some guidelines for finding Christ in the Old Testament.*

It is beyond the scope of this book to treat exhaustively every messianic passage in the Old Testament. It is not my purpose to provide a "Christology" of the Old Testament. There are many of those available. Rather, I want even those who are not skilled specialists in theology or Hebrew linguistics to be able to read and profit from the Old Testament in the light of the Lord Jesus Christ. The approach is basic. In **Part 1** we will identify *whom we are looking for*. We will consider basic truths about Christ's person and work that will help us recognize Him when we see Him. **Part 2** is the principal focus: *where to look*. Here we will consider some of the key places in the Old Testament where Christ is revealed. We will look at topics such as predictive prophecies, preincarnate personal appearances, important names or titles, typology, covenants, and worship. If we know whom we are looking for and where to find Him, we ought to be able to find Him. "Those things which are revealed belong unto us" (Deuteronomy 29:29). Searching for Christ in the places God has revealed Him is not a vain game of hide and seek; it is a sure thing. God's promise throughout the Bible is that those who seek Him will find Him. Beginning at Moses and ending with Malachi, we want to be on Christ-alert.

It is my prayer that throughout this study the Lord Jesus Christ will be "evidently set forth" (Galatians 3:1) and that the Holy Spirit will lead into truth (Psalm 25:5) by showing Christ and glorifying Him (John 16:14).

Part 1
Whom to Look For

PART 1

WHOM TO LOOK FOR

When John the Baptist sent representatives to ask Jesus, "Art thou he that should come? or look we for another?" (Luke 7:19), Jesus said, "Go your way, and tell John what things ye have seen and heard; how that the blind see, the lame walk, the lepers are cleansed, the deaf hear, the dead are raised, to the poor the gospel is preached" (Luke 7:22). The Lord's answer to John suggests an important principle: we can identify a person by what he is like and by what he does. Healing the sick and preaching to the poor were among the works that Isaiah predicted the Spirit-filled Messiah would do (Isaiah 61:1). Christ expected John to put "two and two" together. It is as though Christ said to John, "The Messiah will do these things; I am doing these things; I am Messiah, the one that should come." As we read the Old Testament, we should learn to do the same thing in our search for Christ. If we know who Christ is, what He does, and what He is like, we should be able to put "two and two" together and see Him even if He we are not using a red letter edition.

The simple truth is that the more we know Christ, the more likely we will be able to recognize Him in the Scriptures. Part of the problem with many Christians is that their inability to find Christ in the Old Testament stems from their limited knowledge of who He is and what He is like. If I am told to pick someone out of a crowd and I have no idea what that someone looks like, it becomes purely a guessing game. Indeed, I could be looking right at him and not know it. If we do not know what we are looking for, we will most likely find nothing. Looking for nothing in particular, we find nothing in particular. This is the sad fact with many who read the Old Testament: because they read with no particular objective, they can read the most explicit of messianic texts and not even know that they have looked at Christ. If,

19

on the other hand, I know someone well, I can pick him out in the largest crowd, even without seeing all of him. The better we know a person, the easier it is to find him in a crowd of strangers. I know my wife so well that I could recognize her anyplace. I can recognize the back of her head, the way she stands, sits, or walks. I don't have to see all of her to know her when I see her. So it is that the better we know Christ, the easier it will be to see Him in the Old Testament—even if we don't see all of Him at once. One more thing is true about seeing someone we know in a crowd of strangers. Although we may often feel lost and uncomfortable as we look at a sea of unfamiliar faces, as soon as we recognize a familiar face in the crowd, it is as though an "eye magnet" attracts our attention and fixes our gaze on the one we recognize. There is a sense of relief; we are not alone. So should it be in our reading of the Old Testament. If we know Christ, even in the thick of those texts that seem so strange on the surface our attention will be attracted to and fixed on Him. To find Christ in our reading of the Old Testament is a blessed relief. We may not immediately recognize anything else, but to see the Savior will help put everything else in the proper perspective. If we come to the Old Testament looking for Christ, we will find Christ.

It is therefore the purpose of **Part 1** to identify essential elements and characteristics of the person and work of the Lord Jesus Christ. This section will function as a briefing of what to look out for as we begin the search to find Christ in the Old Testament. Since the New Testament is the complete and consummate revelation of the person and work of Christ, we will not hesitate to use it to provide much of the important data. And since the New Testament relies so heavily on the Old Testament to prove and validate that Jesus of Nazareth is the Christ of God, we are right to focus our attention on it as a guide to the Old Testament's teaching about Christ. Our approach is essentially opposite to that of the first disciples of Jesus. When John the Baptist admonished men to "behold the Lamb of God," Andrew believed and told his brother Simon, "We have found the Messias, which is, being interpreted, the Christ" (John 1:36, 41). After Philip believed, he told Nathaniel, "We have found him, of whom Moses in the law, and the prophets, did write, Jesus of Nazareth" (John 1:45). When Jesus gave evidence of His messianic authority to Nathaniel, he confessed, "Rabbi, thou art the Son of God; thou art the King of Israel"

(John 1:49). These men knew well what the Old Testament taught about Messiah, and they knew how to apply that teaching in their assessment of Jesus. They put "two and two" together and concluded in the light of Old Testament theology that Jesus was the Christ. Whereas their knowledge of the Old Testament helped them identify Jesus as the Christ, our knowledge of the New Testament will help us identify the Old Testament's teaching about Christ. They read the Old Testament into the New; we have the advantage of reading the New Testament into the Old. Frankly, most Christians today know the New Testament better than the Old, and there is nothing wrong with using the advantage that God has given us.

I do not want to digress into a discussion on the theories of interpretation, but I do perhaps need to justify my suggestion of taking advantage of the New Testament in Old Testament interpretation. There are some that consider reading the New Testament back into the Old to be a serious crime of interpretation, a sin against proper hermeneutics. Too often interpreters rely on one element in the entire interpretation process to the exclusion of other essential parts. For instance, one discipline of Bible study is Biblical Theology. This discipline tends to be descriptive of what the Bible text says rather than systematic or deductive. It is a legitimate and profitable means of analyzing the message of Scripture, either by book or by topic. For years I have taught a course in Old Testament Theology based upon the discipline of Biblical Theology. In fact, it is one of my favorite courses. One of the common emphases of Biblical Theology is the concept that God progressively revealed truth. This is an accurate emphasis and one that we will consider later in our study. Obviously, if we are seeking to interpret and describe truth in the order in which it was revealed, we cannot assume later statements into our analysis. Reading the New Testament back into the Old Testament would be a violation of the strict Biblical Theological method; but the Biblical Theological method is not the end of the whole interpretative process. It is an important part but not the only part. I am not proposing in this work to do a Biblical Theology on the doctrine of Messiah. That would be extremely profitable in and of itself. It would help answer questions concerning what and how much people in the Old Testament era knew about Christ at any given time. But the focus of this book is not how much Old Testament saints knew, but how much

Christians today should know, given all the advantages they have. We have in the New Testament, among other things, a divinely inspired commentary on the equally divinely inspired Old Testament. Since truth is timeless, universal, and unchangeable, we must conclude that the New Testament never changes the meaning of any Old Testament text; it always gives the correct and originally intended meaning. Rather than ignoring this inspired evidence, it should be the safeguard and guide to all correct understanding of the Old Testament. Therefore, if the full revelation of Jesus Christ in the New Testament helps us to discover and learn from the progressing revelation of the Old Testament, that is good.

Now we can come back to the purpose of this section: *whom are we looking for*. We want to construct a profile of Christ so that when we see Him we will know it. The following chapters will define the concept of "Messiah" or "Christ," discuss His person as the God/Man, and detail essential aspects of His unique work. This profile of what Christ is like and what He does will get us started on our search for Christ in the Old Testament.

Throughout this work and especially in **Part 1**, I will quote passages from the *Westminster Confession of Faith* and the *Larger* and *Shorter Catechisms*. The Confession gives summary statements of the doctrines of Scripture in declarative paragraphs. The Catechisms use an effective system of teaching that is not often employed today. Catechisms simply ask questions and then provide concise answers. Both the synopsis paragraphs of the Confession and the questions/answers of the Catechism provide a helpful compendium of Bible Doctrine. This will be the only "outside," nonbiblical source I refer to for a couple of reasons. First, the passages concerning Christ represent and express concisely the biblical and historically orthodox statements of doctrine. I quote them to demonstrate that what I am saying is not novel or new. I tell my students constantly that novelty in my profession (teaching and preaching the Bible) is not a virtue. Second, the Confession and Catechisms, which date to the seventeenth century, are part of public domain and easily attainable. Therefore, if you want to check the accuracy of the quoted sections or do further reading, it should be easy enough to find the documents.

CHAPTER 1
JESUS THE MESSIAH

According to Peter, the Old Testament prophets knew both what they were writing about and whom they were looking for. They were looking for the *Christ*. "Of which salvation the prophets have enquired and searched diligently, who prophesied of the grace that should come unto you: searching what, or what manner of time the Spirit of Christ which was in them did signify, when it testified beforehand the sufferings of Christ, and the glory that should follow" (I Peter 1:10-11). Though they were uncertain when He *would* come, they had no doubt that He would come. Although they perhaps did not understand that His sufferings and following glory would constitute two separate advents, they knew that *Christ* was salvation. Not only is Christ the key to salvation: searching for Christ was the key that unlocked the Old Testament message even for those who wrote the Old Testament.

My thesis is that searching for and finding Christ is still the key that unlocks the Old Testament. The basic question, therefore, is *who is Christ?* Whom are we looking for when we are looking for Christ? Understanding the significance of this title is essential for our search. Interpreting the Scripture accurately requires that we consider fully and define properly the names and titles used to refer to the Lord. Too often we regard the names of God as nothing more than labels with little significance other than serving as the means of distinguishing God from someone else. That's how we tend to regard names in our culture. A name is a means of getting someone's attention or distinguishing and identifying one person from another. What a name means is sometimes a point of curiosity or a cute motto for a plaque or coffee cup, but hardly an element that conveys essential information about a person. My parents named me Michael ("who is like God?"), not because they were making a theological assertion but because for whatever reason they liked the name. My wife bought me one of those coffee cups that supposedly defines "Michael," but it says nothing about the Hebrew etymology of the name and instead has a flattering poem that I can only wish were true. The point is that we use names without necessarily thinking about what the name means. That, however, was not the case for the writers of Scriptures. Names, particularly and especially the names of God, were never used haphazardly or casually in the Scripture. Names conveyed something about the nature or character of the one so named. "Thou shalt call his name JESUS: for he shall save his people from their sins" (Matthew 1:21). That "Jesus" means "Jehovah saves" is certainly a significant statement given the purpose of the Savior's being born. What God called Himself was always an important means of His revealing Himself. It is an important part of Bible interpretation to pay attention to the names and titles of the Lord. One way of finding Christ in the Old Testament is to identify and define the titles used to reveal Him. We will consider some of those specific titles in **Part 2**, where to find Christ. But even before we identify some of the more particular titles, we must define the very basics. What does "Christ" mean? It is more than simply Jesus's "last name" in the common New Testament expression of the name of the Lord Jesus Christ. Although each of the terms reveals vital truth, "Christ" is a term that is theologically charged and that brings us to the heart of God's provision for a Savior for sinful men. Understanding what the title "Christ" means is a key initial step in our Old Testament search for the Savior.

Definition of the Term

The word "Christ" is a transliteration of the Greek word that is the equivalent to the Hebrew word "Messiah." "Messiah" and "Christ" mean exactly the same thing; therefore, it is not appropriate or legitimate to speak of the Jewish or Old Testament Messiah in contrast to the Christian or New Testament Christ. The only difference between the words is that one is Hebrew and the other Greek. In biblical context, they mean the same thing and refer to the same ultimate and ideal person, Jesus of Nazareth. John makes this explicitly clear in his record of Andrew's testimony to Simon Peter: "We have found the Messias, which is, being interpreted, the Christ" (John 1:41). The Old Testament, being antecedent to the New Testament, supplies the key data in defining the word. Andrew obviously understood the significance of the title "Messiah" and testified to his expectancy of the promised Christ. What a confession of faith there was in that single word! That the New Testament uses the term "Christ" well over five hundred times to refer to the Savior without defining the concept indicates that the apostles understood the Old Testament implications of the word and assumed their readers did as well. This is a good example of the impossibility of understanding the New Testament fully without reading the Old Testament into it.

The noun "messiah" is based on a verb that means "to spread a liquid over." The verb occurs frequently in various contexts. Though not uniquely so (see Jeremiah 22:14; a house "painted" with vermilion, i.e., a bright red pigment), the liquid most often used was olive oil, and the objects smeared were both things and people. The Authorized Version often translates the verb "to anoint." Most of the anointed objects had some function in the ceremonies of the worship rituals. For instance, Exodus 29:36 instructs that after offering a sin offering "thou shalt cleanse the altar, when thou hast made an atonement for it, and thou shalt anoint it, to sanctify it." Exodus 40:9-11 includes, in addition to the altar, the laver and the entire Tabernacle with all its vessels for the purpose of sanctifying the objects. Sanctifying refers simply to the separation of those objects from other things; the anointed objects were set apart for a distinct purpose and use. They were consecrated or dedicated to a particular function. The same meaning applies to the people anointed. The people anointed were usually in some leadership role, either civil or religious leadership: the most common were kings (I Kings 1:34), priests (Exodus 28:41), and prophets (I Kings 19:16). In each instance, the anointing was a symbolic gesture setting the person or the thing apart for a particular function. Samuel took a vial of oil, poured it on Saul's head, and told the first king that God had anointed him to be the captain (I Samuel 10:1). It is not without significance that the Holy Spirit then came upon the appointed king (I Samuel 10:6, 10). Similarly, when Samuel took the oil and anointed David to be king, the Spirit of the Lord came upon David (I Samuel 16:13). The obvious association between the olive oil and the Holy Spirit is an important element in the anointing ritual and one that adds to its significance. This association will have particular importance when we consider the special anointing of the Savior Himself.

Although the Old Testament uses the noun "messiah" most frequently of kings (28 out of 39 occurrences), any person anointed could be accurately referred to as a "messiah." Kings, priests, prophets–all were messiahs. The noun form "messiah" in Hebrew conveys essentially the passive idea of the verb: *a messiah is one who has been anointed.* Being anointed identified the person as being qualified and chosen to perform the task for which he was anointed. He is one consecrated or set apart for a special task. In other words, there was to be an active demonstration of the office to which the passive anointing pointed. An anointed king was to rule; an anointed priest was to minister; an anointed prophet was to preach. Defined simply as "an anointed one," "Messiah" is a comprehensive word that applies well to the ministry of the Lord Jesus Christ as the only one identified, qualified, and chosen to be the Savior of sinners.

Implications of the Term

It is obvious from the examples used to define the "Messiah" that the term in the Old Testament was not uniquely reserved for the one, true, ultimate, and ideal Messiah, Jesus. Many were anointed and therefore regarded as messiahs. None of these "lesser" messiahs were, however, in any way ever identified as the promised Savior, but their functions were and are instructive about the ministry and work of THE MESSIAH. Highlighting some of the key facts about these messianic officers will help us see why the term "Messiah" is such a fitting designation of the Savior and will help us recognize messianic aspects of His person and work even when the term itself does not occur. Although each of the three messianic offices–prophet, priest, and king–maintained distinct duties and responsibilities, they had some factors in common. Bear with me as we consider some of them: the thrilling and satisfying part comes when we see how they apply to the Lord Jesus.

The Election of Messiah

First, a messiah was a *chosen* individual. God never opened these offices to volunteers, and He dealt severely with those who tried to usurp the positions. This is true for kings. Moses declared specifically that when it came time to crown a king, it had to be the one "whom the Lord thy God shall choose" (Deuteronomy 17:15). In Genesis 49:10 God chose the tribe of Judah to be the royal tribe through which the ultimate king would come. When David, the first of Judah to become king, was anointed, it was explicitly clear that God chose him over all his brothers. When his brothers repeatedly paraded before Samuel, the Lord revealed to His prophet that He had not chosen them in spite of what appeared to be their outward qualifications (I Samuel 16:7-10). But as soon as David appeared, the Lord said, "Arise, anoint him: for this is he" (I Samuel 16:12). Later when David sinned so grievously, the Lord reminded him through Nathan, "I anointed thee king over Israel" (II Samuel 12:7). Although Saul, David's predecessor, was seemingly the "people's choice" for king, the Scripture makes it clear that God chose him. It was the Lord who revealed to Samuel that Saul was the man he was to anoint to reign over the people (I Samuel 9:15-17). Significantly, God's choice of kings extends beyond the borders of Israel. In interpreting Nebuchadnezzar's dream of coming kingdoms, Daniel declared that the Lord "removeth kings, and setteth up kings" (Daniel 2:21). The prophet Isaiah gives a most significant example. Of all the Old Testament prophets, Isaiah has the well-deserved reputation of being one of the most messianic. There is hardly a truth about Christ that you cannot find in Isaiah, from His virgin birth to His Second Coming. Isaiah wrote a Gospel in the truest sense. Yet the only time he actually used the term "messiah," he referred to Cyrus, the pagan Persian king. The Lord called Cyrus "his anointed" (Isaiah 45:1) because He chose him to be the instrument for delivering Israel from the Babylonian captivity, opening the way for Israel to return to their homeland. Adding to the significance is the fact that the Lord revealed this through Isaiah almost two hundred years before it happened. Throughout this section of the prophecy, the Lord made it clear that He would raise up Cyrus (Isaiah 41:25; 44:28; 45:13). Cyrus was foreordained, chosen, anointed, and set apart to perform a special task of deliverance for God's people. That is a pretty good synopsis of a messianic king.

Though most of the focus is on the kingly office, the Scripture is clear that priests and prophets were also chosen to their respective offices. Hebrews 5 gives a synopsis of the Old Testament priesthood. In the list of the requirements and duties is the statement that the priesthood is reserved only for those ordained: "And no man taketh this honour unto himself, but he that is called of God, as was Aaron" (Hebrews 5:4). Deuteronomy 18:5 says concerning the Levites, "the Lord thy

God hath chosen him out of all thy tribes, to stand to minister in the name of the Lord, him and his sons for ever." Numbers records both God's choice of Aaron and his sons to the priesthood as well as the serious consequences of "volunteering" for the office. The Lord declared the names of the sons of Aaron, "the priests which were anointed" (Numbers 3:3), and then explained, "I have taken the Levites from among the children of Israel instead of all the firstborn …: therefore the Levites shall be mine" (Numbers 3:12). Chapter 16 records the rebellion of Korah who, along with Dathan and Abiram, thought that he could do just as well as Aaron in conducting the priestly ministry. We all know the story. In immediate and unique judgment, God caused the earth to open and swallow the rebels, because by seeking this office for themselves they had provoked the Lord (Numbers 16:30). Then in Numbers 17 the Lord miraculously caused Aaron's rod to blossom as a public testimony that He had chosen Aaron to be the priest. The lesson was obvious: only the priest of God's choice could do business with the Lord.

There are many examples of God's choice of men to be prophets. Jeremiah, whose name means "Jehovah establishes, or appoints," is a casebook example. He records a detailed testimony of God's call to the prophetic office (Jeremiah1:4-10). The Lord's word to Jeremiah in verse 5 is particularly instructive: "Before I formed thee in the belly I knew thee; and before thou camest forth out of the womb I sanctified thee, and I ordained thee a prophet unto the nations." Three verbs express the nature of the divine choice. First, the Lord said, "I knew thee." This is more than simple awareness or intellectual knowledge. It is, rather, an intimate, special and selecting knowledge. This knowledge is part of the Old Testament's vocabulary of election. God's selection of Jeremiah was before His conception. Humanly speaking, God knew Jeremiah before there was anything to know. Second, the Lord said, "I sanctified thee." This is the same word that occurs in many of the "anointing" passages to designate the purpose for which something or someone was anointed (cf. Exodus 29:36). Before he was born, God had set Jeremiah apart for the special purpose of being a prophet. His service was divinely determined before he knew what was happening. Third, the Lord said, "I ordained thee a prophet." This is the verb that normally means "to give" but that also has the special sense of appointing or assigning to a specific task. God chose Jeremiah to be a prophet; He called Jeremiah to be a prophet; and Jeremiah was a prophet. What God determined and purposed in heaven happened on earth. There was no slip between the eternal purpose and the temporal fulfillment of God's intent. That is an important "messianic" lesson.

The Authority of Messiah

Second, a messiah was an *accredited* individual. In other words, a prophet, priest, or king had the authority to exercise the office to which he was anointed. The nature of priestly and kingly work rendered the accreditation and authority of these offices obvious and incontestable. God had made a covenant of life and peace with the priests and designated them as messengers of the Lord of hosts (Malachi 2:5-7). God's choice of Aaron and his sons confirmed them as the only ones with the authority to officiate the sacrifices, the holy ceremonies of worship. Their very consecration to the worship service gave them the right and authority to perform these exclusive duties. They also had the authority to judge and settle disputes that were too complex for ordinary magistrates (Deuteronomy 17:8-11). In fact, they had such authority in this regard that those who disregarded their decision received the death penalty (Deuteronomy 17:12). And then who could look at Aaron's royal garments with breastplate, ephod, and turban declaring "HOLINESS TO THE LORD" (Exodus 28) without standing in absolute awe and wonder at this one anointed to represent man before the Lord? Indeed, Aaron himself was called the holy one of the Lord (Psalm 106:16). The very sight of the High Priest exuded authority and honor.

That kings were anointed to rule over the people (Deuteronomy 17:15; I Samuel 10:1; II Samuel 12:7; 23:3) of necessity elevated them to a position of distinction and authority. When Samuel tried to dissuade the nation from installing a king, he enumerated all the things that a king would have the right and authority to do by virtue of his kingship. The people wanted a king to judge them and fight their battles (I Samuel 8:20). He would certainly do those things, but Samuel warned them that along with those benefits to them, the king would have the authority to demand and take from them everything they had, from their possessions to their children (I Samuel 8:11-17). Honor, majesty, and glory are attendant with the throne of the king

(Psalm 21:5); the greater and more extensive his kingdom, the closer to absolute his sovereign power and authority becomes. All who are subject to the king owe him allegiance, honor, and obedience. Ecclesiastes says, "Where the word of the king is, there is power"; none can question the king's will (8:4). Solomon, the wise king and inspired author of Ecclesiastes, also counsels "to keep the king's commandment, and that in regard of the oath of God" (8:2). That is real authority.

Prophetic authority was just as real but not always as obvious. The prophet's authority rested in the fact that he was the representative of God before men, speaking the Lord's word to men. The Hebrew word translated "prophet" implies something of the inherent authority in the prophet's words. It is formed from a verb which most likely means simply "to speak." The word "prophet" itself evidences the same pattern as the word "messiah" in that it conveys the passive idea of the verb. A prophet, therefore, is one who has been spoken to and who in turn conveys that divine message to men. Notwithstanding the clear and direct call of Jeremiah to the prophetic office, he was overwhelmed by the awesome prospect of the ministry and confessed ignorance of what to preach. The Lord, in essence, told him not to worry because He would put His words into his mouth, and all he had to say was what God commanded (Jeremiah 1:6-9). When God commissioned Ezekiel to his prophetic ministry, He told him to speak His words. Ezekiel's message was simply to be "Thus saith the Lord God" (Ezekiel 2:4, 7). Perhaps one of the clearest statements that the prophet was God's messenger with God's message is Haggai 1:12, 13. Verse 12 actually equates obeying the voice of the Lord God with obeying the voice of Haggai the prophet. Verse 13 identifies Haggai's speaking as the "Lord's messenger in the Lord's message unto the people." Although miracles and fulfilled prophecies were visible means to validate the authenticity of the prophet (Deuteronomy 13:1-3; 18:21, 22), his ultimate accreditation was his faithfulness in proclaiming the word of the Lord.

When self-proclaimed prophets voiced their opinions, God forthrightly dismissed them; they had no authority. Concerning the false prophets competing with Jeremiah, the Lord said, "The prophets prophesy lies in my name: I sent them not, neither have I commanded them, neither spake unto them: they prophesy unto you a false vision and divination, and a thing of nought, and the deceit of their heart" (Jeremiah 14:14). But regardless of whether the people received or rejected the prophet's word, if the chosen prophet spoke the word of the Lord, then one way or another there would be the evidence that a prophet had been there (Ezekiel 2:5). The sin, rebellion, and unbelief of the people would often rob a prophet of his honor, but they could not nullify his authority. The authority of the prophet was in the Word.

The Power of Messiah

Third, a messiah was an *empowered* individual. When the Lord anointed one for some sphere of service, whether priestly, prophetic, or kingly, He did not abandon that individual to his own abilities or ingenuity. The Lord always supplied the power for that service, with the ultimate agent of power being the Holy Spirit. This empowering for service was the most vivid element in the anointing ceremony. As the olive oil was poured and smeared on the head of the appointed "messiah," so the Holy Spirit came upon him to enable him to perform the ministry for which he was being consecrated and set apart. The Spirit's activity in Israel's first two kings is explicitly recorded. Samuel told Saul after his anointing that the Spirit would come upon him (I Samuel 10:6). The Spirit's coming on Saul transformed him into another man, giving him ability to rule and be recognized as king (I Samuel 10:9). Apparently, before this empowering the only thing Saul had going for him was that he was taller than anyone else. His leadership ability was the consequence of his anointing and not the cause of it. Similarly, when Samuel anointed David to replace Saul, "the Spirit of the Lord came upon David from that day forward" (1 Samuel 16:13).

Likewise, prophets received the Holy Spirit to enable them to prophesy. Immediately preceding his call to the prophetic office, Ezekiel witnessed a mysterious and magnificent vision of God's absolute glory and fell on his face in worship and recognition of self-insufficiency. Then the Lord commanded him to stand, and the Spirit entered him and caused him to stand (Ezekiel 1:28-2:2). This is the beauty of the Spirit's empowering: He enables the one He fills to fulfill his duty and obey God's command. Contrasting his ministry with that of false prophets, who caused the people to err, Micah testified, "Truly I am full of the power by the spirit of the Lord, and of judgment, and of might, to declare unto Jacob his transgression, and to Israel his sin" (Micah 3:8). That spiritual power gave him boldness to preach the Word of God regardless of its popularity among the people. The Lord assured Isaiah in connection with a profound messianic prophecy of the Redeemer coming to Zion, "My spirit that is upon thee, and my words which I have put in thy mouth, shall not depart out of thy mouth…" (Isaiah 59:21). The Spirit's empowering guaranteed the ultimate success of the word that was preached.

Even priests ministered in the power of the Spirit. II Chronicles 24:20 says that the "Spirit of God came upon Zechariah" the priest, making him a bold witness to the people. That bold and powerful witness so inflamed the people that they conspired and killed him in the court of the temple with the authority of the king's commandment. Although the role of the Holy Spirit in the priestly work is not as commonly stated in the Old Testament as it is for the other offices, consistent interpretation of the significance of the anointing justifies the conclusion that priests were indeed empowered for service. Also, the fact that the actual anointing of priests is more frequently recorded than the anointing of kings and prophets warrants the understanding that what the anointing symbolized was realized in fact. I am certainly not suggesting that every wicked king or false prophet had this special enabling of God's Holy Spirit, but I am suggesting that the Old Testament makes it abundantly clear that legitimately anointed "messiahs" were spiritually empowered for their service. That is the key lesson that we must learn as we apply all of this in our search for THE MESSIAH.

Application of the Concept to Jesus Christ

How does all this help us in our efforts to find Christ in the Old Testament? Knowing that He is THE MESSIAH of all messiahs and knowing what a messiah is and does should draw our eyes to Him magnetically whenever and wherever we read of messianic business.

Specific Evidence of Messiahship

Even though the Old Testament only rarely applies the term "messiah" to THE MESSIAH, the messianic concepts and implications are attributed to the Savior throughout. There are, however, some significant passages that do use the term directly of the Lord Jesus Christ. For instance, though disputed by some interpreters, there are good exegetical, theological, and logical grounds for seeing in Hannah's prayer of thanksgiving a confession of her anticipation for the coming of the ultimate Messiah. She begins by expressing her heart's joy in God's salvation (I Samuel 2:1) and ends with the confident declaration that the Lord "shall give strength unto his king, and exalt the horn of his anointed" (I Samuel 2:10). In between she praises the Lord for His uniqueness, His infallible justice, His sovereignty over life and death, His sovereign disposition of the affairs of men, His creating power, His providential care for His people, and His eschatological judgment of the wicked. That is a lot of good and profound theology from an Old Testament woman! It is with that future judgment of the ends of the earth that Hannah associates the Messiah King. Given the eschatological reference and the fact that there was no king of Israel at that time at all, it stands to sound interpretational reason that Hannah had in mind THE MESSIAH.

Psalm 2 is another unmistakable application of the word "messiah" to THE MESSIAH. Although the entire Psalm has reference to Christ, verse two speaks of the conspiracy of rulers against the Lord and against His anointed, that is, His Messiah. The New Testament settles any doubt that this Psalm refers to the Lord Jesus Christ. Acts 4:25-27 quotes the opening of Psalm 2 and singles out Herod and Pilate as specific conspirators against Jesus, whom God anointed. In Acts 13:33 Paul quotes Psalm 2:6 and applies it directly to the resurrection of the Lord Jesus. There is at least one more explicit use of the term in reference to the Lord Jesus. In Daniel's mysterious vision of the seventy weeks, the word "messiah" occurs twice (9:25, 26). Given what this prophesy says concerning the Messiah and what we know about some of the details that have been fulfilled, we can be in no doubt that Daniel's Messiah is the Lord Jesus Christ. Psalm 2 and Daniel 9 are pregnant with messianic teaching and will require our detailed attention in **Part 2**, where to find Christ. My point now is simply that the Old Testament does use the word "Messiah" in its fullest sense to refer to the Savior.

We know that the Lord Jesus is the promised Messiah, and we know what messiahs did. It remains for us to consider how the Lord Jesus fulfilled those key messianic operations as the ultimate and ideal Prophet, Priest, and King. When we read about the ideal manifestations of these operations in the Old Testament, we know that we are reading about our blessed Savior. If we know what we are looking for, we will know it when we find it. This is our objective: to find the Messiah.

Understanding the Lord's place and function as Messiah is essential to understanding the full implications of His being the Mediator. Paul forthrightly declared, "There is one God, and one mediator between God and men, the man Christ Jesus" (I Timothy 2:5). This is a timeless and universal truth. That Christ is the only Mediator is not uniquely a New Testament doctrine. He was, is, and will forever be the only Mediator between God and men. The Old Testament taught the need for a Mediator and predicted His certain coming to do the necessary mediatorial work. It certainly declared what the Mediator must do. As the Mediator, He executes the power of three offices to redeem sinners. The *Westminster Shorter Catechism* asks, "What offices doth Christ execute as our Redeemer?" The answer is "Christ, as our Redeemer, executeth the offices of a prophet, of a priest, and of a king, both in his estate of humiliation and exaltation" (question 23). This brings us right back to what Christ, or Messiah, means. The title "Christ" and the office of Mediator are essentially synonymous.

A Prophet, a Priest, and a King are essential needs for man, whose sin necessarily separates him from God and precludes him from approaching God on his own. Before the fall, man enjoyed a perfect communion and fellowship with God, his Creator. But with the fall came a tragic and drastic change in man and his relationship with the Lord. Iniquity separated man from God, and sin hid God's face from man (Isaiah 59:2). When man fell, he lost the knowledge of God that must be renewed if man could be saved from sin (Colossians 3:10). Man needed a *Prophet to reveal God*. When man fell, he lost the righteousness and true holiness in which he was created (Ephesians 4:24). Man needed a *Priest to reconcile* him to God. When man fell, he became prey to the enemy of his soul who had power to hold him subject to bondage (Hebrews 2:14, 15). Man needed a *King to reign*, to subdue every enemy of his soul. What man needed, God in His wondrous and amazing grace provided in the person of His own dear Son, His and our Messiah.

As the ultimate and ideal Messiah, the Lord Jesus Christ brought together in His single person both the common features shared by all the lesser messiahs, and all the specific duties and responsibilities of each of the three distinct offices. The Lord Jesus Christ did it all.

Common Features of Messiahship

Remember that three common features applied to all "messiahs." They were chosen, accredited, and empowered. Each of these is beautifully and ideally true of the Lord Jesus, thus providing irrefutable evidence that He is the promised Messiah of the Old Testament. All of these features, then, in the Old Testament directly point to the Savior. Recognizing these features to be true of the Lord Jesus will stimulate us to mark those Old Testament passages that express a messianic focus. In other words, we are on our way to finding Christ in the Old Testament.

The Election of the Son of God

First, the *Son of God was chosen for His work as the Savior*. The frequent references to Christ's being sent by the Father imply at the very least that He was chosen for His mission. For example, Christ said, "I came down from heaven, not to do mine own will, but the will of him that sent me" (John 6:38). In His most solemn and sacred High Priestly prayer, the Lord defined eternal life as knowing "the only true God, and Jesus Christ," whom the Father had sent (John 17:3). Hebrews 3:1 identifies Christ Jesus as the "Apostle and High Priest of our profession." The simple significance of an apostle is being specially chosen and sent to perform a specific mission. As Christ Himself called and commissioned His apostles for their mission work, so the Father called and commissioned His Son for His mission to save His people from their sins. Although Hebrews 5 does establish clearly the superiority of Christ's priesthood to Aaron's, it nevertheless draws a significant parallel: just as the Old Testament prohibited usurpers to the priesthood and required divine calling, "so also Christ glorified not himself to be made an high priest; but he that said unto him, Thou art my Son, to day have I begotten thee" (Hebrews 5:4, 5). That Paul in Acts 13:33 used this statement from Psalm 2 as prophetic evidence of the resurrection of Christ and that the apostle in Hebrews used it to establish the election of the Son of God to be the mediating priest illustrate the deep and far-reaching messianic significance of the passage.

The New Testament makes the eternal election of Christ to be the Redeemer explicitly clear in connection with His atoning death. His sacrificial death on the cross was no accident nor was it a secondary plan implemented when He failed to establish an earthly kingdom. On the contrary, He was the Lamb slain from the foundation of the world (Revelation 13:8). The imagery of Christ as the Lamb, when understood in the light of Old Testament theology, demands attention to His special choice as the appropriate sacrifice. Not any lamb would do; it had to be our Christ, "a lamb without blemish and without spot: who verily was foreordained before the foundation of the world, but was manifest in these last times for you" (I Peter 1:19, 20). What happened in time was the fulfillment of God's eternal purpose. Peter also declared that although wicked men had their hands in the plot to crucify the Lord, in fact He was "delivered by the determinate counsel and foreknowledge of God" (Acts 2:23). Again in Acts 4:28 it is clear that what Pilate, Herod, and the people conspired to do in killing Christ was according to what God's counsel had "determined before to be done." Luke records that "truly the Son of man goeth, as it was determined..." (Luke 22:22). If "messiahs" are chosen, there can be no doubt that Jesus is the Messiah.

The Authority of the Son of God

Second, the *Son of God was accredited for His work as the Savior*. The Lord Jesus had the authority and approval from heaven to perform His duties as the anointed Mediator. The New Testament's documentation of Christ's authority and heavenly approval is abundant. To identify and discuss all the relevant New Testament teaching on this theme would require a volume by itself. My concern now is simply that we understand that those passages that speak of Christ's power or authority and His pleasing the Father provide irrefutable and unquestionable proof that Jesus of Nazareth was in fact the long-awaited Messiah of Old Testament prophecy.

Heaven's approval and verification of Jesus were declared first at His baptism. This remarkable event marked the beginning of the public ministry of Jesus. I don't think that we can ever fully fathom the significance of the Lord's baptism, which He said was necessary to fulfill all righteousness (Matthew 3:15). When we remember that John's baptism was a baptism of repentance (Mark 1:4), we perhaps can understand something of John the Baptist's reluctance to baptize Christ. When John saw Christ approaching, he declared, "Behold the Lamb of God, which taketh away the sin of the world" (John 1:29). Being a prophet, John understood well the significance of his announcement: the Lamb for sacrifice had to be pure, absolutely free from defect. There was no need for the sinless Lamb to be baptized with a baptism of repentance, for He had done nothing demanding repentance. Despite His personal sinlessness, the Lord Jesus submitted to that baptism and thereby publicly identified Himself with sinners. As Hebrews says, He was not ashamed to call brethren those whom He came to save (2:11). Having identified Himself with sinners at the inauguration of the public manifestation of His messianic ministry, Jesus and all who were there at the Jordan heard the voice from heaven affirming, "This is my beloved Son, in whom I am well pleased" (Matthew 3:17). The Father approved His Son's humiliation.

Another similar declaration occurred at the Transfiguration of Jesus on Mt. Hermon. There Peter, James, and John witnessed something of the magnificent glory that belonged to Christ's eternal nature as very God. As the visible glory again faded, the voice from heaven declared, "This is my beloved Son" (Mark 9:7). The Father approved His Son's glory. No lesser messiah ever enjoyed such express endorsement from heaven itself.

There was perhaps no greater declaration of God's approval of His Son than at the resurrection. Paul proclaimed that Christ was "declared to be the Son of God with power...by the resurrection from the dead" (Romans 1:4). In Acts 13:33 Paul interpreted the resurrection of Jesus from the dead to be the climactic declaration from God to Christ: "Thou art my Son" (quoting Psalm 2). By making such a declaration at the resurrection, God stamped His Son's atoning death with divine approval. It assured the success of the atonement and, indeed, of the Lord Jesus's entire messianic work. It is striking that both at the beginning and at the end of His earthly public work, the Father accredited His Son and our Savior with such powerful affirmations and validations of His mission. Sandwiched between those heavenly pronouncements was a work well done.

Not only did the Lord Jesus have the Father's approval; He also had the necessary authority and power to fulfill His mission as Messiah. In

His intimate High Priestly prayer the Son acknowledged that the Father had given him "power over all flesh" (John 17:2). The word "power" connotes more the idea of rightful authority than that of ability. This authority extended to every sphere of His influence and operation. He had the authority to give eternal life (John 17:2). He had the authority to forgive sins and heal the sick (Mark 2:10). He had such authority over the natural elements, the winds and the waves, that even His disciples feared as they pondered "what manner of man is this" (Mark 4:41). He had authority to order and demand obedience even from the demons (Mark 1:27). Even His critics had to acknowledge that "he taught them as one that had authority" (Mark 1:22). It was on the ground of the authority given Him in heaven and in earth that He commissioned His church to evangelize the world (Matthew 28:18-20). All of these instances constitute only a sampling of the authority He exercised while on earth. And they say nothing about the further authority and power he possesses in His exaltation (see Revelation 1). Only unfamiliarity with messianic theology would preclude identifying Jesus as the Old Testament's promised Messiah. The evidence is irrefutable and overwhelming.

The Power of the Son of God
Third, *the Son of God was empowered with the Holy Spirit for His work as the Savior*. Though the earthly ministry of Jesus does not reveal extensive direct evidence of spiritual empowering, the Spirit did clearly exert a vital influence in that ministry. So significant was the Holy Spirit's anointing and empowering of Christ at His baptism, the beginning of the public ministry, that each of the four Gospel narratives records the event (Matthew 3:16; Mark 1:10; Luke 3:22; John 1:32). John's account is perhaps the most instructive for our purpose. In it we read not only that John the Baptist witnessed the Spirit descending on Jesus at His baptism but also that "the Baptist" was told beforehand that this would be the unmistakable sign that the one upon whom the Spirit came would be the Son of God. "Upon whom thou shalt see the Spirit descending, and remaining on him, the same is he which baptizeth with the Holy Ghost" (John 1:33). The Spirit's anointing was messianic evidence. But John the Baptist, the transition prophet between the Old and the New Testaments, was told something and witnessed something that marked Jesus as unique. As we have seen, all the lesser messiahs experienced the enabling of the Holy Spirit for

their service. The nature of spiritual empowering in the Old Testament dispensation tended to be temporary and repetitive. Whenever there was a specific task to perform, there would be the special empowering by the Spirit. However, the Lord told John that the Holy Spirit would remain with the Ideal Messiah, and that is exactly what John saw happen (John 1:32, 33). The simple fact that the Holy Spirit never left the Lord Jesus explains why we never read of the Spirit's coming on Him again. His entire ministry was conducted in the power of the Holy Spirit. This is admittedly a mysterious truth. At the very least it highlights the cooperation of the Godhead in the work of salvation. The Father elected the Mediator; the Son executed the Mediation; the Spirit empowered the Mediator. The *Westminster Confession of Faith* summarizes well the evidence of Scripture:

> It pleased God, in His eternal purpose, to choose and ordain the Lord Jesus, His only begotten Son, to be the Mediator between God and man; the Prophet, Priest, and King…. The Lord Jesus, in His human nature thus united to the divine, was sanctified, and anointed with the Holy Spirit above measure…to the end that…He might be thoroughly furnished to execute the office of a Mediator and Surety. Which office he took not unto himself, but was thereunto called by His Father; who put all power and judgment into His hand, and gave Him commandment to execute the same. (Chapter VIII, sections 1, 2, 3.)

Recognizing that all of these common messianic features apply to the Lord Jesus will go a long way in ultimately helping us to see Him in the Old Testament. We know whom and what we are looking for. So, for instance, when Isaiah says, "Behold my servant, whom I uphold; mine elect, in whom my soul delighteth; I have put my spirit upon him…" (Isaiah 42:1), we have a pretty clear clue who the servant is. "Mine elect"–He is chosen. "In whom my soul delighteth"– He is accredited. "I have put my spirit upon him"– He is empowered with the Spirit. He must, therefore, be the Messiah. We have every warrant for seeing Jesus. At this point in our search, our excitement should be growing.

Distinct Duties of Messiahship

In addition to evidencing all the general characteristics of Messiahship, the Lord Jesus Christ also executes the distinct duties and responsibilities of the three principal messianic offices. As the

Ideal Messiah, He is the Ideal Prophet, the Ideal Priest, and the Ideal King. A synopsis of how Christ fulfills these mediatorial offices will provide necessary data for our Old Testament search. Because in the Lord Jesus all these offices unite in a single person, it is not always possible to identify aspects of His work as distinct operations of any single office. What He did and what He does are the work of the entire person. As the Christ, He fulfilled, is fulfilling, or will fulfill everything expected from a prophet, priest, and king.

The Ideal Prophet

Christ is the Ideal Prophet. The *Westminster Shorter Catechism* succinctly defines how Christ carries out the prophetic office: "Christ executeth the office of a prophet, in revealing to us, by his word and Spirit, the will of God for our salvation" (question 24). Put simply, a prophet is God's representative to man. Who better than the very Son of God, Himself God, could represent God to man? Speaking of the Lord Jesus in prophetic terms, Hebrews declares that God spoke in various ways through the prophets but has now revealed His final word to man by his Son, "whom he hath appointed heir of all things" (Hebrews 1:1, 2). By now, we should be recognizing the messianic vocabulary in that statement about Christ's being appointed. The more of that theological terminology we know the more we will appreciate how wonderfully the Scripture interweaves and integrates truth. Hebrews makes it so very clear that Jesus is the promised Messiah. Although all the Old Testament prophets were spokesmen for God and men of God, how imperfectly they represented God when compared to the Lord Jesus, who was "the brightness of his glory, and the express image of his person" (Hebrews 1:3). Similarly, Paul said of Christ that He is "the image of the invisible God" and that "in him dwelleth all the fulness of the Godhead bodily" (Colossians 1:15; 2:9). The bottom line, then, is this: Christ is the Ideal Prophet because Christ is God.

Christ's preaching, teaching, and working during His earthly mission constituted what we call His *immediate* or direct prophetic work. As we will see, in the Old Testament dispensation this immediate work was limited to the periodic Christophanies, or preincarnate appearances of the Son of God. But during the thirty-some years of the earthly life, that immediate prophetic ministry was unceasing.

40

JESUS THE MESSIAH

Examining the ministry of Christ reveals significant evidence of his prophetic ministry.

Evidence 1: Divine Source of Message

First, He claimed that His message was from the Father. Christ plainly claimed, "My doctrine is not mine, but his that sent me" (John 7:16). Remember that the authority of any prophet was contingent upon his speaking only the word that God had revealed to him. God would put words in the prophet's mouth, and he would in the place of God declare those words. Christ's unique relationship to the Father gave Him an authority that was without equal. The preaching and miracles of Jesus raised such division and debate among the Jews that they demanded of Him, "If thou be the Christ, tell us plainly" (John 10:24). Even these skeptical Jews knew the Old Testament well enough to recognize the messianic implications in what Jesus was saying and doing. So perfectly did Jesus, as the Ideal Prophet, represent God to men that He forthrightly answered their challenge with the profound assertion that no lesser prophet would dare think, let alone utter: "I and my Father are one" (John 10:30). They understood well the implications of that statement, but because of their hardness they sought to stone Him rather than humbly submit to Him in faith. To see Christ was to see God; indeed, to see Christ is the only way to know God. "No man hath seen God at any time; the only begotten Son, which is in the bosom of the Father, he hath declared him" (John 1:18).

As the obedient prophet, whose authority was validated in his insistent proclamation of "thus saith the Lord," Jesus testified that "all things that I have heard of my Father I have made known unto you" (John 15:15). He declared plainly, "I do nothing of myself; but as my Father hath taught me, I speak these things" (John 8:28). In another place He said, "For I have not spoken of myself; but the Father which sent me, he gave me a commandment, what I should say, and what I should speak" (John 12:49; see also 14:10, 24; 17:8). Christ over and over gave convincing testimony that He said and did only what the Father instructed. In some ways these appear to be strange statements coming from God Himself. But they must be understood in the context of "messianic" theology. By so confessing, He made it clear that He was the prophet who was promised and who had to come. Peter specifically identified Jesus as the long-promised prophet whose words had awesome authority and urgency: "For Moses truly said unto the fathers, A prophet shall the Lord your God raise up unto you of your brethren, like unto me; him shall ye hear in all things whatsoever he shall say unto you. And it shall come to pass, that every soul, which will not hear that prophet, shall be destroyed from among the people" (Acts 3:22-23; see Deuteronomy 18:15, 19).

So ingrained was this messianic prophetic anticipation in the time of Jesus that even the Samaritan woman acknowledged, "I know that Messias cometh, which is called Christ: when he is come, he will tell us all things" (John 4:25). Immediately the Lord Jesus declared to her that He was that Messiah (John 4:26). In that New Testament world it was virtually common knowledge what the Messiah would be and do. The tragedy is that notwithstanding that knowledge so many rejected the divinely revealed and authoritative words of the Prophet of all prophets. The implications and applications of this rejection are far-reaching. To trifle with or to ignore the words of this Ideal Prophet is to put the soul in eternal jeopardy. That was true in the days in which He walked on earth; it is true today. It behooves every man everywhere to hear and heed the words of Christ. He had and has authority like no other.

Evidence 2: Predictive Message

The second evidence of the prophetic office of the Lord Jesus is His foretelling the future. Predicting the future, after all, was something that prophets did. In fact, this ability to predict the future accurately was a key test that God specified for judging whether a prophet was genuine or not. The Lord issued a stern warning to any prophet who would presume to speak anything that God had not commanded him to speak (Deuteronomy 18:20). He then declared that unfulfilled prophecy would be an unmistakable sign that the Lord had not spoken through that prophet (Deuteronomy 18:22). If the Lord Jesus was to give credible evidence of His being the Father's prophet, it was necessary for Him to make some predictions.

Perhaps Christ's most extensive predictive message was the Olivet Discourse (Matthew 24), in which the Lord spoke of events that would occur in both the near and the distant future. Some of this complex preview of things to come concerned the fall of Jerusalem to the Romans in AD 70, whereas some await fulfillment in the great cataclysmic events surrounding His own second coming. However, the one single prediction upon which Christ staked His entire prophetic and messianic credibility was the prophecy of His own resurrection from the dead. When the cynical scribes and Pharisees asked Christ for a sign to verify His claims, the Lord first excoriated them as an evil and adulterous generation and then limited the verifying sign to one, the sign of the prophet Jonah. Professing Himself to be greater than Jonah, Christ plainly predicted, "As Jonas was three days and three nights in the whale's belly; so shall the Son of man be three days and three nights in the heart of the earth" (Matthew 12:40). Among other things, the resurrection of Christ was heaven's validation and verification of His entire prophetic office. If this most remarkable prediction were to come true, the Lord is saying, how much should men give heed to every other claim and statement Jesus made. That is the point. All men should listen well. On another occasion when the Jews wanted a sign, the Lord said, "Destroy this temple, and in three days I will raise it up" (John 2:19). In their mocking unbelief, they interpreted Him literally and missed the point completely. He was speaking of the temple of His body. His disciples, however, after the resurrection remembered this specific prediction, and they "believed the scripture, and the word which Jesus had said" (John 2:22).

Evidence 3: Signs and Wonders

Third, Christ performed wonders. According to Deuteronomy 13, this was another thing that prophets did. Jesus would leave no room for doubt concerning His identity and office. If anyone failed to believe who He was, it was not for lack of evidence; it was for lack of spiritual sense and perception. The Gospel narratives are filled with accounts of Christ's healing the sick, casting out demons, giving sight to the blind and hearing to the deaf, and even raising the dead. There is no question that motivating all these acts of mercy was a heart of compassion for those He delivered. In fact, Mark says as much in recording the healing of the leper who humbly sought out Christ for healing (Mark 1:40-41). But in addition to revealing the kindness of Jesus, the friend of sinners, these miracles, as well as those that were just flat-out demonstrations of sovereign power (calming the storm, feeding the thousands, etc.), provide more irrefutable evidence that Jesus was the true prophet of God.

The proof that Jesus of Nazareth was the Ideal Prophet was and is overwhelming. It is not surprising that many in Jesus's own day, having witnessed His works, "glorified God, saying, That a great prophet is risen up among us" (Luke 7:16; Matthew 21:11, 46). It is not surprising that after His resurrection–the "test" prophecy–even some of the religious leaders who called for His death called on Him for life and salvation (Acts 6:7–"a great company of the priests were obedient to the faith"). The same Spirit that empowered Christ for His immediate prophetic ministry worked mediately (indirectly) through all the Old Testament prophets who spoke of Him and through the New Testament apostles who witnessed and recorded His gospel. Although we cannot hear Christ with our natural hearing or see Him with our natural sight, we can and must see and hear Him by faith in the written word. Knowing a prophet when we see one will help us in our search for Christ wherever we read in the Scripture, including the Old Testament.

The Ideal Priest

Christ is the Ideal Priest. The *Westminster Shorter Catechism* cogently describes how Christ carries out the priestly office: "Christ executeth the office of a priest, in his once offering up of himself a sacrifice to satisfy divine justice, and reconcile us to God; and in making continual intercession for us" (question 25). In simple terms, a priest is man's representative before God. It is obvious from the catechism's statement that the priesthood of Christ brings us to the heart of His mission and the ultimate purpose of His incarnation. Christ came to save His people, and saving His people required the shedding of His blood in sacrifice. We will consider the nature of Christ's atoning work in some detail later. It is my purpose here simply to link these most vital works of Christ to His priestly office. As the Lord Jesus performed those distinctively priestly duties, He confirmed again that He was the promised Messiah. He proved that He was the anticipated Savior of the Old Testament. Christ's establishing a link between "priest" theology and Himself was evidence to the contemporary generation that the long-awaited Messiah had come; it is a clue for us as we read about the priestly function in the Old Testament that we should be seeing Christ.

Although much of the New Testament declares the gospel of Christ's dying for our sins, no place more specifically explains that death in priestly terms than the book of Hebrews. The message of the book was primarily to Jews within the Church who were for some reason being tempted to abandon the finished sacrifice of Christ and return to the ritualistic ceremonies of the Temple. They knew they needed a priest, but they were putting their souls in eternal jeopardy by rejecting the Ideal Priest. The whole book of Hebrews argues for the absolute superiority of Jesus Christ over the temporary Old Testament order. It does so not by abrogating the message of the Old Testament but by showing that everything in the Old Testament points to Him. The purpose of "pointing" is to direct attention to an object other than self. If we see a crowd pointing at something in the distance, our curiosity focuses on the distant object, not on the different forms or styles of pointing. If we focus on the latter, we will most certainly "miss the point." Hebrews argues similarly. The intent of the Old Testament sacrifices and ceremonies was to point men to the only Savior of sinners. Hebrews proves that Christ is better, infinitely better, than the pointers. He is better than Moses, whom God called and used to explain the whole sacrificial system (Hebrews 3). He is better than Aaron, whom God called to officiate the rituals of the sacrifices (Hebrews 7). He is better than all the bulls, goats, and lambs that were selected to be the sacrifices (Hebrews 9).

Everything that was necessary for a priest to do, the Lord Jesus Christ did in supreme fashion. The book of Hebrews develops each of the essential elements delineated in the statement of the Shorter Catechism. *He offered Himself as a perfect sacrifice to God.* Declaring the superiority of Christ's sacrifice over any animal, Hebrews says, "How much more shall the blood of Christ, who through the eternal Spirit offered himself without spot to God...bear the sins of many" (9:14, 28). *He became a reconciliation for the sins of His people:* "Wherefore in all things it behoved him to be made like unto his brethren, that he might be a merciful and faithful high priest in things pertaining to God, to make reconciliation for the sins of the people" (Hebrews 2:17). He offers continual intercession for His people on the authority of a continuing, unchangeable, untransferable priesthood. "But this man, because he continueth ever, hath an unchangeable priesthood. Wherefore he is able also to save them to the uttermost that come unto God by him, seeing he ever liveth to make intercession for them" (Hebrews 7:24, 25).

As our Priest, the Lord Jesus has done what is necessary for our salvation. He procured it by His once-for-all sacrifice; He preserves it by His unceasing intercession for us at God's right hand. According to Revelation, the Lord Jesus is now "clothed with a garment down to the foot, and girt about the paps with a golden girdle" (1:13). This "to the feet garment" is the glorious high priestly dress that among other things would include the breastplate and ephod. On the breastplate and ephod were the names of the people of God. What an amazing and reassuring thought this is. As our Savior intercedes for us, He does not just pray in general terms for "all those people down there." He bears our names over His heart in expression of His compassion; He bears our names upon His shoulders in demonstration of His ability to keep us from falling.

Perhaps Hebrews 5 is the most explicit exposition of the link that God intended between the Old Testament priesthood and the Lord Jesus Christ. The chapter begins with the example of the necessary mediation between God and men: Aaron illustrates the priesthood (vv. 1-4). There are five key elements of Aaron's priesthood that point directly to Christ: (1) the priest represents man; (2) the priest mediates for men before God; (3) the priest officiates the sacrifices; (4) the priest sympathizes with the people because he experiences the same infirmities; (5) the priest is chosen.

Following this Old Testament illustration, the chapter gives the evidence of the existing mediation: Christ fulfills the priesthood (vv. 5-9). These verses particularly highlight the Ideal Priest's divine appointment to office and His experiences during the days of His flesh when He suffered, learned obedience, and became the author of salvation unto all who obey Him. He is able to feel for His people as He functions mediatorially in their behalf. Although Christ's priesthood was like Aaron's in significant details, it was so much more. In fact, rather than being exactly like Aaron's, it was "after the order of Melchisedec" (Hebrews 5:10). We will have to consider the significance of this later; my concern now is simply that we recognize the work of Christ in terms of messianic priesthood.

Recognizing this connection will direct our thoughts to Christ when we read about the priests in the Old Testament. We will want to look away from them and their work to the One to whom they are pointing. The more we understand about the priestly ministry, even by looking at the imperfect illustrations, the more we can learn to enjoy and appropriate its many benefits. This is what Hebrews exhorts us to do when it encourages us to come boldly to the throne of grace (4:12). We are to do so because we know about our high priest, who knows firsthand our problems and truly cares for us. What benefits are ours because Jesus is our Ideal Priest!

The Ideal King

Christ is the Ideal King. The *Westminster Shorter Catechism* concisely explains how Christ carries out the kingly office: "Christ executeth the office of a king, in subduing us to himself, in ruling, and defending us, and in restraining and conquering all his and our enemies" (question 26). Ironically, the kingship of Christ is one of the most obvious of His messianic operations yet in some ways the most confusing. Here is the problem. As the Second Person of the holy Trinity, the Son of God is the absolute sovereign over all things. God is essentially independent, unaffected by anything outside Himself. He exercises His absolute dominion over the entirety of His creation. There is, therefore, a kingship that our Savior has by virtue of His being God. On the other hand, as the Christ, the Son of God was anointed and commissioned with a kingship that is vitally connected to the mediatorial work of grace. This messianic kingship refers specifically to Christ's official authority to rule for God's glory and for the ingathering of the whole number of God's elect. By this special kingship, the Lord Jesus procures, protects, and perfects the church. This kingship, like the priestly and prophetic offices, is a vital link to the Old Testament. If we can identify the claims of Christ's kingship from the New Testament and then discover those same claims in the Old Testament, we should perceive the revelation of King Jesus. The following observations about Christ's royal authority should help in our Old Testament search for Him.

Universal Rule

Christ's kingship is universal. When Jesus commissioned His disciples to preach the gospel throughout the world, He backed up His command with the reassuring word that all power—or, more precisely, all authority—was given to Him in heaven and in earth (Matthew 28:18). The reference to heaven and earth is a frequent figure of speech in the Bible called merismus. This is a literary device that uses polar or opposite expressions to include everything in between as well. When, for instance, Christ identifies Himself as the Alpha and Omega, He is not saying that He is merely the first and last letters of the Greek alphabet. Rather, He is saying He is infinite; He is all and in all. So when Christ claims that He has been given authority in heaven and earth, He is not limiting that power to two specific places. On the contrary, He is emphasizing the universality of His rule. There is no place outside the sphere of His dominion. The authority of a sovereign is always limited by the size of his kingdom. Once a king or president or national leader leaves his borders, his right to rule is gone. As a husband and father, I have a God-given right and responsibility to be the head of my home and family. God has graciously given me a family that respects and honors my authority. My next-door neighbors, however, do not recognize my authority at all. My "kingdom" is very small. Christ's kingdom is universal. The world would be a fearful and intimidating place to preach the gospel if Christ were not in ultimate control. Paul explains that this messianic kingship is ultimately for the good of the church, stating that God has exalted Christ "far above all principality, and power, and might, and dominion, and every name that is named, not only in this world, but also in that which is to come: and hath put all things under his feet, and gave him to be the head over all things to the church" (Ephesians 1:21-22).

Irresistible Rule

Christ's kingship is irresistible. In one way or another Christ's kingdom will always be victorious; it conquers all. Christ, the king, will subdue either by grace or by wrath. The day will come when "at the name of Jesus every knee should bow, of things in heaven, and things in earth, and things under the earth: and that every tongue should confess that Jesus Christ is Lord, to the glory of God the Father" (Philippians 2:10-11). Paul's language is not without messianic significance. Notice his reference to Christ, that is, the Messiah, and his reference to "Lord," which must be understood here in its full sense of sovereign master. All will one day confess the messianic kingship of Jesus. One aspect of this irresistible kingship is in the salvation of His people. In one of his early sermons, Peter declared concerning Christ that God had exalted Him to be "a Prince and a Saviour, for to give repentance to Israel, and forgiveness of sins" (Acts 5:31). The word translated "prince" (archegos) does not refer here to the son of a king, who has only a potential or future authority; it refers to a leader who rules from the front. Christ is the champion of His people. The other side of this irresistible kingship is judgment. The Father has committed judgment to Christ (John 5:22, 27), and He will with unrelenting success take "vengeance on them that know not God, and that obey not the gospel of our Lord Jesus Christ" (II Thessalonians 1:8). Revelation vividly declares the certainty of His irresistible judgment when He returns to earth armed with the sharp sword in His mouth and bearing the name "KING OF KINGS, AND LORD OF LORDS" (19:15-16).

Providential Rule

Christ's kingship is providential. Providence refers to the constant ruling and preserving of the affairs of the kingdom. Speaking specifically of the Lord Jesus, Paul identifies Him as the firstborn or preeminent one over all creation. Then he says, "For by him were all things created, that are in heaven, and that are in earth, visible and invisible, whether they be thrones, or dominions, or principalities, or powers: all things were created by him, and for him: and he is before all things, and by him all things consist. And he is the head of the body, the church..." (Colossians 1:16-18). Similarly, Hebrews says that He upholds "all things by the word of his power" (1:3). The point is that Christ is not a king in waiting or a king without a kingdom. He rules now, and He rules well. If we should ever doubt whether Christ is on the throne, we need only look to see if we can see anything. If we can see something, that should be all the evidence we need. If Christ were to stop ruling, there would be nothing left.

Millennial Rule

Christ's kingship is millennial. I readily admit that not all Bible believers share this particular notion about Christ's rule. That disagreement is fine but at the very least, all Bible believers agree that there is a future aspect to His kingdom and that there will be a definite time when Christ will "appear the second time without sin unto salvation" (Hebrews 9:28). At that time the kingship that believers know now by faith will be manifest for all to see. Christ will return to earth personally, visibly, bodily, gloriously, really. It is my opinion that the Scripture teaches that the glorious return of Christ will commence His visible reign on the earth. On the basis of Revelation 20, that reign will last for a thousand years. This passage prophesies that Satan will be bound for a thousand years and that there will be a group of people who will live and reign with Christ that thousand years. At the end of that millennium Satan will be loosed and will instigate a rebellion from the four quarters of the earth. All in all, it seems fairly clear that the whole venue is on the earth. Peter writes about the Day of the Lord that he describes as the "new heavens and a new earth, wherein dwelleth righteousness" (II Peter 3:10–13). This prophetic interpretation is called Premillennialism, which simply means Christ will return before an actual thousand-year reign. Interestingly, although the New Testament, I believe, teaches this, most of our information about this reign of righteousness comes from the Old Testament. We will certainly consider that data when we search for Christ in the prophecies of the Old Testament. I want to be perfectly clear that I am not suggesting that Christ is not now king. He is not an exiled or banished king waiting to reclaim His usurped throne. He is right now an exalted, powerful, and most active Sovereign. But there is to be yet another glorious manifestation of His reign. Even so, come quickly, Lord Jesus. Indeed, let your kingdom come.

Now that we have surveyed what a Messiah is and how the Lord Jesus Christ satisfies the requirements for Messiahship, we are well on our way to finding Him in the Old Testament. Discerning the messianic motifs will always point us to the Savior because He is the One whom the Lord ultimately intends us to see, even if we are looking for a while at one of the lesser messiahs. If we are to interpret the Scripture properly, we must understand that God from the beginning of His revelation and declaration of grace to sinners has centered that message of grace in the one person of the Messiah, the one finally revealed as the Lord Jesus Christ.

CHAPTER 2
THE PERSON OF CHRIST

There is something exciting about seeing someone famous in person. Sport fans go wild when they go to a game and see in person the athletes they have watched on television. Seeing in person the President of the United States or the leader of any country is a memorable event, even if we don't particularly agree with his political philosophy or his policies. Just to see a president is something to remember. It is strange how otherwise normal and mature people will push and shove and strain their necks just to get a glimpse of somebody famous. I must confess that notwithstanding my normally reserved demeanor, even I have fallen victim to this seeing-someone-famous frenzy. Forever etched in my memory is the opportunity extended by a friend to go to Augusta, Georgia, to see the famous Master's Golf Tournament. I have virtually no skill at playing the game but have for years been a fan. To see those professionals on television make look so simple what I find to be so impossible fascinates me. To have a chance to see those guys in person was a dream come true. I will never forget my first sight of Palmer, Nicklaus, Watson, Norman, and all the rest. I was straining my neck like everybody else. While I was duly impressed with what I saw in terms of their skills, there was something that surprised me. Not a one of them was as "big" as he appeared on the television. Not all of them behaved in person the way they appeared on commercials. In some ways they disappointed me. This is the point I want to make. In one way or another people are disappointing, no matter how famous they are. There is only one person who has ever lived or will ever live on this planet who has never disappointed any who have seen him or known him. That person is the Lord Jesus Christ.

Seeing and knowing Jesus Christ in person result in not just a memorable but a life-changing experience. There were times during the earthly ministry of Jesus when for various reasons He was famous. The Scripture relates that His fame spread throughout the country; people were talking about Him everywhere. Huge crowds followed Christ, with the people pushing and shoving and straining their necks just to get a sight of Him. Some climbed trees, and others tore open rooftops just to get to Jesus. Some were nothing more than curious spectators; some were enemies trying to entrap Him; some were genuine seekers of salvation. But Jesus was always Jesus; He was always the same. No one has ever been disappointed in what he has seen in Jesus. Seeing Jesus in person is essential to spiritual and eternal life. Obviously, because Jesus lived on earth some two thousand years ago, we cannot see Him in the same sense that His earthly contemporaries saw Him. Nonetheless, there is a way that God has given us to see Jesus in person—indeed, a superior way. This is clear from Peter's account of his eyewitness experience of Christ's transfiguration. As wonderful as that was, he says that we have a more sure testimony that requires our attention: "We have also a more sure word of prophecy; whereunto ye do well that ye take heed, as unto a light that shineth in a dark place, until the day dawn, and the day star arise in your hearts" (II Peter 1:19). He then identifies that more sure testimony as the inspired Scriptures. Seeing Jesus at the transfiguration was good; seeing Jesus in the Bible is better. This should be our overwhelming desire: to see Jesus. Really seeing Jesus in person is more the operation of spiritual sight than physical. Many saw Christ with their physical eyes who now writhe in hell with the memory of that sight haunting them. The Lord Jesus said to a great crowd, "But I said unto you, That ye also have seen me, and believe not" (John 6:36). There is an old saying that "seeing is believing." Spiritually speaking, this is not true. But the converse is. Seeing is not necessarily believing, but *believing is seeing*. It is through the eye of faith that in the Scripture we will see Jesus for who He really is. The Bible is the only place that we can, for now, see Christ in person.

Seeing Christ in person in the Scripture is the theme of this chapter. But what exactly does "seeing Christ" mean in this context? Certainly, it does not mean that we are to conjure up images or visualize what we think He may have looked like. It is natural as we read the narratives of Scripture to allow the Word of God to generate "pictures" of the scenes and characters, including Jesus. We cannot read in a mental vacuum; God has not designed our minds that way. The point, nevertheless, is that Jesus is not what we imagine Him to be; He is what the Scripture reveals Him to be. What is it that makes Christ Christ? If we can answer that, we are seeing the Lord in person. If we know what constitutes His person, we will recognize Him when we see those personal traits. What I propose doing in this chapter is providing a snapshot of some of the personal traits of Christ so we can recognize Him when we see Him, even in the Old Testament. The Old Testament never explicitly says, "Here is Jesus," but over and again it does reveal His person. As I have contended, a big part of finding Christ in the Old Testament is knowing what and whom we are looking for.

A Special Person

In the last chapter we identified the Messiah by His principal "occupations": prophet, priest, king. We now focus on His person. There are some jobs that virtually anyone can do, whereas other jobs require a special knowledge or ability. Further, some jobs require a special kind of person. Some people just do not have what it takes to be an elementary school teacher, who must deal patiently with other people's little children. And some people with the brains and technical ability to become a surgeon don't have the stomach for such a job. Certain people and certain jobs just don't mix. Here is the point. It takes a special person to be the Messiah, and the Lord Jesus has what it takes. He has all the necessary qualifications to be the only mediator between God and men. In fact, He is the only person who is qualified, able, and willing to perform the "job" that He does. Jesus is a uniquely special person.

Function of the Mediator

We have already identified the main offices that compose the Christ's mediatorial function, and we will consider some of His specific and unique works. For now, though, let's just say that the Mediator's job is to settle the differences between two opposing parties: God and men. Both prophets and apostles make clear the issue that separates the two. Isaiah declares, "Your iniquities have separated between you and your God, and your sins have hid his face from you" (Isaiah 59:2). Paul speaks of men as being "alienated and enemies" against God (Colossians 1:21). By nature men are sinners subject to divine wrath, and by behavior they are disobedient to God's law, liable to condemnation (see Ephesians 2). There is an immeasurable distance between God and man that man cannot begin to bridge and that God cannot close simply by an act of His will. What is required is a mediator who can relate to both parties. Job, in one of his dark moments, desperately felt the need for such a mediator. He all too well recognized that God was not a man with whom he could dispute face to face. At that moment he felt helpless, lamenting, "Neither is there any daysman betwixt us, that might lay his hand upon us both" (Job 9:32, 33). A "daysman" is simply one who could arbitrate between two, a mediator. This text well defines what such a mediator must be able to do: he must be able to touch both sides of the dispute. He must be able to address the needs and concerns of both parties. Man's need is drastic: he cannot on his own approach God. God's concerns are inflexible: He cannot allow justice to fall, not even to grace. The grace of God, notwithstanding its sovereignty, will not and cannot declare bygones to be bygones without something to satisfy His justice. So long as God is God and man is man, there must be a mediator between them. That mediator is the Lord Jesus Christ. Christ is the answer to man's needs; Christ is the answer to God's concern. To be without Christ, therefore, is to be without hope and without God (Ephesians 2:12).

Before moving on, let's be sure we are fair to Job. In his moment of despair, he wondered if God or anyone else really cared. If we are honest with ourselves, we have wondered the same thing when experiencing troubles that do not even approach the severity of Job's suffering. In one of his high moments of faith in the throes of his suffering, Job confidently confessed his knowledge that such a mediator did exist. He confessed a pretty advanced theology for someone living so many years before Christ was born, declaring, "My witness is in heaven, and my record is on high" (Job 16:19). Both "witness" and "record" are personal terms. The word "record" could well be translated "advocate," referring not to a written history of Job's life in heaven but to one taking up his cause. The following verses expand on that confession. The Hebrew of Job is notoriously difficult and some portions can be legitimately translated in different ways. Learning and teaching Hebrew have consumed a big part of my life, so allow me to offer a simple literal rendering of Job 16:19-21. I think it will help to highlight the messianic hope enjoyed by one of the most ancient of

THE PERSON OF CHRIST

Old Testament believers. (Note that when I put a word in parenthesis, it indicates it is necessarily supplied to make sense in English syntax. The Authorized Version does the same thing with italics.)

> Also now, behold in the heaven (is) my Witness
> And my Advocate (is) in the heights
> My Middleman (is) my Friend
> To God my eyes weep
> And He settles quarrels for man with God
> Even (as) a son of man for his friend

Having rescued Job's orthodoxy, we can return to the issue at hand. Jesus Christ is the only qualified mediator between God and men. The question is what qualifies Jesus to be the effective advocate who can touch both God and man. The answer to this question brings us to the essence of His special and unique person. He can do the "job" because He is both God and man.

Qualifications of the Mediator

The above statement is easy enough to say, but comprehending it is a different matter. That Jesus Christ is the Son of God, the eternal Second Person of the Holy Trinity, and at the same time the Son of Man, who was made of a woman in the likeness of sinful flesh, absolutely boggles the mind. It is a profound truth that *defies explanation but demands belief.* It is not my purpose to address all the deep theological and logical issues and problems surrounding the truth. That would require a whole treatise. But there are some fundamental matters that we must consider if we are going to be able to recognize the person of Christ when He is revealed to us in Scripture.

The facts are simple: Christ is God and Christ is man. The problem is how both of these can be true. This union of God and man heads the list of what the New Testament aptly terms "the mystery of godliness": "God was manifest in the flesh" (I Timothy 3:16). That Paul calls this a mystery means that it is a truth that is totally beyond human invention; it is a truth that could not possibly be known apart from the fact that God revealed it to us. Trying to explain this union of the human and divine was the subject of many early church councils and the theme of some of the most profound confessional statements. The affirmation and the creedal declarations of the Westminster Standards are classics which deserve our attention. As you read the statements, pay particular attention to how they use the terms "nature" and "person." Defining these terms properly and keeping them distinct are crucial. Whereas "nature" refers to the intrinsic and essential characteristics of something, "person" refers to the individual being. Whereas nature determines both what a person is like and what a person does, a person is the living entity that has a nature.

The *Westminster Confession of Faith* declares about Christ:

> "...two whole, perfect, and distinct natures, the Godhead and the manhood, were inseparably joined together in one person, without conversion, composition, or confusion. Which person is very God, and very man, yet one Christ, the only Mediator between God and man" (Chapter VIII, section 2).

The *Westminster Larger Catechism* declares about Christ:

> "It was requisite that the Mediator, who was to reconcile God and man, should himself be both God and man, and this in one person, that the proper works of each nature might be accepted of God for us, and relied on by us, as the works of the whole person" (question 40).

The *Westminster Shorter Catechism* declares about Christ:

> "The only Redeemer of God's elect is the Lord Jesus Christ, who, being the eternal Son of God, became man and so was and continueth to be God and man in two distinct natures, and one person, for ever" (question 21).

These declarations are masterpieces of orthodox confession and Scriptural synopsis. They suggest some important focus points crucial for our understanding about the person of Christ.

First, *Jesus is God*. He is a divine person with all the attributes of essential deity. Every thing that God is, Jesus is.

Second, *Jesus is man*. He possesses the human nature with all of its essential attributes. It is vital to remark at this point that sin is not an essential element of human nature. Everything about our human nature is defiled and depraved by the Fall. But Adam, who was created a true man, was not created defiled or depraved. Christ's humanity is, therefore, that of the original creation; His is a pre-sin humanity. In a sense, Christ's humanity is more originally real than ours.

Third, *in the one person of Jesus the two natures of deity and humanity are inseparably united.* The two natures did not act independently. The incarnate Christ was not God sometimes and man sometimes; He was always God and always man. Theologians often refer to Christ as the *Theanthropic* person. This is simply a Greek word that combines the word for God and the word for man. It is the equivalent of our saying the God/Man.

Fourth, *the two natures did not combine to form a distinct third nature.* The Lord Jesus was not a hybrid mixture of deity and humanity. It is important to note that whereas the term *theanthropic* applies appropriately to the person of Christ, it does not apply to the natures of Christ. His deity was not humanized; His humanity was not deified. The finite did not become infinite nor the infinite finite. The God/Man is both finite and infinite. Theologians call this the *hypostatic* union. *Hypostasis* is just a Greek word meaning essence or substance that has been used to describe this otherwise inexplicable union of a perfect human nature with the eternal divine nature in the Second Person of the Trinity.

Fifth, *the person of Christ was not created by the union of the divine and human natures.* The human nature of Christ did not have any independent existence apart from the eternal person of the Son of God. The person of Christ is eternal; He never came into existence. His divine nature is, therefore, necessarily eternal. It had no beginning and it will have no end. The eternal Second Person of the Trinity took to Himself in time a real human nature and now and forever continues as the one eternal Person with two distinct natures. The truth is not that man became God but that God became man.

Don't get frustrated if all of this is difficult to understand completely, because this truth is ultimately beyond comprehension. We can attempt to describe what the Scripture tells us, but to explain the mechanics of the incarnation is humanly impossible. In fact, most of the ancient heresies concerning the mystery of the person of Christ were heresies because they tried to define too much. Some denied the genuineness or completeness of His deity; some counterbalanced by denying the genuineness or completeness of His humanity. Still other heresies wrestled with and defined away the uniqueness of His person. Sadly, versions of these old and specious attempts to explain the supernatural are still floating around. Just remember that we are never expected to explain the miraculous; we are expected to *believe*.

The incarnation, God's manifesting Himself in flesh, is the most stupendous event in the history of the world. Instead of allowing our inability to comprehend it to frustrate us, let us be overcome with a sense of absolute awe as we begin to see how very special is the person of our blessed Savior. Seeing Him in person as He is revealed in the Scripture ought to excite us and cause us to strain our necks to see more and more of Him. We have in the person of Jesus Christ the only one who can solve the problem of our sin and thus resolve the tension between God and us. I want to look at some of the New Testament evidence of the deity and humanity of Christ in order to reinforce in our minds that the union of these two natures is absolutely and invariably unique to one person. Then when we read in the Old Testament about a person who is described in both human and divine terms, we will know that we have found the one and only Christ. He is the one we are looking for.

The Divine Nature of the One Person

The New Testament is dogmatically clear that Jesus of Nazareth is God. The evidence is irrefutable, and it is undeniable except by blind and blatant disbelief. I believe that one of the grandest statements of the deity of Christ in the New Testament is Romans 9:5. In listing the spiritual advantages of the Jewish nation, the apostle Paul climaxes the impressive list by identifying Israel as the national lineage through which Christ came in the flesh. I have taught Greek as well as Hebrew for many years, so again permit me to offer my translation of the verse. Pay attention to the punctuation marks that I will use to highlight the inherent clarity of Paul's statement regarding who Christ is: "Whose are the fathers, and out of whom (is) the Christ according to flesh, the one who is God over all things, the blessed one forever. Amen." Often the New Testament just flat out declares that Jesus is God. That evidence is easy to see. However, there is other evidence of His deity beyond just the names of God applied to Him. Perfections of God, works of God, and the worship of God are all attributed to the Lord Jesus Christ, and they therefore witness to His absolute deity.

THE PERSON OF CHRIST

Perfections of Deity

It is impossible to define God because the very nature of definition is to set limits or restrictions around the subject being defined. The best we can do is to describe God in the terms by which He has chosen to reveal Himself. These descriptions of what God is we refer to as attributes, characteristics, or perfections. Perhaps one of the simplest, yet most profound, confessional statements describing God is in the *Westminster Shorter Catechism*: "God is a Spirit, infinite, eternal, and unchangeable, in his being, wisdom, power, holiness, justice, goodness, and truth" (question 4). The perfections listed here are in two broad categories that theologians call incommunicable and communicable. The communicable attributes of God are those that are infinitely, eternally, and unchangeably true with reference to Him, but also that He communicates or shares with the creature. So for instance, though God's holiness is incomparably more holy than ours, we are to be holy as He is holy. Therefore, someone's being holy is not evidence of deity. Incommunicable attributes, on the other hand, are those that are uniquely true of God. If someone has one of these attributes, he must be God. This is my focus here. If these incommunicable perfections are true of Christ, then the only logical and legitimate conclusion must be that Christ is God. There are five essential perfections of deity that the Scripture applies to Christ, giving evidence of His deity. My temptation is to develop these themes thoroughly, but that would take us too far from our thesis. I will simply identify each perfection and offer some New Testament evidence of it. My purpose is to create a theological database for finding Christ in the Old Testament. Seeing these perfections applied to Christ in the New Testament and seeing the same perfections applied to Messiah in the Old Testament should convince us that we are looking at the same person. We are collecting clues for finding Christ.

Absolute Independence

Christ is *infinite in being*. Independent self-existence is an essential element of deity. God is without beginning or end; He is the ever-living One. God owes His existence to none. The truth is that God is. The New Testament clearly asserts this independent self-existence to be true of the Lord Jesus. John 1:4 expressly declares, "In him was life." John 5 records Christ's response to angry Jews seeking to kill Him because He had healed a man on the Sabbath. The Lord's defense focused on the intimate relationship between Himself and the Father, the significance of which even the unbelieving Jews recognized. If all these things were true, there was no doubt who Jesus really was. They knew that to call God "Father" in the way that Jesus was calling Him "Father" was to make Himself equal with God (John 5:18). They were right. In that self-defense Christ made a statement that proves the point concerning self-existence. "For as the Father hath life in himself; so hath he given to the Son to have life in himself" (John 5:26).

During another confrontation with unbelieving Jews, the Lord said that their father Abraham rejoiced to see His day. This led to a most significant exchange. The Jews said, "Thou art not yet fifty years old, and hast thou seen Abraham?" (John 8:57). Christ's answer astounded them and intensified their anger: "Before Abraham was, I am" (John 5:58). The "I am" is an unmistakable application to Himself of the name *Jehovah*, the unique covenant name of the one true and living God. This is the name the Lord explains to Moses at the burning bush: I AM THAT I AM (Exodus 3:14). To understand the full significance of the assertion requires understanding the rich "Name" theology of the Old Testament. To develop that theology is for now outside our scope, but I will say briefly that one of the essential declarations that God makes about Himself in the name Jehovah is His absolute, independent self-existence. One thing is for sure. Notwithstanding the Jews' hatred of Jesus, they well understood the implications of His theology. When they heard Him apply the divine name to Himself, they took up stones to kill Him. But Christ, in a skillful display of His self-existence, escaped by going through the middle of the angry crowd.

One more passage will evidence this point. Revelation 1 records John's glorious vision of the exalted Christ. In verse 8 the Alpha and Omega identified Himself as the "Lord, which is, and which was, and which is to come." The verbal forms and order of the assertion are noteworthy. Perhaps a more pedantically literal rendering will highlight the significance: "the One who is being, the was One, the One who is coming." The statement is obviously out of order temporally, thus accenting the constant "present tense" of this One who was in the same state and who will be in that same state. In other words, His "was" and His "will be" are necessary corollaries to His "unceasing is." That almost makes sense! Verse 18 also reveals His absolutely independent life: "I am he that liveth, and was dead, and, behold, I am alive for evermore." Sandwiched between two assertions that He is constantly and unceasingly living is the rather unusual statement, "I became a dead one." I would suggest that this implies a voluntary and controlled entering into the state of death rather than the inevitable "out of our hands" dying that is the natural end of all men. That the verse ends with His possession of the keys (authority) over the entire realm of death further substantiates His independence of Being.

Eternity

Christ is *infinite in regard to time*. He is eternal; He is not bound to the limitations of time. Because we are creatures of time, we tend to define everything in terms of the time we know. That's okay; we have to think the only way we can. Eternity past is, in our way of thinking, that time beyond the creation of time. Eternity future is that everlasting time beyond the end of time. There is a sense, however, in which eternity is not just a past with no beginning and a future with no ending. If time consists of a succession of moments, eternity is timelessness. That's why with God there is no difference between a day and a thousand years. There is a sense in which eternity is a constant, unceasing present, which for us is the one thing about time that is so indefinably fleeting. It is easy for us to recognize the past times of life and anticipate the future. But what is the present time for us? How long is the present time for us? Is it today or this hour or this minute or this second or this fraction of a second? For us the present is here and gone before we know it. For us the "present" is more of a philosophical notion than a reality. But eternity is a constant present; in eternity everything is "now." This is one reason that God is unchangeable. Change is something that occurs with the passing of moments; but if there are no moments to pass, there is no change. Nothing "occurs" to God. I confess that thinking about eternity makes my head swim. But rather than quit thinking about it, let it be a thought that reminds us of how infinitely great is our God.

When we see evidences of Christ's eternity, let it remind us how infinitely great is our Savior. The New Testament certainly gives evidence of the Savior's eternal existence as the Son of God. John begins his Gospel with that express testimony: "In the beginning was the Word, and the Word was with God, and the Word was God" (John 1:1). The expression "in the beginning" is one way Scripture speaks to our comprehension. It refers to "eternity past," before the creation of time. The text makes it clear that "before time" the Word, the Second Person of the Trinity, and God, the First Person of the Trinity, co-existed. They are both eternal. The passage goes on to say that the Word was made flesh (John 1:14). In a very real sense, the *Incarnation was eternity breaking into time*. In His great high priestly prayer, the Lord Jesus prayed, "O Father, glorify thou me with thine own self with the glory which I had with thee before the world was" (John 17:5). Similarly, He speaks of the intimate relationship He enjoyed with His Father "before the foundation of the world" (John 17:24). "Before the world" is before time, a reference, therefore, to eternity. When Hebrews 13:8 declares, "Jesus Christ the same yesterday, and to day, and for ever," it is declaring His unchangeableness, or immutability, the necessary corollary to His eternity.

Omnipotence

Christ is *infinite in power*. This is what theologians refer to as *omnipotence*. There is not one particular word in either Testament that labels this perfection, but the Scripture makes it abundantly clear that God has power over everything. There is one title of God in the Old Testament, however, that, as well as revealing other truths, specifically declares God's power: *El Shaddai*. The Authorized Version translates this title "God Almighty," reflecting the translation of the Septuagint, the ancient Greek Version of the Old Testament. I say this to indicate the full significance of Revelation 1:8. The exalted Lord Jesus identified Himself to John as the "Almighty," the same word the Greek Old Testament used. Not only does Christ intentionally identify Himself as the God of the Old Testament, but also He declares His omnipotence. The Greek word is rather transparent. It is a compound word with the components "all" and "powerful." The theological word "omnipotence" comprises the same components from Latin.

In addition to this forthright declaration of omnipotence, the New Testament demonstrates Christ's power over things that men have no power over. His power over nature caused even the disciples to marvel, "What manner of man is this, that even the winds and the sea obey him" (Matthew 8:27; cf. Jeremiah 5:22, where control of the sea is a divine prerogative). His power over demons caused both the evil spirits and the people to acknowledge His uniqueness. When the Lord rescued the man with the spirit of an unclean devil in the synagogue at Capernaum, the demon had to admit, "I know thee who thou art: the Holy One of God" (Luke 4:34; see also 4:41). Most likely, the word "God" is an appositive of "Holy One." An appositive or apposition is a noun which renames another. The idea would be "the Holy One, which is God." It is not without significance that "Holy One" is a divine title in the Old Testament. This demon illustrated well the apostolic warning: "Thou believest that there is one God; thou doest well: the devils also believe, and tremble" (James 2:19). The people had to admit that Christ's power over the demons was not within the sphere of human authority: "What a word is this! for with authority and power he commandeth the unclean spirits, and they come out" (Luke 4:36). Even a cursory reading of the Gospel narratives discovers the manifestations of His infinite power extending over disease and even death itself. It is not surprising that throughout His earthly mission, people were "astonished with a great astonishment" (Mark 5:42).

Omniscience

Christ is *infinite in wisdom*. Theologians refer to this as *omniscience*. Paul's famous doxology places this divine perfection in connection with God's eternity, immortality, and spirituality: "Now unto the King eternal, immortal, invisible, the only wise God" (I Timothy 1:17). Then he asserts explicitly that in Christ "are hid all the treasures of wisdom and knowledge" (Colossians 2:3). Make no mistake, then: where there is evidence of Christ's infinite knowledge, there is evidence of His deity. The description of the exalted Christ in Revelation 1 is pregnant with proof of both Christ's deity and His continuing humanity. Verse 14 depicts the Savior as having pure white hair, like wool and snow, and eyes as "a flame of fire." Both of these are images that highlight absolute wisdom. The white head represents age and the acknowledged wisdom that goes with it. This parallels Daniel's title and description of the Lord as "the Ancient of Days" in his vision of the coming of the Son of Man (Daniel 7:9-13). Interestingly, what Daniel says about the Father in his vision, John applies to Christ in his vision. What is true of God is true of Christ.

The statement in Revelation 1:14 about the fiery flaming eyes also refers to penetrating intelligence. By a figure of speech called *metonymy*, the Scripture often uses the eyes to designate the mind and knowledge. Metonymy occurs when one word is used to refer to the meaning of another because there is some obvious connection between the two words. For example, after someone unknowingly put some poisonous gourds in the soup pot, the sons of the prophets told Elisha, "there is death in the pot" (II Kings 4:40). Poison was in the pot, but because they thought the soup was going to kill them, they called it death. The effect (death) was used to refer to the cause (poison). This is what I mean by metonymy; the Bible uses this figure frequently, so being able to recognize it will be helpful. Now, let me return to eyes. Since the eye is a key part of the body that takes in facts, it is a fitting word to designate the understanding of the facts taken in. When the Psalmist declares that the pure or radiant commandment of God enlightens the eyes, he is saying that God's word shines light into his mind to give him understanding (Psalm 19:8). Therefore, when John says that Christ has eyes like flaming fire, he is saying that the intelligence of Christ is infallibly penetrating. Nothing escapes His knowledge: all things are openly known before His eyes.

On more than one occasion during his earthly life, the Lord Jesus gave evidence of His omniscience and, therefore, of His deity. When Jesus told Nathanael that He had seen him under the fig tree, Nathanael, aware that such knowledge was humanly impossible, confessed, "Rabbi, thou art the Son of God; thou art the King of Israel" (John 1:49). It is always remarkable to me how theologically astute these "Old Testament" saints were. Nathanael obviously knew that such knowledge belonged to God and the coming Messiah alone. As soon as he saw Jesus exercise such knowledge, he knew Him to be the Christ. Remember that he knew all that from the Old Testament. It is our ultimate objective to learn there the same messianic theology that Nathanael had learned.

John 2:23-24 reveals that Christ acted before men on the basis of what He knew about men. Not only did He know all men, but He knew them without learning about them. That is, His knowledge was not gained; it was innate. John said that he "needed not that any should testify of man: for he knew what was in man" (2:25). I suppose there are some things that we know by instinct, whatever that means, but certainly most of our knowledge is learned. Our knowledge is always limited and often wrong. Christ's knowledge is immediate and accurate–always. His demonstration of omniscience occurred often enough to convince men that He was the Messiah. After her encounter with Jesus, the Samaritan woman rushed back to the city, inviting others to "come, see a man, which told me all things that ever I did: is not this the Christ?" (John 4:29). Even the Samaritans knew enough Old Testament theology to make the proper identification. And later, after Christ explained some parables to His disciples, they confessed, "Now we are sure that thou knowest all things, and needest not that any man should ask thee: by this we believe that thou camest forth from God" (John 16:30).

Omnipresence

Christ is *infinite in regard to space*. Theologians refer to this as *omnipresence*. This means that God is not bound to any physical location; He is everywhere present simultaneously. Remember Solomon's confession at the dedication of the Temple: "behold, heaven and the heaven of heavens cannot contain thee; how much less this house which I have built" (II Chronicles 6:18). Remember the Psalmist's assurance that God was with him constantly and that he could not be where God was not. That rightly amazed him: "Such knowledge is too wonderful for me; it is high, I cannot attain unto it" (Psalm 139:6-9).

Recognizing this perfection in terms of Christ is confessedly "too wonderful," but true. Obviously, when we talk about Christ's being present everywhere simultaneously, we are talking about His eternal deity and not His human body. The humanity of Christ was under the same limitations as those of any other body. The body of Jesus could be and still is only in one place at a time. If that were not true, it would not be a real human body. But His divine spirit is another matter. Just as Solomon's ornate Temple could not contain or box in God, neither could the Lord's Temple, His body, confine or box in His full deity. Jesus made a startling statement to Nicodemus that declares this mystery: "And no man hath ascended up to heaven, but he that came down from heaven, even the Son of man which is in heaven" (John 3:13). There was a sense in which the Incarnate Son of man who was there talking to Nicodemus was still in heaven–absolutely astounding! If Christ were not omnipresent, His promises to His people would not be particularly comforting. In the Great Commission, He guarantees that He will be with us always, even to the end of the world (Matthew 28:19). In Matthew 18:20, He promises His church, "For where two or three are gathered together in my name, there am I in the midst of them." Because Christ is God and therefore omnipresent, His people do not have to "take a number" or take turns to know and experience His presence.

Works of Deity

Not only does the Scripture attribute God's incommunicable perfections to the Lord Jesus Christ, but it also attributes to Him the works of God. The logic is the same. If there are certain things that only God does and Christ does those things, then Christ is God. Again I want to look at some of the express evidence for this in the New Testament so that we will have the foundation to recognize the same truths in the Old. Theologians typically summarize the general works of God in three broad categories: creation, providence, and miracles.

Creation

Christ is the *Creator*. Although the New Testament affirms that God created the world and all in it, most of creation theology is developed in the Old Testament. From the opening word in the Bible, God declares that He created the heaven and the earth. That declaration immediately established His ownership of the creation, His authority over it, and the creation's accountability to Him. It also declared His absolute power, because if anything is clear from the way the Old Testament uses the special word for "create," it is that only God can do it. Creation is a uniquely divine activity. And yet though creation is uniquely the work of infinite power, the Scripture portrays the seeming ease with which God created all things. When we read the creation account, we do not get the impression that this required any exertion of divine energy. God spoke. What He spoke happened. His creating word was always irresistible. The darkness did not, and could not, resist the "let there be light" command from God. Every time I think of this, my mind goes to II Corinthians 4:6, which compares God's command to cause the light to shine out of darkness to the command He gives to shine the light of the Gospel in the darkened heart of sinners. Both commands are creative words, and both are irresistible. When God commands the light to shine, the light shines. What a beautiful assertion of grace! That is a great point, but for now beside the point. But it illustrates nicely how the New Testament builds on Old Testament theology.

THE PERSON OF CHRIST

The significance increases as we realize that the New Testament specifically acknowledges that Jesus Christ is the Creator and that therefore He is God. All that creation implies about God, therefore, applies to Jesus Christ. He owns all; He rules all; all creation is accountable to Him. Colossians 1:16 is one of the great explicit New Testament texts that identify Christ as Creator. Paul's theme throughout the book is the pre-eminence of Christ over everything. But chapter 1 is without question one of those theological and Christological high-water marks in Scripture. Verse 15 says of Christ that He is "the image of the invisible God," the ideal manifestation of God, and therefore the ideal Prophet. It also begins the thought continued in verse 16: "the firstborn of every creature: for by him were all things created, that are in heaven, and that are in earth, visible and invisible, whether they be thrones, or dominions, or principalities, or powers: all things were created by him, and for him."

The word "firstborn" is not a temporal word but a word of rank. It certainly does not mean that Christ was the first one created; the statement of verse 16 precludes that. It is impossible for any creature to create; the entire creation theology of the Old Testament established that clearly. The phrase "firstborn of creation" means that creation is subordinate to the one of pre-eminent rank. Christ is over creation because He is the creator. John 1 gives the same evidence of Christ's deity: "All things were made by him; and without him was not any thing made that was made" (John 1:3). The argument of Hebrews 1 is significant. Hebrews 1:2 says that it was by the Son that God made the worlds. Beginning at verse 8, the apostle records a series of Old Testament passages that the Father Himself said to His Son. Verse 10 begins a quote from Psalm 102:25-27, all of which God the Father says is true of His Son and our Savior: "Thou, Lord, in the beginning hast laid the foundation of the earth; and the heavens are the works of thine hands." Who can dispute the Word of God? Who can dispute God's own interpretation of His word?

Providence

Christ is the *ruler and preserver of creation*. This is the work of *providence*. The *Westminster Larger Catechism* offers a succinct definition of God's works of providence: "God's works of providence are his most holy, wise, and powerful preserving and governing all his creatures; ordering them, and all their actions, to his own glory" (question 18). The key words are *preserving* and *governing*. Providence is the necessary corollary to creation. Because God is the creator, He owns creation and has the authority to rule it and keep it according to His own purpose. Let us be careful here not to equate a belief in divine providence with a "whatever happens happens" theology. That is fatalism; and fatalism is paganism. There is a world of difference between believing in an uncontrollable operation of blind fate and believing that all things are working together toward a prescribed and purposeful end by One who is infinitely wise, infinitely good, and infinitely powerful so that His purpose cannot be threatened, frustrated, or jeopardized. It ought to be most comforting for believers to know and rest in the constant truth that they are part of God's unfailing purpose.

The same two New Testament texts that declare Christ as the Creator also prove that the Lord Jesus is engaged in the ongoing work of providence. Creation and providence are inseparable truths. In Colossians 1:17 Paul says about the pre-eminent Christ, "He is before all things, and by him all things consist." The word "consist" means "to cohere or stand together." It is by Christ that the created world stands or sticks together. Hebrews 1:3 tells us exactly how Christ not only makes things stick together but moves them along to their prescribed end. The apostle says that He upholds all things by the word of His power. The word "uphold" means literally "to bear or carry along." The word "word" refers to an individual spoken word. The word "power" speaks of ability. As the Lord spoke the world into existence, so His spoken word ably and successfully keeps and directs the world. An interpretative translation of this text, then, would sound like this: "By speaking an irresistible and unfrustratable word, He carries everything along."

Miracles

Christ is the *miracle worker*. The *Westminster Confession of Faith* says that "God, in his ordinary providence, maketh use of means, yet is free to work without, above, and against them, at his pleasure" (Chapter V, section 3). The ability to do the supernatural or miraculous is another logical extension of creation theology. Since God has the power to create, He has the right to govern creation as He sees fit. He who ordered and defined "nature" has the right and ability to override the rules whenever He desires. It should be noted, however, that His desire to override the rules of nature has not occurred often. His supernatural activity, the performance of miracles, is not capricious or whimsical. Sometimes when we read the Bible we get the impression that miracles were commonplace. In fact, they were quite rare. But when they occurred, they were phenomenal.

With few exceptions, most miracles are confined to set time periods. The first great display of supernatural power occurred in the middle of the fifteenth century BC, when God through Moses demonstrated His power against Pharaoh and the gods of Egypt. The second display was some six hundred years later in the ninth century BC during the ministry of Elijah and Elisha, when these two prophets battled the apostasy of Baal worship. The third display was over eight hundred years later during the earthly ministry of the Lord Jesus and His apostles. And finally, there will be one more occurrence at least two thousand years later, when the two witnesses stand and proclaim the Gospel in the face of the antichrist (Revelation 11). One common thread ties these periods together. At times of crisis when the one true religion has been threatened, the Lord has verified Himself and His claims by supernatural acts. The Incarnation marked such a necessary time. True religion reached its visible manifestation and definition. In order to prove "Christianity" against entrenched Judaism and empirical paganism, the supernatural occurred. What marked this period of miracles as distinct from the others is that God in person was visible to work the miracles immediately, rather than mediately, through His agents. Even a cursory reading of the Gospel narratives underscores the miracles of the Lord Jesus, from changing the water to wine, to feeding the thousands, to walking on the water, to raising the dead. Among other things, the miracles of Jesus proved His absolute deity.

The Object of Worship

That Jesus Christ is the proper object of worship is express evidence of His deity. The Law of God is unmistakably clear that there is only one true and living God that man must worship. The *Westminster Shorter Catechism* summarizes well both the requirements and prohibitions of the first commandment not to have other gods before the Lord. "The first commandment requireth us to know and acknowledge

God to be the only true God, and our God; and to worship and glorify him accordingly" (question 46). "The first commandment forbiddeth the denying, or not worshipping and glorifying the true God as God, and our God; and the giving of that worship and glory to any other, which is due to him alone" (question 47). The New Testament both reveals that men rightly worshipped Christ and commands that worship be given Him. When Thomas saw the resurrected Christ he confessed, "My Lord and my God" (John 20:28). When John saw the exalted Christ, he "fell at his feet as dead" (Revelation 1:17). Revelation also uncovers that glorious scene in which the population of heaven falls down before the Lamb and worships "him that liveth for ever and ever" (Revelation 5:8, 14). Hebrews 1:6 records the command that God gave the angels to worship the Son: "Let all the angels of God worship him." Paul speaks of that time when every knee will bow before Him and confess that "Jesus Christ is Lord, to the glory of God the Father" (Philippians 2:10-11).

Because Christ is God, all the work of His person had infinite value and efficacy. His deity assures for Christians the eternal salvation that He personally procured for them. We are going to see that this is Old Testament truth as well as New.

The Human Nature of the One Person

The New Testament is as dogmatically clear that Jesus of Nazareth is man as it is that He is God. The evidence of His humanity is equally irrefutable, and it is likewise undeniable except by blind and blatant disbelief. Again, the *Westminster Confession of Faith* gives a concise synopsis of the doctrine:

> The Son of God, the second person in the Trinity, being very and eternal God, of one substance, and equal with the Father, did, when the fullness of time was come, take upon him man's nature, with all the essential properties and common infirmities thereof, yet without sin; being conceived by the power of the Holy Ghost, in the womb of the Virgin Mary, of her substance... (Chapter VIII, section 2).

Perhaps reacting to liberal and apostate views of Jesus that He was just a good man, conservative theologians in their necessary defense of the deity of Christ have sometimes been guilty of minimizing or at least ignoring the full implications of His humanity. The humanity is essential to His mediation and His Messiahship. Because He was a true man, Christ personally suffered all the infirmities and miseries of life so that He can sympathize and intercede continuously for His people. Because He was a true man, Christ vicariously and actively obeyed the law of God to earn a righteousness that is imputed to every believer. Because He was a true man, Christ vicariously paid the penalty of the broken law by offering Himself a sacrifice of sin. Because He was a true man, Christ was raised bodily from the grave to guarantee the justification of all His believing people. Because He was a true man, Christ ascended triumphantly into heaven as the forerunner of His "sure to be glorified" people. Because He is a true man, Christ will return gloriously to complete God's eternal redemptive plan. From His virgin birth to His glorious return, Christ performs His messianic duty in the body God prepared for Him. We will consider more of the implications of both His deity and His humanity as we deal with Old Testament passages. I want at this point just to survey some of the New Testament evidence of His humanity so that when we see the same in the Old Testament, we will know that we are seeing Christ in person.

Facts of Christ's Humanity

First, the New Testament often calls attention to the human *ancestry of Jesus*. It thus links Him to the Old Testament promise that a Messiah would come not only into the human race but also into a specifically defined nation and family of the human race. I am well aware that the genealogies in the Bible are not particularly exciting reading and are often skipped over in daily devotional reading in the search for more obvious blessing and instruction. I am not suggesting that you may find your life verse in the fact that somebody begat somebody, but I am suggesting that those lengthy family trees are there by divine purpose. The New Testament begins with Matthew's "book of the generation of Jesus Christ, the son of David, the son of Abraham." Matthew worked forward from Abraham to Jesus, concluding that there were fourteen generations from Abraham to David and fourteen from David to the Babylonian captivity and fourteen from the captivity to Jesus (Matthew 1:1-17). The birth of Jesus, which Matthew records next, was an obvious continuation of those "generations" (Matthew 1:18). After introducing the public ministry of Jesus that commenced with His baptism, Luke gives an extensive genealogy. Immediately after recording God's declaration from heaven that Jesus was His "beloved Son," Luke gives evidence that this one just identified as God was also man. Beginning with Joseph, the earthly guardian of Jesus, Luke traces the human ancestry right back to Adam, who was "the son of God" (Luke 3:23-38). Without going into all the same details, Luke records Paul's explanation of the same essential evidence. In his sermon at Antioch in Pisidia, Paul introduces Christ with a synopsis of Hebrew history. After mentioning David, a man after God's own heart, he said, "Of this man's seed hath God according to his promise raised unto Israel a Saviour, Jesus" (Acts 13:23). In Romans, his great theological treatise, Paul twice calls attention to the human ancestry of the Lord. In Romans 1:3 he speaks of God's Son, "Jesus Christ our Lord, which was made of the seed of David according to the flesh." In Romans 9:5, the same verse so important in declaring the deity of Christ, the apostle speaks of Christ's coming through the nation of Israel: "Whose are the fathers, and of whom as concerning the flesh Christ came...." The conclusion is clear enough by applying the words of Christ Himself: "That which is born of the flesh is flesh" (John 3:6). Note that that is not necessarily a bad thing; it is just a statement of fact.

Second, the New Testament *refers to Christ as man.* I think it will suffice here just to note the way the Lord Jesus liked to refer to Himself. His most common self-designation was "the Son of Man." Daniel was the first to assign messianic significance to this title (7:13), and following his lead, the New Testament uses the term in reference to Christ's second coming as well as the circumstances of His earthly sufferings, death, and resurrection. Understanding the significance of the title will show why it is such a clear expression of the humanity of Christ. Two observations will help. First, the word "son" means more than just being a male child. It often conveys the sense of "belonging to a class." For instance, when the Old Testament refers to the "sons of the prophets," it is not referring to "preachers' kids." It means those who belong to the class of prophets; in other words, the sons of the prophets were prophets. Second, the word "man" means more than male in contrast to female. This is the general word for mankind that would include both males and females. It is the word for humanity. Therefore, to designate Christ as the Son of Man is to identify Him as belonging to the class of humanity. To be the Son of Man is truly to be man. His humanity was real.

Third, the New Testament reveals that *Christ had a real body and a rational soul.* Hebrew 10:5 quotes Psalm 40:6-8, putting the words directly in the mouth of Christ: "a body hast thou prepared me." In our discussion of His deity, we argued that an evidence of deity was doing divine works and having divine perfections. So it is for His humanity. If human "stuff" is true about Him, we can only conclude that He is human. As God He is omnipresent, but His human body was as finite as any body. He could be only one place at a time. As God He is an infinite living Spirit, but as man He had a body consisting of flesh and blood. As God He is omnipotent, but in His body He knew most of the same physical limitations as other men (remember that He could walk on water). He knew what it was to hunger and thirst and eat and drink. He knew what it was to be physically tired and to rest and sleep. As God He is immutably the same, but in His body He grew from infancy to adolescence to manhood. In that body He was born, experienced pain, and died. As God He is omniscient, yet in His humanity He increased in wisdom. As God He is absolutely independent, unaffected by the creature, but in His humanity Christ reacted and responded to the people and circumstances. He experienced common human feelings. He knew what it was to weep with those who wept and rejoice with those who rejoiced.

Apparently, not long after the Lord Jesus ascended to glory, some in the professing church denied His real humanity. The book of I John proves the real humanity of Christ and warns about the serious consequences of denying that essential truth of the gospel. From the beginning of his letter, John accents the reality of Christ's humanity. He had a body that was both seen and touched (I John 1:1-2). To deny the incarnation, that God was manifest in the flesh, was to be anti-Christ. The line between theological orthodoxy and antichristian heresy is as distinct now as it was then. "Every spirit that confesseth that Jesus Christ is come in the flesh is of God: and every spirit that confesseth not that Jesus Christ is come in the flesh is not of God" (I John 4:2-3). Considering all that the New Testament says Christ did in His prepared body highlights how absolutely essential this truth is. It should not surprise us, then, that the Old Testament will identify the Messiah in human as well as divine terms. Both Testaments reveal the same person.

The Problem of Christ's Humanity

The problem issue concerning Christ's humanity is His relationship to sin. It is part of our evangelical message to sinners that they are born in sin and therefore need the gospel of saving grace. Since Christ was truly born, how was He exempt from sin? That's the problem. It is outside the scope of my purpose and thesis to discuss the question of whether Christ could have sinned, though in fact He *did not*. But allow me a brief digression to address this important question. It is important to maintain that the humanity of Christ was real and that since Adam's fall, sin has been a part of human nature. How then could Christ's humanity be real if He was without sin? We must start with the clear statement that His humanity was as real as that of any other human being except for the fact that He was absolutely sinless (see Hebrews 4:15; 7:25; I Peter 1:19; etc.). All orthodox theologians agree that the Lord Jesus Christ was perfect and sinless in every way. But not all agree on the ultimate reason for that perfection. Some contend for the *peccability* of Christ; He could have sinned but did not. Others contend for the *impeccability* of Christ; He could not have sinned and therefore did not. Although I cannot develop all of the theological and Scriptural reasons for my position at this point, I must, nonetheless, make my position clear. I would argue strongly for the impeccability of Christ. He was not sinless just because He did not sin; rather, He did not sin because He is sinless. It was impossible for Him to sin because of who He was, the God/Man. It is foolish to suggest that His human nature could have sinned but His divine nature could not have sinned. Remember that His human nature did not and could not exist apart from or independent of His person.

Let me offer just one final observation that may help you get a handle on this issue. Remember that sin is not an essential element of human nature as it was originally created. Follow Paul's argument and logic in Romans 5 and I Corinthians 15 and you will find that God established Adam and Christ as representative heads of a people. Although Jesus was a natural descendent of Adam and a real part of the human race, He was not under Adam's representation and headship and not subject to that disobedience that plunged the rest of humanity into sin. Therefore, Adam's sin had no effect on Him. As the second Adam, He is the representative Head whose complete obedience is the basis for redeeming a believing humanity from Adam's curse. God ultimately deals with all humanity in terms of those two men. In Adam all die; in Christ all live. This concept is referred to as Federal Theology and warrants your study sometime. It is an important part of the doctrine of Christ.

Synopsis of Key Texts

Throughout the New Testament are statements affirming Christ's deity and His humanity. There are, however, some classic texts that bring these two essential truths about the person of Christ together. It would be worthwhile to expound these texts fully, but I will simply offer a synopsis of the salient points for your consideration as you study through these passages.

Romans 1:2-5; 9:5

Referring to the only Redeemer, Paul identified the two natures of the promised Christ. He is the Son of David according to the flesh; He is the Son of God according to the spirit of holiness. It is noteworthy that this comment on the two natures in one person follows his testimony that he was separated unto the gospel which was "promised before" by the "prophets in the holy scripture." When you remember that for Paul the "holy scripture" was the Old Testament, this text is all the more significant for our present study. Paul makes it clear that his Christ was the Old Testament Christ and his gospel was the Old Testament gospel. We want to be able to see from that same Old Testament what Paul saw. In the other statement in 9:5, the apostle declares the same person, Jesus, to be both God over all and a descendent from Abraham.

I Timothy 3:16

In this inspired hymn, Paul lists facts about the Lord Jesus Christ that he heads with this exclamation: "Great is the mystery of godliness." By using the word "mystery," Paul emphasizes that this is something that we know by revelation—because God has told us. These are truths beyond human invention. It is clear that all the predicates in this list, from the manifestation in flesh to the reception into glory, belong to one person and that person is Christ. The key statement is "God was manifest in the flesh." Eternal deity was exposed to full view in the body of real humanity.

Hebrews 1 and 2

These two chapters are significant not only for declarations about the full deity and full humanity of Christ, but also for the manner in which the declarations are made. Both chapters are jammed full of Old Testament "proof-texts." The first chapter identifies the Son as being the brightness of the Father's glory, eternal and immutable. The second chapter identifies the same person as being man, fulfilling the ideal and universal dominion assigned to man at creation and sharing the same nature as those He was not ashamed to call brethren. Hebrews certainly warrants our search for Christ in the Old Testament.

John 1:1-14

What a gold mine of truth this passage is. It is clear that the entire passage is referring to one person, the Lord Jesus Christ. Several amazing statements jump out. This person is eternal (v. 1). This person has an eternal, intimate relationship with God (v. 2). This person created everything (v. 3). This person is the essence and source of life (v. 4). This person is the revealer of true knowledge and holiness (vv. 4, 5, 9). This person entered the world that he made (vv. 9, 10). This person assumed human nature by becoming flesh (v. 14). This person revealed God's glory as the only begotten Son of God (v. 14).

Philippians 2:6-11

This text is a high-water mark: no passage is more explicit in uniting the divine and human natures in one person. Note the key points. (1) Jesus was, is, and continues to be in the form of God. The word "form" refers to the essential nature or essence of something. Jesus is everything God is. (2) Jesus knew He was God. Here is a literal translation of verse 6 that shows the precise logic of the statement: "Who, because he was the very essence of God, did not regard equality with God to be something seized." The point is that equality with God was not something Jesus had to acquire; it was already His by virtue of His eternal existence. He did not grow into deity or divine consciousness. Striving for deity was not necessary, because He was God. (3) He became man. As He was the essence of God, so He became in essence a servant and assumed the appearance of ordinary man. Eternally used to glory, our Savior entered the realm of natural frailty and infirmity. The eye of flesh would have seen nothing but an ordinary man; but the eye of faith would have seen—and still sees—the God/Man. (4) He submitted to death. This indeed was the purpose of His coming. He came to pay the price for our sin and redeem us by His blood. (5) He is exalted with absolute authority. This testifies to a mission successfully accomplished. This important passage, then, teaches clearly that the humiliation of the incarnation did not consist of the Son of God's giving up divine attributes; rather, it consisted of His taking to Himself human attributes. This one passage could well be the biblical foundation for the Shorter Catechism's classic statement. "The only Redeemer of God's elect is the Lord Jesus Christ, who, being the eternal Son of God, became man, and so was, and continueth to be God and Man in two distinct natures, and one person, for ever" (question 21). I love that statement.

There is no question that the details about the person of Christ are more specific in the New Testament than in the Old. We wait until the New Testament to learn, for instance, that the Messiah's name would be Jesus, that He would live in a carpenter's home in Nazareth, that He would ultimately die on a Roman cross. But the Old Testament does reveal and eagerly anticipate the Messiah, who would be God/Man and who would be cut off in violent death for the sins of the people. By keeping in focus the clear picture of the person of Christ that we see in the New Testament, we will know Him so well that we can see Him when and where He appears in the Old Testament. If we realize that Christ is in the Old Testament, we will want to "strain our necks" to be sure that we see Him. Knowing whom to look for is essential to knowing we have found Him.

CHAPTER 3
THE WORK OF CHRIST

In our house an empty coffee cup is my signature. My wife can see an empty coffee cup in any room and know I was the one who left it there, because she knows what I do with empty coffee cups. I belong to a hunt club with a membership ranging from university professors to students who apparently have more free time than I did when a student. Some of these members are carpenters by trade, but when it comes to making tree stands, they apparently fail to employ their considerable skills. In fact, there is a standard joke that you can always identify stands made by a carpenter because they tend to be awkward and uncomfortable. It's a trademark. In a similar manner, by evaluating brush strokes or other peculiarities of technique, art experts can detect forgeries of the genuine works of the artists they know. Literary experts can identify famous authors by the style of writing. Architects have their trademark styles that easily identify their work. Criminals often give themselves away because they have a standard "MO," or method of operation, that law enforcement recognizes.

For purposes of identification, someone's work is often as good as a signature. Linking someone to a particular work requires knowledge of both who the person is and what he does. The better we know someone, the more likely we will recognize him by his work. Art experts and literary experts can identify certain artists and authors only because they have studied their works so thoroughly. I know a "carpenter's stand" when I see one because I have had firsthand experience with carpenters' stands. The point is that works can identify people.

Identifying people by their works is also a Scriptural principle. The apostle James argues that genuine believers evidence certain works as proof of real faith (James 2:18ff.). A profession of faith without the works of faith is not genuine faith. The apostle Paul throughout the Epistle of II Corinthians gave evidence of the works of his ministry to verify the legitimacy of his apostolic office to those who questioned his authority. He did apostolic works; therefore, he was an apostle. The Lord Jesus Himself taught this principle of "works identification" often. Christ concluded His famous Sermon on the Mount with a warning to beware of false prophets who appear in sheep's clothing but who are in fact ravening wolves. His recommended test for recognizing false prophets was to evaluate their work. Shifting from the sheep/wolf image to that of a fruit tree, the Lord plainly said, "by their fruits ye shall know them" (Matthew 7:15-20). What they produce or what they do is the sure evidence of what they are. What is true about false prophets is also true for genuine prophets. The principle is true for the Lord Jesus Christ Himself. His works identify Him as the only Redeemer and Mediator for sinners. Consequently, knowing the works of the Messiah is one more way of being able to recognize His presence in the Scripture, even if His name does not directly appear. If we see the work, we see the person.

The ability to see Christ in the Old Testament when seeing His works requires that we know what those peculiar, unique works are. An art or literary expert cannot link particular masterpieces to particular artists or authors unless he knows intimately the unique characteristics of the masters. I confess that I could look right at a Rembrandt without having a clue it's a Rembrandt. I really know nothing about the man or the peculiarities of his style. But those who know Rembrandt and what he has done recognize his works immediately. This is the issue I want to make about finding and seeing Christ in the Old Testament. Many can look right at His works recorded there and have no idea that they are looking at the Christ simply because they don't know what they are looking for. In this chapter I want to identify some key works that belong uniquely to the Lord Jesus Christ. I want to expand our list of clues that will help us find Christ in the Old Testament.

Our focus must be on those works that are peculiar to the Second Person of the Trinity, the Son of God and Son of Man. As the eternal God, the Son of God performs the "common" works of the Godhead, such as creation and providence. Those are essential works but they do not identify Christ specifically. For instance, when the Psalmist states that the heavens declare the glory of God, he is crediting Christ along with the Father and the Holy Spirit for having made the world. We have already considered some aspects of Christ's mediatorial work in our survey of the significance of the word "Messiah." Prophet work, priest work, and king work all help to identify the Christ. We must keep those in mind; they are important clues in our search. But there were many prophets, priests, and kings. The Lord Jesus is in every way the ideal manifestation and fulfillment of each of those offices, but there are some aspects of prophet, priest, and king work that are not unique to Him. In this chapter I want to concentrate on those particular works that only the Lord Jesus Christ has done, is doing, and will do. These unique works center on His necessary accomplishing of the full salvation of His people. He did what was necessary to redeem His people, is doing what is necessary to preserve His people, and will do what is necessary to vindicate His God, His name, and His people. That we can expect to find these works in the Old Testament as well as the New is evident from Peter's statement that the Old Testament prophets having the Spirit of Christ "testified beforehand the sufferings of Christ, and the glory that should follow" (I Peter 1:11). In fact, Peter's statement suggests the best way we can outline these saving works of Christ: His first advent works, His present works, and His Second Advent works.

First Advent Works

The Book of Hebrews gives an inspired synopsis of Christ's first advent works: "he appeared to put away sin by the sacrifice of himself" (9:26) that "through death he might destroy him that had the power of death, that is, the devil" (2:14). The purpose of the Incarnation was that the Son of God might shed His blood and die on the cross to save His people. Saying that He came to die is one thing; understanding why He came to die is the essence of the gospel. Strangely enough, understanding the gospel requires understanding the law of God. The tension between the gospel and law exists in theological discussion but not in the Scripture. The gospel of free salvation in and through the Lord Jesus Christ does not replace the law of God; it is the fulfillment and satisfaction of the law of God. The gospel is the one and only answer to the desperate plight man faces because of sin.

The Need for Christ's Work

God's law demands a total obedience. From the greatest commandment to love God completely to whatever may be the least
commandment, God demands absolute righteousness. The word
"righteousness" means conformity to a standard. It is an absolute term;
there is no such thing as being almost righteous in terms of God's law.
Man must exhibit perfect conformity in both spirit and letter or he is
unequivocally unrighteous. The law is inflexible and the least breach
of the law carries severe penalty. Because of his sin–that is, his failure
to conform to the standard required by the holy law of God–every man
has earned death. Death is the fair wage of sin (Romans 6:23). The
justice of God demands the full payment of that earned wage, and,
therefore, sinners are doomed to the full payment of not only physical
but also spiritual and eternal death. Man left to his own devices and
efforts in the face of the law of God can never earn any claim to life.
Man needs divine pardon, but the question is how God can grant pardon and at the same time retain His eternal and immutable justice.
How can God be just and the justifier (Romans 3:26)?

Jesus Christ, God's Son and our Savior, is the solution to that problem. What man cannot do in earning life under the weight of God's
holy law, Jesus Christ did. This is to me the great beauty of Gospel:
what man cannot do for himself, God in His grace through His eternal Son has done. In his classic and inspired exposition of the gospel,
Paul declared that Christ Jesus has provided freedom from the law of
sin and death, "for what the law could not do, in that it was weak in
the flesh, God sending his own Son in the likeness of sinful flesh, and
for sin, condemned sin in the flesh" (Romans 8:2-3). The weakness of
the law stemmed from man's helplessness and spiritual inability in the
throes of his sinful nature; Christ had to come to free man from that
bondage. He freed us not by changing the rules but by obeying the
rules in our place and suffering the consequences of our disobedience.
This brings us to Christ's first advent works: what He did in living and
what He did in dying. Two things were necessary for God to be just in
saving sinners: the demands of the law had to be completely obeyed,
and the penalty of the broken law had to be completely paid. Jesus
Christ did both, and both are foundational essentials of the gospel.

THE WORK OF CHRIST

The Living of Christ

Throughout His earthly life, the Lord Jesus obeyed the law of God, earning both life and the right to die in the place of His people. Theologians refer to this righteous living of Christ as His *active obedience*. It is important to realize that this active obedience of Christ, or His life, was just as vicarious as His death. Not only can a Christian say, "Jesus died for me," but he can also say, "Jesus lived for me." In fact, had the Lord Jesus not lived the life that He did, His death could not have counted as a substitutionary death at all.

An Earned Righteousness

The New Testament places significant emphasis on Christ's obedience as an essential part of His mission. Galatians 4:4 plainly says, "when the fulness of the time was come, God sent forth his Son, made of a woman, made under the law." "Made of a woman" implies the virgin birth and asserts the real humanity of the Savior. If I may put this colloquially, though reverently, "made under the law" means that Christ did not receive any "special break" or "special treatment" in regard to the law. He was not exempt from the rules; He was born under the same rigid, inflexible, unchangeable law that every other man is born under. In fact, according to words attributed to Christ Himself, He came to fulfill that law, which reflects God's perfect will: "Lo, I come (in the volume of the book it is written of me,) to do thy will, O God" (Hebrews 10:7; quoting Psalm 40:7-8). But whereas that law condemns us and calls for our death, it vindicates Christ as having been absolutely righteous. I Timothy 3:16 says that the God who was manifest in the flesh was justified by the Spirit; that is, He was vindicated or proven to be righteous. In absolutely every way Jesus Christ conformed to the absolute standard of righteousness, God's Law. We earn death; Christ earned life.

I must clarify that I am not referring to the inherent and eternal righteousness that Christ has by virtue of His deity. It is wonderfully true that as God He is righteous. But the righteousness that "counts" for our salvation is that which He earned or merited every day and every moment for the thirty-some years He lived on earth. Paul in that great Christological text in Philippians 2 declares that an essential element in the Lord's self-humiliation was that He became obedient all the way to death. As strange as it may sound, the Lord Jesus had to learn obedience. Although He was impeccably perfect, He had to achieve perfection. Hebrews 5:8-9 says, "Though he were a Son, yet learned he obedience by the things which he suffered; and being made perfect, he became the author of eternal salvation unto all them that obey him." Literally verse 9 says, "He became one who was perfected." Ethically and morally, Christ matured to evident perfection (cf., Hebrews 2:10). Never a wrong deed, never a wrong thought—He kept the law in its perfect spirit to the minutest detail of its letter.

A Vicarious Righteousness

Although the Gospel narratives and General Epistles give evidence of Christ's sinless life, it is Paul who explains the theology of it. Romans 5 is a crucial text. Here the apostle expounds the relationship between Adam and Christ. Through the sinful disobedience of Adam, the entire human race is justly guilty before God and under the necessary sentence of death (5:12, 17-19). Through the righteous obedience of Christ, the entire "believing part" of the human race is justly righteous before God and freed from the necessary penalty of death: "So by the obedience of one shall many be made righteous" (5:19; see also 15, 17, 18). As God justly imputed or regarded Adam's sin to apply to the human race, which was in Adam and which consequently, was involved in his sin, so He justly imputes or regards Christ's obedience to apply to those who believe in Christ. Adam's disobedience was not confined to himself; Christ's obedience was not confined to Himself. This is precisely how God maintains His absolute justice while at the same time pardoning the sins of everyone who trusts in Christ and Christ alone. When God saves a sinner, He considers the demands of the law to be completely, righteously satisfied because of the righteousness earned by the perfect, active obedience of Jesus. Theologians like to debate the mechanics and logic of this legal imputation, often confusing the matter, making it more complicated than God wants it to be for us. Let me make it as simple as I possibly can. Here are the basic facts. (1) God demands perfect obedience to His law or else. (2) Man cannot obey perfectly; so he earns death, the penalty for breaking the law. (3) The man Christ Jesus obeyed the law perfectly; so He earned life, the reward for keeping the law. (4) God graciously lets the perfect obedience of Christ "count" for all and any who trust Christ, thereby freeing them from the penalty of death. This is why Paul says that Christ is the end of the law for righteousness to those who believe (Romans 10:4). For believers Christ has fulfilled the law. Unbelievers are still on their own, and they continue, therefore, under condemnation. Being in Christ is man's only hope.

An Imputed Righteousness

This active obedience of the Lord Jesus Christ is particularly central to that aspect of salvation called *justification*. I like to think of justification as dealing with the legality of the gospel. In light of what we've discussed, consider how ably and succinctly the *Westminster Shorter Catechism* defines justification: "Justification is an act of God's free grace, wherein he pardoneth all our sins, and accepteth us as righteous in his sight, only for righteousness of Christ imputed to us, and received by faith alone" (question 33). Always remember that this is the merited righteousness of Christ's active obedience that satisfied the law's demands. Therefore, as far as the law is concerned, God sees believers the same way He sees Christ: legally perfect and innocent. There can be no condemnation for those who are in Christ Jesus (Romans 8:1). The law has nothing against believers. This is why I emphasize that the life of Christ is an essential element in His mission to save His people. We are going to see that this is not just a New Testament truth. Certainly the doctrine of justification is in the Old Testament, because Abraham and David are the common New Testament examples of justified sinners (Romans 4). But the basis of that justification is also part of Old Testament messianic theology. I want us to understand that when the Old Testament refers to the Messiah as righteous or doing righteousness, it is referring to His active obedience. The very word "righteous" will be a clue that identifies the person and work of Messiah (e.g., see Isaiah 60:16-17).

The Dying of Christ

The life of Christ took care of the positive demands of the law, but something had to be done to pay the penalty of the broken law. God cannot let bygones be bygones when it comes to sin. Christ's perfect obedience earned two things: for His people, life, and for Himself, the right to die in payment for their sins. His death could pay the penalty for our sins because it did not have to pay the penalty of His–He had no sin. In His saving work, the life and death of Christ are inseparably linked. Theologians refer to His dying for His people as His *passive obedience*. This does not appear a precisely accurate expression because Christ was not a passive victim in His death. No man could take His life; He voluntarily, deliberately, lovingly, and joyfully submitted Himself to the shame and suffering of the cross (John 10:17-18; Hebrews 12:2). Perhaps we should see His death as the last, triumphant demonstration of His active obedience in completely fulfilling the will of God. The coiners of this expression, however, did not intend to imply that Christ was inactive in His death; rather, they used the term "passive" according to its Latin derivation that meant "capable of suffering." This is better, although it may suggest that there was no suffering during His life of active obedience. Nevertheless, as long as we define the term properly and understand that passive obedience refers to His obedient death on the cross (Philippians 2:8) without implying that He was just a victim of uncontrollable circumstances or that He experienced no suffering before His passion, we can use the term legitimately.

Although infirmities, miseries, and sufferings filled the whole life of Christ, they reached their indescribable climax at the cross and in the events immediately leading to the cross. Although the Old Testament does predict the active obedience of Christ, it gives greater attention to the passive obedience. This is no doubt what Peter was directly referring to when he said that the Old Testament prophets were searching diligently concerning the sufferings of Christ. Because so much of the Old Testament points to the cross, it is important for us to remember some essential truths about the cross-work of Christ that will help us to identify that work in the Old Testament, even though the word "cross" does not appear. When we consider the atonement of Christ, we are coming to the deepest and highest theological truths in the Bible. Theologians have argued about the purpose of the death of Christ, the extent of its application, even the shape of the cross. It is not my purpose here to consider all the theories of the atonement, but to set down key aspects of Christ's death that are essential and fundamental to the gospel message.

A Literal Death

The death of Christ was real. The death of Christ is not just a theological doctrine; it is a historic fact. On an actual day in history, Jesus of

THE WORK OF CHRIST

Nazareth shed His blood and died on a Roman cross. His death testified to His real humanity, for it is appointed unto man once to die (Hebrews 9:27). What He achieved by His death testifies to His being the Christ of God, the one and only Savior. It is not without significance that the Gospel narratives devote so much attention to the crucifixion of the Lord Jesus. Although Christ lived over thirty years and accomplished so much that John said the world would not be able to contain the books if everything about His life were written (John 21:25), all four Gospels focus on the events of the last week of His life. The Gospels may be temporally lopsided, but they are theologically balanced. This is one reason we call them the Gospels and not the biographies of Jesus Christ. Each of the Gospels narrates the real sufferings and agony that Christ endured at the hands of wicked men. These historic narratives necessarily prove that every Old Testament prophecy about the suffering Messiah was actually fulfilled in time and also that the apostolic preaching of the cross was not religious myth or legend. The gospel of salvation in Christ is only religious theory unless founded on the real historic fact of the death of the Son of God.

A Vicarious Death

The death of Christ was a substitutionary sacrifice. We often speak of this aspect as the vicarious atonement. A vicar is simply one who fulfills the duties of another as a substitute. That the atonement was vicarious, then, means that it was substitutionary. Christ died instead of us; He died in place of us. Christ fulfilled our obligation to die in payment of our sins. This is the very heart of the gospel. The line in the old hymn says it well: "It is enough that Jesus died and that He died for me." For us to pay the penalty of our own sins would take forever because we have offended the infinitely holy God. There could never be salvation if sinners were left to themselves either to obey the law or to make full payment for breaking it. Salvation for sinners requires a Savior outside themselves. Salvation for sinners requires that the penalty of sin be paid by one whose death could have infinite value. Jesus Christ is the only One qualified to be such a Savior of sinners. Because He was completely pure and holy with no unpaid debt to the law for Himself, He was able to suffer and die for others. As we will see, the Old Testament is rich in the theology of substitutionary sacrifice. Similarly, the New Testament declares over and again that Jesus died not for Himself but for sinners. I could offer many texts as evidence, but consider these few. Christ "was delivered for our offences" (Romans 4:25). "In due time Christ died for the ungodly" (Romans 5:6). "While we were yet sinners, Christ died for us" (Romans 5:8). "Christ hath redeemed us from the curse of the law, being made a curse for us" (Galatians 3:13). "Who his own self bare our sins in his body on the tree" (I Peter 2:24). "Christ died for our sins according to the scriptures" (I Corinthians 15:3). "For he hath made him to be sin for us, who knew no sin" (II Corinthians 5:21).

This last verse requires explanation. Paul is not saying that Christ became a sinner. There are two orthodox interpretations of the statement. Some interpret it to mean that Christ was made a sin offering for us. This is certainly true and would establish a clear link between Christ's sacrifice and the Old Testament that uses the word "sin" to designate the sin offering. Others interpret the statement as using the language of imputation. Christ was considered or regarded as guilty of sin and liable for its penalty. On the cross God dealt with Christ as though He were legally a sinner, though in actual fact He was always the pure and spotless Lamb. For what it's worth, I favor the second interpretation. I believe this imputation aspect of Christ's passive obedience parallels the imputation aspect of His active obedience. Legally, God deals with believers in terms of Christ's righteousness, which He imputes to them. Legally, God dealt with Christ in terms of our sins. By God's legal transaction, the life that Christ earned becomes ours and the death that we earned became His.

A Planned Death
The death of Christ was God's eternal purpose. Christ was "the Lamb slain from the foundation of the world" (Revelation 13:8). The real, sacrificial death of Christ was planned in eternity. To suggest that the cross was a contingent plan resulting from Jewish rejection of Christ's kingdom defies the clear teaching of Scripture and denigrates the precious blood of the Savior. It makes God subservient to sinners. The New Testament makes it absolutely clear that Christ's dying for sinners was God's only and eternal plan for saving sinners. Sinners did not dictate what God did; God's purpose dictated what sinners did. In one of his first sermons, Peter declared that even though wicked men crucified Christ, He was "delivered by the determinate counsel and foreknowledge of God" (Acts 2:23). When Paul defines the gospel by

saying Christ died according to the Scripture, he highlights the eternal plan of God. The Scripture he refers to is the Old Testament, which I am suggesting is filled with revelation concerning this atoning work of Christ. If the Old Testament reveals His death, then obviously it was not a contingent move on God's part.

The implications of Christ's death as eternally planned are twofold. First, it implies that the sacrifice of Christ was, is, and will be the only basis for salvation. God's eternal plan guaranteed its reality, and the effect of its reality is applicable to the time before its actual occurrence as well as after. In other words, Christ's blood washed away Abraham's sin as effectively as it does ours. Second, it implies the absolute necessity of the atonement as the only possible way of salvation. Paul makes it clear that if salvation could be possible any other way apart from Christ's death, then Christ died for no reason, uselessly (Galatians 2:21; 3:21). What a mockery of God's justice it would be if Christ's sacrifice were not essential for man's salvation. God's nature and will made the atonement necessary. His justice demanded penalty; His grace gave His only begotten Son.

A Successful Death

The death of Christ was effective. The atonement successfully accomplished its purpose concerning God, sin, and man. Every time we meditate on the cross-work of the Lord Jesus Christ, our hearts ought to warm, overflowing with gratitude and praise for His amazing love to us. To read the Gospel narratives, which describe the indescribable sufferings, tortures, and agonies that our Savior endured for us, ought to generate ever-increasing love, devotion, and dedicated service to Him. Having judged that He died for us, how can we possibly live for ourselves (II Corinthians 5: 14-15)? Indeed, the love of Christ ought to constrain us, that is, hold us fast in custody; it ought to arrest us. This kind of subjective response is good and is an intended effect of the sufferings and death of the Lord. There is no more appropriate motive for service than a sight of Christ. Nevertheless, the atonement possesses an objective aspect that is vitally important, too. By objective, I mean something outside of and independent of our subjective, personal responses: something that is true regardless of feeling. In fact, if these objective aspects were not true, the cross of Christ could not save us no matter what we thought about it. When we understand what the atonement did "objectively," it warrants more and more of our "subjective" confidence, joy, and praise. These objective features are detailed in numerous Scriptural passages, and they carry with them many implications that I can only briefly mention. However, our awareness of just three principal truths about the atonement will aid us in recognizing the work of Christ in our Old Testament search.

Success with God

First, Christ's death was effective with God. This Godward effect of the atonement is called *propitiation*. Propitiation refers to the satisfaction or appeasement of God's just wrath against sin and sinners. The death of Christ satisfied the penalty of the broken law; the blood of Christ appeased the divine wrath against the sinner. The blood of Christ removed every legal impediment to man's coming to God. This thought brings us to one of the great mysteries of the cross of Jesus Christ. The crucifixion was at the same time the greatest display of God's love for sinners and the greatest display of His justice and wrath against sin. It was ultimately on the cross that mercy and truth met together and righteousness and peace kissed (Psalm 85:10). The inflexibly holy and just God poured out His infinite wrath on His dear and only Son. Because the Lord Jesus took for us the full brunt of God's wrath, there is absolutely no wrath left for us. To be in Christ is to be free from divine wrath because that wrath was appeased. God is no longer angry with those reconciled by the blood of His Son. The mystery is that the God who is justly angry at sin is the God who lovingly gave His Son "to be the propitiation for our sins" (I John 4:10; Romans 5:8-10; II Corinthians 5:18-20). This gospel of propitiation is rich in the Old Testament.

Success against Sin

Second, Christ's death was effective regarding sin. This sinward effect of the atonement is called *expiation*. Expiation refers to the removal of sin and guilt, the forgiveness of sin. The Scripture forthrightly states that "without the shedding of blood is no remission" (Hebrews 9:22). Christ came to "put away sin by the sacrifice of himself" (Hebrews 9:26), and this is exactly what He did. John said the purpose of Christ's coming was to "destroy the works of the devil" (I John 3:8; cf., Hebrews 2:14). This in no way means that Christ offered Himself to Satan, but rather that His death was the ultimate bruising of the serpent's head that reversed the curse of sin (Genesis 3:15). His sacrificial death paid the penalty of sin; it provided cleansing for sin; it defeated the power of sin; it guaranteed the final escape from the very presence of sin. Through the blood of the Lord Jesus is "the forgiveness of sins, according to the riches of his grace" (Ephesians 1:7). Little wonder that Paul exclaims, "sin shall not have dominion over you" (Romans 6:14). The old hymn answers its own question well. "What can wash away my sin? Nothing but the blood of Jesus." This gospel of expiation is rich in the Old Testament.

Success for Man

Third, Christ's death is effective for man. My point here is simply that the gospel works. Because the atonement satisfied God and defeated sin, it can save man. The emphasis of Scripture is on the redemption and deliverance every believer enjoys through Christ (see I Corinthians 7:23; Galatians 3:13; I Peter 1:18-19; I Timothy 2:6; Revelation 5:9). Believers are delivered from every curse of sin and threat of the law. Believers are assured access to God—now only spiritually, but someday completely. The death of Christ is the basis for every benefit that we enjoy in salvation: union with Christ, justification, adoption, sanctification, assurance of divine love, peace, joy, perseverance, eternal security, hope of certain resurrection, eternal glorification, and whatever else God has promised and Christ has guaranteed. The more we learn to relate every aspect of our salvation to the precious blood of Christ shed for us, the more we will know and enjoy the certainty of our salvation.

What a glorious work the Lord Jesus performed during His first advent! His first advent addressed the problem of sin and the problem of the law. He lived a life that none else could possibly have lived; He died a death with consequences that none other could possibly have. Paul defined the gospel in the simple terms of Christ's death and resurrection, both according to the Scripture (I Corinthians 15:3-4). (I will say something about the resurrection in the next section.) His life and death and life constitute the gospel, the good news for sinners. Once we understand that this is the only good news for sinners, it should not surprise us that its proclamation is just as prevalent in the Old Testament as in the New. Knowing His work is a clue to finding and identifying Him in our Old Testament study. And finding Him is the secret to a spiritually happy life.

The Rising of Christ

The resurrection of the Lord Jesus Christ is the second bedrock element of the gospel. In his famous definition of the gospel in I Corinthians 15, Paul identifies two key components: Christ's death and His resurrection. That Christ died and rose again is the good news. Notice how the apostle frames these two fundamental facts of the gospel with the statement "according to the scriptures." He then offers two key pieces of historical evidence to verify the gospel claims. The evidence of the real death of Christ was that He was buried; the evidence of the real resurrection was that He was seen by many witnesses. That framing statement, "according to the scriptures," reminds us that both of the essential gospel truths were as much Old Testament theology as New. Therefore, the resurrection will be one more clue to look for in our search for Christ in the Old Testament. Keep in mind that this is what we are doing now: gathering clues.

The Fact of the Resurrection

Life after death and glory after suffering are common messianic themes in the Old Testament and well-developed theology in the New. The resurrection was the obvious means to that life and glory. Christ's resurrection is more than theological doctrine; it is historic fact. Every genuine Christian affirms that Jesus Christ, having been crucified on a Roman cross, bodily rose from the dead on an actual day in history. To deny the resurrection is to deny the gospel. But to believe in a resurrection that did not occur is still to perish in sins. The objective, historical certainty of the resurrection is essential to salvation (I Corinthians 15:17). Indeed, Paul makes it clear that believing in the resurrection of Christ is worthless folly if Christ did not in truth rise from the dead. Believing it and preaching it do not make it so (see I Corinthians 15:14). Notwithstanding the necessary emphasis on the historicity of the resurrection, we must not ignore the equally important theology associated with it that is so wonderfully a part of our salvation. Too often it is the neglected part of the gospel.

The Implications of the Resurrection

Let me just suggest some of the theological implications of Christ's resurrection. I would encourage you to look up these Scripture texts to establish these summary statements. I am using here the main points of a sermon I once preached. *(1) The resurrection affirmed Christ's identity*: as the promised Messiah (Luke 24:44-46), as the true prophet (Matthew 12:38; John 2:18), and as the Son of God (Romans 1:4). The point is that His resurrection verified and validated every claim the Scripture made concerning the Messiah and that Christ made about Himself. Remember we have already learned that Jesus staked His whole prophetic authority on the prophecy that He would rise from the dead. The implications are significant: if He was right concerning this astounding prophecy, then everything else He said deserves careful hearing and obedience. *(2) The resurrection accredited Christ's atonement* (Romans 4:25). It is the guarantee that God received His sacrifice as the full satisfaction of His wrath against sin, the full payment for sin's penalty. Significantly, in this connection most of the references to the resurrection focus on God's activity in raising up Christ. Although it is true that Christ arose, it is theologically vital that we understand and believe that He was raised by the power of God's Spirit. This was the great "stamp of approval" on a mission accomplished. *(3) The resurrection acclaimed Christ's authority* (Acts 2:32-36): as the mediatorial ruler (Ephesians 1:20-22) and as the mediatorial representative (Hebrews 7:25; Romans 8:34). This is the session work. *(4) The resurrection achieved our salvation* (I Peter 1:3; Romans 5:10; I Corinthians 15:14). If by His death Christ fulfilled every condition to purchase life for those united to Him, then those united to Him will be certainly saved in and by His life. In fact, the resurrection of Christ stands as the great guarantee of the success of His whole mission. *(5) The resurrection assures our immortality* (John 14:19; I Corinthians 15:20-23). Christ's life after death not only revealed the destiny of believers but also guarantees the life of every believer. It is impossible for those in Christ to perish. Christ redeemed us completely, and not one part of redeemed man will ever perish, not even his body. It is a tragic shame that we tend to think of the resurrection only on Easter Sunday. The New Testament apostles included it in almost every sermon. The Old Testament prophets from Moses forward, as we will see, included it in their preaching as well.

The Ascending of Christ
Although not many texts focus directly on this single event, it is nonetheless important. Luke records the historic fact of Christ's being

taken up into heaven (Luke 24:51; Acts 1:9,11). Hebrews speaks of our great high priest "that is passed into the heavens" (4:14). This could be rendered more literally, "a great high priest, that had gone through the heavens." The bodily ascension of the Lord Jesus testifies to His finished work, which earned His entrance to glory and commenced a new, intensified, manifest ministry of the Holy Spirit (John 16:7-17). In one sense, Christ's return to heaven was to be expected. He Himself said, "I came forth from the Father, and am come into the world: again, I leave the world, and go to the Father" (John 16:28). As the Son of God, He had every right to reside in His eternal glory. What made the ascension theologically special was the entering into glory of the Son of Man. The inspired apostle recognized the significance of this when he applied Psalm 8 directly and uniquely to Christ: "What is man, that thou art mindful of him? or the son of man, that thou visitest him? Thou madest him a little lower than the angels; thou crownedst him with glory and honour, and didst set him over the works of thy hands" (Hebrews 2:6-7). For a little while the Son of Man was being perfected through sufferings, but because of His perfect life He earned everlasting glory as the Ideal Man. In the person of Jesus Christ, man achieved heaven. His entrance prepared the way for all His followers. Speaking of Christ's entering within the veil, the most holy place of heaven itself, Hebrews plainly says, "whither the forerunner is for us entered, even Jesus" (6:20). Christ is the pioneer who has blazed the trail for His people to enter fully into His glory. Heaven is ours because Heaven is Christ's. "He the pearly gates will open–so that I may enter in."

Present Works

"The estate of Christ's exaltation comprehendeth his resurrection, ascension, sitting at the right hand of the Father, and his coming again to judge the world" (*Westminster Larger Catechism*, question 51). The first advent of Christ marked His humiliation and commenced His exaltation; His present work continues His exaltation. The humiliation was temporary, never to be repeated. His exaltation is everlasting, never to cease. The New Testament ends with a grand and glorious revelation of the Lamb of God's being all the glory of eternity (Revelation 21); indeed, as the hymn repeats, "the Lamb is all the glory in Immanuel's land." This messianic exaltation is the earned reward of His divinely accepted active and passive obedience. It is the irrefutable evidence that His atoning work was well done and that heaven guaranteed its absolute success. The New Testament makes the link between His obedience and His exaltation explicitly clear. After delineating the extreme humiliation of the Lord Jesus, Paul declared, "Wherefore God also hath highly exalted him" (Philippians 2:9). The little Greek particle translated "wherefore" means simply "on account of this." Because Christ perfectly obeyed the law and perfectly paid the penalty of sin, God exalted Him to a position of unique honor. Similarly Peter, relying on Old Testament theology, proclaims that Christ is now exalted at the right hand of God (Acts 2:33, applying the theology of Psalm 110:1).

Theologians refer to this exalted status and station at the right hand of God as the *Session of Christ*. Just as the first advent of Christ witnessed His work in behalf of His people, so does this current work of His session. Hebrews says plainly that Christ has entered into heaven "now to appear in the presence of God for us" (9:24). As there was nothing passive about His first coming, there is nothing passive or inactive about His present position at God's right hand. Although He is sitting there, He is not idle. It is a huge mistake to assume that Christ is just sitting around heaven waiting for the Father to tell Him the time for His Second Coming. Christ is currently, constantly, and wonderfully active for His people. The two principal works of Christ between His advents are His intercession and His administration.

In His exalted session work the Lord Jesus continues to exercise His mediatorial operations. As Prophet, He sends His Spirit to "reprove the world of sin, and of righteousness, and of judgment" (John 16:8). As Priest, He constantly intercedes for His people. As King, He administers the affairs of His kingdom, particularly His church. The *Westminster Larger Catechism* gives a clear synopsis of this work.

> Christ is exalted in his sitting at the right hand of God, in that as God-man he is advanced to the highest favor with God the Father, with all fullness of joy, glory, and power over all things in heaven and earth; and doth gather and defend his church, and subdue their enemies; furnisheth his ministers and people with gifts and graces, and maketh intercession for them. (question 54)

Prophetic Administration

His prophetic work is primarily mediate. This means He works indirectly, but He works nonetheless. Interestingly, Paul links Christ's prophetic administration with His ascension. Ephesians 4:9-10 is an interesting passage that is often misunderstood: "Now that he ascended, what is it but that he also descended first into the lower parts of the earth? He that descended is the same also that ascended up far above all the heavens, that he might fill all things." Let us be careful to follow Paul's logic. There is no question that he is referring to Christ's ascension into heaven. This ascension from earth to heaven is possible only because Christ first descended from heaven to earth. Paul's reference to lower parts is in contrast to heaven, not some lower region inside the earth. The word "earth" stands in an appositive relationship to "lower parts." In other words, "earth" identifies what the "lower parts" are. Nothing in the language or the context permits interpreting this passage as saying Christ went down into Hades. The descending refers to His Incarnation; the ascending refers to His glorious entrance to heaven. On the basis of this ascension, Paul declares that Christ "gave gifts unto men" (Ephesians 4:8). Included in this gift distribution were some "apostles; and some, prophets; and some, evangelists; and some pastors and teachers; for the perfecting of the saints, for the work of the ministry, for the edifying of the body of Christ" (Ephesians 4:11-12). Even while in heaven, Christ has not left His people without a Word. What adds significance for our particular consideration is that Paul asserts all this on the basis of his inspired and therefore correct interpretation and application of Psalm 68:18. This is not just New Testament revelation.

Priestly Intercession

Christ's priestly work, on the other hand, is immediate. We are given the amazing privilege of listening in on Christ's great intercessory prayer just prior to His sacrifice on Calvary (John 17). The wonderful depth and beauty of that prayer require that we remove our shoes, for it is holy ground. One thing we can learn from that recorded prayer is that Christ prays with His people on His heart. He prayed both for His disciples and for every believer in every generation to follow: "I pray for them: I pray not for the world, but for them which thou hast given me; for they are thine ... neither pray I for these alone, but for them also which shall believe on me through their word" (John 17:9, 20).

What He prayed on earth, He continues to pray in heaven. Although John does not again record the actual words of Christ's intercession, he assures us that "we have an advocate with the Father, Jesus Christ the righteous." The word "advocate" is *paraclete*, that one who is called alongside. Christ is the one near to the Father and near to us to intercede for us with the Father. Although we do not know His exact words as He intercedes for us, we do know the basis of His argument. That John immediately identifies the Lord as our propitiation suggests that He pleads His own blood (I John 2:2-3). God is forever satisfied with His Son and forever satisfied with His sacrifice. None who have been saved by the blood can ever be the object of God's wrath. I don't want to keep breaking out into song, but how well Wesley's hymn expresses the truth: "Five bleeding wounds He bears, received on Calvary; they pour effectual prayers, they strongly plead for me; Forgive them O Forgive they cry ... nor let that ransomed sinner die." This intercessory work is our guarantee of the irrevocable application of the blood of Christ to save us and keep us saved forever. We will never know how much we owe to the successful intercession of Christ in our behalf. The very thought ought to stop us short and move us to praise and thanks for His faithfulness and effective representation of us before the throne at God's right hand. The statement of the *Westminster Larger Catechism* about Christ's intercession warrants thought:

> Christ maketh intercession, by his appearing in our nature continually before the Father in heaven, in the merit of his obedience and sacrifice on earth; declaring his will to have it applied to all believers; answering all accusations against them; and procuring for them quiet of conscience, notwithstanding daily failings, access with boldness to the throne of grace, and acceptance of their persons and services. (question 55)

How tremendous!

There is no book in the New Testament that more thoroughly instructs us concerning Christ's priestly intercession than the book of Hebrews. This is perhaps doubly significant for our present study because no book in the New Testament is so thoroughly dependent on Old Testament theology as Hebrews. Hebrews teaches us that the Old Testament properly understood leads to the knowledge of Jesus Christ. It certainly gives us clues that inform us that Messiah's intercessory ministry is an Old Testament theme. Although the apostle does not record the words of any heavenly prayer, two things emerge as remarkably clear from Hebrews: Christ constantly intercedes for us, and nobody can do so like Him. Hebrews 7:25 says, "Wherefore he is able also to save them to the uttermost that come unto God by him, seeing he ever liveth to make intercession for them." "To the uttermost" means literally completely, entirely, or perfectly. Salvation begun is always salvation finished. Hebrews 7:24 says, "This man, because he continueth ever, hath an unchangeable priesthood." The word "unchangeable" means untransferrable. His priesthood cannot be passed on to anyone else. Only He has the credentials; only He has the heart to pray as He does for His people.

Kingly Administration

The kingly work of Christ is administrative, especially relating to His church. Once again we appeal to the evidence of the apostle Paul. His writings express both his knowledge of Old Testament truth and the relevant application of that truth to the new administration of the church. In Ephesians 1 Paul first links Christ's resurrection to His session at God's right hand, alluding to Psalm 110. He equates the regenerating power of the Holy Spirit in the heart of believers with the same power "he wrought in Christ, when he raised him from the dead, and set him at his own right hand in the heavenly places" (Ephesians 1:19-20). The corollary to Christ's sitting down in heaven is that God "put all things under his feet, and gave him to be the head over all things to the church" (Ephesians 1:22). During His session Christ rules His kingdom.

John's initial apocalyptic vision of the exalted Lord illustrates the reality of Christ's superintendence of His church. When John turned to see who was speaking to him, he saw "one like unto the Son of man" in the middle of the lamp stands, having seven stars in His hand (Revelation 1:13, 16). Happily, the vision interprets itself for us. The lamp stands represent the churches, and the stars represent the ministers of those churches (Revelation 1:20). The point is beautifully obvious. Although John was exiled because of the gospel and the church was being persecuted, Christ was with them, holding tightly in His hand those whom He had appointed to lead, pastor, and teach His church. Everything was under control. Adding to the significance of this vision of the glorified Christ is the preponderance of Old

Testament terminology and imagery used to describe this aspect of Christ's session. If you have cross-references in your Bible, just look how rich is the Old Testament influence. It follows that if Christ uses these terms and images to describe Himself, then those terms and images in the Old Testament were direct references and pointers to Him. These are the kinds of clues we are looking for.

If the New Testament is clear about anything, it is clear that Christ is now at work for His people. He accomplished a wonderful work at His first advent and will do so again at His second, but He is now active for the good of His kingdom. The Old Testament is not silent concerning this present aspect of the glory of Messiah.

Second Advent Works

Although the Old Testament did not always clearly address the time gap between the sufferings of Christ and the glory that would follow, the works of Christ that we now know belong to His Second Coming are very frequent topics of Old Testament Christology. Discussions about the Second Coming concern that area of theology called eschatology, the doctrine of last things. Sadly, many today get so taken up with trying to figure out the timing and sequence of predictive details that they miss the main message. Even more sadly, many become so confident and dogmatic in their sequential schemes that they deny the orthodoxy and almost the Christianity of any who interpret differently. I am well aware of the controversy and for now want to avoid it. I have my own views of prophecy, and I suppose I am just as confident as anyone else that I am right. My principal concern, however, is not to discover and order the events of predictive prophecy, but to discover the person of predictive prophecy. The main theme of eschatology is not events but Christ. As believers, even if we cannot agree on the sequence of events, we ought to be able to rejoice in the knowledge of a soon-coming Christ.

Hebrews 9:28 plainly says that Christ will "appear the second time without sin unto salvation." Whereas His first advent dealt with the sin problem for His people, His Second Advent will bring the full consummation of the salvation of His people. The biblical focus on His Second Coming is twofold: He comes in glory to judge, and He comes in glory to reign. The Scripture links many important events to the time immediately before, at, and immediately after the Second

Coming of Christ, such as the rise and fall of the Antichrist and his False prophet, "the time of Jacob's trouble," the great battle of Armageddon, the binding of Satan, the marriage supper of the Lamb, the resurrection of all the dead (righteous and wicked) and the Great White Throne Judgment. By the way, please don't try to figure out my eschatological scheme by the order in which I listed these attendant circumstances. I listed them on purpose randomly as they crossed my mind. All are extremely important, and all warrant study and appropriate application. But resisting the temptation to discuss the attendant circumstances of Christ's Second Advent, we want simply to identify His work—what He does—so we can see Him as the central figure not only in the times to come but in the Scripture that reveals those times.

The Infallible Judge

First, *Christ will judge.* The New Testament asserts both that Christ is the Judge and that His right to judge is part of His messianic appointment. The key texts really need no comment. John 5:27 says that God has "given him authority to execute judgment also, because he is the Son of man." Peter declared that God had commissioned the apostles to preach that Christ "was ordained of God to be the Judge of quick and dead" (Acts 10:42). Paul preached that God has "appointed a day, in the which he will judge the world in righteousness by that man whom he hath ordained; whereof he hath given assurance unto all men, in that he hath raised him from the dead" (Acts 17:31). II Timothy 4:1 says that the Lord Jesus Christ "shall judge the quick and the dead at his appearing and his kingdom." John records in his apocalyptic vision, "Behold a white horse; and he that sat upon him was called Faithful and True, and in righteousness he doth judge and make war" (Revelation 19:11). The Lord Jesus said there would be a judgment between the sheep and goats at the time of His glorious return: "When the Son of man shall come in his glory, and all the holy angels with him, then shall he sit upon the throne of his glory" (Matthew 25:31).

This judging of the wicked is an essential part of His kingship. It is an essential element in His continuing exaltation. Note how Paul in the Acts 17 text linked the righteous judging of Christ with His resurrection. The first element in Messiah's exaltation guarantees the ultimate

manifestation of that exaltation. One way or another men will acknowledge and experience the authority of Christ. As King, He
conquers either by grace or by the wrath of just judgment. Both are irresistible and effective. As certainly as He saves, preserves, governs,
and protects His people, so will He take "vengeance on the rest, who
know not God, and obey not the gospel" (*Westminster Larger
Catechism*, question 45). One way or another, every knee will bow and
every tongue will confess that Jesus Christ is Lord (Philippians 2:10-
11). The book of the Revelation pictures the Lamb of God both in His
Sovereign kindness in leading His people (7:17) and in His Sovereign
wrath, against which none can stand except those who are sealed
(6:16-7:3). It is most assuring that He knows the difference: His judgment is both certain and infallible. "The foundation of God standeth
sure, having this seal, The Lord knoweth them that are his ..." (II
Timothy 2:19).

The Supreme Ruler

Second, *Christ will reign.* I want to be clear here that I am not saying
Christ's reign is limited to or will not commence before His Second
Coming. We have already established the fact that Kingship is an inherent part of the messianic operation. It is a serious and tragic
mistake to say that Jesus will not become King or begin to rule until
the Second Coming. He now rules His kingdom with absolute authority and success. My point is that at His Second Coming a new
manifestation and administration of that existing Kingship will commence. Paul dogmatically proclaims that Christ must reign until He
puts all enemies under His feet, the last enemy being death (I
Corinthians 15:24-26). When that last enemy falls may be a matter of
interpretation, but it is not an interpretation issue that He must reign
until every enemy falls. Remember that in Matthew's Gospel Christ
said that the Son of Man would sit on the throne of glory when He
would come in His glory (25:31). This indicates that there is going to
be a public display of His glorious reign. That is a key difference between now and then. Now, by faith we believe and enjoy Christ's
active reign; then, even the sight of the most wicked will recognize
His reign. Revelation, alluding to Psalm 2, says that when the Lord
smites the nations, He will rule them with a rod of iron (19:15).
Revelation 20:4-6 says that participants in the "first resurrection" will
live and reign with Christ for a thousand years. This is a key piece of

New Testament evidence that suggests the "premillennial" return of the Lord Jesus to earth to rule and reign personally, visibly, and actually for a thousand years. Nevertheless, I said I would not address that issue now: forgive me, but I couldn't help myself! It just seems so clear to me.

The *Westminster Larger Catechism* identifies the salient points of the Second Advent work of Christ that all orthodox believers can affirm.

> Christ is to be exalted in his coming again to judge the world, in that he, who was unjustly judged and condemned by wicked men, shall come again at the last day in great power, and in the full manifestation of his own glory, and of his Father's, with all his holy angels, with a shout, with the voice of the archangel, and with the trumpet of God, to judge the world in righteousness. (question 56)

The certain fact of the Lord's Second Coming should, regardless of prophetic interpretations, draw men to salvation, deter men from sin, drive Christians to purity, and assure and comfort believers that He who has begun a good work will perform it until the day of Jesus Christ (Philippians 1:6). By seeing the Christ of prophecy may we be able to pray sincerely with John, who saw the Christ of prophecy, "Even so, come, Lord Jesus" (Revelation 22:20).

Our focus has been on the past, present and future work of the Lord Jesus Christ. These works are unique to Him and stand as telltale evidence of His person. His works point to Him. The logic is simple. If only Christ does certain things and we see someone doing those things, then we are seeing Him. This is our clue to finding Christ in the Old Testament. Admittedly, the details may not be as sharp in the Old Testament expectations as in the New Testament expositions, but the work is the same. As we read the Old Testament, we want to have our eyes open for One who is the Lord's righteous servant, who dies for the sins of His people, who after offering Himself as a sacrifice enjoys life because His body could not corrupt in the grave, who is an exalted priest, who sits on a throne with a universal kingdom, and who will come proclaiming and accomplishing both the day of salvation and the day of vengeance. If our eyes are open, we will see all this and more. When we see this One, we are seeing the Lord Jesus Christ because all thee things are true only about Him.

Part 2
Where to Look

PART 2

WHERE TO LOOK

Having identified whom we are looking for, it remains for us to find Him. The question before us is where we can find Christ in the Old Testament. It is important to begin our search with the assurance that we will find Him. If we have the mindset that the Old Testament is nothing but Israeli history, endless genealogies, and useless instructions about how to arrange wilderness camps and distinguish between animals that chew the cud or not, we most likely will not see much of Christ. But if we can come taking Christ at His word that He is the central topic of discussion of the entire Old Testament (remember Luke 24:27, 44), then we will be anticipating Him at every turn of the page. It's kind of like the difference between fishing in a bathtub or fishing in a pond that has been stocked with fish. Fishing in the bathtub may pass away some time, but it would not create much expectancy since we know there are no fish there. Fishing in a stocked pond may not guarantee a fish every time, but knowing that fish are there generates excitement and anticipation that sooner or later we will catch something.

Too many Christians approach the Old Testament as if they were fishing in the bathtub, expecting nothing, but at least fulfilling "devotion" time. It is my desire that we can open the Old Testament with the certain knowledge that it is filled with Christ and with eagerness to search for Him, knowing that we will find Him. I am not saying that we will find Him in every verse in the Old Testament or even on every page, any more than we would catch a fish in a stocked pond every time we cast the line. But I am saying that He is there everywhere. Let it be on the top of our list of objectives as we read all of Scripture, including the Old Testament, to discover what it reveals about Christ. If we seek Him, we will find Him. Then we can rejoice like the bride in the Song of Songs, "I found him whom my soul loveth" (3:4).

It has been one of my great desires in the ministry that God has given me both in the classroom and in the pulpit to encourage the reading and study of the Old Testament with a view to Christ. It is my desire through this vehicle of teaching to create an excited expectancy in you, as you read the Old Testament, that Genesis to Malachi is a Living Word that cannot ultimately be understood apart from its central message: the Messiah, our Christ and Savior.

The premise that underlies our confidence that Christ is the message of the Old Testament is twofold. First, we believe what Christ said about the Old Testament. We have already considered His statements that the Law, the Prophets, and the Psalms all spoke about Him. If that were all the evidence we had, that would certainly be enough to warrant our diligent effort to understand what the Old Testament revealed concerning Him. Second, we believe that Christ is the only Mediator between God and men. It necessarily follows that since He is the only Mediator, He is the only message of grace and salvation that God has ever given to man. It is the person of Christ that gives grand unity to God's plan and purpose of salvation. This does not mean that God revealed everything about Christ all at once; there was a progressive revelation of truth. And this does not deny that in the Old Testament era there were differing dispensations or administrations of the gospel message; the New Covenant or Testament is indeed a better covenant. What I am saying is that Christ is the only way that God has ever offered to save sinners.

I do not believe that God made this offer of Christ surreptitiously. I do not believe He told them one thing (for instance, that they could be saved by animal sacrifices), and then did something else behind their backs without their knowledge. If we understand that the work Christ did was of infinite value, then we should have no problem understanding that God could regard the virtue and merit of His sacrifice as the sole ground for salvation on both sides of the cross. After all, Christ was in fact the Lamb slain from before the foundation of the world. We are obviously dealing with a mystery. The *Westminster Confession of Faith* summarizes this idea well.

PART TWO

Although the work of redemption was not actually wrought by Christ till after his incarnation, yet the virtue, efficacy, and benefits thereof were communicated unto the elect, in all ages successively from the beginning of the world, in and by those promises, types, and sacrifices, wherein he was revealed, and signified to be the seed of the woman which should bruise the serpent's head; and the Lamb slain from the beginning of the world; being yesterday and to-day the same, and for ever. (Chapter VIII, section 6)

In **Part 2** I want to suggest some places you can find Christ in the Old Testament. "If there—where?" Much of what I will consider can function as material for entire treatises, so I can only be suggestive. In this part I want simply to be a guide pointing out some of the great sights and providing you a map whereby you can discover on your own. I will try to give some hints for reading the map as well. Here are the some of the places we are going to find Christ: the covenants, the pre-incarnate appearances, the titles of Christ, the types of Christ, the Predictions of Christ, and the patterns for worship that focus on Christ. If I can return to my earlier analogy: these are the well-stocked ponds that we will find throughout the Old Testament.

CHAPTER 4

CHRIST IN THE COVENANTS

When Gabriel announced to Mary that she had been chosen as the mother of Messiah, he identified Jesus as the fulfillment of God's covenant promise to David. "He shall be great, and shall be called the Son of the Highest: and the Lord God shall give unto him the throne of his father David: and he shall reign over the house of Jacob for ever: and of his kingdom there shall be no end" (Luke 1:32-33; see II Samuel 7:12-16). When Zacharias opened his mouth in praise to God after the birth of his son John, he recognized the dawning of the messianic era. Not only did he identify his son as Messiah's forerunner, but he saw in Christ's coming a link between the promised salvation associated with David's throne (Luke 1:69) and God's holy covenant oath to Abraham (Luke 1:72-73). He blessed the Lord for raising up "an horn of salvation for us in the house of his servant David ... to perform the mercy promised to our fathers, and to remember his holy covenant; the oath which he sware to our father Abraham." As the writer of Hebrews enumerates and expounds the many excellencies of Christ, he identifies Jesus as "the mediator of a better covenant" (8:6) and ends his discourse with reference to the resurrected Christ and the "blood of the everlasting covenant" (13:20). These New Testament statements make a definite connection between the Lord Jesus Christ and the covenants, thereby warranting our search for Christ in those Old Testament passages that reveal God's covenant promises.

That Christ is central to the covenant promise is not just a New Testament tenet; it is Old Testament theology. The prophet Isaiah in one of his famous messianic Servant Songs records God's words to His Servant: "I will preserve thee, and give thee for a covenant of the people" (49:8). The Old Testament ends with the promise that God would send "the messenger of the covenant," who is identified as the

"Lord, whom ye seek" (Malachi 3:1). All of this suggests that Christ is not only a topic of covenant themes but the very heart, the essence of the covenant itself. To miss finding Christ in the study of God's covenant revelations is, therefore, to miss the main message of the revelation. God's gracious covenant promise is a good place to begin our search for Christ in the Old Testament.

I want to begin our search for Christ in the covenants for a couple of reasons: first, because God's earliest revelation of a Savior can be understood in terms of a covenant promise, and second, because of my personal experience in Old Testament study. I don't know exactly when or how I discovered this clue to seeing Christ in the Old Testament, but I can testify that more than anything else it became the key that unlocked the Old Testament for me. It is a rather simple concept, and why it took so long for me to see it perhaps testifies only to my dullness. But when it finally hit me that Christ is the unifying theme of all the covenants, it was like the proverbial light bulb going on in my head. Seeing Christ in the covenants is significant because of the importance of the covenant theme itself throughout Scripture. To recognize in all the specific covenant institutions, with their particular elements and attendant circumstances, this one, constant, unchanging, unifying message has helped me immensely to discover God's purpose and irresistible, unfrustratable plan in providing the necessary Redeemer to save sinners. It is this covenant promise of Christ that unites the Old Testament together and links it to the New Testament. Indeed, at the core of every covenant institution–whether with Adam, Noah, Abraham, Moses, or David–was the "better covenant," the Lord Jesus Christ Himself. Too often the study of Old Testament covenants has focused on attendant circumstances and has ignored or missed the core message. My concern, while not dismissive of the importance of the peculiar elements of each covenant, is to center our attention on the core issue. I want us to find Christ in the covenants.

Before we begin our search, I need to offer a word of caution and explanation. I am well aware that the simple mention of the word "covenant" is a "red flag" word associated with theological debate and controversy. It is not my purpose to enter into that controversy, except to say that what I am going to discuss with you is not a distinguishing element of any particular system of theology. Seeing Christ in the covenants is an issue that should be nonoffensive to all Christians. Seeing Christ and elevating Him to a central and pre-eminent position ought to be desires embraced by every orthodox Christian. As we will see, the word "covenant" occurs about three hundred times in the Old Testament. It is an important biblical word. My plan is to define the word "covenant" biblically and develop simply its messianic message. My desire is that the light will come on as we study this portion of the Old Testament with a view to Christ.

Definition of Covenant

Part of the difficulty in Bible study is reading words without fully realizing what the words mean. Communication depends on understanding the words that are being used. Since the Bible is God's communicating to us, it is vital that we take the time to make sure we know the definitions of the words and concepts He uses. Much of the misunderstanding surrounding the covenant concept is due to our not fully understanding the significance of the word. Although we rarely use the word "covenant" in modern English apart from legal contracts and marriage ceremonies, it was a well- known concept in the Old Testament world and thus a most fitting vehicle by which God revealed Himself and His gracious promises to man.

The Authorized Version occasionally translated the Hebrew word for "covenant" as "league" (Joshua 9:6; Judges 2:2; II Samuel 3:12, etc.) or "confederacy" (Genesis 14:13; Obadiah 7), but in the vast majority of the approximately three hundred occurrences of word it uses "covenant." Some interpreters have speculated about the etymology of the word, trying to factor their assumptions into the definition. Etymology simply refers to the history of a word and frequently in Hebrew involves linking the word to some foundational root which is often evidenced in another Semitic language besides Hebrew. Opinions concerning the etymology of "covenant" range from root words meaning "to fetter," "to eat bread with," or "to decide." This sort of speculation can be interesting, but it can prove distracting in the absence of definitive proof. When a word appears as frequently in the Old Testament as "covenant," my opinion is that etymology is irrelevant and that the contexts of word usage better provide the clues for definition. In view of all the Old Testament evidence, I would define "covenant" as a *mutually binding agreement between two parties*. This agreement obligated the parties to certain duties and guaranteed certain issues.

Human Covenants

Various covenants between men illustrate something of these basic and essential elements of a covenant. In a dispute over a well, Abraham and Abimelech entered a covenant and confirmed it with an oath that they would respect each other's property (Genesis 21:25-32). Genesis 31:44-55 records a covenant between Jacob and Laban that set the terms for their future relationship. They called God to witness, swore by God, and offered a sacrifice to God promising each other that they would not cross their established border in hostility. Joshua entered a covenant with the Gibeonites that obligated them to servitude but guaranteed their lives in spite of their devious behavior during the negotiations (Joshua 9:15ff). In II Samuel 5:1-3 David entered a covenant with the elders of Israel that guaranteed his throne, obligated him to provide for the people, and required them to submit to his authority. We could go on and on with these illustrations, but I think these few establish the point I want us to see—that a common feature of all these man-to-man covenants is the sense of obligation and guaranteed behavior between the parties. Obligation and guarantees are likewise essential elements in God's covenants with men.

Observing some of the attendant actions and events that occur in conjunction with covenant ratifications also helps to define the concept. And not only do they help define, but they also help identify a covenant context even if the term "covenant" does not occur. Again, if we see those actions and events that are attendant to the making of a covenant, we have sufficient warrant to assume the existence of a covenant.

Covenant Oath

First, an oath often accompanied the establishing of the covenant. Taking the oath, or swearing, was a pledge of allegiance to the terms of the covenant agreement and the declared promise to fulfill those terms. Isaac showed the association between oath and covenant when he negotiated with Abimelech about the wells: "Let there be now an oath betwixt us ... and let us make a covenant" (Genesis 26:28). II Chronicles 15:12-15 vividly illustrates the close connection between the covenant and oath. In fact, so close was the connection that the word "oath" could represent the covenant itself. In verse 12 Judah "entered into a covenant to seek the Lord God of their fathers with all their heart and with all their soul." Then verse 14 says that they "sware unto the Lord" in confirming that agreement. Finally, verse 15 says, "All Judah rejoiced at the oath: for they had sworn with all their heart, and sought him with their whole desire." In this last verse, the word "oath" by metonymy designates the covenant to seek the Lord. Remember that metonymy is a common figure of speech whereby one word can be used for another because of a connection or association between those words. So here, "oath"–the pledge to keep the covenant–stands for the covenant itself. The oath taken at the institution of the covenant was a means of affirming and declaring the intended resolve to fulfill the obligations and assure the terms. The oath was the guarantee.

Covenant Sacrifice

Second, a sacrifice often accompanied the establishing of a covenant. Interestingly, the common designation for making a covenant was "to cut a covenant." Although multiple explanations exist for this idiom, it most likely has some connection to the common practice of offering a sacrifice as part of the ratification of a covenant. The full expression may have been something like "cutting the animal for the covenant." The idiom was used even when no actual sacrifice occurred. For instance, David's covenant with Abner to consolidate the nation after Saul's death did not involve a sacrifice, but David nonetheless said, "I will make a league" (II Samuel 3:13). Translated literally, he said, "I will cut a covenant with you." However, the Old Testament often mentions the sacrifice as an integral part of making the covenant. For instance, part of Jacob's covenant ratification with Laban involved the offering of a sacrifice, the killing of animals (Genesis 31:54). Jeremiah 34:18 is a key text that provides some explanation of the significance of the sacrifice. The Lord declared judgment on those who broke the terms of His covenant by not performing the "words of the covenant which they had made before me, when they cut the calf in twain, and passed between the parts thereof." That passing between the parts of the sacrifice is similar to the Lord's passing through the pieces of the sacrifices that Abraham had made in ratification of the Lord's covenant with him (Genesis 15:17). Theories abound concerning the significance of this act. I can only give my opinion. Without question, the blood that was shed in the sacrifice was extremely important, and I will consider the importance of blood when we look at the sacrifices specifically. My thoughts here concern that "passing through the parts." I think that perhaps this part of the ceremony was to convey the reconciliation between the parties and in effect to declare what by covenant they now shared. The two halves most likely represented the two parties of the covenant, and the mutual passing through the parts symbolically represented the binding of the parties into a single unit. Each had his part; each had his duty to fulfill in maintaining the agreement. The covenant was to be a mutually binding contract.

Covenant Meal

Third, a fellowship meal often accompanied the establishing of a covenant. This component is particularly significant because eating together signaled an affirmation of friendship and peace. Though speaking of betrayal, Psalm 41:9 clearly suggests the significance of the common meal in referring to "mine own familiar friend, in whom I trusted, which did eat of my bread." Several covenant contexts expressly mention the parties' eating together. After Isaac and Abimelech came to terms about the water rights, Isaac "made them a feast, and they did eat and drink" (Genesis 26:30). Similarly, Jacob and Laban ate bread together after reaching their agreement (Genesis 31:54). After Abner made good his word to David in convincing Israel to submit to David's kingship, David "made Abner and the men that were with him a feast" (II Samuel 3:20). The fellowship meal clearly evidenced the reconciliation of the parties. Whatever it was that had alienated them was resolved, and they could sit together in peace.

Covenant Guarantee

Fourth, salt was sometimes associated with a covenant. When Abijah, a king of Judah, warred against Jeroboam, a king of Israel, he referred to the Lord's giving David the kingdom of Israel as a "covenant of salt" (II Chronicles 13:5; see also Numbers 18:19). Although I'm sure they used salt primarily to make food taste good, the symbolic significance was more likely in salt's use as a preservative than in its savory quality. In other words, Abijah was arguing that the house of David still had legitimate claim to the northern tribes and territory. The salt of the covenant asserted the continuing and perpetual aspect of the agreement. A covenant was not to be broken. A covenant was a binding agreement.

Although not every covenant context includes all of these features, each of the features testifies to an important element in the covenant. Many of the covenant contexts recorded in the Old Testament were between parties of more or less equal standing. Because the parties were equal, the terms of agreement were often negotiable yet mutually binding once the deal had been struck. These are called parity covenants. Other covenants, those between superiors and inferiors, are called suzerainty covenants. More technical terms identifying these two types of contracts are "dipleuric" and "monopleuric," but I prefer the simpler terms. A suzerain is a sovereign, a king. Suzerainty covenants were both non-negotiable and mutually binding. The sovereign had the right to set the terms to which the subjects submitted. In both the parity and suzerainty covenants, all the parties assumed certain obligated duties that were guaranteed by a pledge of allegiance or oath. Obviously, the covenants that God "cuts" with men are suzerainty covenants. He is infinitely superior, with the divine right to set all the terms and the divine power to fulfill His pledge.

Divine Covenants

The covenant was a widespread phenomenon in Israel and throughout the ancient Near East. It was, therefore, a most appropriate vehicle through which the Lord revealed His Word. All the salient features that define and identify covenants reach the ideal in God's gracious covenants. The people would have understood well the implications. The major difference between the human-to-human agreements and the God-to-man covenant is that God could and would keep His end of the agreement. Men often reneged on the terms of their contracts, and sovereigns often made promises they were incapable of keeping. But God was—and is—unfailingly faithful to His covenants. One of the great covenant terms throughout the Old Testament highlights the absolute loyalty of God to His covenant promise and to His covenant people. It is the word the Authorized Version translates as "kindness," "lovingkindness," or "mercy." It is the word that occurs in every verse of Psalm 136: "for his mercy endureth forever." The Psalmist is saying over and again that God is loyal in keeping His covenant. Psalm 111:9 affirms that God has "commanded his covenant forever." Psalm 105:8

says, "He hath remembered his covenant for ever, the word which he commanded to a thousand generations." God takes His covenant seriously. These wonderful statements become all the more significant in view of our premise that Christ is the essence of the covenant.

Consider these facts:

1. As covenants were confirmed with oaths, so God confirmed His covenant promise of Christ with an oath. The prophet Micah ended his message with the assurance that God would perform the truth to Jacob and the mercy to Abraham which He had "sworn unto our fathers from the days of old" (7:20). When reaffirming His covenant with Abraham, He swore by Himself (Genesis 22:16). Hebrews explains that He did so because He could swear by no greater and that the oath was the direct means "wherein God, willing more abundantly to shew unto the heirs of promise the immutability of his counsel, confirmed it by an oath" (6:13, 17). Significantly, Hebrews immediately identifies the irrevocable promise as referring to the Lord Jesus, the sure and steadfast anchor of the soul (6:19). God, therefore, guaranteed with a pledge of infinite worth the certain coming and successful mission of Christ to fulfill every term and promise set down by covenant.

2. As covenants were ratified by sacrifice, so God ratified His gracious covenant by the sacrifice of His dear Son. Hebrews again gives us the inspired commentary that Christ as the mediator of the new covenant died to redeem sinners, even sinners under the old covenant (Old Testament believers), that the called might "receive the promise of eternal inheritance" (9:15). It is not without significance that Jesus Himself in instituting the Lord's Supper referred to the cup as the new testament, or covenant, in His blood (I Corinthians 11:25). Similarly, as the Old Testament covenant sacrifices pictured the reconciliation of the parties, so Christ made "peace through the blood of his cross ... to reconcile all things unto himself" and especially those alienated from and enemies of God (Colossians 1:20-21).

3. As covenants were affirmed with communal fellowship meals, so God now receives to a place of peace and pardon those who have accepted Christ. Being justified by faith in Christ, we have peace

with God and access by faith into grace (Romans 5:1-2). That we so often refer to the Lord's Table as "Communion" testifies to the enjoyment of peace and the experience of divine presence we know in union with Christ, the covenant promise.

4. As the salt of the covenant pictured the certain perpetuity of the covenant, so God has made Christ the surety, or guarantee, of the better covenant (Hebrews 7:22). There is not the slightest possibility that any part of God's covenant purposes regarding Christ can fail, because "all the promises of God in him are yea, and in him Amen, unto the glory of God by us" (II Corinthians 1:20). By covenant, God has graciously and sovereignly entered into a binding agreement that He will save all and any who come to Him through the Lord Jesus Christ. By covenant, He has obligated Himself to keep the promise. Christ is the guarantee of salvation.

I pray that this covenant concept will sink into our souls. It truly boggles the mind that the God who owes nothing to anyone obligates Himself to fulfill all the terms of the covenant and make good on every promise. The gospel of Christ is no "maybe" gospel; it must work or God is not God. As we begin our search for Christ in the covenants, we need to keep in mind this full definition of covenant. Do not skip lightly over the word or its attendant actions and circumstances. It is a great word. It is a concept filled with Christ, the promise and the guarantee of life.

Development of the Covenant

God initiated covenants with man at various stages of Old Testament history. Beginning in the Garden of Eden and ending with the promised New Covenant, God revealed to man more and more about His plan and purpose for His people in Christ. The principal messianic covenants are those with Adam and Eve (Genesis 3), Noah (Genesis 6-9), Abraham (Genesis 12-17), Moses (Exodus 19), David (II Samuel 7), and the prophets (e.g., Jeremiah 31). Every promise of salvation made in these covenants focused on and culminated in Christ, but not every promise highlighted every aspect of Christological truth. God did not reveal everything at once. Each new institution renewed earlier promises and advanced knowledge about God's promised salvation.

Progressive Revelation Defined

Because the nature of redemptive truth is complex, God progressively revealed His truth in ways that man could understand. I have already suggested that the covenant theme was something man was familiar with and understood; it was an appropriate vehicle to communicate truth. Although most Bible interpreters recognize the concept of progressive revelation, not all agree on the nature or direction of the progression. But the concept is really quite simple. Understanding complex ideas requires a comprehension of fundamental or elementary ideas. For instance, a grasp of basic rules of mathematics and physics is essential to our understanding quantum theory. Attempting to teach quantum theory to first graders would be disastrous, even if some in the class might eventually become brilliant physicists. Furthermore, full comprehension of the complexities of quantum theory does not imply our rejection of basic rules of mathematics and physics. Advanced knowledge does not contradict or invalidate elementary knowledge; it builds upon it. I teach Hebrew classes, ranging from elementary to advanced courses. I do not teach the beginning students what I teach the advanced, but everything I teach the advanced students rests on the foundation of what I teach the beginners. If I were to require my beginning students to know and do what I expect of my advanced students, I would most likely never again have advanced students. The casualty rate would be so high none would be left to advance. So I go slowly (at least from my perspective), establishing foundations on which to build more understanding. This principle is true for all education.

And this, simply, is the nature of God's progressive revelation of redemptive truth. His goal is to reveal and give understanding, not to conceal and confuse it. He gives first the foundation and continues to build, increasing the capacity to understand. Progressive revelation does not change the essence of truth; it expands, clarifies, and details the truth. Progressive revelation is never from wrong to right or from partial to complete. It is from general to specific, from macroscopic view to microscopic view, from overview to thorough view. The elementary or foundational revelation has few components and broad definition; the advancing revelation adds more and more specifying, identifying, and defining components. The closer the promise gets, the clearer the details about the promise become.

Let me give one more illustration of how progressive revelation works. Some years ago when my children were young, one of my sons, having gone to the supermarket with my wife, came home with a plastic egg that he purchased from one of the machines designed to seduce children into spending their quarters. I tried to give him a lesson in being frugal and resisting temptation. But he assured me that what was in that plastic egg was worth the price. Inside was a little fish of some "magical" substance that would increase in size when left in water. So we tried it. We put the little fish in a pan of water and sure enough it grew overnight. When we examined the enlarged fish, we were able to see details that were invisible on the little fish. We saw a mouth, eyes, and even what appeared to be scales. The point is that all of those details were on the little fish, but we just could not see them until the enlargement occurred. To this day, I regret not putting that little fish in the bathtub. Who knows what would have appeared–maybe even Jonah? I have forgotten my son's reaction, but I will never forget mine. I said to myself, "What a classic example of progressive revelation." The expansion of the little fish revealed details about the fish that were there all the time. Similarly, in progressive revelation, God is not altering the essence of the truth; He is enlarging our view and thereby revealing more and more details. That was a quarter well spent.

The Covenant Progressively Revealed

God's covenant revelations illustrate well the nature of progressive revelation. It is vitally important to realize that God did not change the essence of the covenant every time He made a covenant with men. The Edenic, Noahic, Abrahamic, Mosiac, Davidic, and New Covenants are not different covenants; they are the same covenant that God renewed and enlarged, each time revealing more and more of the essential details. For instance, in one way or another each institution of the covenant advanced knowledge about the "Seed" that would come. This reference to the "Seed" is an obvious seam that binds each of these covenant institutions together. At times it has both a collective and a specific identification, but its ultimate and ideal identification is the Messiah. I know I am right here because the inspired apostle Paul flat-out declares that the seed promised to Abraham was Christ (Galatians 3:16). Paul's inspired statement ought to alert us that if we are not seeing Christ as the promised seed in the

Old Testament, we have not been looking at the text correctly. Remember that the New Testament never changes the meaning of the Old Testament text. One inspired text may refer to or explain another, but it never alters the truth. This makes sense when we acknowledge that God is the ultimate author of both. My contention here is that the messianic "Seed" is in view in each of the covenants, and each of the covenants identifies Him more specifically. In no way did advancing revelation revoke any part of the preceding truths. Rather, there was a constant building on the foundations with incremental definition. Recognizing this, we understand why the New Testament begins by linking the birth of Jesus to both Abraham and David.

A Synopsis of Covenant Development

Immediately after Adam and Eve sinned, God promised that the Seed of the woman would destroy the serpent. The first sinners received the direct, quite general, but most encouraging promise that a Savior for humanity would arise from the human race. Humanity had just been cursed by sin, and one coming into the human race through the woman would reverse that curse of sin. Reversing the curse was good news; in fact, we could call it the gospel!

The sin of Adam spread and intensified. When man's sin grew worse and reached the point of judgment, God sent the flood to destroy mankind. With the exception of Noah and his family, God eradicated the entire human race. Sinful humanity deserved no less. But destroying the human race was not the promise made to Adam and Eve. Reversing the curse through another human was the promise, but the only humans left on the earth were Noah and his family. There was no Savior in the crowd. The promise to Adam and Eve appeared to be in jeopardy, but God made a covenant with Noah by which He secured and renewed the first promise and disclosed more information. The Lord declared that He would never again destroy the world by flood, thus guaranteeing the continuation of the human race into which the promised Seed, the Savior, was to come. In this progression of Gospel revelation, the Lord singled out Noah's son Shem as the progenitor of the specific race into which the Seed would come. The Lord identified the Semitic nations as the specific peoples through whom He would fulfill His promise to reverse the curse. As we will see in our detailed examination, this enlarged truth included the amazing information that God Himself would come into Shem's family line. The Seed would be unique, to say the least.

But once again, sin intensified and earned God's direct intervention. After man rebelled against God at Babel, God scattered and confused the nations, and He called Abraham out of Ur of the Chaldees. The Lord made a covenant with Abraham, a Semite, and the promise became even more specific. God pledged to Abraham that a seed, "the Seed," would come into his line who would bless all the people on earth. By repeating the promise to Isaac and Jacob, God identified the specific Abrahamic line through which the worldwide blessing would come. Interestingly, when Jacob blessed his children before he died, he gave a prophecy that narrowed the lineage of Messiah to the specific tribe of the specific Semitic nation of Israel. The prediction revealed not only that Messiah would come from the tribe of Judah but that He would be a king.

The next incident that more precisely defined the lineage of the Seed occurred about a thousand years later, when God made a covenant with David that the ideal King would be from his family and that He would rule forever. A long time had passed, but God had not forgotten His covenant. Every promise and every seeming delay was making the way ready and increasing the expectancy for Christ. God's covenant revelation concerning Christ progressed generally from the human race to a group of nations to a specific nation to the tribe within the nation to the family in that tribe.

Illustration of Key Features

The following summary illustrates the salient features of the messianic "Seed" identity in successive covenants. The statements are intentionally unabridged to highlight the inherent unity and growth of the revelation. Although the promise to David exhibits more definition than the promise to Adam, the general promise to Adam remains true throughout the development. There is no reason to doubt that the ideal Son to come into David's family is the ideal Man that was promised to Adam's race. Little by little, God made it clear who the Redeemer was going to be.

A Man (Genesis 3:15

A Semitic God/Man (Genesis 9:27)

A Semitic Man from the line of Abraham (Genesis 12, 15, 17)

A Semitic Man from the line of Isaac from the line of Abraham (Genesis 17:19)

A Semitic Man from the line of Jacob from the line of Isaac from the line of Abraham (Genesis 26:3, 4)

A Semitic Man from the tribe of Judah from the line of Jacob from the line of Isaac from the line of Abraham (Genesis 49:10)

A Semitic Man from the family of David from the tribe of Judah from the line of Jacob from the line of Isaac from the line of Abraham (II Samuel 7:12-16)

Each new covenant was better because each revealed more data concerning the promised Redeemer. These gracious covenant developments express just one way in which God was directing events toward the fullness of time into which Christ would come. The Gospel accounts of Christ's birth and identity are in no way startling to those who see the messianic theme in Old Testament covenant revelation. Matthew's genealogy of Christ as "the son of David, the son of Abraham" (Matthew 1) and Luke's genealogy, which traces Jesus's human ancestry all the way back to Adam (Luke 3), stand as testimonies to every covenant promise of God. Though the covenant promises moved slowly at times they always moved steadily, from Eden's paradise to Bethlehem's manger. They had to do so because they were covenant promises that were guaranteed by the oath of God. This particular synopsis of covenant development does not include the Mosaic and New Covenants because they are more concerned with Messiah's work than with narrowing down His identity. We will consider their truths in the next section.

Details of the Covenants

Now that we know to look for Christ in the covenants, I want to discuss some of the truths about Christ that these covenants reveal. It is not my intention to expound every aspect of the covenant contexts because each includes elements that are not directly messianic. But knowing that Christ is in the covenants requires directing our attention to what about Christ is there. Understanding what each covenant reveals about Christ will aid in interpreting the other elements as well because every part in one way or another links to God's ultimate promise and guarantee of the Lord Jesus Christ.

The Covenant with Adam and Eve

For obvious reasons, I like to refer to this as God's covenant with humanity: not only because Adam and Eve were the only people alive but also because the extent and intent of the covenant included the human race that would follow by natural generation from this first man and woman directly created by God. Genesis 3:15 is the text that I want to address specifically. Although the term "covenant" does not occur in this context, the evidence of a covenant exists. The old saying about ducks is applicable here. If it looks like a duck and walks like a duck and quacks like a duck, it is most likely a duck. Throughout this text covenant implications abound. There are two parties; there are terms; there are promises. In addition to these attendant circumstances associated with covenants, the analogy of Scripture justifies interpreting the opening chapters of Genesis in terms of covenants. This means that we allow the Scripture to interpret itself. When we follow the Scripture's own interpretation, we can be confident that we have the correct interpretation. In the eighth century BC, Hosea was preaching to the northern tribes, which were on the eve of national disaster because they had been unfaithful to the terms of the covenant God had made with them. Hosea contrasted the sinful behavior of Israel with the covenant mercy and knowledge of God, which the Lord required of them (Hosea 6:6). He then forthrightly accused them of breaking the covenant: "But they like men have transgressed the covenant: there have they dealt treacherously against me" (6:7). The word the Authorized Version translates as "men" is the word *adam*. Although this word often refers to mankind or humanity, it is also the name of the first man. The question of interpretation is whether Hosea refers to mankind generally or Adam specifically. I would suggest that it is a specific reference to Adam. If this is the proper interpretation, then the inspired prophet justifies our interpreting God's dealing with Adam and Eve as a covenant. I think there is a sense in which even if Hosea meant "mankind," the word presents a purposeful ambiguity, taking us back to this first covenant because God, when dealing with Adam, was also dealing with humanity.

Need for the Covenant

The covenant to which Hosea refers is that recorded in Genesis 2:16-17. This is the immediate backdrop and reason for the covenant promise of Genesis 3:15 that we want to consider. Sometimes designated as the Adamic covenant or the covenant of works, this first covenant required Adam's total obedience to the terms God defined. God had set two special trees in the Garden of Eden with sacramental or symbolic significance. One tree represented life, and the other represented the knowledge of good and evil (Genesis 2:9). The terms of this covenant arrangement were simple and clear: God gave Adam freedom to eat from all the trees of the Garden except the tree of the knowledge of good and evil. The Lord made it explicitly and unmistakably clear to Adam that he would certainly die if he ate from that one tree. Obedience would earn life; disobedience would earn death. We know both the story and the consequences of Adam's disobedience. "By one man sin entered into the world, and death by sin; and so death passed upon all men, for that all have sinned" (Romans 5:12). The immediate results of the first couple's disobedience of the covenant terms were shame (Genesis 3:7), alienation from God (3:8), guilt (3:10), the curse on both the tempter and the tempted (3:14ff.), the sentence of death (3:19, 22), and grace (3:15). This is remarkable beyond words and comprehension. In the very statement of the curse, God announces His purpose of grace to reverse the curse He has just pronounced. As Paul puts it: "Where sin abounded, grace did much more abound" (Romans 5:20). Paul's contrast between Adam's disobedience and Christ's obedience is a significant clue that the "Reverser" of the curse in Genesis 3:15 is the Lord Jesus (Romans 5; I Corinthians 15).

Essence of the Covenant

Genesis 3:15 is often called the "protevangelium," the first gospel. The Lord said, "I will put enmity between thee and the woman, and between thy seed and her seed; it shall bruise thy head, and thou shalt bruise his heel." This verse certainly highlights the beauty of grace: as soon as man needed the gospel, God announced the gospel. But this grace goes far beyond just answering man's need. Although salvation is certainly good for man, it is ultimately more about God's glory than man's good. This is why Paul, expounding the great benefits of the gospel in Ephesians, kept repeating that all the blessings of salvation were to the praise of the glory of God's grace (1:6, 12, 14). Similarly, Ezekiel made it clear that what God does and will do in saving His people is for His own "holy name's sake" (36:22, 23, 32). I think the strategic placement of this first gospel message in the threefold curse pronouncement highlights this truth. Rather than being directed to man, this first declaration of the gospel is part of the curse against the serpent, Satan himself. Man would certainly benefit, but God's glory was the issue. The serpent's defeat and man's salvation were the means of declaring that glory.

God's Idea

The text emphasizes the Lord's sovereign, non-negotiable resolve in declaring His purpose and means of reversing the curse: "I will put...." The almighty God demonstrated His power and resolve to destroy a being who was His inferior but nevertheless His archenemy. Satan stood no chance against God; the devil's doom was sealed from the beginning. God also demonstrated His sovereign grace by promising a Savior for cursed men, who deserved wrath and condemnation. His justice sentenced the race to death; His wondrous grace devised the means whereby the banished might not be expelled (see II Samuel 14:14). Even this first, general promise of salvation warrants Micah's question of praise and wonder: "Who is a God like unto thee, that pardoneth iniquity, and passeth by the transgression of the remnant of his heritage?" (7:18).

God's Plan

This text declares not only what God's grace will do in reversing the curse but also how He will accomplish it. The first thing the Lord would do was to change the relationship between the woman and the serpent. The woman had agreed with Satan against God; now grace would reconcile her to God. I believe the woman here is specifically Eve. Therefore, the statement testifies to God's grace in saving the very one who had led her husband to disobey the terms of the covenant. This enmity or disposition of hostility was not an aversion to snakes; it was an awakened conscience that recognized the lie of the serpent and attracted the heart back to God.

The second thing the Lord would do would be to enlarge the scope of that enmity between the seed of the serpent and the seed of the woman. Understanding this requires understanding the significance of the word "seed" and identifying the referents to the two seeds. By referent I simply mean the actual object or person being referred to by the less specific word. So if I say that Christ is the seed of the woman, I am saying that the seed refers to Christ or that Christ is the referent of seed. It's a useful grammatical term. Identifying the referents to seed is important because as suggested earlier, "seed" is going to be one of the great clue words that points to Christ and ties this first gracious covenant with those that follow.

This word refers both to seeds produced by plants and to the offspring or descendants produced by men. This gets a little complicated, but thinking it through proves rewarding. Part of the problem is that although the word is singular, it can have a collective as well as a purely singular sense. In any given context we have to determine whether the writer has in mind a singular or plural idea. The word "crowd" in English is an example of a collective noun. The word is singular, but a crowd consists of a plurality of individuals. Unlike the Hebrew word for "seed," however, the English word "crowd" would never refer to a single individual. I am suggesting that Genesis 3:15 includes both a collective sense in regard to the serpent's seed and a singular sense in regard to the woman's seed. The seed of the serpent would refer to all those who, untouched by grace, retain Eve's pre-conversion hostility to God and affinity to Satan. It refers to all sinners who in their natural state are the enemies of God. Obviously, they are related to Satan "spiritually" and not "physically." This is an association made in the New Testament. The Lord Jesus attributed the Jews' inability to understand Him and refusal to believe Him to the fact that they were of their father the devil (John 8:44). Similarly, the apostle John declares that those who are given over to the practice of sin are "of the devil; for the devil sinneth from the beginning" (I John 3:8). The serpent's offspring are the race of unconverted sinners.

The woman's seed, on the other hand, is a singular identity and brings us to the One who is the real enemy of Satan and the only Savior of sinners. The woman's seed is the promised Christ. That He is identified as the woman's seed hints of the miraculous virgin birth and most certainly declares that the Savior will be part of the human race. As a real man He will reverse the curse of sin. There can be little doubt that Paul had this text in mind when he declared that in the fullness of time God sent His Son, "made of a woman" (Galatians 4:4). This first promise of a Savior makes it clear that the Savior must be a man. It is imperative to keep this foundational truth in focus when you begin to read about the animal sacrifices lest you think they had anything to do with reversing the curse of sin. God announced from the beginning that the seed of the woman, not the seed of an animal, would be the Redeemer. That Christ came to destroy the works of the devil expresses the open hostility between Him and Satan (see I John 3:8). Indeed, Hebrews says that Christ became flesh so that He could "through death ... destroy him that had the power of death, that is, the devil" (2:14).

God's Intent

The final statement of the verse reveals God's purpose by predicting the outcome of the hostility: "it shall bruise thy head, and thou shalt bruise his heel." The victory of the woman's seed over the serpent is absolutely guaranteed. The outcome is that the head of the serpent will be bruised. The word "bruise" literally carries the idea of crushing. *Crushing the head is fatal.* So the Lord Jesus effectively defeated and destroyed the devil. The New Testament identifies this fatal crushing with Christ's work on the cross, with the operation of the church, and with the end times. The Lord Jesus links the casting out of the prince of the world and His being lifted up from the earth (a reference to the cross) in the same context (John 12:31-32). Paul alludes to this verse when he assures the Roman church that "the God of peace shall bruise Satan under your feet shortly" (Romans 16:20). The final outcome is at the end of time when Satan is bound and ultimately cast into the lake of fire forever (Revelation 20:3, 10).

That the serpent will bruise the heel of the woman's seed suggests the ineffectiveness of the serpent to frustrate or alter the mission of Christ. *Crushing the heel is futile.* Some interpreters see this as referring to the cross, but I am not so inclined. I do believe Genesis 3:15 points to the cross, but not in this part of the verse. It is far better to see the cross in the declaration that the serpent's head will be crushed. Even if the heel crushing does predict the cross, Satan's objective in the death of Christ was hampered and overruled. Ironically, what he would have intended for his ultimate victory became his ultimate defeat. The cross was not Satan's blow against Christ; it was Christ's ultimate death blow against Satan. Paul said in no uncertain terms that the cross of Christ was the means of disarming and humiliating all powers and authorities, including Satan, and publicly triumphing over them (Colossians 2:15). The cross of Christ was not God's making the best of a situation generated by the devil; it was the climax of His eternal plan to redeem fallen and needy sinners.

It may be that the word "crush" in this statement actually derives from another root, a *homonym*, meaning "to snap at." A *homonym* is a word that sounds identical to another, but is a completely different word (e.g., *there–their*). If this is the root, it intensifies the total futility of all Satan's annoying efforts to prevent the inevitable from occurring. If crushing a heel is futile, snapping at the heels is even more so. I think the evidence of the New Testament is that Satan tried everything he could to kill Christ before He could make the eternally planned atonement. From moving Herod to kill the children in hopes of murdering Jesus, to attempting to discredit Christ during the temptation, to attempting to have the crowds stone Him, to fiercely attacking Him in the garden of Gethsemanæ on the eve of crucifixion, Satan was constantly nipping and snapping at Christ's heels. But he could not frustrate God's plan to reverse the curse of sin by the Seed of the woman.

This first gospel message does not reveal all the details about Christ that we know. But it does guarantee the Savior and sets the groundwork for more revealing truths. Every other revelation about Christ fits nicely within the sphere of this first promise. Once we know the actual details, it becomes relatively easy to see how all-encompassing was the first promise. Remember that it is not our objective to speculate about how much the Old Testament saint could see; it is to see for ourselves. Although they could not know all the specifics of the crushing and the nipping, these saints would know that there was to be a crushing and a nipping. That is the key. Eve did not know how it would all work out, but her faith and anticipation of God's promise were so intense that she thought for a slight moment that the birth of her first son Cain was the promised Seed. Genesis 4:1 contains some translation difficulties, but it could fairly be rendered, "I have acquired a man, even Jehovah." It was a brief case of mistaken identity, but it suggests that saved Eve was looking for the right one. We want to follow her example in this.

The Covenant with Noah

The word "covenant" appears the first time in the Old Testament with reference to God's covenant with Noah. The story of the flood is tragic testimony to the consequences of Adam's sin. Man's sin, rebellion, and hatred of God had so increased that God, being grieved, issued His just sentence of death upon the entire race (Genesis 6:3-6). Notwithstanding His justice and His right to destroy the race, He could not and would not destroy it completely because there was a covenant promise He had obligated Himself to keep. The Seed of the woman was going to crush the serpent's head, and that fact required a continuing human race until the Seed should come. Once again, God demonstrated His grace. From that sinning and death-deserving human race, the Lord singled out Noah: "Noah found grace in the eyes of the Lord" (Genesis 6:8). As a consequence of God's gracious salvation of Noah, Noah was "a just man and perfect in his generations, and Noah walked with God" (Genesis 6:9). It is imperative not to reverse the order of these two verses. It was grace that made Noah a just man; it was not his being a just man that earned him grace. Grace never leaves a man where it finds him. When God found Noah, "every imagination of the thoughts of his heart was only evil continually." That had to be true because Noah was a descendant of Adam and therefore depraved and dead in sins. But what a difference grace makes; it always does. In grace, God entered a covenant with Noah that spared him and his immediate family from the devastating flood that would destroy the rest of the human race and change the world forever (Genesis 6:18, the first occurrence of "covenant").

Link to the Past

Although the fact of the covenant is announced in Genesis 6 before the flood, the details are given in Genesis 9 after the flood. The Lord said, "And I, behold I establish my covenant with you, and with your seed after you" (Genesis 9:9). The language is emphatic and certain in declaring God's initiative and guarantee. And there's that word "seed" again. Though not discernible from English, the pronouns "you" and "your" are plural, including Ham, Japheth, and Shem in the promise. As in the first covenant promise, so here the entire human race is included. The principal focus of this covenant was God's guarantee not to destroy the world again by the flood. We will miss the intent if we do not recognize in this guarantee God's vouchsafing His initial gospel promise to send a Savior into humanity. God's preserving the world was tantamount to preserving His promise to send His Son in the likeness of sinful flesh. As a visible token or symbol of this guarantee, God set the rainbow in the sky. The bow was a constant reminder both to man and to God Himself of God's mercy and faithfulness to fulfill all the terms of His gracious covenant. That the Lord calls this "the everlasting covenant" (Genesis 9:16) heightens the sense of assurance and confidence that His purpose and promise in Christ are unfrustratably fixed. The same promise that was good for Noah is good for us.

The Advancement of Truth

Not only did God's covenant with Noah continue the covenant with Adam and Eve, but it also advanced knowledge about the identity of the Seed. Interestingly, this advance occurs in connection with another curse declaration. Not long after the flood, the unfortunate and sinful incident involving Noah and Ham occurred (Genesis 9:20ff.). When Noah learned about the transgression, he pronounced a curse on Canaan, one of Ham's sons, that ended with a declaration of blessing on the entire human race (Genesis 9:25-27). Admittedly, difficulties of interpretation associated with this section arise in identifying the nature of both the curse and the blessing. All I can do is suggest what I believe to be the best way of handling the text. Because the focus of our concern is to identify the messianic elements, I will address primarily the blessing problem.

Perhaps I should first say something about the curse. The sentence placed on Canaan illustrates at the very least the principle of judgment called *lex talionis*, the law of retaliation. This simply means that the punishment fits the crime. As a son, Ham transgressed against his father. As a father, Ham witnessed the toll of his sin on one of his sons. Any father knows that that is no easy thing to witness. The curse was that Canaan would become the servant of Shem. The fulfillment of this curse reached its climax many years later when Joshua, leading the new nation of Israel which had descended from Shem, conquered the land of Canaan. In this conquest, Israel both executed and enslaved many Canaanites (read Joshua). But as we will see, even the fulfillment of the curse was a necessary precursor to greater blessing. That brings us back to the blessing problem.

Verse 27 is the crux. ("Crux" designates a hard verse or puzzling problem of interpretation. Using a technical term to describe our ignorance makes us feel a little better.) The Authorized Version translates the verse, "God shall enlarge Japheth, and he shall dwell in the tents of Shem; and Canaan shall be his servant." The problem is twofold: identifying the subject of the verb "shall dwell" and identifying the antecedent to the pronoun "his." Whereas a translation should retain whatever ambiguities exist in the text, the interpreter must seek to resolve the ambiguity. I would suggest that the subject of the verb "shall dwell" and the antecedent to the pronoun "his" is God. The verb forms are not strictly future tenses but, rather, forms that occur regularly in requests or expressions of desire. Instead of simply being a prediction of what will happen, this is a prayer or petition that Noah makes concerning the solution to the curse just pronounced on Canaan. I suggest the following interpretative translation: "May God provide ample space for Japheth; may God take up residence in the tents of Shem; and may Canaan become God's servant." Japheth, Shem, and Canaan represent the roots from which the restored human race would develop, and the great point of this statement is that there is a blessing in store for all nations and people. As is true in all of these covenants, the more narrow the identification of the Seed, the greater the assurance given that the influence of the Seed would be worldwide.

What is at the heart of the blessing and what reverses the curse is God's dwelling in the tents of Shem. This suggests two significant truths about Messiah's identity. First, it names the descendants of Shem, the Semites, as the particular segment of the human race into which the Seed would come. Second, it suggests that it is God Himself who will come. The language of Noah is remarkably similar to that of John, who spoke of the eternal Word's becoming flesh and dwelling among men (John 1:14). Both Noah and John used the imagery of pitching a tent and taking up residence to describe this dwelling. I would suggest that both have in view the Incarnation, God manifest in the flesh. If this is the correct interpretation, then the second key promise of the Messiah reveals the vital truth that the Savior of sinners, the Reverser of sin's curse, is the God/Man. Right at the beginning of God's gracious covenant promises, He establishes foundational truths concerning the eternal Son of God's becoming man. It only gets better.

The Covenant with Abraham

The years following the flood demonstrated again the tragic consequences and universal extent of sin. The same depravity and bent to sin that characterized pre-flood humanity characterized post-flood humanity (Genesis 8:21). Humanity multiplied in keeping with God's promise and plan, but as it multiplied, so did its open and united rebellion against God. Although man desperately needed the Savior, it seemed that the race as a whole was united in ungodly efforts to prevent the divine purpose. The enmity, that hostile disposition, between the serpent's seed and the Seed was intensifying. That enmity reached a climax in the land of Shinar when men who were united in sin rallied together against the Lord in building a tower to mark their allegiance to self and rebellion against God. The Lord, both in judgment and in mercy, intervened and scattered them, turning their "convention center" to Babel, a place of confusion (Genesis 11). He evidenced judgment in bringing to frustration man's plans; He evidenced mercy in restraining and checking the mad rush of sin. However, with man indiscriminately scattered over all creation, again the covenant promise seemed in jeopardy. But God's guarantees assured the continuation of His purpose of grace. The genealogy of Shem that occurs immediately after the scattering at Babel is not just a boring list of names; it stands as a witness to God's absolute faithfulness in keeping His covenant oath (Genesis 11:10-32). Remember that in the last covenant, Shem was singled out as the specific race into which the Savior would come. The genealogy thus demonstrates that although mankind was now scattered over all the earth, God had not lost track of Shem. The promise was still good, and it was about to become more specific on its steady move to the fullness of time. That genealogy, then, effectively links the covenant with Noah to the covenant with Abraham.

A Covenant of Grace

Genesis 12 records God's call of Abraham and the terms of the new and enlarged covenant. Genesis 15 and 17 are also key texts that detail this vitally important covenant. Abraham's call was a great demonstration of God's grace. Joshua 24:2 makes it clear that Abraham was not a worshipper of the true and living God who courageously took his stand for righteousness in the midst of an idolatrous city. On the contrary, Abraham was as much a sinner as any other human, and he was just as involved in the pagan idolatry of Ur of the Chaldees as any other citizen of the city. God did not choose Abraham because of some merit in Abraham, either potential or realized. God chose Abraham because of grace. That's the only reason God ever saves men. Connected to Abraham's conversion was the covenant that would establish him as the father of many nations, and specifically as the father of the nation into which the Seed would come. This is why the Lord renewed Abraham's covenant with Isaac (Genesis 26:3, 24) and with Jacob (Genesis 28:15; 35:12) and not with Abraham's other sons by Hagar or Keturah or with Isaac's other son, Esau.

A Covenant of Promise

The details and implications of God's covenant with Abraham are far-reaching. In pointing out the salient elements, I will confine myself to the directly messianic features. Although there are significant attendant elements, I think we can summarize the essential aspects of this covenant in terms of three distinct but related promises that God gave to Abraham. (1) He would give him a *seed* (Genesis 17:6; 12:2; 15:5). (2) He would give him a *land* (Genesis 17:8; 12:7; 15:18). (3) He would make him a source of *universal blessing* (Genesis 12:2-3).

A Seed

By now we should not be surprised that the seed promise is crucial. Identifying the seed gets a little complicated because it has multiple referents. But once we know who and what are involved, it is not too hard to keep things straight. The New Testament gives some vital clues that we cannot ignore. Factoring in all the data, we can identify three referents of the seed. Sometimes one, sometimes another aspect is in view. It is the same issue that we saw before regarding the singular collective noun. It is a "pregnant" term; that is, it is full of meaning.

First, Abraham's seed was physical. God promised that Abraham would be a father of many nations (Genesis 17:5). God, in fact, changed his name from Abram, "exalted father," to Abraham, "father of a great multitude," to reflect this destiny. The Jews of Christ's day prided themselves in being "Abraham's seed," a fact that Christ did not dispute (John 8:33, 37). The developing of this physical seed was an essential element in the coming of Christ, for He was in fact and of necessity in the line of Abraham (see Romans 9:4-5). In a real sense Israel, the particular physical seed of Abraham, was a means to the messianic end of God's promise. There had to be physical seed of Abraham if there was going to be God's Christ. That the circumstances of the birth of Isaac were so extraordinary, requiring supernatural intervention for Sarah's conception, demonstrates the direct interest and purpose of God in establishing this chosen line for the future birth of the Messiah.

Second, Abraham's ultimate Seed was Christ. The link to the previous covenants demands this interpretation. The New Testament verifies what the Old Testament demands. Galatians 3:19 says the seed was Christ. The Lord Jesus declared that Abraham rejoiced to see His day (John 8:56).

Third, Abraham's seed was and is spiritual. That God promises Abraham a seed more numerous than the stars of heaven or the sands of the sea at least hints that something beyond physical descendants is meant. The Lord Jesus, in the same context in which He acknowledges Abraham's physical descendants, questions the validity of their claiming Abraham as their father (John 8:39). It was obviously possible to be a physical descendant without being a spiritual descendant. Not all Israel is Israel (Romans 9:6-8). Paul, having argued for the singular significance of the Seed, also recognizes the plurality of it. The children of Abraham are those who have faith (Galatians 3:7). The apostle makes it wonderfully clear that whether Jew or Gentile, bond or free, male or female, "if ye be Christ's, then are ye Abraham's seed, and heirs according to the promise" (Galatians 3:28-29). We should not wonder why Paul equated the terms of God's covenant with Abraham with the gospel (Galatians 3:8).

A Land

The promise of a land was also a key component in the Abrahamic covenant. This is a real, geographic territory. It follows that if there is to be a literal physical seed, there must be a literal place for them to live. Much of the Old Testament concerns Israel's conquest, inheritance, expulsion, and repossession of this land. It is the repossessing of the land that is most significant in our search for Christ. To consider all the aspects of this, however, would take us into matters of eschatological controversy. Premillennialists believe that a future generation of Abraham's physical seed will possess the Promised Land to its fullest borders with the Ultimate Seed personally present to rule the entire world with Jerusalem as His capital. Even this physical promise cannot be fully understood apart from Christ. I am a premillennialist, so that is my interpretation. That is all I can say for now, or this synopsis will turn into a treatise in itself.

A Universal Blessing

That God would bless Abraham and make him a blessing to the entire world brings the focus of the promise directly to Christ. God put His special protection on Abraham and his seed, promising to bless those who blessed and curse those who cursed. This promise entails much more than just signalling God's favor toward those who become Israel's ally in political or military conflict. At the heart of this promise and threat was the declared guarantee that nothing or no one could frustrate God's covenant purpose to send Christ in both His advents. Too often we get sidetracked with the attendant issues and miss the main point. The only thing about the descendants of Abraham that can in any way be construed as a blessing to the entire world is the fact of the Lord Jesus Christ, the ultimate Seed of the promise. Again Paul gives an inspired interpretation of the Abrahamic blessing. He says that Christ became a curse by hanging on the tree "that the blessing of Abraham might come on the Gentiles through Jesus Christ; that we might receive the promise of the Spirit through faith" (Galatians 3:13-14). Even the apostate rascal Balaam had the insight to recognize that his inability to curse Israel was linked to a person yet to come. "I shall see him, but not now: I shall behold him, but not nigh: there shall come a Star out of Jacob, and a Sceptre shall rise out of Israel" (Numbers 24:17).

This element of the promise highlights a messianic theme that I want you to see throughout the Old Testament. The promise of Messiah was never a uniquely Jewish promise. Gentile inclusion in the gospel of Christ is a frequent theme of Old Testament theology and revelation. We have to wait until the New Testament dispensation to see the engrafting of the Gentiles, but the Old Testament signals that Gentile inclusion in many ways. The only unique claim that Israel has on Christ is that He came into the world physically through them. Even this claim came to be realized only after God renewed Abraham's covenant with Jacob. There was no Israel until then, but there was a world of history and revelation about Christ before then. Adam and Noah and Abraham were not Jews. It is significant that in each of the covenant institutions, there is a word of hope for the whole world of sinners. Abraham's line was chosen for the identity of Messiah, but all the nations of the earth would benefit from the Messiah. On the one hand, the covenant with Abraham narrows our understanding; on the other hand, it maintains the inclusiveness of God's purpose of grace for the world.

A Covenant of Faith

One final observation about Abraham and the covenant is in order. Abraham illustrates the necessity of faith in the covenant as the means to justification. Genesis 15:6 is a pivotal text in the Old Testament and is frequently used in the New Testament to define the nature of justifying faith: "And he believed in the Lord; and he counted it to him for righteousness." Resisting the strong urge to expound this text and the whole doctrine of justification, I will simply note the object of Abraham's faith. The bottom line is that if Abraham believed the covenant promise, he believed in Christ, the essence of the covenant. It is not the mere exercise of faith that saves; it is the object of faith that saves. The object of faith determines the value of faith. Saving faith is saving faith because its object is Christ, the only Savior of sinners ever. To interpret Abraham's believing God to mean only that he believed it when God said he would have a lot of kids is to miss the message of the covenant promise and pervert the very nature of saving faith. Abraham indeed believed every single component of the covenant, including his having children. But we must not substitute the attendant aspects of the covenant for the foundational aspect. Faith in Christ is the first step to believing everything else God says. That was true for Abraham, and it is true for us. Again, Christ said, "Abraham rejoiced to see my day: and he saw it and was glad" (John 8:56). I believe Christ!

The Covenant with David

I have not forgotten the Mosaic covenant; I will address it below. But the covenant with David is the next clear advance in establishing the identity of the Messiah. It is closely associated with the covenant with Abraham. When Jacob declared his last will and testament to his twelve sons, as a prophet he issued a significant prediction concerning Judah: "The sceptre shall not depart from Judah, nor a lawgiver from between his feet, until Shiloh come; and unto him shall the gathering of the people be" (Genesis 49:10). Judah would function as the tribe of kings until the appearance of king to whom kingship really belonged. That's the significance of "Shiloh"– to whom it belongs. When that rightful king should come, then all the people would submit obediently to him. Theologically, we expect II Samuel 7 to follow Genesis 49 immediately. But for almost a thousand years, there was no evidence or advancing of that prophecy. The long delay seemed to jeopardize the promise; but God is always faithful. In His good time, the Lord renewed and confirmed that promise in a covenant with David, Israel's first king from the tribe of Judah. The Old Testament prophets and Psalms allude to God's covenant with David over and over again, but two principal texts will define it for us: II Samuel 7 is the historical account of its inception, and Psalm 89 is the inspired commentary on its significance.

The Seed

God had rejected David's proposal to build a house of worship and announced His own plan and purpose to build a house for David– not a palace, but a dynasty that would culminate in the Ideal King, the Messiah. Right at the beginning of this covenant affirmation is the now expected reference to a seed: "I will set up thy seed after thee" (II Samuel 7:12). That God promises to set up David's seed is a key factor that links this covenant to all the preceding seed promises. The main advance of knowledge is that David's seed would occupy an everlasting throne, ruling over an everlasting kingdom. The king would enjoy a unique relationship with God: God would be his father and he would be God's son. The Psalmist comments that the Lord would make this king his "firstborn, higher than the kings of the earth" (Psalm 89:27). Interestingly, the same curious ambiguity exists here as in the earlier promises. The seed is seen sometimes in collective or plural terms, sometimes as the single Ideal. That some of the seed commit iniquity speaks collectively of all of David's seed, except One. That the promise is unconditional, regardless of the iniquities, points singularly to the ultimate Seed, whose coming was guaranteed by every covenant institution (II Samuel 7:11-16; see the inspired commentary at Psalm 89:29-33).

The prophet Isaiah obviously understood the essence of the covenant with David in terms of a single individual. In his great gospel invitation, following the great prophecy of the Suffering Servant, he speaks of the "everlasting covenant," even "the sure mercies of David." The word "mercies" is that significant covenant term that highlights the unfailing loyalty of the Lord to guarantee and perform every detail of His covenant promise. In this text, Isaiah interprets the "sure mercies" as a person. He says about those sure mercies, "Behold, I have given him for a witness to the people, a leader and commander to the people" (Isaiah 55:3-4; cf. II Samuel 7: 15; Psalm 89:27-28). There is little doubt, if you follow Isaiah's development, that the Suffering Servant and the Sure Mercies of David are one and the same. Please recall that one of our means of differentiating between Christ and all the "lesser" messiahs–kings in this text–is statements that are inapplicable to "mere" humans. Certainly all the talk in this covenant about an everlasting kingdom points to One who is beyond any of David's natural sons, all of whom have long since died.

The Divine Oath

One of the most remarkable features of this covenant institution is the obvious divine initiative that stands as testimony to God's unbreakable oath. Just count in these verses the first person verbs which God uses to proclaim what He will do. The great commentary of this covenant seems to interpret all these statements in terms of God's oath to David: "I have made a covenant with my chosen, I have sworn unto David my servant" (Psalm 89:3). Again the Psalmist reports, "My covenant will I not break, nor alter the thing that is gone out of my lips. Once have I sworn by my holiness, that I will not lie unto David" (Psalm 89:34-35). It is not surprising that this sure promise to David became the theme of so many of the sweet psalmist's songs of praise and worship. As we will see when we search for Christ in worship, the Psalms were a key vehicle for keeping the messianic hope vividly and constantly before the people.

The Universal Scope

Although God's covenant promise to David narrowed the identity of the Messiah to the family of David, David realized that the ramifications of the Greater Son who would sit on his throne went far beyond the concerns of his family and his little kingdom. When David heard these amazing promises, he was overwhelmed: "Who am I, O Lord God? and what is my house that thou has brought me hitherto?" (II Samuel 7:18). He confessed his awareness that the implications of this promise extended temporally way beyond his time. Then he made a profound statement reflecting his faith and insight into the worldwide significance. According to the Authorized Version, the last line of II Samuel 7:19 has David questioning, "And is this the manner of man, O Lord God?" The word translated "manner" is actually the Hebrew word *torah* that means "instruction." It is the most general word in the Old Testament for God's special revelation to man. The word for "man" is the Hebrew word *adam*, which designates humanity. Although the quotation can legitimately be construed as a question, nothing actually demands it. I would suggest, therefore, a translation that renders this as a declarative statement and treats the word "manner" a bit more literally: "And this is the revelation for mankind." David sees his promised Seed as the source of blessing for the entire world. David's promise was our promise. What was good for David is good for us. That's the nature of the gospel.

The Covenant with "Israel"

Because God had chosen the nation of Israel to be the particular nation through which and into which He would send His Son, He graciously explained and renewed the covenant with them (see again Romans 9:4-5). Although all nations were to enjoy the benefits of the coming of Christ, Israel had a unique place in God's plan and purpose. What a privilege! The great tragedy is that "He came unto his own, and his own received him not" (John 1:11). Yet, Paul declared, "All Israel shall be saved: as it is written, There shall come out of Sion the Deliverer, and shall turn away ungodliness from Jacob: for this is my covenant unto them, when I shall take away their sins" (Romans 11:26-27). Comparing Paul's two texts (Romans 9 and 11) suggests two principal parts of God's covenant dealings with Israel: one past, one future.

The Mosaic Covenant

The past part occurred immediately after God had "remembered his covenant with Abraham, with Isaac, and with Jacob" (Exodus 2:24) and delivered the enslaved people establishing them as a nation. The exodus from Egypt was Israel's "Independence Day," the birth of a nation. When the people reached Sinai, God entered into a covenant with the nation (Exodus 19). To define this covenant in terms essentially different from the covenant with Abraham, the developing fulfillment of which brought the nation to this point, is hermeneutically and theologically unsound. It ignores both the immediate context and the whole foundation of previous revelation. It would be odd for God to deliver the people from bondage in terms of the Abrahamic covenant and then replace that covenant once He had delivered them. This Mosaic covenant is a renewal and expansion of the earlier promises. We must remember that we cannot jump into the middle of a text in isolation; God expects that we remember what He has already said. I will be suggesting that the essence of the Mosaic covenant is exactly the same as all the others, the message of the gospel of Christ.

The Work of Christ

As in all the covenants, however, there is an advance of knowledge and special focus of concern. Two things stand out in the Mosaic covenant. First is the focus on the work of Christ. Whereas the covenants with Adam, Noah, Abraham, and David identify the person of Messiah more and more specifically, the covenant with Israel through Moses explains the Messiah's mediatorial ministry. I see the Mosaic covenant as a theological deliberation in which the Lord explains what the Seed must do if He is to reverse the curse of sin and become that worldwide blessing. By all the complex tabernacle operations, the sacrifices, and the ceremonies, God is picturing what Christ will do. These pictures are full of Christ and therefore are a key place that we must search for Him. So rich are these pictures that we have to devote a separate study for them. I will guide you through the Mosaic rituals in the chapter on typology.

The Condition of Faith

The second focus is on the necessary response to the promise of Christ. It is not the fact of Christ that saves. If that were all that was necessary, none would ever perish, since Christ is an indisputable fact. It is the personal appropriation of Christ by faith that saves. The covenant promise of Christ's certain coming and sufficient work is unconditional; nothing could or can frustrate it. But there are conditions for salvation. Personal faith and repentance condition the personal experience of Christ and His work. This is what the Lord sets before the people in Exodus 19:5, a text that is often grossly misinterpreted. The Lord graciously offers them the covenant: "If ye will obey my voice indeed, and keep my covenant, then ye shall be a peculiar treasure unto me above all people...." Unless we impose a completely different definition of the word "covenant"–and there is no warrant for doing so–then obeying this command is tantamount to obeying the gospel. To agree to the terms of this covenant is far from rejecting the promise; it is accepting grace.

God commanded Abraham, "Walk before me, and be thou perfect. And I will make my covenant between me and thee" (Genesis 17:1-2). We have already seen how Abraham believed God. The great patriarch had to respond to what the Lord had revealed. Abraham obeyed and kept the covenant. Similarly, the New Testament declares the necessary terms for personal salvation. Conversion consists of faith and repentance. The apostle Paul describes those who are ultimately sentenced to everlasting destruction as those "that obey not the gospel of our Lord Jesus Christ" (II Thessalonians 1:8-9). Jeremiah virtually defined Paul's language when he declared, "Cursed be the man that obeyeth not the words of this covenant" (Jeremiah 11:3).

I submit that there is no difference between obeying the gospel in II Thessalonians and obeying and keeping the covenant in Exodus 19. Not obeying the covenant is tantamount to rejecting the gospel message of Christ. Keeping the covenant is believing the gospel. We must personally appropriate the promise. That Moses renewed this same covenant with the next generation in Deuteronomy emphasizes the necessity of personal appropriation. How the parents responded did not insure the same response from the children. Everyone is personally responsible to trust and obey. This is what Moses preached through this gracious covenant with the nation. It is what every faithful gospel preacher proclaims today. To be confronted with the claims of Jesus Christ, whether then or now, demands a personal response. Once a man knows about Christ, the question is always, "What will you do with Jesus?"

The Canonical Context

Let me suggest one final thought that may help to keep the Mosaic covenant in the proper perspective with the preceding covenants. Although the historical contexts of Genesis and Exodus are hundreds of years apart, the canonical context is the same. By this I mean that the books were written by the same man, at approximately the same time, and for the same people. In other words, Genesis, which demonstrates the unfailing resolve and faithfulness of God in guaranteeing the coming Savior-Seed, was given to the same people who were going to learn about the work of that Seed through the various tabernacle rituals. Genesis, which records Abraham's justifying faith—the very faith that even the New Testament uses to explain saving faith—was given to the same people who were told to obey and keep the covenant. The focus on the Seed and faith in the Seed defined what obeying the covenant meant. It always helps to interpret the Bible in its context. Genesis is the theological context in which Exodus must be interpreted, both for ancient Israel and for us. It is the theological "corrective" to prevent Israel from misinterpreting the ceremonial laws in isolation from the Promised Seed. The fact that some did not believe and misinterpreted the gospel did not nullify God's faithful purpose (see Romans 3:3) any more than unbelief and perversions of the gospel today alter God's purpose in Christ.

The New Covenant

The future aspect of the covenant with Israel is in terms of the New Covenant. Jeremiah 31:31-34 is the only Old Testament passage that employs the term "new covenant," but its essence is a common prophetic theme (see, for instance, Isaiah 24, 55, 61; Ezekiel 34, 37). Like the Mosaic covenant, the new covenant does not so much advance knowledge about the person of Messiah as it does the benefits and application of His work. Throughout his message, Jeremiah had explained God's judgment on Judah in terms of Judah's breach of the covenant. In this text, he proclaims God's gracious salvation of a future generation of Israel in terms of covenant renewal. It is important to include in the word "new" the idea of "renewed." This new covenant certainly contains some grand and brand-new elements that advance our previous knowledge and explain more of the promise, but some things in it link the new covenant with the preceding promises as well.

The New Testament clearly expresses that this new covenant is not uniquely for Israel. Various New Testament texts allude to the new covenant and Hebrews 8:8-12 and 10:16-19 quote the passage completely. The New Testament makes it clear that the personal benefits of the new covenant are applied to every individual believer of the gospel: regeneration (a change of heart), reconciliation (a change in relationship with God), pardon (a change in legal standing, or justification). All of this is possible because of Jesus Christ. But we learn from Jeremiah that a day is coming in which God will apply these benefits to the nation of Israel as a whole; there is going to be a universal knowledge and acceptance of the covenant. That has never happened before; it has not happened yet. Other Old Testament passages reveal that Gentiles are included in that glorious day, but Jeremiah's special focus is on Israel (see, for instance, Amos 9:11-12; Zechariah 8:22-23). Zechariah spoke of a day when God "will pour upon the house of David, and upon the inhabitants of Jerusalem, the spirit of grace and of supplications: and they shall look upon me whom they have pierced..." (Zechariah 12:10). God will send His Spirit to administer saving grace, regenerating the people and causing them to call upon the Lord as they look in faith to the Messiah, who so many years earlier had died for them. I believe that this is what Paul refers to when he says that all Israel will be saved. Interestingly, he explains that coming salvation in terms of Jeremiah's new covenant prophecy: "For this is my covenant unto them, when I shall take away their sins" (Romans 11:27; compare this with Jeremiah 31:34). I believe that this national conversion will occur as one of the great attendant acts of the Second Coming of the Lord Jesus. Although the nation as a whole will be saved, it is important to note that the grace of the new covenant is applied individually to the hearts of the people. Nowhere does Scripture ever hint that people are saved by virtue of nationality. Even the physical seed of Abraham can become the spiritual seed only by exercising the same faith as did Abraham himself.

Knowing that Christ is at the heart of every covenant should alert us to look for Him in every covenant context. It would be a good exercise to take your concordance and look up not only the word "covenant," but also other words and expressions associated with "covenant theology." For instance, when God says, "I will be their God and they will be my people," that is covenant talk. Don't forget the great covenant term "loyalty," which the Authorized Version tends to translate as "mercy," "kindness," or "lovingkindness." You can be sure that when you see that word, you are right in the middle of God's covenant faithfulness, which finds its ultimate expression in the Lord Jesus. You may be surprised at how much of Old Testament theology revolves around and flows directly from God's gracious covenants. From the first coming of Christ as the Seed of the woman to the Second Coming of Christ as the Deliverer of Sion, God has revealed His plan of salvation in covenant terms. By covenant He issued the unconditional and unbreakable promise that Christ would come, and He has entered into a binding agreement with all who will trust and obey that covenant promise. Salvation is sure for all who emulate the faith of Abraham and become the heirs of the promise. It is not surprising that the message of the Old Testament closes with the prophecy that the "messenger of the covenant" would be coming suddenly (Malachi 3:1). It is not surprising that the New Testament begins with "the book of the generation of Jesus Christ, the son of David, the son of Abraham" (Mattew 1:1). You recognize now that that "Seed" of David and Abraham is convenant language and is the first divinel inspired link between the Testaments. Find God's covenant, and you find God's Christ.

CHAPTER 5
CHRIST IN PERSON

God is not what we think or imagine Him to be; He is what He is. What we know about God is what He has graciously revealed about Himself. The Lord has made Himself known to man by two principal means: General and Special Revelation. General Revelation testifies to God's existence, His essential Deity, and His glorious perfections, but it communicates no saving message to fallen and needy sinners. Special Revelation, on the other hand, is God's gracious communication of the good news of salvation in and through His Son, the Lord Jesus Christ. In one way or another, all of Special Revelation merges in that revelation of Christ. Faith in Christ is necessary for salvation, and faith comes by hearing and hearing by the Word of God (Romans 10:17). For us, Special Revelation is the Scripture, the inspired, written Word of God. Sometimes I think the wonder of this does not impress us as it ought to. The Bible is something we can purchase, possess, and read at will. We are too often more concerned about the quality and beauty of the leather binding than about the content of the message. What a tragedy that we do not cherish this Book for what it really is: the Word of the Living God. If that simple truth were to sink into our hearts, it would unquestionably increase our desire to know, understand, and heed every word in the Book. We are greatly privileged to have in this written Word all that is necessary for our eternal destinies as well as our temporary sojourns.

Although the Bible is currently man's only record of Special Revelation, it has not always been so. God did not drop the Scripture from the sky in one complete leather- bound volume. The Scripture was written over a period of more than fifteen hundred years by human authors dating from Moses in the fifteenth century BC to John the Apostle at the close of the first century AD. The world had a considerable history before God inspired Moses to write the first word. But Special Revelation did not begin with Moses; it began in the Garden with God's communicating His will to Adam and Eve. How the Lord revealed His Word before inscripturation varied. Hebrews 1:1 indicates that in the former times God spoke in diverse ways. Sometimes He communicated through dreams and visions; sometimes He revealed Himself through theophanies. A *theophany* literally means an appearance of God and refers to those visible manifestations of His presence that God gave from time to time. For instance, the cloud and fiery pillar that led Israel in the wilderness is an example of a theophany. It was a visible reminder and declaration of the Lord's constant presence and guidance.

A *Christophany* was a particular kind of theophany: *a pre-incarnate appearance of Christ in human form.* From time to time, the eternal Son of God visibly appeared to give a special word. The Old Testament records various instances of this revelation of Christ, (although–with some notable exceptions–as the written word increased, the manifestations of the visible "Word" decreased). These Christophanies reveal significant truths about God and His purpose for His people. What these appearances teach about the Godhead and the work of the Messiah is profound and more theologically advanced than we might expect. Christophanies provide a richly rewarding place to pursue our objective of seeing Christ in the Old Testament.

Precautions Concerning Christophany

Before considering some of the great issues taught by the Christophanies, we must emphasize that these several appearances of the Son of God were pre-incarnate. Incarnation means "in flesh" and refers to the eternal Son of God's being conceived by the virgin through the operation of the Holy Spirit and being born in the barn at Bethlehem. Pre-incarnate, then, designates the time before the eternal Son took to Himself human flesh. Christophanies, therefore, were occasions when the Second Person of the Holy Trinity appeared as a man but was not a man. He took the form of man but not the nature of man.

It is imperative not to confuse "form" and "nature." By form, we mean the outward appearance; by nature, we mean the essence of being. If sinners were to be saved, then the Son of God did have to become man. Remember that great catechism statement: "The only Redeemer of God's elect is the Lord Jesus Christ, who, being the eternal Son of God, became man, and so was, and continueth to be, God and Man in two distinct natures, and one person, for ever" (*Westminster Shorter Catechism*, question 21). To deny that Christ came in the flesh is serious heresy (I John 4:2-3). To assert that He was a real man before the Incarnation is a serious error as well. For Christ to be man before He became man is logically inconsistent; furthermore, it would attribute eternity to essential humanity, a perfection that is true only of God. The person of Christ is eternal, but His human nature had a beginning. It now has no ending, but it did have a beginning. That is important.

A well-known "Christmas" passage suggests this truth. Let me cite the verses because I want you to see the theological precision of the prophet. Micah 5:2-3a reads:

> But thou, Bethlehem Ephratah, though thou be little among the thousands of Judah, yet out of thee shall he come forth unto me that is to be ruler in Israel; whose goings forth have been from of old, from everlasting. Therefore will he give them up, until the time that she which travaileth hath brought forth....

This famous text does much more than merely identify the birthplace of Messiah. In addition to putting Bethlehem "on the map," it emphasizes three truths. First, a ruler was going to come. Kingship is one of our messianic clues. Second, this ruler's coming into Bethlehem would not be His first manifestation. The text says literally, "His exitings have been from before, from days of long ago." Though some have interpreted this as referring to the Son's eternal generation, I suggest that it refers rather to those before-the-Incarnation instances when the eternal Son of God appeared visibly on earth to men. Both interpretations, however, emphasize the eternal existence of the Son. His coming into Bethlehem would not mark the beginning of His existence. To have existence prior to a point in time requires eternity, a unique perfection of deity. So for this coming ruler to have been active from everlasting means that He is God. Deity is another of our messianic clues. Third, this One will be born through the labor pains of a woman. This is a normal, human birth. Humanity is also a messianic clue. Note Micah's logic. The humanity of this coming ruler follows multiple appearances. I suggest that Micah is referring to what we are calling Christophanies. Micah prophesied that a King would come who was God and would become Man and that prior to His birth, the incarnation, this Messiah "had left" heaven from time to time. It is to these "prior-to-birth" appearances that we want to give our attention.

Person of the Christophany

One of the key lessons taught by Christophanies is that God is a person. He is not a force or an abstract energy: He is a personal being. But He is a spiritual being. God is an infinite, eternal, unchangeable Spirit. Unfortunately, we are incapable of comprehending what pure Spirit is. It defies definition. This is one reason the Bible so frequently uses anthropomorphisms (human forms) to describe God. Although God is without body parts, He reveals Himself with human terms to enable finite man to understand something about Him. God's having an arm or eyes does not mean that He has these body parts shaped in some ghost-like outline. The resemblance is one of function, not appearance. That God has an arm means that He is powerfully able to act. That God has eyes means that He sees and knows. Anthropomorphisms aid our finite minds in understanding something of the infinite. A Christophany was in one way a visible, rather than verbal, anthropomorphism—an effective means of revealing that God is a person. That it was the Second Person of the holy, eternal Trinity who made these special appearances reveals something of the mystery of the Godhead. These Christophanies introduce to man extremely profound theology concerning Christ and His place in the Trinity. And this is the Old Testament.

The Christophany as the Angel

The most common designation that identifies a Christophany is "the Angel of the Lord." This title is also the most instructive concerning the nature of the divine manifestation. The reference to the Angel of the Lord does not occur in every Christophany, but it is safe to say that the Angel of the Lord always refers to Christ. Most of the appearances of the Angel occurred in actual circumstances of life, but sometimes He was part of a prophetic vision (particularly Zechariah's visions) or a historical account of an actual appearance. We may also identify some of the "unnamed" Christophanies in terms of the Angel of the Lord. For instance, Jacob wrestled all night with an unidentified man whom he ultimately recognized as God. After the wrestling match, Jacob named the place Peniel, explaining, "for I have seen God face to face" (Genesis 32:24-30). More than a thousand years later, the inspired prophet Hosea, referring to this historic episode, specifically identified the opponent as the Angel of the Lord (Hosea 12:4). On the basis of this inspired interpretation, we may very well conclude that all the Old Testament Christophanies can be understood as appearances of the Angel of the Lord.

Before considering what this Angel reveals about the person of God, we need to understand the expression itself. Part of the difficulty is the immediate association we make between the word "angel" and that great host of ministering spirits (Hebrews 1:14) that God created as agents of His providence. If this Angel is in the same class as Michael, Gabriel, the cherubim, and seraphim, then we cannot claim that this is a Christophany, because the Son of God is the Creator, not the created. The Old Testament word translated "angel," however, literally means "messenger"; it does not demand that we automatically classify any given messenger with the assembly of the created ministering spirits. Interestingly, the New Testament word for "angel" carries this same idea, as evidenced by its referring to the ministers of the seven churches in Revelation 3-4. The Angel of the Lord, therefore, is the Messenger of the Lord. It is the word's function or activity that applies to the Christophany. It is similar to the New Testament's referring to Jesus Christ as "the Apostle" (Hebrews 3:1). Obviously, the Lord was not one of the twelve whom He Himself had called and commissioned, but He was called, commissioned, and sent to save His people. He was the ideal Apostle. Even before His Incarnation, Christ was the ideal Messenger.

A second issue of interpretation concerns the logical relationship between the word "Angel" and the word "Lord." This "X of Y" type of construction is very common yet sometimes ambiguous. Although there are times when the context seems to warrant the idea that this is the Messenger *from* the Lord, I suggest that interpreting the word "Lord" as being in apposition to the word "angel" best explains and accounts for the mystery of this person. (Remember that apposition is a renaming of a noun, usually in a more specific manner.) In other words, the Angel of the Lord is the Angel *who* is the Lord.

The significance of this identification is profound when we recognize that the word "Lord" refers to Jehovah. Jehovah, of course, is that unique name of the one true and living God. Therefore, to equate the Angel with Jehovah irrefutably proves His deity. The significance of the name "Jehovah" is manifold, but at its heart is the declaration of God's covenant promises to His people. Consequently, the coming Messenger, or Angel, of the covenant in Malachi 3:1 is the same Being as the Angel of the Lord. This Messenger is Jehovah Himself, who graciously enters into covenant with His people and graciously reveals Himself for the benefit of His people. Further, this interpretation is distinctively Christological in that by identifying God as the Second Person of the Trinity, it accounts for the times the Angel seems to be distinct from God the Father. These Angel contexts are complex, but what, after all, is more complex than the Trinity? Granted, the term "Trinity" does not occur in these texts, but neither does it in the New Testament. Nevertheless, Scripture does make clear that the Angel is Christ, who is God.

The Christophany as God

The evidences of the deity of the Christophany are both explicit and deduced. Remember that we can identify God not only by His titles but also by what He is like and what He does. If the person of the Christophany is called God or if He possesses divine perfections or performs divine works, He is God. I am not going to address all of the texts here, but let me show you some of the indications of deity to look for when you encounter a Christophany in Scripture.

Explicit Statements of Deity

Notice the explicit equations of the Angel with God. These equations were made sometimes by the recipients of the Angel's message, sometimes by the Angel Himself. Consider these examples. The Angel of the Lord found Hagar in the wilderness after she had been banished from Abraham and Sarah. After receiving the message of promise from the Angel, Hagar "called the name of the LORD that spake unto her, Thou God seest me" (Genesis 16:13). Even Hagar had enough spiritual acumen to recognize the Angel as a visible manifestation of Jehovah, confessing by her name for Him that He was omniscient, a divine perfection. When Manoah, Samson's father, realized that the mysterious visitor who had announced the birth of his son was the Angel of the Lord, he confessed, "We shall surely die, because we have seen God" (Judges 13:21-22). Not only did Manoah correctly identify the Angel as God, but my guess is that he was plugging into his evaluation all the previous revelation about the Angel: the Pentateuch had already been written (see the similar response of Gideon in Judges 6:21-24).

Sometimes the Angel identifies Himself as God, either expressly or by speaking as Jehovah in the first person. In Genesis 31:11-13 the Angel of God plainly said to Jacob, "I am the God of Bethel." When the Angel of the Lord appeared to Moses from the burning bush, He identified Himself as "the God of thy father, the God of Abraham, the God of Isaac, and the God of Jacob" (Exodus 3:2, 6). As Moses is responding to the Angel speaking with him, the Scripture says directly, "Moses said unto God" (Exodus 3:11). When the Angel of the Lord spoke to Abraham after preventing the sacrifice of Isaac, He said, "By myself have I sworn, saith the Lord" (Genesis 22:15-16). He spoke directly as Jehovah because He was Jehovah.

Acts and Prerogatives of Deity

Not only do express statements reveal the deity of the Angel but so do His actions. To deduce from the works and behavior of the Angel that He is God requires applying our theological knowledge. Remember my contention developed in Part 1: if we know what we are looking for, we will know it when we see it. What we know about the doctrine of God, particularly the unique aspects of His person and work, will warrant our deductions concerning the deity of the Christophany. If things about God are true of the Christophanic person, then He must be God. That is both good logic and good theology. I will not consider every relevant text at this point, but I will give some examples to illustrate the kind of things to look for in your own study.

The context of the Angel's appearance to Hagar is instructive. It most likely was this evidence of divine behavior that led to Hagar's confession that the Angel was "Thou God seest me." Genesis 16:10-12 records the specific promise the Angel gave to Hagar. The Angel promised that He would multiply her seed and that Ishmael would be a source of contention wherever he would go. We should note two things here. (1) The angel had power to give life ("I will multiply thy seed exceedingly"). (2) The angel knew the future as though it were present ("he will be a wild man; his hand will be against every man, and every man's hand against him"). Authority over life and immediate knowledge are characteristics of God.

Exodus 23:21 is a most significant text. Here Jehovah speaks concerning the Angel: "Beware of him, and obey his voice, provoke him not; for he will not pardon your transgressions: for my name is in him." The authority to forgive sins is uniquely the prerogative of Deity. When Jehovah graciously descended and stood with Moses declaring His own name, one of the significant self-descriptions was that He forgives iniquity and transgression and sin (Exodus 34:5-7). According to Micah, what marked the uniqueness of God was that He pardons iniquity and forgives transgressions (Micah 7:18). Even the Pharisees knew enough theology to know that only God can forgive sins (Mark 2:7). Tragically, they did not have enough spiritual sense or perception to deduce legitimately from the fact that Jesus was forgiving sins that He must, therefore, be God. We certainly do not want to be guilty of the Pharisees' blindness in our identifying the Angel of the Lord. He had the power to forgive; therefore, He must be God.

Another conclusive piece of evidence of deity is that the Angel accepts worship, something that created angels always refused. Indeed, He demanded worship. When the Angel appeared to Moses from the burning bush, He commanded Moses not to approach and to take off his shoes because he was standing on holy ground (Exodus 3:5). The only thing that made that wilderness ground holy was the presence of the Angel, the presence of God. The Christophany in Joshua 5:13-15 is identified not as the Angel of the Lord, but as the "captain of the host of the Lord." But it is the same person. He commanded Joshua, "Loose thy shoe from off thy foot; for the place whereon thou standest is holy" (5:15). In light of the first commandment that forbids the worship of any other god, these commands to submit in reverence to the Christophany demand His identification as Deity. Certainly, the Scripture would not command sin. Similar to the demands for worship are the demands for obedience to the Angel (see Exodus 23:21-22). All in all, the overwhelming evidence is that the Angel, who is Jehovah, and every other Christophany are visible manifestations of the eternal God.

CHRIST IN PERSON

The Christophany Distinct from God

The person of the Christophany is God, and yet He is distinct from God. The principal evidence for this is that the Angel, who often speaks as Jehovah in the first person, also speaks of Jehovah in the third person. For instance, when the Angel tells Hagar what He will do, giving evidence of His Deity, He also says "the Lord hath heard thy affliction" (Genesis16:11). Again, in Genesis 21, when Hagar is cast out for good, the Angel of God calls to Hagar and tells her, "God hath heard the voice of the lad" (21:17). Genesis 22:12 hints at this mysterious distinction when the Angel says to Abraham, "Now I know that thou fearest God, seeing thou hast not withheld thy son, thine only son from me." Similarly, when Jehovah speaks, He sometimes distinguishes between Himself and His Angel. In Exodus 23 it is Jehovah who is giving the instructions concerning the proper response to the Angel that will go before the nation (23:20-23). Significantly, the Lord calls Him "mine Angel" (23:23). The prophet Isaiah in his prayer argument for the Lord to look down from heaven and visit his generation referrs to the Lord's gracious presence with ancient Israel in the wilderness. His historic reference corresponds to the episode in Exodus 23. Isaiah similarly distinguishes between the Lord and the Angel: "In all their affliction he was afflicted, and the angel of his presence saved them" (Isaiah 63:9, 15). Yet, it is His own presence that God promised Moses: "My presence shall go with thee" (Exodus 33:14).

The Old Testament evidence that the person of the Christophany is God, yet distinct from God, is clear. What conclusions are possible from this evidence is not as clear. Given all the revelation we possess in the completed Scripture, it is legitimate for us to see in this sameness and difference the eternal relationship between the First and Second Persons of the Holy Trinity. At the least, the Old Testament data teaches that the Godhead is complex, beyond complete human comprehension. It teaches that God, who is transcendent, infinitely high above all creation, is also immanent, graciously near His people. It teaches that God is not just an abstraction, but a personal God who is vitally interested in His people and who will graciously make Himself known to His people in their times of urgent need. The Christophany was an effective, unmistakable means of revelation whereby God not only made Himself known but also introduced the unique person who would be the only One in whom the invisible God would be visible.

But the issue for us is not speculating about how advanced or primitive was the Old Testament saint's creedal statement on the Trinity. Our concern is seeing what we can see about Christ in our reading of the Old Testament, and the New Testament warrants our seeing in these Christophanies our Lord Jesus Christ. Stephen links the Angel with the Ideal Prophet, claiming that He was with the "church in the wilderness" (Acts 7:30-38). Paul specifically says that Christ followed the nation of Israel in the wilderness as the "Rock" and that the Israelites, in fact, tempted Christ in their various wilderness sins (I Corinthians 10:4-9). Although this particular form of revealing Christ is no longer possible, the truths about His mission and purpose remain. Since Christophanies are visible manifestations of Christ in human form without human nature, they are no longer possible because Christ at the Incarnation took to Himself a real human nature and now continues and will forever continue as God and Man in two distinct natures, yet one person.

Purpose of the Christophany

Apart from what the Christophanies revealed about God in general, they were most effective in preparing the way for the Incarnation. They helped to generate the theological mindset that expected and anticipated the visible manifestation of God. The Christophanies were tokens of that time when in Christ all the fullness of the Godhead would dwell bodily, when the "light of the knowledge of the glory of God" would shine in the face of Jesus Christ (Colossians 2:9; II Corinthians 4:6). In addition to providing a foretaste of the fact of the Incarnation, the Christophanies give a foretaste of the messianic mission. Knowing what we now know about that messianic work is another reason we are warranted in seeing the Lord Jesus in these Old Testament passages. The Messiah is the anointed Prophet, Priest, and King. Remember that we are able to identify Christ by His works.

A Foretaste of the Prophetic Mission

A prophet is God's representative to men with God's word for men. Without question, this prophetic mission is the most outstanding of the functions of the Christophany. That the Christophany is so often defined in terms of the Angel or Messenger highlights this prophetic work. He appeared with a message from the Lord, revealing God's purposes, encouraging with God's promises, and instructing God's people.

Some key texts will illustrate. Malachi's title of Christ as the "Messenger of the covenant" (3:1) is clearly pictured in what I would identify as the first of the Christophanies. Though not designated the Angel of the Lord, I would suggest that "the voice of the Lord God" that Adam and Eve heard walking in the garden while they were hiding from the Lord's presence after their sin was not just a mysterious shuffling and rustling of leaves (Genesis 3:8). It was indeed a pre-incarnate appearance of the soon-to-be promised Seed. That He is called the "voice of the Lord God" parallels closely the apostle John's title for Christ as the "Word" (John 1). Similarly, when the exiled apostle heard the words of his exalted Christ speaking, he "turned to see the voice" (Revelation 1:12). That He is called the "voice of the Lord God" and that the next verse records the Lord God speaking (Genesis 3:8) draw attention to the prophetic ministry. Here was One who was the visible manifestation of God declaring the will of God. Significantly, right at the heart of the first Christophanic message was the announcement of the gospel: the Seed was coming to reverse the curse of sin. This "voice" was the "Messenger of the covenant."

The first appearance of the Angel of the Lord was to Hagar in her banishment from Sarah. He spoke to her as the Lord with words of assurance and promise (Genesis 16:10). In Genesis 18, the Lord visibly appeared to Abraham and announced both the word of judgment on Sodom and the imminent conception and birth of Isaac. Notice that one of those visitors to Abraham is specifically identified as the Lord (18:13). The Angel of the Lord that spoke to Moses from the burning bush announced the divine purpose to deliver Israel from Egypt and instructed Moses concerning his own call and mission (Exodus 3). Similarly, the Christophanies during the time of the judges announced God's deliverance for the people and instructed the chosen judge (see the call of Gideon in Judges 6:12ff.). In the case of Samson, the Angel appeared to announce his birth and predict the deliverance that would come through him (Judges 13:3ff.).

If Christ executes the office of prophet "in his revealing to the church, in all ages, by his Spirit and word, in divers ways of administration, the whole will of God, in all things concerning their edification and salvation" (*Westminster Larger Catechism*, question 43), then without question the Old Testament Christophany evidences His prophetic office. These periodic visitations of the pre-incarnate Christ were vivid assurances that God would never leave His people without a word. They were gracious tokens that increased anticipation for the Word's becoming flesh. Even though we cannot physically see what they saw, the lesson about Christ in these Christophanies is as relevant for us as for them.

A Foretaste of the Priestly Mission

A priest is man's representative before God who deals with God in man's behalf. Although not as prevalent as indications of the prophetic mission, hints of the Angel's priestly operation do occur and contribute to the messianic identity of the Christophany. The most significant examples are in Zechariah's visions. Before considering Zechariah's revelation, though, I need to justify my inclusion of these texts. Technically, what Zechariah witnessed were not Christophanies. That is, they were not actual appearances of the pre-incarnate Christ on the earth. They were real manifestations of the same Angel, but they were revealed to the inner consciousness of the prophet. I cannot begin to explain the mechanics of any form of divine revelation, but visions were a common vehicle through which God revealed truth. What the prophet saw was real, but he saw it in himself and not in front of him; the vision was internal, not external. He did not imagine the vision; the vision was the work of God's supernaturally controlling the prophet's mind. Therefore, Zechariah's internal vision of the Angel of the Lord was a revelation of the same person who appeared externally to Hagar, Abraham, Moses, and all the rest. It was a Christophany as far as Zechariah was concerned. All of the preceding knowledge about the Angel would have been a factor both for Zechariah who saw the vision and for his contemporaries who read his message. It should be a factor for us as well. Zechariah's visions warrant our consideration here. Notwithstanding the particular mode of the revelation, they are most instructive about Christ.

Zechariah records a series of eight night visions that he received from the Lord, revealing an overview of God's gracious purpose for His people (Zechariah 1-6). The vision of the man on a red horse standing among the myrtle trees and the vision of Joshua the high priest being accused by Satan are instructive for us regarding the Angel of the Lord. In the first vision, the rider of the red horse is identified as the Angel of the Lord (1:8-17). His standing among the myrtle trees most likely represents His presence among His people: He identifies Himself with His people. That's one thing priests do. But most significant in this passage is the Angel's interceding for the people. In 1:12 the Angel pleads with the Lord to show mercy on the nation by fully ending the seventy-year demonstration of His indignation. Intercession is priestly work.

Zechariah 3 is one of the most beautiful passages in Scripture. Joshua the high priest stands before the Angel of the Lord with Satan at his right hand accusing him. He is clothed with disgustingly filthy garments and he can offer no excuse or self-defense against Satan's accusations. But the Lord silences Satan, refusing to entertain the accusations. The Lord commands that the filthy garments be removed and replaced by royal attire. That action is explained as being symbolic of the forgiveness of sins. It leads to a prophecy of the Messiah/Branch who will remove iniquity in one day. I believe that this is a reference to the atoning work of the Messiah. While all this is going on, "the angel of Lord stood by" (3:5). In addition to being a vivid picture of what the Lord does in justifying guilty sinners, this vision suggests the important role Christ has in the justified sinner's legal defense. Not only is it His death that one day removed iniquity, but it is His constant "standing by" as the representative and the advocate for His people that assures their continuing acceptance before the Lord. As our High Priest, He ever lives to make intercession. What Zechariah saw in vision is not much different from what John forthrightly declared. "And if any man sin, we have an advocate with the Father, Jesus Christ the righteous: and he is the propitiation for our sins: and not for ours only, but also for the sins of the whole world" (I John 2:1-2).

If Christ executes His priestly office "in his once offering himself a sacrifice without spot to God, to be a reconciliation for the sins of his people; and in making continual intercession for them" (*Westminster Larger Catechism*, question 44), then without question the Old Testament Christophany is evidence of His priestly office. The Christophany was a momentous token of the certain coming of that One who would take human flesh to become forever qualified to be the Ideal and Perfect Priest through whom men would be able to approach God. We can learn from the Christophany not only that God required such mediation but that He provided such mediation in our Lord Jesus Christ.

A Foretaste of the Kingly Mission

A king is a sovereign with authority to govern, guide, and protect his subjects as well as execute whatever punishment necessary for infractions of his law. Although the Old Testament Christophany is not directly identified as a king, the person of the Christophany is often engaged in kingly operations. His appearances foreshadow the incarnate revelation of the Messiah/King. Some examples will illustrate. The episode of the three visitors to Abraham who declared both the birth of Isaac and the sentence of judgment on Sodom and Gomorah is instructive (Genesis 18). One of those visitors was a Christophany who spoke to Abraham as the Lord (18:17). The text states that "Abraham stood yet before the Lord" and then that he "drew near" and began his intercession for the city (18:22, 23). Standing before the Lord and speaking to the Lord in the person of this visitor, Abraham argued, "Shall not the Judge of all the earth do right?" (18:25). The right to execute judgment is a kingly prerogative.

According to II Samuel 24:16 (see also I Chronicles 21:16), it was the Angel of the Lord that executed the plague judgment on Israel after David's sin of numbering the people. Interestingly, in this passage it is clear that the Lord assigned the role of executing judge to the Angel. Not only does this text maintain that "same as the Lord, yet distinct from Lord" mystery, but it also hints that judgeship is part of the messianic commission. Remember that the Lord Jesus said that the Father had given him "authority to execute judgment also, because he is the Son of man" (John 5:27).

Leading and defending His people were common functions of the Christophany. Abraham told his servant that the Lord's angel would go before him and give success to his mission in finding a wife for Isaac (Genesis 24:7, 40). When Jacob blessed the sons of Joseph, he testified that it was the Angel who had delivered him from all the dangers and troubles of his life (Genesis 48:16). In Exodus 14 the operations of leading and defending are linked together. The Angel that was before the camp of Israel, having led them out of Egypt, "removed and went behind them" at the Red Sea to defend the people and to be a barrier between them and the pursuing Egyptians (14:19-20). The Lord promised Moses that the Angel would go before them to drive out the inhabitants of the land (Exodus 33:2). In Judges 2:1 the Angel appears and declares that is what He has done: "I made you to go up out of Egypt, and have brought you unto the land which I sware unto your fathers; and I said, I will never break my covenant with you." The Angel's intervention for Hezekiah stands as a classic demonstration of kingly defense and protection. Jerusalem was surrounded, and Hezekiah, the king of Judah, did not have the military resources to deliver his people from what seemed to be unavoidable defeat. But the godly king prayed, confessing his total dependence on the Lord, and the Lord sent His Angel. In a single moment, the Angel of the Lord went to the very camp of the enemy and slew one hundred eighty-five thousand (II Kings 19:35).

If Christ executes the office of a king by "subduing us to himself, in ruling and defending us, and in restraining and conquering all his and our enemies" (*Westminster Shorter Catechism*, question 26), then without question the Old Testament Christophany is evidence of His kingship. Considering some of the more detailed statements of the *Larger Catechism* increases the evidence that the Christophanic person revealed Himself as the good king of His people: "preserving and supporting them under all their temptations and sufferings; restraining and overcoming all their enemies, and powerfully ordering all things for his own glory, and their good; and also in taking vengeance on the rest, who know not God" (question 45). All of the kingly operations of the Christophany were manifest tokens of this messianic function. These tokens instructed and increased desire for the complete manifestation. A little sight of the coming King aided faith. Faith cannot occur in a mental vacuum: you have to know what you believe. The Christophany was a means of giving the Old Testament saint some necessary knowledge about the only effective object of faith.

Not only were these tokens good for them then, but they are also good for us now because they are part of the inspired Old Testament history, recorded for our benefit and edification. Though the vehicle of revelation is different for us (we read what they saw), the truths revealed by Christophany are as valid for us as for them. Although we may not experience or need the same kind of kingly operation as those in the wilderness or those surrounded by Assyrians, we still need guidance and protection daily. We can learn from the Christophanies that God always is for His people and always does for His people what they need at the appropriate times. That has always been true, and that is good.

Passages Revealing Christophanies

Christophanies are easy enough to recognize. Apart from the wilderness wanderings where it seems that the Angel of the Lord was a consistent, prolonged presence, most of the appearances of the pre-incarnate Christ in human form were momentary epochs. Certainly, as you read your Old Testament these epochs should cause you to pause and reflect on what messianic truth is being presented. It would be a profitable study as well to search out the relevant passages and systematically discover the great truths about Christ. To get started on that search, consider the following passages. I make no claim that is an exhaustive list, but it identifies some of the key passages and offers a brief descriptive synopsis. As you study the passages, try to identify on your own what messianic ministry is being revealed in each one.

Reference	Synopsis
Genesis 3:8	The Voice of the Lord finds fallen man, pronounces the curse, and reveals the Gospel.
Genesis 16:7-13	The Angel of the Lord appears to Hagar, promising the birth of Ishmael and offering comfort in her trial.
Genesis 18	The heavenly visitors, one of which was a Christophany, announce the birth of Isaac and the judgment on Sodom and Gomorah.
Genesis 21:17	The Angel of the Lord comforts Hagar again.
Genesis 22:11-18	The Angel of Lord stops Abraham from sacrificing Isaac, directs him to the ram provided for a sacrifice, and repeats the covenant blessing.
Genesis 24:7, 40	The Angel leads Abraham's servant in his search for Isaac's bride.
Genesis 31:11-13	The Angel of God warns Jacob about Laban's deceit.

Genesis 32:24-32	Jacob wrestles with a man whom he admits was God. Jacob requests a blessing from the man and the man changes Jacob's name to Israel (Years later Hosea identifies the man as the Angel of the Lord.)
Exodus 3:2-10	The Angel of the Lord appears to Moses in the burning bush, announcing deliverance for the covenant people, identifying Himself as God, and demanding worship.
Exodus 14:19	The Angel of the Lord is present with Israel at the Red Sea, protecting them from the Egyptians.
Exodus 23:20-23 (33:2; cf. 33:14)	The Lord promises that His Angel will lead and preserve the people in the wilderness and warns against disobeying and provoking the Angel's anger, because He alone has the power to forgive sins. Note in the 33:14 text that the presence promised is the Lord Himself.
Numbers 22:22-35	The Angel of the Lord stands as an adversary to Balaam, preventing him from cursing the covenant people.
Joshua 5:13-15	The Captain of the Lord's host appears to Joshua on the eve of the conquest to give assurance for the wars to come and instructions for the conquest of Jericho.
Judges 2:1-4	The Angel of the Lord appears to the entire nation, reminding them of His operation in the Exodus and conquest, assuring them that He would not break the covenant, and exhorting them to separate from the heathen.
Judges 6:11-23	The Angel of the Lord appears to Gideon, calling him to judgeship and promising deliverance from the enemy.

Judges 13:3-23	The Angel of the Lord appears to Samson's parents, announcing his birth and mission. Once Manoah recognizes it is the Angel, he confesses that they have seen God and consequently expect to die.
II Samuel 24:16-17 (I Chronicles 21:15-16, 18)	The Angel of the Lord executes God's chastening of Israel after David's sin of numbering the people. Afterward, the Angel instructs Gad to tell David to build an altar to the Lord.
I Kings 19:4-8	The Angel of the Lord comforts and instructs Elijah in the wilderness during his flight from Jezebel.
II Kings 1:3-4 (II Chronicles 32:20; Isaiah 37:36)	The Angel of the Lord instructs Elijah to tell the messengers from Ahaziah that the king will certainly die.
II Kings 19:35	The Angel of the Lord defends Hezekiah and Jerusalem by slaying almost two hundred thousand Assyrians in a single night.
Psalm 34:7	God's delivering David from Abimelech prompts David to confess, "The angel of the Lord encampeth round about them that fear him, and delivereth them." (If not referring to an actual Christophany, the statement illustrates that David knew the significance of the Angel and how to apply the implications of "Christophany theology." If it is not a Christophany, it is still a good illustration for us about how to apply the truth of Christ's presence with us.)
Isaiah 63:9	The prophet refers to the Angel's sympathetic presence with Israel during the wilderness wanderings.
Daniel 6:22	It is God's angel that shuts the mouths of the lions, thus preserving Daniel. (This may not be the Angel of the Lord, but the mission per-

formed is in keeping with His typical operations.)

| Zechariah 1:8-12; 3:1-9 | These are Christophanic visions in which the Angel of the Lord exercises priestly intercession in behalf of His people. |

I suppose that one of the questions I am asked most frequently is how much of Christ Old Testament saints really knew. My typical response is that I don't know how much they knew, but I do know how much they should have known in the light of God's revelation to them. In addition to all the things God said to them, from time to time He allowed them to see with their eyes the promised Savior. Maybe they knew more than we want to give them credit for! Each of these Old Testament manifestations of Christ before the Incarnation testifies to God's eternal, immutable purpose to provide the necessary Mediator, the Prophet, Priest, and King. Even before the arrival of the fullness of time that would bring the climactic fulfillment of that purpose in the birth, life, death, resurrection, Ascension, Session, and Second Coming of Jesus of Nazareth, the Lord gave gracious tokens of His promise in these epoch appearances of the Second Person of the Trinity, the Mediator-elect.

In some ways, I think these gracious Christophanies parallel what we know and experience of the Holy Spirit. The New Testament says that the Holy Spirit is the "earnest of our inheritance" (Ephesians 1:14). In other words, the Holy Spirit is the down payment, the guarantee of the full and final salvation we will enjoy eternally. The Holy Spirit is a gracious and wonderful token of complete salvation. The evidence that we will be forever in the presence of the Lord is the Lord's abiding presence with us now in the person of His Spirit. Salvation is good now, but the best is yet to be. Similarly, the Old Testament Christophanies were guarantees that the Messiah was on His way. "The messenger of the covenant...behold, he shall come, saith the Lord of hosts" (Malachi 3:1). Those temporary manifestations were good, but the best was yet to come. Although we live on this side of the fullness of time, we can still profit from these impossible-to-be-repeated pre-incarnate appearances because they testify to the Lord's unfailing faithfulness. Afer all, it is the same Christ.

CHAPTER 6

CHRIST IN HIS NAMES

A rose by any other name may smell the same, but a rose is a rose. In our culture, our given names are usually nothing more than labels for identification. The name we use to address a person, for instance, often indicates our relationship to him. We tend to call only good acquaintances by their first names. Further, we may address by his first name someone whom we consider beneath our station in life, such as an employee, but we would not presume to call a superior by his first name. Nevertheless, we tend to be thrilled when a boss addresses us by our first name, inferring correctly or incorrectly, that he really knows and cares about us. I suppose I will never forget the day my principal Old Testament professor and mentor called me "Mike" for the first time. I took that as a sign that I was worthy and capable in his estimation of pursuing my degree. I was such an impressionable kid. We have now been colleagues and friends for years, but to this day I find it awkward to address him by his first name. I'll call him by his last name without using his degree title, but that irreverent circumlocution is as far as I can go. Too, although our first names are in some way special, their use or nonuse does not depend on what the names may mean etymologically or historically. They're just labels. They can identify us, but they do not describe us.

Nicknames are something else. Not only do they identify an individual, but they also describe something about him. We assign nicknames to public figures as well as those who are close to us. Husbands and wives often refer to each other with particular and sometimes peculiar names. Some terms of endearment like "honey" and "sweetheart" are well-worn and may show little imagination, but they are nonetheless special, communicating something only to each other. My wife's name is Sandra, but I call her Sander. That's my special name for her and the fact that it communicates nothing to anyone else is okay. We do have a couple of others that we will take to the grave. Nicknames flourish in the world of sports. Some years ago there was a baseball player who was known as "Mr. October" because his bat always seemed to come alive in the playoff season. Those who follow professional golf can immediately identify "the Bear" and "the Shark" and make the connection between the name and some characteristic of their play. I am told professional wrestlers, too, are known by certain descriptive nicknames, but I suppose if I knew what they were I would not be writing this book, and that if you knew, you wouldn't be reading it! I think that's a different world, but you get my point. Nicknames communicate something about a person. We sometimes refer to people by the position they hold or occupation they perform: Mr. President, Mr. Chairman, Pastor. These are not exactly nicknames, but the titles effectively reveal something about the person.

There is a point to all this. I suggested earlier that the names of God are more than simply labels: they are means by which God reveals something about His person, His perfections, and His work. They both identify and describe. What is true about the names of God generally is true about the names of Christ specifically. The Old Testament contains many names or titles of Christ that draw attention to some particular aspect of His person or His work. The use of these special titles for Messiah was an effective way for advancing knowledge about Him in the Old Testament dispensation and an effective way for teaching us about Christ in this dispensation, because He is the same yesterday, today, and forever.

I call them special titles because they are not proper names in the technical sense. Many of them are just common nouns or expressions that are used for personal designation. The technical term for this is an *appellative*, a common noun used as a descriptive name. Because many of these messianic titles are common nouns, they are not always immediately recognizable. The Authorized Version helps at times by capitalizing the expressions, but it does not do so consistently. For instance, one of the key titles we will consider is "branch." Twice in Zechariah the Authorized Version has "BRANCH," twice in Jeremiah it has "Branch," and yet in Isaiah it simply has "branch." In each instance it is the same word in the original, referring each time to the same Messiah. Recognizing it as a title for Christ is easy enough when we come across it in Jeremiah and especially easy in Zechariah, but it requires a bit more attention in Isaiah because the translation does not give us any obvious clue. That's fine, because the Hebrew text never distinguishes words in that way. It does not use what we would call capital or small-case letters; all the letters are the same size.

We need to be able, then, to identify these descriptive "names" even when the words do not appear to be names. When we see personality or personal traits or activity associated with what seems to be a common noun or expression, we should at least pause to consider whether this could actually be a title for Christ. So when I see "wisdom" in Proverbs speaking and acting, I need to compare what wisdom says and does with what I know Messiah says and does to see if there may be some connection. This analogical method—or "analogy of Scripture" principle of interpretation—will often suggest and justify identifying certain common nouns as titles for Messiah. If we can find the titles of Messiah in the Old Testament, we have obviously found Him and we will learn some important lessons about Him. Since finding Christ in the Old Testament is our objective, His names are a good place to look.

In this chapter, I want to get you started on this search for Christ in His titles. My list cannot be exhaustive, but I do want to identify some of the most important of these titles and define their significance. The key element in your own reading of the Scripture is simply to be sensitive to this means of revelation. We have the big picture of who Christ is and what He does; these specific titles tend to provide details of some aspect of His person or some element of His work. Because the person of Christ is inseparable from His work, many of these titles overlap in their revelation. Herein lies my struggle: How can I best organize this synopsis? It would be easy to discuss the terms alphabetically in dictionary style. On the other hand, it would be interesting to discuss them chronologically, highlighting the progressive nature of the revelation. I am going to attempt to classify them according to what they teach about Messiah's person and work. Admitting overlap, I will discuss each title in only one category and make the cross-references to other implications of the title. However, before I begin that synopsis, let us consider two texts that deserve special attention because of the concentration of messianic designations.

Two Name-calling Texts

It is perhaps not without significance that these two name-calling texts occur in Isaiah and Zechariah, the most intensely messianic of all the prophets. For good reason, we could well refer to these books as the Gospel according to Isaiah and Zechariah. There is hardly any essential truth about Christ's person or work not addressed by these two. We will examine some of their key prophecies in the next chapter, but here we simply want to set the context and define the descriptive titles in these two texts.

Isaiah 9:6

This famous Christmas verse occurs in the middle of what is often called the "Immanuel trilogy." Isaiah 7 announces the virgin birth of the Messiah; Isaiah 11 describes the ministry and work of the Messiah; Isaiah 9 identifies the character of the Messiah and the amazing difference His presence will make in the world. When Isaiah issued this prophecy, the nation was in the darkness of Assyrian domination and oppression. With prophetic foresight and vision, Isaiah saw a time when "the people that walked in darkness" would see a great light. With messianic consciousness, the prophet linked that great light to the birth of a child who would be the rightful king upon David's throne (the fulfillment of the Davidic covenant) and who would perpetuate an everlasting rule of absolute justice. As the guarantee of assured success to this messianic mission, the prophet declared, "The zeal of the Lord of hosts will perform this" (9:7). All the energy, passion, and fervor of the "Commander-in-Chief" would insure that nothing could frustrate or alter the messianic mission and that no part of the work could fail. The New Testament removes any interpretational doubt that this text refers to the ministry of Jesus Christ when it quotes Isaiah 9:1-2 as being fulfilled at the beginning of Christ's Galilean ministry (Matthew 4:12-16).

Right in the middle of this rich messianic prophecy is a list of titles that describe the character of Christ. When we remember that one of our clues for finding Christ is the linking of humanity and deity in a single person, there can be no question that Isaiah 9:6 uniquely refers to the Lord Jesus. That a male child would be born indicates a real birth and therefore a real humanity. Remember that this is part of the larger context that began with the prophecy of the virgin birth (7:14).

Here is the coming of the Seed of the woman promised way back in Genesis 3:15. The promise never changed. That He is born "unto us" literally means "for us," for our benefit. In a nutshell, it declares the blessings of His vicarious life and death for His people. That a son is given speaks of the appointing and anointing of the eternal Son of God as the chosen mediator. This special selection refers to His deity. The language suggests that the sonship was antecedent to the giving and parallels closely that most famous of gospel texts: "God so loved the world that he gave his only begotten Son" (John 3:16). If we have no problem recognizing the significance of John 3:16 in declaring the eternal sonship of Christ and amazing grace of God, we should have no problem seeing the significance of Isaiah 9:6. John and Isaiah are saying the same thing; they are speaking of the same person. Rather than reading John back into Isaiah, let's say that we are reading John in the light of Isaiah. The Incarnation that Isaiah prophesied was revealed in Christ's explanation of Himself to Nicodemus. Having identified the coming Messiah as God/Man, Isaiah describes His character with four titles.

Wonderful, Counselor

First, He is the *Wonderful, Counselor*. Although the Authorized Version separates these as individual titles, it is better to link them together: *the Wonder of a Counselor*. The word "wonder" or "marvel" refers to something that is extraordinary and humanly incomprehensible. It is a word associated with the supernatural acts of God, and it therefore attests to the Messiah's deity. The word "counselor" implies the wisdom that is required not only for giving advice but also for issuing decrees. The fact that Isaiah governs it with the word "wonderful" suggests that the appointed Son has infinite wisdom or omniscience, a unique perfection of Deity. Isaiah shows his understanding of the implications of this title when he uses the same words to describe Jehovah of hosts, "which is wonderful in counsel" (Isaiah 28:29). The uniqueness and superiority of divine counsel are evident in Isaiah 40, which declares that God takes counsel from none (40:13-14). What is true of God is true of Christ (see also Isaiah 11:2).

Mighty God

Second, He is the *Mighty God*. This literally says "God, the defender/guardian." The term "God" (El) applies only to Deity and designates God in His power and transcendent majesty. The term "defender/guardian" is not uniquely a divine word, but the Scripture does apply it to the Lord, designating Him as the security of His people. Intriguingly, Isaiah uses the same expression in referring to Jehovah, the Holy One of Israel (10:20-21). Years later, Jeremiah used the expression as he addressed the Lord in prayer: "the Great, the Mighty God, the Lord of hosts, is his name" (Jeremiah 32:18). In fact, in the very next verse (32:19), Jeremiah describes the Lord as "great in counsel," an expression similar to that in Isaiah 9:6. And years earlier, Moses declared, "For the Lord your God is God of gods, and Lord of lords, a great God, a mighty ..." (Deuteronomy 10:17; see Zephaniah 3:17). These are the same terms that Isaiah 9:6 assigns to Messiah, the divine Defender and Guardian. That this title became part of messianic theology is clear from Psalm 45, an unmistakably messianic psalm. Verse 3 entreats the Messiah, "Gird thy sword upon thy thigh, O most mighty...." The Lord Jesus is the great Defender of His people.

Father of Eternity

Third, He is the *everlasting Father*. A more literal translation eliminates any possible Trinitarian confusion that the Son is also at the same time the everlasting Father. The Hebrew expression is the "father of eternity." It is not speaking of the Son's relationship to the Father but rather His relationship to time. The word "father" is an honorific title of authority. Christ is above time; He is eternal and therefore of necessity God, because eternity is a uniquely divine perfection. He is the absolute and everlasting authority. The title highlights His everlasting sovereignty.

Prince of Peace

Fourth, He is the *Prince of Peace*. The term "prince" does not refer to the son of a king, someone who has royal position but no royal authority. This prince is not a king-in-waiting. Instead, the word designates a ruler, a chief, or an official with the power and authority to administer. Daniel 8:25 uses the term to refer to God as the Prince of princes, a superlative expression meaning that God is the absolute Ruler, the most authoritative Ruler that exists. Here the term applies to Christ as the Sovereign Administrator of peace. Embodied in this title is His whole work of salvation whereby He removed the impediments to peace, harmony, and fellowship with God. He is the reconciliation for His people to God.

This verse will appropriately remain a Christmas text, but I trust that we will go beyond its surface reminder of the Christmas story to reflect on the great revelation about the Lord Jesus in the simple list of names.

Zechariah 10:4

"Out of him came forth the corner, out of him the nail, out of him the battle bow, out of him every oppressor together." This verse is not nearly so famous as Isaiah 9:6, and some even question its messianic relevance. However, I believe it does refer to Christ and thus warrants a summary statement here because it illustrates how effectively and economically special titles can communicate. The person described in Zechariah 10:4 is God's answer to the bad shepherds (rulers) who had troubled the flock of His people (10:2-3). The Lord of hosts would visit His people and reverse their fortunes. The agent by whom the bad shepherds would be punished and the flock blessed is the corner, the nail, the battle bow, and the absolute ruler. The statement "from him" (from the Lord) precedes each of these four titles, suggesting the divine anointing and commission of the Messiah to conduct His ministry.

Corner

That Christ is the Corner testifies to His being the sure and stable foundation. This same word occurs in Isaiah's more extensive description: "Behold, I lay in Zion for a foundation a stone, a tried stone, a precious corner stone, a sure foundation: he that believeth shall not make haste" (Isaiah 28:16). Likewise, it is the word in Psalm 118:22: "The stone which the builders refused is become the head stone of the corner." The New Testament demands the Christological interpretation (see Matthew 21:42; Acts 4:11; I Peter 2:4-8). In contrast to the vain and worthless objects of trust mentioned in Zechariah 10:2 (idols, diviners, dreamers), from the Lord would come the Corner, the only trustworthy object for faith. That was true then and it is true now. The object of faith determines the value of faith, and the only object of saving faith is Christ.

Nail

That Christ is the *Nail* testifies to His ability to bear the load in supporting His people. This nail is a peg in the wall for hanging items. Unless the peg is solid, it will be useless for hanging anything. Ezekiel plays on this thought when he says that the "wood" of a vine would be a worthless pin for hanging vessels (Ezekiel 15:3). Isaiah's report of Eliakim's promotion to administer the keys to David's house illustrates this function of the nail: "And I will fasten him as a nail in a sure place ... and they shall hang upon him all the glory (weight) of his father's house" (Isaiah 22:23-24). Sadly, Eliakim's nail loosened and the burden hanging on it fell off (Isaiah 22:25). This failure of what seemed to be a sure support points to the fact that there is only one Nail that is strong enough and sure enough to hold any burden. That unfailing Nail is Christ. In contrast to the bad shepherds who took advantage of and increased the burden of the people, the Lord would fix an immovable Nail that would hold up under any weight and load. It is good to know that not only did Christ bear the load of our guilt and sin, but that He is ever able to bear the load of our troubles and cares. We can hang it all on Him.

Battle Bow

That Christ is the *Battle Bow* testifies to His being the active champion and warrior for His people. This highlights that aspect of His mediatorial kingship in which He subdues and conquers all of His and our enemies. The Psalmist speaks of the same activity in that great royal and messianic Psalm 45: "Thine arrows are sharp in the heart of the king's enemies; whereby the people fall under thee" (45:5). This kingly behavior is on the surface of the Zechariah text. It is this divinely sent *Battle Bow* that will execute God's anger against the bad shepherds and punish the goats. Certainly, the final manifestation of this warrior King will come when He rides in on that white horse with a sharp sword in His mouth to smite the nations (Revelation 19:12-15). In the meantime, Christ is the able and unfailing Defender of His people.

Absolute Ruler

That Christ is the *Absolute Ruler* testifies to His certain sovereignty. The translation of this last line is notoriously difficult. The word the Authorized Version translates as "oppressor" is the word I am focusing on when I say that Christ is the absolute Ruler. There is no question that the word designates a ruler, and many occurrences of the word in the Old Testament refer to hard taskmasters or slave drivers who would use whatever means they desired to force their subjects into compliance. This explains the translation "oppressor." However, I would suggest that the word itself simply defines one who has ultimate authority over another. The character of the ruler determines whether his rule is cruel and oppressive. The parallelism with the other three expressions demands that this title refer to the same person. Therefore, the Ruler with absolute authority over His subjects is Christ. His rule is not oppressive, but it is absolute nonetheless. This is a most fitting designation of Christ in the immediate context. The people knew well the oppression of the bad shepherds (rulers). What a relief it would be to know the kind despotism of the Messiah King. Submitting to the absolute authority of Christ is always a relief; moreover, it is the wise thing to do. He will rule either by grace or by the rod of iron. The advice of Psalm 2 is appropriate in view of this absolute rule of Christ. "Kiss the Son, lest he be angry, and ye perish from the way, when his wrath is kindled but a little. Blessed are all they that put their trust in him" (Psalm 2:12). If He is the Absolute Ruler, it is best to be a citizen rather than an enemy of His kingdom. That was true then; it is true now.

Having considered the two outstanding texts that use special titles to describe Christ, we now move on to select and reflect on other names that are scattered throughout the Old Testament. Of necessity, this discussion cannot be exhaustive of all the titles. All are important and all contribute to our knowledge about Christ. My only criterion for selecting the titles that follow is that they are some of my favorites. I think that the selected names will suffice to illustrate the kind of expression we are looking for as well as provide me an opportunity to discuss these great names. I will supply at the end of the chapter a summary of other titles that you may study on your own.

Titles Focusing on Christ's Person and Perfections

Although most of the titles of Christ focus on some aspect of His messianic ministry, a few describe Him both in terms of His two natures and in terms of His perfections that mark Him as the sole and sensible object of saving faith. Christ is a unique person: He is the God/Man.

The evidence of this dual nature is overwhelming throughout Scripture, and the truth of it is essential to messianic theology. Many times in the Old Testament the Messiah is expressly identified as God. Psalm 45:6, quoted in Hebrews 1:8 and speaking of Christ, says, "Thy throne, O God, is for ever and ever." That is pretty clear. That He is called the Seed of the woman, the Seed of Abraham, and the Seed of David is equally clear evidence of His real humanity. We certainly want to learn from these explicit statements and factor in that information as we meditate on the theology of Messiah. Each name tends to focus on some particular about this unique person. The significance of some of these titles is transparently obvious; others will require more explanation.

Thou God seest me

I want to start here because this title is frequently overlooked. This is the name assigned to Jehovah by Hagar when she encountered the Angel of the Lord in the wilderness (Genesis 16:3). In the previous chapter, we established the identity of the Angel as a Christophany, a pre-incarnate appearance of Christ. That this is a title for the Messiah is somewhat disguised by the English translation. Although the Authorized Version correctly interprets the expression as a declarative statement, "Thou God seest me," it more literally says, "You are *Elroi*." Amazed by this unexpected meeting with the Lord, Hagar expressed her spiritual perception by calling the Lord "God sees me." Not only did she explicitly call the Angel "God" (*El*), but she also included her personal confession of His omniscience, "sees me" (*roi*). El is a term for deity that highlights divine power and majesty. Omniscience, or infinite knowledge, is one of those unique and unmistakable divine perfections. This title of Christ that declares His deity is a fitting climax to this episode that in other ways identifies the Angel as Jehovah Himself (see the discussion of this text in the preceding chapter).

Immanuel

"With us is God" is the literal meaning of Immanuel. This well-known title occurs in Isaiah 7:14 and 8:8, 10. Whereas the Authorized Version transliterates the term in 7:14 and 8:8, it translates it in 8:10 as "God is with us." This name occurs in the famous virgin birth prophecy. I will deal with the prophetic implications and context of this prophecy in the next chapter. Here I simply want to focus on this remarkable title that links Messiah's real humanity, evidenced by the miraculous birth, to the fact of His essential deity. The name is an explicit declaration of the Incarnation: God was going to be manifest in the flesh. Although the Messiah would bear the name "God with us," the spiritual truth expressed by this name is not unique to the Incarnation. This is part of the beauty of the name. That God is with His people has always been and always will be true, although the manifestations of that divine presence have varied. To understand the full force of this title requires a survey of all the Old Testament data that declares God's presence with His people. That is outside our scope, but it should be easy enough to do. Take a concordance and look up the preposition "with." Observe all the places where the Lord says, "I am (will be) with," or where someone confesses to the Lord, "Thou art with me"; note also direct statements that say the "Lord will be with."

Let me suggest three truths you will learn from that study. First, God's presence is always timely. In periods of crisis, when His people are in jeopardy needing special help or guidance, God assures them of His presence. Second, God's presence is always consistent. His promise is that He will never leave or forsake His people. His presence never fails. Third, God's presence is always comforting. It eliminates fear and anxiety in the crisis times and generates contentment in all the circumstances of life.

This synopsis of "Immanuel" theology must be plugged into this prophecy of the Incarnation. Christ was the visible manifestation of the unchanging truth; He is the climax of "Immanuel" truth. Theologians may argue concerning the mechanics of God's constant, unceasing, comforting presence with Old Testament saints, but they agree that it was a real presence. Today, believers experience "Immanuel" in the abiding presence of the indwelling Holy Spirit. But what a special manifestation of Immanuel there is in the person of Christ: God was manifest in flesh. In Christ, the invisible God became visible; the eternal Word became flesh and dwelt with us (see Colossians 1:15; Hebrews 1:3; John 1:14). The identification of Messiah as "Immanuel" was a fitting word for the crisis that Isaiah was addressing. It is a fitting word for us, too.

Before I leave this text, I want you to see how Isaiah links in this single verse the gospel promises of Genesis 3:15 and 9:27. Remember the first promise was that the Seed of the woman would reverse the curse and the second promise was that God would dwell in the tents of Shem. The virgin bearing a son is the Seed of the woman; Immanuel is God's dwelling in the tents of Shem. What a unity and continuity there is in God's Word. It is exciting to see it all come together.

Branch

This is one of the most significant of messianic titles, occurring in five passages: Isaiah 4:2; Jeremiah 23:5 and 33:15; and Zechariah 3:8 and 6:12. Its import is augmented not only by the imagery suggested by the word itself, but also by the specific contexts that heap up important information about the identity and mission of the Branch. At first consideration, this does not appear to be a particularly flattering expression. This common noun is based on a root verb that means to sprout or bud. It refers to a new shoot that buds on a stump or in unexpected and unwanted places.

Although Ezekiel does not use the word with messianic significance, he illustrates the basic sense of the term in his allegory of the two eagles and the transplanted cedar branches (Ezekiel 17). The verb form occurs at the beginning of verse 6. Not long after the cut-off branch was planted, it "sprouted," showing signs of new life. The noun form occurs in the middle of verse 9, where the Lord asks whether the leaves on this new sprout will wither. There was a sign of new life, but it was so fragile that survival seemed unlikely. For illustrative purposes, let's move from Ezekiel's transplanted cedar to a tree in my front yard that is a nuisance in many ways. One of its ongoing annoyances is the sprouting of fresh green shoots right from the trunk of the tree. I can tolerate them only so long before I find myself impelled to cut them off. This obviously is not a biblical example, but it illustrates what I want you to understand about this word "branch." It is not referring to the large, strong boughs that extend majestically from a well-rooted tree; it refers to something that is tender and fragile yet full of promising life in an unlikely place.

General Significance

This imagery underscores each of the messianic references in two ways. First, that the Messiah is a "Branch" vividly pictures His humiliation. The Messiah would not and did not appear with all the pomp, circumstance, and manifest glory that He deserved and that inherently and eternally was His. On the contrary, He humbled Himself, becoming man and becoming obedient as a humble servant unto the death of the cross (Philippians 2:6-8). There was nothing about Christ that to natural sight would identify Him as the eternal Son of God; He appeared as an ordinary man. Using different words but the same imagery, Isaiah prophesied, "He shall grow up before him as tender plant, and as a root out of a dry ground: he hath no form nor comeliness; and when we shall see him, there is no beauty that we should desire him" (Isaiah 53:2). So many who saw Christ with their natural eyes during the years of His earthly life saw Him as I see those annoying green shoots on my front-yard tree. He was despised and rejected of men (Isaiah 53:3); He came unto His own and they did not receive Him (John 1:11). What condescension it was for God to become manifest in flesh.

Second, that the Messiah is a "Branch" vividly testifies to God's faithful fulfilling of the covenant promise. This title has a special link to the Seed promise that reached its Old Testament climax in the covenant promise to David. Remember that in the Davidic covenant God promised that David's Seed would sit forever on the throne, ruling a universal and everlasting kingdom (II Samuel 7). King after king sat on David's throne, each one disqualified as the ultimate and unconditional fulfillment of the promise. When the Seed finally came, there was no king at all from David's family, and there had not been for hundreds of years. From every natural perspective, it appeared that David's dynasty was defunct and the promise *passé*. But from the stump of David's fallen kingdom, there appeared a new green shoot of life. There was life in the promise; the Ideal King had arrived. Summed up in the title "Branch" is Paul's declaration, "For all the promises of God in him (that is in Christ) are yea, and in him Amen" (II Corinthians 1:20). The title "Branch" discloses the real humanity of Messiah by linking His lineage to David's. As we look briefly at the specific Branch passages, keep in mind that in addition to the particular focus of the text, each reference declares the humble humanity of Christ as the fulfillment of the covenant promise.

The Branch as God

Isaiah 4:2 is the first messianic reference: "In that day shall the branch of the Lord be beautiful and glorious." Although the Authorized Version does not capitalize the word, I believe that it is used here as a title of Messiah. The temporal statement "in that day" that begins the verse marks this as a Day of the Lord. The Day of the Lord designates those special, epochal times when God interrupts the affairs of history to directly accomplish His purpose either in judging the wicked or in blessing the righteous. The Day of the Lord is eternity breaking into time. The Old Testament speaks of many different days, some now past (e.g., the destruction of Edom, Babylon, and Jerusalem; the blessing of Pentecost) and one climactic Day still to come in the eschatological future. I believe that this passage describes something of the millennial blessing of the future day. The essence of the blessing of that day is the beautiful and glorious presence of the Branch of the Lord. The special contribution this text makes to Branch theology is the association between the Branch and Jehovah. We have already considered the interpretation challenge presented by this "X of Y" relationship between words. Remember how we interpreted "the Angel of the Lord": the Angel who is the Lord. We took "Lord" as an appositive to "Angel." I suggest the same apposition relationship here: the Branch who is Jehovah. Given that the humanity of Messiah is declared by the term "branch," and that Jehovah is the unique name of the one true and living God, the full expression "Branch of the Lord" declares the Messiah to be the God/Man. He is one person with two distinct natures. This is singularly true of Christ. Traditionally, interpreters have paralleled Isaiah's affirmation of the deity of the Branch to John's particular emphasis in his Gospel of Christ as the Son of God.

The Branch as King

Jeremiah 23:5 and 33:15 constitute a single context; these texts say virtually the same thing. Like Isaiah, Jeremiah sets this text within the framework of the Day of the Lord, and some of the blessings and benefits to Israel occur in the eschatological future. But the Scripture always in one way or another weds blessings—whether spiritual, historical or eschatological—to Christ. The saving of Judah and safety of Israel that Jeremiah foresees are possible only because of the Branch. Jeremiah, more explicitly than Isaiah or Zechariah, links the Branch title directly to David: "I will raise unto David a righteous Branch" (23:5); "will I cause the Branch of righteousness to grow up unto David" (33:15). Two features about the Branch stand out in Jeremiah's description: The Branch will be righteous, and the Branch will be King. His kingship is expected as the natural descendant (Seed) of David. His righteousness marks Him as the fulfillment of the Ideal Kingship promised to appear in the tribe of Judah and perpetuate in the family of David. David himself understood this. In his last words, the sweet Psalmist repeated God's word to him: "He that ruleth over men must be just (i.e. 'righteous'), ruling in the fear of God." He then confessed, "Although my house be not so with God; yet he hath made me an everlasting covenant, ordered in all things, and sure: for this is all my salvation, and all my desire, although he make it not to grow" (II Samuel 23:3, 5). The delay in the coming of that King did not dissuade David from seeing in Him the fulfillment of God's requirements for Kingship and God's promise of that King who would be both the salvation and the desire of His people. What David anticipated, Jeremiah in this context describes. Traditionally, interpreters have paralleled Jeremiah's Branch to Matthew's presentation of Christ as King.

To understand the full beauty of the text, we have to know what righteousness means. I am going to use a couple of words that may be unfamiliar, but stay with me: I will define what I mean. The concept of righteousness can be either stative or fientive. *Stative* refers to a condition of existence; *fientive* refers to activity. In other words, righteousness refers either to what someone is or to what someone does. The essential idea of righteousness is straightness or conformity to a standard. It is an absolute term. There is no such thing as "almost righteous." The slightest deviation from the standard renders someone unrighteous. Further, what the standard is determines the significance of righteousness. Although the righteousness of Christ extends to every single aspect and element of God's perfect law, in this context the standard is the requirements of God for the King. Jeremiah draws particular attention to the active sense of the word; the Branch always does the right thing ("He does justice and righteousness in the earth"). The Branch actively behaves according to the demands of God, accomplishing everything God has promised and purposed in the Davidic covenant. He is the Ideal messianic King. No other son of

David ever came close or ever could come close to doing everything demanded by the law of God. Remember that when we see statements that transcend mere human application, we may discern a messianic clue.

Jeremiah removed all doubt concerning the identity of the Branch when he said, "This is his name whereby he shall be called, THE LORD OUR RIGHTEOUSNESS" (23:6). It is little wonder that the translators capitalized that whole title. What a name! I can only be suggestive here, but I want you to think about two great truths in this name. First, the Branch is Jehovah, an explicit declaration of His deity. Second, the Branch is the justification of His people. Encapsulated in this statement is the doctrine of justification. The stative sense of righteousness is in view here: God regards us to be in a state or condition of perfect conformity to His standard not on the basis of our acts, but on the basis of Christ's acts. Christ's acts of righteousness result in our state of righteousness. Jeremiah's subtle variation of the statement in 33:16 suggests this: "This is the name wherewith she shall be called, The LORD our righteousness." Notice that the word "name" is italicized in the Authorized Version, and it says "she" instead of "he." The "she" refers to the nation of Israel which in that future day will be gloriously saved. What the text says about her is true for believers in every age. Whereas Jeremiah named the Branch in chapter 23, in chapter 33 he declared that name as having reference to and benefit for His people. The literal translation is "and this will be called for her—The Lord our righteousness." Rather than being the name of the future people, it is the message of the gospel that will be preached to them whereby they will be saved. That Christ is our righteousness is the everlasting gospel. How much Jeremiah declared in that name!

The Branch as Servant

Zechariah 3:8 identifies the Branch as the servant of the Lord. Traditionally, interpreters have paralleled Zechariah's naming of the Branch as servant with Mark's presentation of Christ as the Servant of the Lord. The significance of the title "servant" is itself far-reaching, warranting its own discussion (it's one of my favorite topics). But for now, let's focus on how Zechariah uses the title "Branch." It is important to note that Zechariah did not employ the title without factoring in all the preceding revelation. We must keep this in mind when we interpret what Zechariah says. It is also a good example for us to follow when doing our Bible study: we must factor in what God has already said about a matter when considering the topic in the context being studied. By Zechariah's time (6th century BC), the "Branch" was part of official and inspired messianic vocabulary. No doubt Zechariah knew well the prophecies of Isaiah (8th century BC) and Jeremiah (7th-6th centuries BC). He knew that the Branch was the God/Man who is the ground of the justification of all believers. It is particularly Jeremiah's special name of the Branch as "the Lord our Righteousness" that Zechariah builds upon in this text. I regard Zechariah's vision in this chapter to be one of the most vivid pictures anywhere of God's gracious act of justifying sinners.

Four things stand out in this text. *First is the need for justification.* The passage begins with a judicial scene in which Joshua, the high priest, is standing before the Angel of the Lord and is being accused by Satan. As the high priest he is serving as man's representative, an accurate picture of how every man on his own stands before God. He stands silently, dressed in detestably filthy garments with no self-defense before the Judge. This scene vividly and graphically pictures how man appears before God in all the filthy rags of his own righteousness. Because of unrighteousness, all men are guilty before the just God.

Second is the act of justification. Seemingly out of the blue God rebukes Satan and rescues Joshua as a brand plucked from the burning. Joshua was accepted before the Lord and allowed to stand in His presence. The text highlights two essential elements of that acceptance. (1) The Lord graciously pardoned sin. This is pictured by the removal of the filthy garments and explained directly: "I have caused thine iniquity to pass from thee" (3:4). The guilt and, therefore, the liability for punishment and penalty were removed. (2) The Lord provided righteousness. Not only were the filthy garments removed, but they were replaced with costly and glorious clothes. This represents that robe of righteousness, the garment of salvation, that renders the wearer presentable before the Lord. In justification, God both pardons sin and imputes the righteousness of Christ.

Third is the grounds of justification. God's pardoning sinners is gracious, but it is not capricious. This brings us to the Branch. It is the Lord's sending the Branch that would be the meritorious grounds by which He justifies sinners. That the Branch is called the servant, charged with all Isaiah's theology, speaks of His humble obedience both in life and to death. I would suggest the reference to iniquity's being removed in one day (3:9) points to His cross, the only place where iniquity was effectively removed.

Fourth is the demand of justification. Zechariah makes it clear that a change in legal standing demands a change in moral behavior. Justification always issues in sanctification; position always effects experience. Grace never leaves a man where it finds him. Those justified are to persevere in godliness by walking in God's ways, keeping His charge, and maintaining justice (3:7). Those justified are to be like Christ; they are to imitate and represent Him. Zechariah described Joshua and his fellows as "men wondered at" (3:8). Literally, they were "men of a sign," men who were to be types of something else; they were to signify the Branch. These implications of justification would make a pretty good sermon!

The Branch as Man

Zechariah 6:12 is the last reference to the messianic Branch: "Behold the man whose name is The BRANCH." Traditionally, interpreters have paralleled Zechariah's identification of the Branch as man with Luke's presentation of Christ as the Son of Man. The particular focus of this text is the uniting of the offices of priest and king in the person of the Branch. Remember the important dichotomy between these two mediatorial offices. We have already established as an inviolable messianic clue that whenever these two offices are united in a single person, it must be referring to Christ. As an object lesson of the coming Priest/King, Joshua the high priest is crowned with a splendid royal crown (6:11). That visible picture prophecy of a priest wearing a crown led to the declaration that the man named Branch would come, build the temple of the Lord, and "sit and rule upon his throne; and he shall be a priest upon this throne" (6:12-13). The significance is obvious. Inherent in the term "Branch" is the identification with the royal line of David. That the Branch is identified as man helps establish the priestly connection with Joshua because a priest had to be one of those he represented. Humanity is an essential qualification for messianic priesthood. The evidence is overwhelming in this context: the Branch is the Ideal Messiah.

One More

Although translating a different Hebrew word from the one we have been considering, the Authorized Version uses the word "Branch" one other time to designate the Messiah. Although it is a different word, the imagery and theology are the same. In fact, the text contains several words that suggest the Messiah's unpretentious lineage to the line of David. Isaiah 11:1 says, "And there shall come forth a rod out of the stem of Jesse, and a Branch shall grow out of his roots." The word translated "rod" designates either a switch or a shoot, neither of which would seem to have much substance. Since the word "stem" is actually the stump of a tree, the rod most likely pictures that new sprout that shoots from what is left of the tree. Similarly, the "branch" is just a tender shoot that springs forth from the rootstock. Both lines of this text emphasize the humanity and humble origin of the Messiah. Bypassing the connection to royal David by linking the Branch to pre-royal Jesse intensifies the lowly, unassuming, unobtrusive life of the messianic descendant.

Matthew plays on both the significance and the sound of this word "Branch" in his explanation of Christ's dwelling in Nazareth (Matthew 2:23). That Nazareth was regarded as the "boondocks" of Israel is suggested by Nathaniel's telling question to Philip when he was introduced to Jesus of Nazareth: "Can there any good thing come out of Nazareth?" (John 1:46). Apparently no one of any reputation would ever live in Nazareth; it was a village without honor. Consequently, Matthew said Jesus's living there fulfilled the prophecy, "He shall be called a Nazarene." You will look a long time to find any prophecy in the Old Testament that identifies Nazareth as the home of Messiah. In fact, the Old Testament makes no reference to Nazareth at all. However, the word "Branch" in Isaiah 11:1 is netser. With theological and linguistic insight, Matthew puns, playing on the sound of words. (The more narrow, technical word for this device is "paronomasia," but we'll just call it a pun.) Nazareth was an insignificant, unlikely place for the Messiah; the netser was an insignificant sprout growing on a stump, an unlikely place. Matthew saw in Christ's living in Nazareth a fulfillment of the prophet's description of the Messiah's humiliation in terms of the Branch. Translating rather than transliterating the word in Matthew 2:23 would transmit this idea. Christ dwelt in Nazareth "that it might be fulfilled which was spoken by the prophets, He shall be called a Branch." Matthew certainly knew the significance of names.

Wisdom

 This title occurs in the book of Proverbs and highlights one of the essential divine perfections that characterize the person of Christ. Remember that God is a spirit, infinite, eternal, and unchangeable in His being, wisdom, holiness, justice, goodness and truth. Wisdom is one of the communicable attributes, but it is nonetheless an essential attribute of God. That Proverbs calls the Messiah "Wisdom" is not much different from Isaiah's calling God "the Holy One of Israel." Both titles use one of the Lord's perfections to designate Him. Not all agree, however, that Wisdom is a messianic title; therefore, I must provide some explanation and defense of my interpretation.

The Meaning of Wisdom

 Essential to understanding the significance of this title is an understanding of the meaning of the word "wisdom." The word simply refers to skill or ability. The sphere of application of that skill or ability is defined by the context in which the word occurs. For instance, God called Bezaleel to be the foreman in the construction of the Tabernacle, filling him with His Spirit and thereby giving him the necessary wisdom or skill to do the work (Exodus 31:3). Similarly, Solomon hired Hiram as his chief craftsman because "he was filled with wisdom, and understanding, and cunning to work all works in brass" (I Kings 7:14). Joseph instructed Pharaoh to look for a wise man who had the necessary administrative skills to govern; he chose Joseph (Genesis 41:33). The point is simply that whatever someone was good at was considered his wisdom. So when Jeremiah said that Israel was "wise to do evil" (Jeremiah 4:22), he claimed that they were skillful at sinning–that they were really good at it. Wisdom, as a divine perfection, highlights God's infinite ability to do whatever is appropriate for God to do. It is obviously related to His infinite knowledge, omniscience, in that He knows all things. In His infinite wisdom, God uses the best possible means to achieve the best possible ends; He is all-wise. To put it plainly but reverently, God is good at everything He does.

Essential to understanding how Solomon uses "Wisdom" as a messianic title is a knowledge of how wisdom functions in the book of Proverbs. Proverbs defines wisdom in terms of morality and ethical behavior. In Proverbs, wisdom is the skill of behaving properly according to the will of God; it is the ability to do those things that are pleasing to the Lord. It is safe to say that in Proverbs a wise man is a saved man because only believers have any heart or any ability to do those things that are pleasing to God. Proverbs is a thorough "how to" book in explaining how to apply religion to every sphere of life. Proverbs teaches that there is no part of life unaffected by one's relationship with God. Although most of the uses of "wisdom" in Proverbs define the proper conduct for believers, in three chapters Wisdom appears as a person rather than an experience: Proverbs 1, 8, and 9. This brings us to the interpretation problem: whether or not this person Wisdom is Christ. Some contend that it is a personification of the divine attribute. Personification is a literary devise whereby something abstract or impersonal is described in personal terms. Others, myself included, interpret this not as a literary device but as a designation of the Second Person of the Trinity, the Son of God. I want to take you through some of the reasons for my interpretation in order to show you Solomon's gospel logic and theology in Proverbs and to illustrate how to employ some of our messianic clues in finding Christ in the Old Testament revelation. Before going any further, let me take care of the surface problem of Wisdom's representation in the feminine gender. This is a grammatical, not a theological, issue. The word "wisdom" in Hebrew is a feminine word, as abstract words tend to be. Consequently, any pronouns associated with the word are going to be feminine as well. That the Authorized Version translates all these pronouns as feminine is grammatically correct and does not militate against the messianic interpretation, nor does it suggest any feminine characteristics about the Messiah. I tell my students often that grammar and reality have little to do with each other.

Remember that part of finding Christ in the Old Testament is knowing what we are looking for. When we use our check list of who Christ is, what He does, and what He is like to ascertain what Wisdom stands for, we find ample support for interpreting this title as a reference to

Christ. In addition, the analogy of Scripture (comparing Scripture with Scripture) justifies our seeing Christ in this title. Other passages in the Old Testament that are indisputably messianic say about Christ what Solomon says about Wisdom. In addition, New Testament evidence sanctions the identification of Wisdom with Christ. Consider these New Testament texts that identify Christ as Wisdom: Matthew 11:19, 25-30; Matthew 23:34; Luke 11:49; I Corinthians 1:24, 30; and Colossians 2:3. Three strands of evidence in Proverbs 8 point to Wisdom as a title of Christ.

Wisdom as God

First is the fact that Wisdom although distinct from God, yet possesses divine perfections and performs divine operations. For instance, in verses 27-30 Wisdom speaks of God in the third person. Read these verses and note the contrast between "he" and "I." It is clear that a distinction exists. Yet there are statements that demand that Wisdom be God. At least ten statements in the chapter suggest that Wisdom existed prior to creation (verses 22-30). To be prior to creation is to be prior to time and therefore eternal. Eternity is one of those incommunicable perfections of Deity. Three verbs, however, seem to suggest a beginning to Wisdom's existence. Before rejecting the messianic interpretation on the basis of these statements, note that whether Wisdom is here the Messiah or just the personification of a divine attribute, it is theologically impossible to say either had a beginning. All the perfections of God, including wisdom, are infinite, eternal, and immutable. Certainly, if the term designates the Son of God, He is co-eternal with the Father and the Holy Spirit. Let me give a brief explanation of the problem words.

The first problem is verse 22: "The Lord possessed me in the beginning of his way." The word translated "possess" is the difficulty. The Hebrew root word is *qanah*. There is a question whether it is a general word that is used in a wide range of contexts or whether there are two different words, homonyms, which the interpreter must choose between. Remember that homonyms are words that sound the same but have different meanings. The general word *qanah* has the idea of possessing something, regardless of the means of or reason for the possession (get, acquire, purchase, etc.). The other root (spelled the same) means to create. It is beyond our scope at this point to do a

186

thorough word study or to enter into the argument as to whether two different roots even exist. Personally, I am not particularly convinced that the root "create" occurs in the Hebrew Scripture. In all the texts where the supposed root occurs, the more general term fits equally well. In other words, no context in which this word occurs demands the meaning "create."(If you are interested, the standard references for the word "create" are Genesis 14:19, 22; Exodus 15:16; Deuteronomy 32:6; Psalm 78:54; and Psalm139:13. The Authorized Version translates the word as "possess," "purchase," or "buy," all of which make perfectly good sense in the respective contexts). I believe the translation of the Authorized Version conveys the proper idea. The word emphasizes a relationship of some sort between the subject and object; "possess" conveys something of that relationship idea. Admittedly vague in this statement, Wisdom simply declares that that there has been an eternal relationship between Him and God.

The historic problem with Proverbs 8:22 really comes from the Septuagint, the old Greek translation of the Hebrew Bible. This version dates from between 250-150 BC; it was the principal version of both New Testament times and the early church. It translated the word "possess" as "create." Your guess is as good as anyone's whether this represents the ancient translator's knowledge of a root meaning "create" or whether it reflects a mistake in either interpretation or translation. My guess is that it is a mistake. What is interesting is that the early church recognized Proverbs 8 to have messianic reference. In one of the early theological controversies attempting to "define" Christ, the Arians appealed to this verse as evidence that Christ was not eternal and therefore not God. They based their argument on a mistranslation. The Arians were rightly condemned as heretics.

The second problem is verse 23: "I was set up from everlasting." On the surface, this sounds again like wisdom's confession of an inception of its being. However, a proper definition of the word "set up" strengthens the messianic interpretation. The verb literally means "to pour out" and has the idea of being consecrated, exalted, or anointed. It is the same word that occurs in the undeniably messianic Psalm 2 when the Lord declares, "Yet have I set my king upon my holy hill of Zion" (verse 6). I would suggest that Wisdom's being poured out from eternity refers to that "time" in eternity when the eternal Son of God was chosen to be the Mediator (cf. Isaiah 42:1). Wisdom was ordained to be the Messiah. It is interesting that in Isaiah 42:1 the Lord declares concerning the chosen Servant that He is the one "in whom my soul delighteth." Compare that with verse 30 of this passage when Wisdom declares, "I was daily his delight." The analogy of Scripture points to Wisdom as Christ.

The third problem concerns the statement in verses 24 and 25: "I was brought forth." Since this word describes the giving of birth, it, too, suggests the beginning of existence. However, that this word typically refers to the mother's role in giving birth prohibits this from being a literal statement of birth. It would be ludicrous, indeed blasphemous, to attribute to the Heavenly Father such activity, regardless of the object of the birth. Part of the interpretive process is ruling out what a text cannot mean when seeking to determine what it does means. This cannot mean that Wisdom was literally born of God. Rather than focusing on the *inception* or establishing of a parent/child relationship, the word stresses the *existence* of such a relationship. Wisdom says that before anything was created, He existed in an eternal relationship with God as parent and child, theologically and specifically as Father and Son. Some, perhaps, will accuse me of saying too much here, so I will not be dogmatic. But I believe we see in this statement at least a hint of the eternal Sonship of the Second Person of the Trinity. These problem verses are not really problems at all but rather further confirmations of Wisdom's identity as the Christ of God.

We have been necessarily digressing, but let me at this point return to the second part of the first strand of evidence. Not only does Wisdom possess a divine perfection (eternity), but He also performs uniquely divine works. Specifically, Wisdom creates. Remember that one of our search criteria is that we can tell who someone is by what he does. We have already established creation to be something only God does. Therefore, if someone creates, He is God. Verse 30 is a key text. Let me give a more literal rendering of the Hebrew text: "And I was beside Him, an Artisan." This is the climax of a series of verses that detail aspects of creation. In verse 27 Wisdom said simply, "When he prepared the heavens, I was there." Verse 30 suggests that it was not a passive presence; He was a craftsman participating in the whole creative process. There was a joint participation in creation between Wisdom and the Lord. Theologically, we know that creation is the work of the Godhead. Now it all fits together. The parallel between

Wisdom's presence with God and Wisdom's participating in creation and the Word's presence with God and the Word's participating in creation is too close to ignore or regard as coincidental. John opens his Gospel with the explicitly clear statement, "In the beginning was the Word, and the Word was with God, and the Word was God ... all things were made by him; and without him was not any thing made that was made" (John 1:1, 3). It seems that the only difference between Solomon and John is that Solomon uses the word "Wisdom" and John uses the word "Word." If we can understand John as declaring the deity of Christ, the Word of God, it would seem that we ought to be able to understand Solomon as declaring the deity of Christ, the Wisdom of God.

Wisdom as Messiah

The second strand of evidence for identifying Wisdom as a messianic title is the fact that messianic descriptions and operations are assigned to Wisdom. In other words, what is said about Messiah in other contexts is said about Wisdom in Proverbs 8. This is particularly true in verses 1-21. If Wisdom performs messianic activity, we have good reason to identify Wisdom as Messiah. One of the mediatorial operations of the Messiah is the execution of the office of prophet. As Prophet, He represents God to man and reveals God's word and will to man. Proverbs 8 begins with Wisdom's preaching. The words of Wisdom are described as excellent, right, true, righteous, without perverseness, and plain to him who understands (verses 6-8). That sounds like prophetic activity. Kingship is another function of the messianic office. Wisdom expresses absolute authority over lesser sovereigns: "By me princes rule, and nobles, even all the judges of the earth" (verse 16). The credentials attributed to Wisdom correspond remarkably to the credentials of the Messiah. Compare Wisdom's claim to have wisdom, counsel, understanding, knowledge, and strength (verses 12-14) with Isaiah's description of the messianic Branch's having "the spirit of wisdom and understanding, the spirit of counsel and might, the spirit of knowledge and of the fear of the Lord" (Isaiah 11:2). It follows that if these are descriptions of Messiah in Isaiah, they could be describing the same Messiah in Proverbs.

Wisdom as the Object of Faith

The third strand of evidence is the fact that man's eternal destiny is linked to his relationship with Wisdom. Proverbs 8 ends with Wisdom's admonition: "Whoso findeth me findeth life, and shall obtain favour of the Lord. But he that sinneth against me wrongeth his own soul: all they that hate me love death" (verses 35-36). This sounds similar to John's declaration: "He that hath the Son hath life; and he that hath not the Son of God hath not life" (I John 5:12). The invitation of Wisdom in Proverbs 1 makes the same promise: "Whoso hearkeneth unto me shall dwell safely, and shall be quiet from fear of evil" (verse 33). Throughout Proverbs 8 it is clear that those who love and choose Wisdom share in His riches and receive the benefits of salvation (particularly look at verses 17-21). Just as Christ promised that He would not cast out any who came to Him, so Wisdom declares, "I love them that love me," and promises, "Those that seek me early shall find me" (compare John 6:37 with Proverbs 8:17). "Seeking early" means to seek diligently; it is an exercise of faith. Saving faith always and only has Christ as its object.

That this book of practical wisdom begins with an invitation to believe Wisdom is good gospel preaching. There is no way a man can do anything that is pleasing to God (the practice of wisdom) without first having a saving relationship to Christ who pleased God in every way (the Person of Wisdom). Theologically, sanctification follows regeneration and justification. That is the order of Proverbs. In this way, Solomon's theology sounds Pauline. Paul said, "But of him are ye in Christ Jesus, who of God is made unto us wisdom, and righteousness, and sanctification, and redemption" (I Corinthians 1:30). It is only in union with Christ, who is Wisdom, that all the benefits of salvation flow. Perhaps we could say that Paul's theology was Solomonic. Better yet, let's just admit that they were preaching the same Christ and the same gospel. We have learned a lot from this name.

Son of Man

Only once does the Old Testament call the Messiah the Son of Man: Daniel 7:13. Daniel sets the theological foundation for this title, stamping it with messianic weight. The title is not difficult to understand, but it deserves attention because it became the favorite self-designation of Christ during the years of His earthly ministry. The

Lord commonly referred to Himself as the Son of Man, thereby announcing Himself as the Messiah and claiming for Himself the implications of the title. We need to do two things here: establish the messianic identity and define the implications of the expression. It occurs in the Aramaic section of Daniel that records his vision of the world empires, represented by the odd-appearing beasts. All the kingdoms of earth will be dissolved when "one like the Son of man" comes in the clouds of heaven. Daniel's using this designation to describe the One to whom God would give an everlasting and universal kingdom identified the Son of Man with the Son of David. By Daniel's time the theme of an everlasting and universal kingdom was a well-established and eagerly anticipated element of messianic theology and hope. At the time of this vision (during the first year of Belshazzar's administration, the eve of Babylon's fall), there was no Son of David sitting on a throne. Worldly kingdoms ruled and more were coming, each more "worldly" than the preceding. It appeared that the promise to David of an everlasting, universal kingdom, although anticipated by the faithful, was in serious trouble. But the promise was not in trouble; a King was coming who would utterly conquer the most nefarious and powerful of the worldly powers (the kingdom of the Anti-Christ) and receive a kingdom like none other.

The point to recognize here is that previously revealed and defined messianic theology is now associated with a new title for the Messiah, the Son of Man. The Davidic Covenant is not specifically mentioned in this context, but it is nonetheless an essential part of the theological context that must be factored into the interpretation. Even though the Scripture has never called Messiah the Son of Man before, we know the Son of Man is Messiah because what we know about Messiah is true about the Son of Man. I don't want to be stating the obvious, but I want you to see how we are using one of our clues in finding Christ in the Old Testament. Remember that we can identify a person by what he does. Here is one who will rule eternally and universally. Only Christ will do that; therefore, this must be Christ. Easy!

Now that we know this is a messianic title, our concern is to learn what "the Son of Man" reveals about the Messiah. Obviously, this title highlights the real humanity of Christ. The Aramaic word for "man" refers not to a specific male, but to mankind, humanity. English uses the word "man" the same way; it can designate the entire human race, both genders. The word "son" in Aramaic and in Hebrew does not always refer specifically to a male offspring. It frequently designates a class or category of something. For instance, the "sons of the prophets" associated with Elijah and Elisha were not "preachers' kids" who were in a summer camp learning how to be prophets like their fathers. This was a group of men that belonged to the class of prophets; they were part of the prophetic order. Simply, the sons of the prophets were prophets. Job's reference to "the sons of God" who appeared before the Lord to give an account of their activity obviously does not designate God's offspring (Job 1:6). It refers to angels, who were in the class of supernatural beings. Messiah's being the Son of Man means, therefore, that He is in the class of humanity; He is human. It is important to see, then, that this title in no way suggests that Jesus was the offspring of a human father. Rather, it describes Him as being a real man, an essential truth about the Messiah. As He is God, so is He man. Given the significance of the title, it is not surprising that it was our Lord's favorite self-designation, seeing that He was not ashamed to call us His brethren (Hebrews 2:11).

Titles Focusing on Christ's Work

The Old Testament is filled with titles that underscore some aspect of the Messiah's mediatorial work. Sometimes the terms of mediation are directly used in pointing to the Ideal Anointed One. Moses said, "The Lord thy God will raise up unto thee a Prophet" (Deuteronomy 18:15). Samuel recorded the Lord's words, "I will raise me up a faithful priest" (I Samuel 2:35). Zechariah echoed other prophets when he declared, "Thy King cometh" (Zechariah 9:9). Each of these refers directly and ultimately to the Lord Jesus Christ as the Prophet, Priest, and King, the only Mediator between God and men. In this section, I will identify and explain some of the more specific and descriptive titles. Again, I cannot be exhaustive and will be arbitrarily selective. But I think this will illustrate the kind of thing to look for.

Shiloh

Jacob's deathbed prophecies about his sons included a messianic announcement. Part of his word to Judah was, "The sceptre shall not depart from Judah, nor a lawgiver from between his feet, until Shiloh come; and unto him shall the gathering of the people be" (Genesis 49:10). We have already considered the advance this prediction made to the continuation of the Abrahamic covenant, further identifying the Seed of promise and anticipating the more specific promise to David. Here we want to focus specifically on the word "Shiloh." The scepter refers to the kingship that will continue in the tribe of Judah until the coming of one called "Shiloh." Note that "until" does not suggest that kingship will cease in Judah when Shiloh comes, but rather emphasizes the absolute certainly that the promised king will come into Judah. God will not allow the promise to fail; the king will come. The word that the Authorized Version transliterates as "Shiloh" seems to be a combination of three distinct parts (*morphemes*, if you want the technical word). The *sh* is a short form of a particle often translated as a relative pronoun, "who or which." The *l* is a preposition meaning "to." The *oh* is a personal pronoun meaning "him." If we put it all together, we could translate the expression: "which is to him," or "to whom it belongs." It refers to the one to whom this kingship really belongs, the rightful king. That rightful king, of course, is the Lord Jesus, "the Lion of the tribe of Juda" (Revelation 5:5).

Although this is only time the form occurs in the Old Testament, it is not the only time the significance of "Shiloh" occurs. Well over a thousand years after Jacob's prophecy, the prophet Ezekiel showed that "Shiloh" theology was still alive. The prophet announced God's judgment on the house of Judah, claiming that He was going to "remove the diadem, and take off the crown" (Ezekiel 21:26; verse 31 in the Hebrew Bible). To emphasize that dethronement the Lord forcefully declared, "I will overturn, overturn, overturn, it: and it shall be no more, until he come whose right it is; and I will give it him (21:27; verse 32 in the Hebrew Bible). Although Ezekiel does not use the specific form "Shiloh," the meaning of this statement is equivalent. Rather than using the short form of the relative particle, he uses the long form, followed by the same preposition and a variant form of the same pronoun ('*∂sher lo*). What the Authorized Version translates "whose right it is" corresponds exactly to the meaning of "Shiloh." History certainly bears witness to the truth of Ezekiel's prophecy. The Babylonian judgment removed Israel's king and the throne was vacant until Christ came, the Rightful King who will reign forever.

Star and Scepter

Balaam said, "I shall see him, but not now: I shall behold him, but not nigh: there shall come a Star out of Jacob, and a Sceptre shall rise out of Israel, and shall smite the corners of Moab, and destroy all the children of Sheth. And Edom shall be a possession ... Out of Jacob shall come he that shall have dominion..." (Numbers 24:17-19). A remarkable thing about these two titles is that God put them in the mouth of Balaam, the prophet for hire, but it is not our purpose here to consider the issue of God's using a wicked charlatan to proclaim His Word. Notice instead how the episode testifies to God's faithful promise to Abraham that those who blessed His people would be blessed and those who cursed them would be cursed (Genesis 12:3). It is not without significance that that specific promise to Abraham was followed immediately by the promise that all the families of the earth would find blessing in Abraham and his Seed. We have already seen how that promise of universal blessing is centered and fulfilled in the Lord Jesus Christ. Therefore, at least in part, the protection of Israel from Balaam's efforts to curse was God's guaranteeing the safe and sure arrival of the Messiah.

There is much more to the Balaam story than just God's enabling a donkey to talk; the whole narrative is ultimately messianic. Nothing and no one could hinder God's unconditional promise to send Christ. Almost comically, every time Balaam opened his mouth to deliver his "prepared sermon," God overruled his tongue and changed his message.

The messianic theme surfaces in Numbers 24 when God forced Balaam to see the Star and Scepter. The similarity to Jacob's Shiloh is obvious: a King will come out of Israel to be a universal ruler. Whereas "Shiloh" emphasized the legitimacy of the kingship (the rightful king), the "Star and Scepter" titles stress the glory and authority of the coming King. As a star is bright and brilliant, so will be the glory and majesty of the coming King. The exalted Christ Himself used this imagery in association with His Davidic royalty: "I am the root and the offspring of David, and the bright and morning star" (Revelation 22:16). The scepter is the sign of royal authority and by metonymy represents the King who wields that sovereign authority. Balaam is not as specific as Jacob that the coming King will come from Judah, but he adds some details to Jacob's closing statement about Shiloh: "unto him shall the gathering of the people be." The word translated "gathering" connotes the idea of obedience or submission. It suggests the irresistibility of Shiloh's authority. Significantly, Balaam predicts that that irresistible authority will extend beyond Israel: Moab and Edom will become His possession, one way or another. It is outside our scope here to develop the fulfillment of that prophecy (see for instance Amos 9:12), but note at least what we have observed before. The promise of Messiah was not in the Old Testament limited to Israel. He is the Christ for the world, and either by grace or by the rod of iron He will bring all into submission.

Redeemer

Redeeming sinners is the sum and substance of the Messiah's work, and appropriately "Redeemer" is one of His important titles. The Old Testament uses a couple of different words to refer to God's redeeming His people, neither of which is limited to God's activity in "salvation" redemption. One of the words (*padah*) often focuses directly on the Lord's rescuing and delivering His people. It is the word David used when he praised the Lord after receiving the covenant promise: "What one nation in the earth is like thy people, even like Israel, whom God went to redeem for a people to himself ...thy people, which thou redeemest to thee from Egypt..." (II Samuel 7:23). The other word (*ga'al*) is what we want to define here; it is the root on which this title of Messiah is formed. In fact, the title "Redeemer" is just a participle of the verb. I have tried to avoid throwing around a lot of Hebrew words, but I think you may be familiar with this one. Though not transliterated precisely, I will use the word *Goel* to refer to this title.

The *Goel* is like the term "Messiah" itself in that it does not refer uniquely to the Lord Jesus. As there were lesser messiahs that pointed to the greater Messiah, so were there lesser *goels* that pointed to the Ideal. Understanding the word generally will help us understand its specific application to Christ. This is the word that frequently specifies the "kinsman redeemer," and that is good because it highlights the distinctive and specifying component in this word's meaning. This word assumes a relationship between the redeemer and the redeemed. The word assumes that the *goel* will perform the appropriate action to alleviate the need of those with whom he has a relationship. In fact, the *goel* is under obligation because of the relationship to do whatever is necessary to do. It is the *goel* that the Authorized Version translates as the "avenger" of blood (e.g., Joshua 20:9), whose obligation it was to execute the death penalty on one who had murdered a relative. Boaz, as the "near kinsman" (goel), did what was necessary to purchase property in behalf of Naomi and even went beyond the call of duty in marrying Ruth. The point is that whether paying a debt, freeing from slavery, reclaiming property for the family inheritance, or avenging a death, the *goel* did whatever was necessary to meet the need of his relatives.

All of this reaches its zenith when applied to the Messiah. Christ is for His people the Ideal *Goel*; He never fails to fulfill His obligation—we may say covenant duty—in behalf of those with whom He is related by virtue of that covenant. This is the information that you need to plug into those texts that refer to God as the Redeemer. I would suggest that the implications of *goel* are relevant in those texts that apply the term generally to God, and that even in those general statements the specific reference may be to the Messiah as the Agent of the Godhead who performs the necessary acts. So when David desires that the meditation of his heart be acceptable in the sight of the Lord, his Strength and Redeemer, we are warranted in seeing Christ (Psalm 19:14). He is certainly not excluded. Other passages are more explicitly messianic. When Isaiah declares that "the Redeemer shall come to Zion," the reference is uniquely to Christ (Isaiah 59:20). Paul verifies that when he uses this verse in Romans 11:26-27 in referring to Israel's future acceptance of Christ. Isaiah 59 describes the heinous sins that separate man from God. What man needs is someone to take care of the sin problem. In answer to man's desperate need comes the *Goel*, who is the means by which men turn from transgressions. It is interesting that Paul, with his inspired theological insight, links the Deliverer's turning away ungodliness to the covenant promise to take away sin. The apostle shows how it all fits together. Man needs to be delivered from sin; Christ delivers from sin; He does so on the basis of a covenant relationship. That is *Goel* work.

One final text will illustrate the beauty of this title of Christ. In the throes of his immense suffering, Job declared, "I know that my redeemer liveth" (Job 19:25). In addition to the physical and emotional torment that Job experienced, he endured the pain of a tarnished testimony and reputation. His friends assumed that he was guilty of sin and so accused him over and over again. Job himself had no clue as to why all of this misfortune had fallen his way. Although Job often and understandably despaired in his situation, he had faith that somehow, some way, some time vindication would come. In this high-water expression of that faith, he confesses that even if the vindication would not come until after his death, it would certainly come. His confidence was founded on his Goel, with whom he had a relationship and who was obligated to come to his defense. That Job knew this coming Redeemer was Christ is suggested by his earlier confession that his Witness was in heaven (Job 16:19). Although Job does not call this Advocate the Messiah, what Job expected that Advocate to do is exactly what Christ does for His people. Vindication is what Job needed; vindication is what his Goel would give him. The point I want us to see from this is that Christ's being our Kinsman Redeemer is not limited to His redeeming us from sin. That is a wonderful part of it, but that He is our Redeemer means that He will always without fail be there for us. He does not save us to leave us. Whatever our need or crisis, the fact that we have a saving and personal relationship with Jesus Christ guarantees that He will meet our every need. "Redeemer" is a great name for our Savior.

Shepherd

In one of the great gospel texts of the Old Testament, the Lord declared that He would raise up a shepherd to save His people: "And I will set up one shepherd over them, and he shall feed them, even my servant David; he shall feed them, and he shall be their shepherd. And I the Lord will be their God, and my servant David a prince among them; I the Lord have spoken it" (Ezekiel 34:23-24). The messianic significance of this title occurs as early as Genesis 49:24. The "shepherd, the stone of Israel" would come from the mighty God of Jacob. The use of the title "Shepherd" was common in the ancient world, and its meaning would have been understood well. Based on the obvious pastoral imagery, the appellative was frequently employed even by pagan kings throughout the ancient Near East to designate their authoritative rule. The title designates sovereign kingship. It is clear that God's condemnation of the bad shepherds at the beginning of Ezekiel 34 is a condemnation of the nation's rulers. Zechariah uses the term in the same way when he announces God's anger against the shepherds

(Zechariah 10:3; see also 11:3). In contrast, God would appoint a Sovereign Ruler who would in every way manifest the beneficent leadership suggested by the title. That we are to understand the royal sovereignty of the Ideal Shepherd is clear from the association of the term with the other titles used: "my servant," "David," and "prince."

I will discuss "servant" in the next section, but let me briefly define the significance of the other two titles. "David" is used in an ideal sense of the greater than David who is the ultimate fulfillment of the Davidic Covenant. This in no way refers to a resurrected or reincarnated David who will again rule. Jeremiah and Hosea also used the name as a messianic title. Both prophets connect the title "David" to the Lord Himself. Jeremiah says the time will come when the people will "serve the Lord their God, and David their king, whom I will raise up unto them" (Jeremiah 30:9). Hosea, looking to the same time, said, "Afterward shall the children of Israel return, and seek the Lord their God, and David their king" (Hosea 3:5). In both texts the "and" should be interpreted and could be translated as an explicative (that which explains) rather than a copulative (that which connects): "the Lord their God, even David their king." The term "prince" does not refer to the son of a king or a king-in-waiting, but to one who is lifted high and exalted, a fitting description of royalty. Similarly, Daniel refers explicitly to Messiah, the Prince (9:25). He uses a different word, but it has the same idea as Ezekiel's word: a sovereign leader or chief. There is no doubt that the Shepherd is a King.

The identity of this one shepherd is clear: it is the Lord Jesus Christ. Even without using any New Testament parallels, we find that applying our other clues for discovering Christ in the Old Testament points directly to Him. He is appointed (a mediatorial commission); He is a king (a mediatorial office); He saves His people (a mediatorial work). He is the ideal King; He is the good Shepherd. Zechariah advances this "Shepherd theology" by pointing to the sacrifice of the Shepherd as the specific means of saving His people: "Awake, O sword, against my shepherd ... smite the shepherd, and the sheep shall be scattered" (Zechariah 13:7). This text is most suggestive and theologically important. The Lord Himself issues the command to slay the shepherd, testifying that the sacrifice of Christ is the eternal plan and purpose of God. The Lord identifies the shepherd as "my shepherd," testifying to the special relationship between the Lord and Christ and suggesting the divine commission of Christ to this mediatorial office. It is similar to the Lord's declaration concerning the Messiah in Psalm 2:6: "Yet have I set my king upon my holy hill of Zion." All this is messianic.

Although we do not need the New Testament to see Christ in this title, we certainly do not want to neglect the New Testament evidence. The New Testament not only validates our seeing "Shepherd" as a messianic title, but it shows how minutely Christ fulfilled the Old Testament. The Lord Jesus quoted Zechariah 13:7 just prior to His arrest in warning the disciples that they would soon be offended because of Him (Matthew 26:31). There is no question that the Shepherd in Zechariah is Christ. How can you argue against the Lord's own interpretation and application of the Old Testament? In one of our Lord's great "I am" declarations, He identified Himself as the Good Shepherd: "I am the good shepherd: the good shepherd giveth his life for the sheep" (John 10:11). The parallels between John 10 and Ezekiel 34 stand out explicitly.

If you compare closely the Good Shepherd passage of John 10 with Ezekiel 34, you might almost imagine that the Lord Jesus had His Bible open to that text as He expounded His ministry. Significantly, He contrasted His being the Good Shepherd who voluntarily and sacrificially would die for His sheep with thieves and hirelings who take advantage of the sheep and abandon them in self-preservation rather than self-sacrifice. Ezekiel 34 begins with God's condemnation of bad shepherds who feed themselves rather than the sheep and leave the sheep to wander aimlessly (cf. John 10:10, 12-13). The Lord announced that He would perform the shepherd's duty by seeking the lost and sick sheep (34:12, 16), bringing them safely and securely into the fold. When He finds them, He graciously meets their needs. He binds the broken and strengthens the sick (34:16); this pictures forgiveness. He feeds the hungry (34:14); this pictures provision. He gives rest (34:15); this pictures peace and security. So the Lord Jesus as the Good Shepherd gives His life in saving His people, bringing them all together into one fold (John 10:11, 15). As the Shepherd in Ezekiel knows His sheep, discriminating between the kinds of cattle (34:16-17, 22), so the Shepherd in John says, "I…know my sheep, and am known of mine" (10:14). As Ezekiel notes the special relationship between the Lord and Shepherd and the Shepherd's divine commission (34:23-24), so Christ highlights His special relationship with the

Father and the commandment that He received from Him (John 10:15, 17-18). Both Ezekiel and John record that there is but one Shepherd (Ezekiel 34:23; John 10:16). I think that I could preach just about the same sermon from either text. They refer to the same Shepherd, the same Christ.

Servant

The designation "Servant of the Lord" is an honorific title expressing both a special relationship between the servant and the Lord as well as a functionary subordination in which the servant performs obediently the will of the Lord. Throughout the Old Testament, specially called and used men of God were labeled as God's servants. Moses, more than any other saint (about forty times), was identified as the servant of the Lord (e.g., Deuteronomy 34:5; Joshua 1:1-2; II Kings 21:8). But several others enjoyed the honor of that designation: Abraham (Genesis 26:24), Joshua (Joshua 24:29), Samson (Judges 15:18), Caleb (Numbers 14:24), David (II Samuel 7:19-20), Elijah (I Kings 18:36), Job (Job 1:8), Nehemiah (Nehemiah 1:6, 10), prophets and priests generally (Jeremiah 7:25; Psalm 134:1), and even the nation of Israel as a whole (Jeremiah 30:10; 46:27-28). Sometimes even the unexpected received the title: Nebuchadnezzar, the pagan Babylonian king, unknowingly was raised up and used by God to accomplish the Lord's will (Jeremiah 27:6; 43:10). Uniting this whole list is the fact that the servant was one who was especially chosen by God to stand at the head of a people to perform a special mission for God in behalf of the people. It was a position of great privilege and grave responsibility. Consequently, the title "Servant of the Lord" when referring to Christ is like the title "Messiah" itself in that there are many lesser referents that in one way or another point to the Ideal Servant. The failures of all the other servants heighten the need and desire for the One who will not fail. Christ stands in a unique relationship to the Lord and performs the divine will to absolute perfection.

It was the prophet Isaiah who under divine inspiration began to make the connection between the title "Servant of the Lord" and the promised Messiah. Referring to the servant theme over thirty times in his prophecy, Isaiah points to the failures of lesser servants to establish the need for the Ideal Servant who faithfully and obediently does whatever is necessary to accomplish God's purpose of saving His people. Isaiah's "Servant theology" reaches its climax in four great messages: 42:1-9; 49:1-12; 50:4-11; and 52:13-53:12. In these Servant Songs, Isaiah with Pauline precision declares the identity and saving work of God's only Redeemer for sinners. I confess that as I come to these Servant Songs as an author, I experience the same mixed feelings I have had when coming to these texts as a teacher and preacher. On the one hand, there is so much here that finding something to say about the text is easy. On the other hand, so much is here that reaching the depths and height of meaning is impossible. When I come to these Songs, I am in over my head, out of my league. But I think that is how we should always feel when we come to look full in the face of the Savior. That is exactly where Isaiah is making us look. I will resist the temptation to give a complete exposition of the Songs, but I will at least point out some of the great messianic elements that you should focus on as you meditate and work your way through these passages. Just take your time; don't be in a hurry to leave.

Isaiah 42:1-9

In this text the Servant is a special person who successfully executes a special mission. Verse 1 focuses attention on the unique relationship between the Servant and the Lord. He is the elect of God, the eternally chosen Mediator set apart to do a work that none other could possibly do. This takes us to that Trinitarian council of redemption in which the eternal Son of God, the eternal object of the Father's delight, received His commission to be the Savior of sinners. You see what I mean about this subject's being deep. Verse 8 suggests something else about the uniqueness of this special person: although a Servant, He is also the glory of God. God gives His glory to none other, but as we know also from the New Testament, Christ is the brightness of God's glory and it is in the face of Christ that God's glory shines (Hebrews 1:3; Colossians 1:15; II Corinthians 4:6). Most of this passage details aspects of the Servant's mission, with a primary emphasis on the prophetic ministry, one of the essential mediatorial operations. His prophetic ministry is unlike that of any lesser prophet because He is both the Messenger and the message (verse 6). As the Ideal Prophet, He reveals truth (verses 1and 3), enlightens blind eyes (verse 7), and liberates from spiritual bondage (verse 7). He conducts His prophetic mission without ostentation and with meekness (verses

2-3). Relate that to the number of times during His earthly ministry that Christ, having performed some act of mercy or miracle, instructed the beneficiary of that act to keep it quiet (e.g., Mark 5:43). Any lesser prophet would have put those accomplishments in bold print in his résumé. Finally, His mission would be successful because of His own faithful resolve (verse 4), the empowerment by the Holy Spirit (verse 1), and the will and sustaining help of God (verses 1, 6, and 9).

Isaiah 49:1-12

This text also develops the prophetic ministry of the Servant, calling specific attention to the Servant's divine commission and assurance of divine aid in achieving every detail of His mission. The theme of worldwide success runs through the entire Song. The Song begins with the Servant Himself addressing His message to the world (verse 1). The middle of the Song declares that not only is He the Savior of Israel, but He is as well "a light to the Gentiles" that salvation may extend to the end of the earth (verse 6). The Song ends with people from the entire world coming by means of the way created by the Servant (verses 11, 12). Reading this is almost like reading Romans 11 and Ephesians 2, which describe so wondrously Gentile inclusion in the body of Christ. We don't have to wait until the New Testament to learn that God intended to save Gentiles as well as Jews, all through the one and the same Christ. Again we learn that the promise of Christ was never a uniquely Jewish promise. What a blessing it is as Gentiles or Jews to know that our salvation was not a divine after-thought; the bringing together of every race and nation to be one in Christ has been God's purpose from the beginning. Check out Revelation 7:9 for a peek into the final fulfillment of that purpose.

In this Song, the Servant testifies to His consciousness of divine call-ing and commission as the Prophet whose message was sharp as a sword (verse 2). This imagery parallels and perhaps prefigures John's sight of the exalted Christ with the sharp sword, which was the Word of God, proceeding from His mouth (Revelation 19:15, 21). It is a cer-tain reminder as to how vitally important it is to hear and heed the words of this Ideal Prophet.

This text also highlights one of the mysterious aspects of the Servant's ministry: His absolute trust and dependence on God. I say "mysteri-ous" because it boggles the mind. Although the Servant is the eternal

God, in the faithful performance of His humiliation work He submitted Himself to the will of His God. During the years of His humiliation, more rejected Him than accepted Him, giving the appearance that the whole work was in vain (verse 4). Yet in unrelenting resolve and faith, He claimed the Lord was His strength (verse 5). The Lord proved to be a reliable object of messianic trust in that He preserved the Servant and guaranteed His success. He is the covenant Head of a people, He establishes a kingdom, He liberates prisoners, He gives sight to the blind, He feeds the hungry, and He opens the way to glory (verses 8-12). This second of the Servant Songs gives us boldness in preaching the gospel and confidence in believing the gospel. The gospel really works because the Servant was absolutely successful in what He came to do.

Isaiah 50:4-11

If any passage in the Bible depicts Christ as the Ideal Prophet, it is this third Servant Song. The passage begins with the Servant's testimony of His constant dependence in receiving the word from God and His faithful dedication in delivering the word. That the Lord gave Him the "tongue of the learned" defines in a nutshell the role of the Prophet (verse 4). Remember that the responsibility of the prophet was to speak only what God had spoken to Him. What the Servant says here about the origin of His message, the Lord Jesus often said during the years of His earthly ministry (see Matthew 11:27; John 5:30; and John 8:28-29). Because God instructed Him daily, He always had the fresh and appropriate word to meet the needs of those to whom He ministered: a word in season for the weary.

The Servant's dedication to the word resulted not only in His faithful proclamation of it to others but also in His own determined, resolute obedience. Many lesser prophets were often reluctant to accept their prophetic orders, but not so the Ideal Prophet. He never resisted, rebelled, or retreated from the path of duty, no matter where that path led. He obediently submitted to scourging, plucking of hair, shame and spitting (verses 5-6). It does not require more than a cursory knowledge of the life of Christ to put this prophetic word in historic perspective. Not only does the New Testament record these specific details in the Passion narratives, but it gives us the theological synopsis, too: He "took upon him the form of a servant ... and became obedient unto death, even the death of the cross" (Philippians 2:7-8).

The Servant's exaltation and vindication follow His obedience, both in this text as well as in the New Testament (see Philippians 2:9-11). The Servant declared His confidence that God would come to His defense, and, therefore, His resolve to do His duty was justified (verses 7-9). I think one of the things I love most about this particular text is that what is said about Christ in verses 8 and 9 is applied to believers in union with Christ in Romans 8. None can condemn Christ, and none can condemn those in Christ. His people share in His success and exaltation. Finally, the Song ends with the admonition to trust the Servant and the warning against rejecting Him. The Servant of the Lord is the only way, the only hope, the only Savior.

Isaiah 52:13-53:12

If this final Song were all we knew of the gospel, we would know the gospel well. It was all that Philip needed; in his witness to the Ethiopian, he "began at the same scripture, and preached unto him Jesus" (Acts 8:35). There is no way in the limited framework of this study that I can come close to doing justice to the fullness and beauty of this depiction of the Suffering Servant. No exposition can ever plumb its depth, yet just reading it lifts the heart to spiritual heights. Not only is the theology profound, but the poetic arrangement of the Song is a literary masterpiece. The Song develops in five stanzas of three verses each. I will limit my analysis to a synopsis of the principal message of each stanza. I encourage you to spend some prayerful time meditating and rejoicing over the message of this Song that encompasses so much of messianic theology. Seeing Christ in this Song does not require using many of our messianic clues; in this Song we look fully at the Savior.

Stanza One (52:13-15) gives an overview of most the specific themes developed in the rest of the Song, but its main focus is on the success and exaltation of the Servant. He will be exalted and extolled, but the path to that success takes Him through the throes of humiliation and suffering. The suffering is so intense that He is disfigured beyond recognition, yet it is the means of purifying many nations.

Stanza Two (53:1-3) describes the humiliation and rejection of the Servant. He was rejected because nothing identified Him as the expected King. Born and bred in humble surroundings and unpretentious in appearance, He had nothing to identify Him as royalty. Consequently, He was treated with contempt, shunned and ignored. His whole life was filled with misery ("acquainted with grief"), earning Him the title "man of sorrows." Natural sight could see nothing attractive about Him; the eye of faith alone beholds His beauty.

Stanza Three (53:4-6) vividly pictures His vicarious (substitutionary) suffering. These sufferings in both body and soul were necessary because of our sins, and the sorrow and grief He bore testified to the terrible consequences of those sins. His sufferings reached a climax when God violently pierced Him in order to achieve our peace and forgiveness. The Lord took the initiative in this vicarious execution and the Servant took the blow that we deserved, thereby bringing us to God (see I Peter 2:24-25). We must wait until the New Testament to learn that He made the atonement on a Roman cross, but we don't have to wait to see the vicarious atonement.

Stanza Four (53:7-9) underscores the voluntary nature of His suffering obedience. Note the explicitly minute prophecies concerning His arrest, trial, death, and burial: the events of His passion. He humbly allowed Himself to be afflicted, offering no self-defense: "who, when he was reviled, reviled not again; when he suffered, he threatened not" (I Peter 2:23). After His arrest and unjust trial, He was violently, brutally, and vicariously cut off from the land of the living. Then He was buried. Essentially, the only details the New Testament adds to Isaiah's account of Christ's Passion are the names of Judas, Pilate, Herod, and Joseph of Arimathæa.

Stanza Five (53:10-12) is the grand climax, coming full circle again to the Servant's success and exaltation. He did not suffer and die in vain. The Servant accomplished God's eternal purpose by offering Himself as the guilt offering, paying the price and making full recompense for sin. God was satisfied with the work of Christ. The Servant in reward for His full obedience would see the promised seed, enjoy prolonged days, and know the pleasure of the Lord. That all of this follows His atoning death points to His victorious resurrection and earned exaltation. Christ was satisfied with His work. Sinners are justified by knowing Him and they share in His inheritance, becoming joint-heirs with Christ. Believers are satisfied with Christ. It is not surprising that we often refer to the Gospel according to Isaiah.

Other Suggested Titles

The titles of Christ reveal something about His person, nature, and work. But like all words in Scripture, they are an integral element of the propositional truth that God reveals. Therefore, in the samples we have considered I have not limited our discussion just to a dictionary definition of the word, but have included at least a general analysis of the context in which the title occurs. In other words, merely defining the word "branch" does not tell me everything I need to know about the Branch in a given context. But the meaning of "branch" is a vital component or building block in the overall communication. Recognizing a title should be a clue for us to stop and evaluate who is being designated and what is being said about him. When we plug in all of our messianic clues about who Christ is, what Christ is like, and what Christ does, we should be able to determine whether we are looking at a messianic title. If by the analogy of Scripture we can recognize messianic truths, then we are warranted in applying the title to Christ. Once again we will have found Christ in the Old Testament. If you read your Old Testament in that search mode, you will find Him.

At the beginning of this chapter, I confessed the arbitrary criterion used in selecting the titles discussed: they were *some* of my favorites. I want to list several others that you can study on your own. This list is merely suggestive and certainly not exhaustive, so keep your eyes open for others as you read the Scriptures. Sometimes it is difficult to discern whether a word or expression is used as a title or just a descriptive statement. That's okay; our task is not so much to formulate a list of names but to learn what the Old Testament teaches about Christ. I would recommend that in your study of these, you use whatever helps you have, such as Bible dictionaries or commentaries.

Reference	Title	Basic Significance
Micah 2:13	Breaker	Performer of kingly duties
Jeremiah 30:9; Hosea 3:5	David	The Ideal King
Haggai 2:7	Desire of all nations	King and Priest (a disputed title, so see commentaries)
Hosea 1:11	Head	King
Malachi 3:1	Lord	Deity (not the usual form of the word; always refers to God)
Isaiah 53:3	Man of sorrows	Real suffering humanity
Malachi 3:1	Messenger of the Covenant	The Angel; Prophetic ministry; the Head of the covenant
Zechariah 13:7	My fellow	Deity; identification of One who is the equal of God
Ezekiel 37:25; Daniel 9:25	Prince	King; the exalted One
Haggai 2:23	Signet	A sign of Kingship
Malachi 4:2	Sun of righteousness	The glorious Savior (a disputed title, so see commentaries)
Genesis 49:24; Isaiah 28:16	Stone (tried stone, precious corner stone, sure foundation)	Christ as the object of saving faith
Job 16:19	Witness and	Record (literally, an Advocate) Priestly mediation

CHAPTER 7
CHRIST IN WORD PROPHECY

It so happens that I am working on this chapter a few days before Christmas. The anticipation of special times with family and friends makes this a favorite season for many. It is amazing how the approach of this holiday affects behavior and mood, even for those with no particular sense of the glorious significance of what it commemorates. How many parents tease their children into a frenzy with thoughts of what Christmas morning will bring? How many parents threaten their children into feigned obedience with the possibility that Santa Claus may not come if they misbehave? How many try to instill patience in their children by deferring gratification of their incessant requests with the assuring reminder that Christmas is coming? Every whisper, carol, card, tree, and brightly wrapped package increases the anticipation and excitement, the "can't wait any longer" tension. Yet the greater the longing for the day, the longer it seems to be before it finally arrives. It is amazing how the annual "coming" of an imaginary character generates such restless expectancy, even in those who know better. On the other hand, some future events that we know are coming can cause dread and anxiety. Thinking about a dentist appointment, for instance, also generates a restlessness, but it is a "hope it never gets here" tension. Yet the day seems to come before we know it. The coming of Christmas or a dentist appointment illustrates the point I want to make: the future and our view of it influences our behavior and attitude. What we think, imagine, or know about the future affects the present.

What is true in terms of mundane affairs is certainly true of spiritual matters. Throughout the Scripture, the Lord sets the future before us, not just to let us know what is coming but to prepare us now for what is coming. The future affects the present. Being prepared for the future increases our longing for it. God's promises guarantee that the future He reveals is as certain as the present. This guaranteed future is nowhere more important than in God's promises concerning Christ. At the first need of Christ, God promised that Christ would come. From the beginning God revealed Christ to be the only Savior, the only object of saving faith. From the beginning believers were taking God at His Word. Saints in the Old Testament dispensation placed their faith in an "unseen" Christ who would come in the future; saints in the New Testament dispensation place their faith in an "unseen" Christ who came in the past and will come again in the future. Whether in the Old Testament or the New, faith is faith and what man knows about Christ and His coming is based on the Word of God. Whether the Christ of prophecy or the Christ of history, it is the same Christ. Although the reality of Christ's person and the efficacy of His work transcend time, Christ had to come into time and history to accomplish the eternal purpose of redemption. Without the temporal accomplishing of redemption through the Incarnation of the Son of God, all the talk about it could ultimately achieve nothing. The time had to come when the person would be manifest and the work done. In the fullness of time, Christ came, just as God promised He would. In the fullness of time, Christ will come again, just as God has promised He will.

The entire history of the world before the Incarnation was moving steadily toward that stupendous event of the condescension of Christ at His first coming, just as the history of the world since the Ascension of Christ is moving steadily toward the stupendous event of His Second Coming. Everything in time is centered in Jesus Christ. It makes sense that everything in Scripture centers in Him. Given the nature of time progression, what the Old Testament reveals about Christ and His work is predictive, whereas what the New Testament reveals is both historical and predictive. There is more to come; it's not over yet. But our attention here is on the Old Testament specifically and what it reveals about Christ. In one way or another, everything in the Old Testament contributes to the development and fulfillment of God's redemptive purpose in Christ, even when His person or work is not directly in view. The Pentateuch laid the foundation; the historical books recorded the sometimes checkered development of the plan that seemed to be in constant jeopardy because of human sin and failure; the prophetic, poetical, and wisdom books defined the appropriate application of redemption to the life of faith, warning of the consequences of unbelief. In every section of the Old Testament, one of the most striking ways that God revealed His purpose in Christ was with direct predictions. He flat out revealed the future. As time progressed, these predictions became more and more precise, keeping the messianic hope alive and increasing the expectancy for Christ. What the Old Testament saint believed about the future affected his present. In a very real way, the Old Testament was God's assuring reminder that Christmas, in its truest sense, was coming. As we read the Old Testament we must adopt the same plan of study as the Old Testament prophets themselves: "Searching what, or what manner of time the Spirit of Christ which was in them did signify, when it testified beforehand the sufferings of Christ, and the glory that should follow" (I Peter 1:11). In our search for Christ in the Old Testament, prophecy is a good place to look. Finding Christ there is a sure thing.

In this chapter, I am using the term "prophecy" in a restricted sense to designate prediction. The biblical word for prophecy, however, is not so limited. It refers to speaking forth whatever God commanded the inspired prophet to speak. It includes what we would call preaching as well as what we would call prediction. The authority for both comes from the Lord. I am also limiting our discussion to actual spoken or written prophecies. This is why I have entitled this chapter "Christ in Word Prophecy." In the next chapter we will consider the revelation of Christ in what I will call "picture prophecy," what is generally referred to as typology. Interpreting prophecy, whether word or picture, is not always easy. Therefore, before considering some specific examples of messianic prophecies, I want to discuss the purpose and nature of prophecy. Understanding this will help not only to interpret the fulfilled first advent prophecies but also the unfulfilled, but just as certain, Second Advent prophecies.

The Purpose and Nature of Prophecy

I suppose there is more fascination with prophecy than with any other part of Scripture. Unfortunately, abuse of prophecy abounds. Everyone has some curiosity about how things are going to end, and plenty of "kooks," using the "key to biblical prophecy," advance their peculiar agendas. Even those who mean well may become so convinced of the correctness of their particular schemes of prophetic interpretation that they close their Bibles, fatalistically ticking off the events of history and plugging in current events as they look anxiously for the next event on the prophetic time chart. To walk by the sight of a prophetic time line rather than by faith is a misuse of prophecy, even if the time line is correct. God never revealed the future to satisfy man's natural curiosity about the future. Both the purpose and the nature of prophecy work to fuel faith, not replace it. God reveals the future to affect the present. A proper use of prophecy always brings the future to bear on the present. That was true in the Old Testament, and it remains true today.

Purpose of Prophecy

I think that I can summarize the overall purpose of prophecy generally and messianic prophecy specifically in four essential statements.

To Glorify God

First, prophecy *indicates that God is in control*. God's absolute control of time and circumstance evidences His complete sovereignty over all. Read through Ecclesiastes 3 some time if you need to be reminded of this. After the Preacher gives the evidence of the Lord's purposes for time, he concludes, "I know that, whatsoever God doeth, it shall be for ever: nothing can be put to it, nor any thing taken from it: and God doeth it, that men should fear before him." He continues, "That which hath been is now; and that which is to be hath already been" (Ecclesiastes 3:14-15). What will be is just as certain as what has been because God is in control; His purpose will prevail.

Prophecy is a dramatic way of displaying God's absolute sovereignty, and thus it brings glory to Him. He knows the end from the beginning because He has decreed the end from the beginning; therefore, He guarantees the end from the beginning. Nothing can frustrate or alter what He has determined.

Every so often He revealed what was going to happen as evidence of that absolute control. As the Lord of time, He could do that. Isaiah 41 is a great text which illustrates this truth. The Lord challenged idol worshippers to bring their "gods" to court to produce evidence of their worth as gods. The key challenge was the ability to predict the future: "Shew the things that are to come hereafter, that we may know that ye are gods" (Isaiah 41:23). When they remained silent, the Lord issued the verdict, "Ye are of nothing" (Isaiah 41:24). The true God can do what idols cannot. In contrast, the Lord gave evidence of His deity by telling how He would raise up one from the north (Isaiah 41:25). Later He identified that northerner as Cyrus, who would perform all of God's pleasure (Isaiah 44:28). He could identify Cyrus by name almost two hundred years beforehand because He is God. Announcing the future and accomplishing the announced future irrefutably prove that God is in control of everything.

The application to us is significant. If God determines the future, it follows that He determines and controls the present as well. If nothing can frustrate His future purpose, nothing can frustrate His present purpose, either. Even if we don't understand all the specific issues of a given prophecy, we can learn well this lesson about God. That God is in absolute control of time means that every prophecy of Christ is certain. He promised Christ and governed the moments from Eden to Bethlehem, and so He continues to govern until moments disappear into eternity when Christ comes again.

To Encourage Believers

Second, prophecy *inspires confidence*. This confidence is the inevitable corollary to the assurance that God controls time and that, therefore, regardless of appearances, the present is part of the execution of God's program. Looking in faith to God's revealed future should inspire confidence for present service and duty by assuring the believer that his "now" fits precisely on the way to "then." A proper application of prophecy produces an active, bold, fervent, and confident performance of duty until God fulfills the promise.

Zechariah provides a good example of using prophecy to inspire confident activity in the present. Remember that Zechariah was preaching to people who had returned to Israel from the Babylonian captivity–people whose first and principal job was rebuilding the temple. Their present was filled with discouragement. The temple and the entire city lay in ruins. Yet the Lord revealed through Zechariah a city of glory, peace, and prosperity that would know the very presence of God (Zechariah 8). If you interpret this passage from a premillennial perspective, as I do, then this passage describes the glory of that future kingdom. Zechariah predicted what is still future even from our time, yet he made direct application to the people of his day. "Let your hands be strong, ye that hear in these days these words by the mouth of the prophets, which were in the day that the foundation of the house of the Lord of hosts was laid, that the temple might be built" (Zechariah 8:9). Just the fact of God's certain blessing, regardless of when it would come, was the motive to encourage them to do what God had commanded them to do.

In one of His kingdom parables Christ teaches the same lesson. He instructed, "Occupy till I come" (Luke 19:13). The word "occupy" means to conduct business. In this parable the one who buried his money and passively waited for the kingdom was strongly rebuked. He believed that the king was coming but did nothing about it. Using the prophetic future as an excuse for passive resignation in the present is an abuse of prophecy. A belief in the Second Coming should produce a confident use of the means of grace and a bold evangelism that seeks to win the world for Christ.

To Intensify Desire for God's Will

Third, prophecy *increases expectant hope.* Knowing what God has promised intensifies the desire to experience and possess the promise. The more we contemplate the promise, the more we want the promise to materialize. The more details we know about the promise, the more intense the desire becomes. Prophecy is a means whereby God keeps hope alive and increases trust and dependence on Him. Prophecy generates that "I can't wait any longer" attitude. Prophecy is a means whereby God incites us to want Him and what He has promised more than anything else.

Both the Old and the New Testaments sometimes use the idea of "waiting" to express this eager anticipation for the Lord to fulfill His promises. Waiting is not resignation; it is a "sitting on the edge of your seat" expectancy. As a hunter, I know what it is to sit "actively" for hours, watching in eager and hopeful expectancy that a deer will materialize. There were those in the Old Testament dispensation who lived in that kind of expectant hope of Christ's coming. Luke describes the devout Simeon as one "waiting for the consolation of Israel," confident in God's promise that he would not die "before he had seen the Lord's Christ" (Luke 2:25-26). Seeing Christ was all that he lived for. Similarly, the prophetess Anna, on seeing the child Jesus, "gave thanks likewise unto the Lord, and spake of him to all them that looked [literally, "waited"] for redemption in Jerusalem" (Luke 2:38). Messianic prophecy fulfilled its purpose in those saints living when Christ was born.

Daniel makes an interesting statement that I believe indicates that same expectancy in those saints living hundreds of years before Christ came, but who by that time had almost as much prophecy about Christ as Simeon and Anna. Chapter 11 has gotten Daniel into trouble with unbelieving critics because his prophecies about the Seleucid period were so minutely accurate. The unbeliever cannot see how Daniel, writing in the sixth century, could prophesy with such precision about events of the second century. They obviously have no knowledge of the Lord who controls time. But my point here is that when Daniel skips ahead from the Maccabbean times to the end times, he says that the one we call the Anti-Christ will not regard "the desire of women" (Daniel 11:37). I suggest that this is a direct reference to Christ, the promised virgin-born Seed of the woman (Genesis 3:15; Isaiah 7:14). It may well indicate the hope of every believing woman in Daniel's time that she might be that chosen woman to bear the Messiah. Obviously, those living at the time of Christ's Second Coming would know who the mother of Christ was, but it was a fitting expression for those in Daniel's day who lived before Christ's first coming. Perhaps Eve herself, to whom that first prophecy was given, interpreted the birth of Cain to be that promised Seed. Upon the birth of Cain, Eve declared, "I have gotten a man from the Lord" (Genesis 4:1). This could be more literally translated, "I have gotten a man, the Lord." It did not take long before she realized Cain was not the Seed, but my point is that Eve was living in the expectant hope of the Curse Reverser whom God had promised.

As Christians, we ought in this way to be waiting for Christ to return—not in fatalistic resignation, but in eagerness and hope (see Romans 8:23; I Corinthians 1:7). How intensely we long for the return of Christ is a sobering check on the level of our desire for Him. Too often Christians profess the desire for the Second Coming, sing songs about it, and repeat John's prayer, "Even so, come, Lord Jesus" (Revelation 22:20), while pursuing a personal agenda that takes precedence. Too often the concerns of life supplant professed theology.

To Motivate Sinners to Repentance and Saints to Purity

Fourth, prophecy *encourages holiness*. The coming of Christ is not without consequence; it behooves us to be ready for His appearing. If the Old Testament prophets teach anything about the use of prophecy, it is that prophecy is a motive to repentance and purity. Joel, for instance, after describing the great and terrible Day of the Lord (Joel 2:11), issued a classic call to repentance: "Therefore also now, saith the Lord, turn ye even to me with all your heart, and with fasting, and with weeping, and with mourning: and rend your heart, and not your garments, and turn unto the Lord your God: for he is gracious and merciful, slow to anger, and of great kindness, and repententh him of the evil" (Joel 2:12-13). The apostle Peter, describing the same Day of the Lord, concluded, "Seeing then that all these things shall be dissolved, what manner of persons ought ye to be in all holy conversation and godliness" (II Peter 3:11). He also admonished, "Wherefore, beloved, seeing that ye look for such things, be diligent that ye be found of him in peace, without spot, and blameless" (II Peter 3:14). Similarly, the apostle John, having addressed Christ's return, said, "Every man that hath this hope in him purifieth himself, even as he is pure" (I John 3:3). I don't think I need to elaborate: if we believe that Christ is coming again and that we will stand accountable before Him, we will live in a way that seeks to please Him. To hear "well done, thou good and faithful servant" (Matthew 25:21) ought to motivate us to purity. The Scripture is clear that any use of prophecy that does not influence the present is inappropriate.

The Nature of Prophecy

Growing up, I heard over and over again that prophecy is simply pre-written history, as clear as yesterday's newspaper. I remember the frustration that assertion caused when I compared the newspaper with something from Daniel or Revelation. Even the stock market reports made more sense than strange-looking beasts with wings and horns. I appreciate the God-honoring sentiment that generated those statements, but the fact is that prophecy is not as clear as history. I maintain that every divinely inspired prophecy will be actually fulfilled; in that sense it is pre-written history.

CHRIST IN WORD PROPHECY

Prophetic Ambiguity

Nevertheless, there is an *intentional* ambiguity inherent in prophecy. Enough is revealed with enough clarity to testify to God's control of time and faithfulness to His Word, but we are not necessarily privy to every single detail of His plans. II Kings 7 illustrates this principle of prophecy plainly because it contains two specific prophecies by Elisha and their literal fulfillments: cheap food and the destiny of the doubter. Samaria was under Syrian siege and was suffering great famine. Elisha's prediction of abundant and cheap food seemed impossible and "a lord on whose hand the king leaned" let him know so. That doubt precipitated the prediction that the lord would see it but not eat it (II Kings 7:1-2). Both of these were very specific predictions. The details of fulfillment, however, make it clear that Elisha left out some key facts. Had he delineated how the lepers would find the camp of the Syrians abandoned with all the cache of supplies and how the doubter would be trampled by the hungry crowd rushing to buy some of the cheap food, the doubter would have been a fatalistic fool to accept the king's appointment to "have the charge of the gate" (II Kings 7:17). But enough was revealed to make it absolutely certain that the whole episode was "according to the word of the Lord" (II Kings 7:16). The prophecy was clear, yet ambiguous.

Prophecy reveals much about the future, but it doesn't reveal everything. Realizing this must temper our interpretation of prophetic texts. We must focus on and emphasize the points revealed and resist the temptation to speculate with dogmatism about what God did not choose to reveal. We have to be honest and admit that were it not for this inherent and intentional ambiguity in prophecy, every God-fearer and Bible-believer would confess the same prophetic perspective.

Let me give another example of a prophecy and its fulfillment that I think illustrates this principle. When the Lord revealed to Isaac and Rebekah that they would have twins, He also said, "The elder shall serve the younger" (Genesis 25:23). We know from the historic narrative how that played out in Jacob's receiving the birthright instead of Esau. The English translation makes the prediction explicitly clear; the Hebrew, however, is a bit ambiguous. It could be translated either "The elder shall serve the younger" or "The younger shall serve the elder." The addition of one simple particle could have eliminated the ambiguity, but the Lord chose not to use that particle. I will not be dogmatic about this, but I would suggest that Isaac and Rebekah interpreted that prophecy differently. It seems unlikely to me that Isaac, who feared the Lord, would have been so bent on giving the firstborn blessing to Esau in conscious defiance of God's revealed purpose. But God's revealed purpose could not be frustrated even by Isaac's misinterpretation. Divinely inspired prophecy results in certain fulfillment; humanly perceived interpretations do not share that certainty.

It's my opinion that if God filled in all the details and removed all the ambiguity, we would all be pretribulationalists and premillennialists. It would not have been difficult for God to say explicitly that the church will be raptured before or in the middle or at the end of the Great Tribulation, but the fact of the matter is He did not. Until we have the fulfillment to seal the interpretation, may God grant His people enough sense not to accuse those of differing prophetic schemes of not believing the Bible. Not believing the Bible is a serious charge; not agreeing with my interpretation of prophecy may be foolish, but it is not to be equated with unbelief.

All of this relates to our search for Christ in Old Testament prophecy. Virtually every element of Christ's person and work is predicted in the Old Testament, but not with "historical" detail. For instance, the Old Testament is clear that Messiah would be the vicarious sacrifice for the sins of His people, but it does not specify that a Roman cross would be the means of His execution. The Old Testament is clear that Messiah will rule as the rightful heir to David's throne, but it does not specify the span of time between His vicarious sacrifice and victorious rule. The Old Testament gives the facts associated with the first and Second Comings of Christ, but it does not specify two distinct comings separated by thousands of years. According to I Peter 1:11, the issue that baffled the Old Testament prophets was not the "fact of" but the "when of" Christ's sufferings and following glory. We have the advantage of history to see how precisely the Old Testament pre-wrote that history; we can easily distinguish between the Advents. Our added insight should help us in our study of the Old Testament prophecies about Christ. That we see so many of the elements precisely fulfilled should increase our faith in those yet to be fulfilled. Although we know more about the details of some of these prophecies than our Old Testament predecessors, the essential truths were as relevant to them as they are to us. Perhaps I should say that they are as relevant to us as to them. We can still learn about Christ from the prophecies.

Prophetic Language

Let me suggest some specific things to keep in mind about the nature of prophetic language. First, note that prophecy tends to use symbolic language that must be interpreted figuratively. Don't confuse a literal or actual fulfillment of prophecy with a pedantically literal interpretation of prophetic language. For instance, Daniel's prediction of world empires in terms of strange, unnatural beasts cannot be interpreted literally without being weird. But there is some connection between the strange beasts and the empires they represent that was and will be actually fulfilled. Interpreting symbolism requires that you determine the point of relevance between the symbol and the actual referent without attempting to find a tit-for-tat parallel. The meaning of symbolic language is not on the surface; discerning the meaning requires careful thought. There is a degree of subjectivism, so we must exercise caution about going too far.

Second, note that prophecy tends to use the language of imminency. This means that regardless of how distant the actual prophecy from its fulfillment, the prediction is made as though its fulfillment were impending, about to occur. This intentional temporal ambiguity is one of the most significant features of prophetic language. Since the time of the fulfillment is not specified, the application of the prophecy is not limited. For prophecies to be precisely dated would effectively rob a given prophecy of its purpose to affect the present of all the pre-fulfillment generations. Had Isaiah specified that the virgin birth would be more than seven hundred years in the future, it would not have been a motivating sign to those to whom he was preaching. But he did not date the fulfillment, and the prophecy was most relevant to his contemporaries.

Third, note that prophecy tends to link distinct epoch events into single predictive contexts, giving the appearance of a single event. This is called progressive prediction or prophetic telescoping. In a single utterance, the prophet makes multiple predictions, juxtaposing them without any indication of time intervals between them. The focus is on the certain fact of the epochs, not the timing of them. It is this regular disregard for chronology that differentiates history from prophecy. Whereas history demands dates, prophecy thrives on their omission. Isaiah 61 is the classic example of this prophetic phenomenon. Verse 2 identifies as part of the Messiah's ministry "to proclaim the acceptable year of the Lord, and the day of vengeance of our God." When at the beginning of His ministry the Lord Jesus read this text in the synagogue at Nazareth, He stopped in the middle of the sentence, closed the book, and said, "This day is this scripture fulfilled in your ears" (Luke 4:17-21). That statement explains His otherwise abrupt conclusion. The proclamation of the acceptable year of the Lord was being fulfilled "this day," but that was not true of the day of vengeance. That yet awaits His Second Coming. Isaiah telescoped the two events separated by at least two thousand years into a single sentence. Similarly, comparing what Daniel says about the resurrection with Revelation illustrates the same disregard for time. Daniel telescoped two types of resurrection without specifying the time gap between them: one to everlasting life and another to everlasting contempt (Daniel 12:2). Later, John revealed that a thousand years would separate these two resurrections (Revelation 20:4-5). It is little wonder that the Old Testament believers were trying to sort out the "when" of these great works of Christ.

Prophetic Fulfillment

A failure to take into account these features of prophetic language has led to some confusion about the nature of prophetic fulfillment. A debate rages as to whether a given prophecy has a partial, single, or double fulfillment—or even multiple fulfillments. Part of the disagreement stems from imprecise definition of terms and part involves fundamental differences in hermeneutics. It is far beyond the scope of our study to deal with these issues in detail, so I will simply give you my opinion. I suggest that a specific prophecy has a single specific fulfillment. That's easy enough to suggest but not always easy to defend. I do believe, however, the single fulfillment axiom works well in almost every instance. If we remember the inherent "timeless" factor in prophecy, we should not be tempted to demand a near as well as a distant fulfillment just to rescue contemporary relevance for the prophet's audience. The temporal ambiguity guarantees its relevance; one fulfillment is all that is necessary.

There is one type of prophecy, however, that lends itself to the appearance of multiple fulfillments. Some prophecies constitute a whole concept that comprises specific constituent elements. The fulfillment of the prophecy develops progressively from element to element until the completion of the whole. For instance, both Isaac and Christ constitute Abraham's promised Seed. Obviously, Christ was the main issue, but there had to be an Isaac before there could be a Christ. Isaac marked the beginning of the fulfillment of the messianic prophecy. I prefer saying it that way rather than that the promise was fulfilled in Isaac and then again in Christ. The prophecy that the Seed of the woman would bruise the serpent's head seems to have a progressive fulfillment as well. Hebrews 2:14 indicates that the death of Christ was the means of destroying "him that had the power of death, that is, the devil." That Paul told the Romans that the God of peace would bruise Satan under their feet shortly suggests that they (or the church as a whole) were going to witness some aspect of that bruising (Romans 16:20). Satan's ultimate sentence to the lake of fire marks the ultimate completion of the prophecy (Revelation 20:10). The cross began the fulfillment that continues now and will end at the final judgment. Prophecy is difficult enough; let's keep the interpretative process as simple as possible. Once we start claiming and trying to identify multiple fulfillments for a single prophecy, we remove any objectivity as to what the text means.

The Content of Messianic Prophecy

The subject matter of Old Testament prophecy is varied, ranging from birth predictions to the cataclysms that will mark the end of the world. Scripture is replete with so many specific predictions that it is almost humanly impossible to keep track of them. But God never forgets His word and every prophecy will be minutely fulfilled. This is wonderfully true about the messianic prophecies, which promise and prepare the way for the coming of Christ. Many of these prophecies foreshadow some aspect of Christ's person, work, or perfection; others, particularly those with an eschatological focus, foreshadow aspects of the attendant circumstances of Christ's coming and presence (peace, prosperity, judgments, etc.). There are so many of these that it is impossible to identify and discuss them all at this time. Before giving some examples that will illustrate how much about Christ these prophecies reveal, I want to remind you of some issues to consider that will help you identify messianic predictions on your own.

Interpretation Guidelines

Let me suggest three "C's" to keep in mind as you read the Old Testament with the purpose of searching for Christ. First, be sensitive to the messianic *clues*. One of my basic premises has been that knowing whom to look for is essential to finding Him. Be sensitive to those unique elements of the Messiah: His unique person (God/Man), His uniquely ideal mediatorial operations (prophet work, priest work, and king work), and His unique perfections or attributes. Be sensitive to statements that transcend application to mere men. This is simple enough: when you see those things that you know are true about Messiah, you can assume that you are seeing Christ in those places. As I say, this is not profound, but it will mark the messianic prophecies, and that's our objective.

Second, rely on Scriptural *confirmation*. This includes both parallel statements in the Old Testament as well as declared identifications in the New Testament. Here is the old analogy of Scripture principle. If a given prophetic text uses terms similar or identical to those another passage has used with reference to the Messiah, then we are safe in identifying that text as messianic. Take every advantage you can from the New Testament. Note the various "fulfillment" formulas and statements that the New Testament uses to link something about Christ to the Old Testament prophecies. Prophecies dealing with the same issues, even if not directly quoted or referred to in the New Testament, by analogy can be identified as messianic as well. Always allow the Scripture to interpret Scripture: that guarantees infallible interpretation. Finding these parallel passages should not be difficult. Any Bible that includes cross-references should at least get you started. I particularly like those supplied in the Cambridge edition, but those in the Oxford edition work as well. I use both.

Third, pay attention to the *context*. I think one of the biggest mistakes made with prophecy generally, including messianic prophecies specifically, is isolating the statement concerning the future and divorcing it from the argument of the immediate context. Remember that just predicting the future is not the purpose of prophecy. Use the context, the flow of thought and argument, as an aid in interpreting the prediction; everything fits together. Often you will find clues in the immediate context that demand messianic identification. There will always be lessons in the context that illustrate the purpose of prophecy.

Specific Prophecies of Christ

With these interpretation keys in mind, let's consider a few examples of messianic prophecies. There are so many of these I must set some delimitation. To avoid digressions into eschatological issues and debates, I will not deal with the yet-to-be-fulfilled prophecies of the Second Coming of Christ. You must understand, however, that you cannot formulate any eschatological theology without taking into consideration the vast number of prophecies in the Old Testament that focus directly on the end times. I dare say that the Old Testament supplies more data for this branch of theological study than the New Testament. Seeing how the prophecies of the first advent have been fulfilled should generate confidence in the sure fulfillment of the prophecies of the Second. Fulfilled prophecy should also mark some guidelines for interpreting unfulfilled prophecy. I will highlight *some* specific prophecies that take us through the life and work of Christ. These are by no means exhaustive of the seemingly countless prophecies, but they will illustrate how specifically the Old Testament foretold the coming of Christ. As you read the Old Testament, be prepared to find messianic prophecies everywhere. They are not limited to the books we call the Prophets.

The Time of the Coming of Christ

The New Testament declares that God sent His Son in the fullness of time (Galatians 4:4). Daniel 9 gives some insight into the last stretch of time leading to that divinely determined fullness and beyond. Daniel's revelation of the Seventy Weeks is a classic example of prophetic telescoping that previews epoch events separated by some undetermined amount of time. The famous prophetic vision illustrates some of the inherent ambiguities of prophetic chronology. Even though the passage is focusing on time periods, some uncertainty inheres concerning the nature of the temporal symbolism (weeks) and the exact circumstance that marks the beginning of the reckoning. Nonetheless, that Messiah is the primary focus stands without question. As noted before, this is one of the few Old Testament texts that actually use the word "Messiah" to designate the coming Redeemer.

Whatever may be unclear about the Seventy Weeks, it is nevertheless clear, as always, that Christ is the answer to every problem. Volumes have been written concerning these weeks, and many writers attempt to squeeze into the weeks or between them notions completely foreign to Daniel's context or argument. It is not my purpose to address or attempt to correct what I regard as erroneous notions about this prophecy. I do, however, want to discuss briefly some of the key points and interpretation issues that should help you to see how marvelously this text pinpoints the fact and the time of Christ's coming to be the Redeemer.

It is significant that this prophecy of Seventy Weeks was God's answer to Daniel's prayer that was generated by another temporal prophecy. Daniel had read in Jeremiah that the Babylonian captivity would last for seventy years (Daniel 9:2; cf. Jeremiah 25:11; 29:10). Calculating how long he had been in Babylon, Daniel claimed that promise and began pleading with God to fulfill His Word. Knowing God's will gave him confidence and expectation in his prayer. This context illustrates two important lessons: one about prayer and one about Christ. It shows the vital link between God's Word and prayer, both of which are means of grace. It teaches how to use God's Word as the basis for prayer. Daniel's praying did not change the date of the divinely prescribed end to the captivity, but Daniel's praying expressed his desire and eager expectancy for God's will to be done. Similarly, our praying for Christ's return will not alter the divinely determined moment of that coming, but it should express our "can't wait until He comes" desire: "Even so, come, Lord Jesus" (Revelation 22:20). The lesson about Christ is one we have seen again and again: God's purpose in Christ is certain regardless of appearances to the contrary. As Daniel prayed, the chosen nation had recently passed from subjugation to one foreign power, the Babylonians, to another, the Persians. There was no king on David's throne; it appeared that it was impossible for God to keep His promise of the Seed of David. This period of the seventy divinely decreed weeks was God's "not to worry" to Daniel. The promised Seed of Woman progressed to the Seed of Abraham and then to the Seed of David. In no way could He fail to appear in the fullness of time.

Three interpretation matters regarding the weeks themselves demand our attention: the symbolism of weeks, the arrangement of weeks, and the beginning and ending of the weeks.

The Symbolism

The first matter concerns the symbolism. Most interpret the weeks to symbolize or represent weeks of years rather than weeks of days. Although ordinarily we would not refer to a week in terms of years, this construction is certainly feasible because the word translated "week" is simply a "unit of seven," most often a unit of seven days, hence a week. But, these seventy weeks are very probably seventy units of seven years each, a total of 490 years.

The Arrangement

The second matter concerns the arrangement. The passage clearly divides the weeks into three segments: (1) one set of seven weeks, 49 years; (2) one set of sixty-two weeks, 434 years; (3) one set of one week, 7 years. Although the first seven weeks are isolated from the next sixty-two weeks, they seem to be consecutive, resulting in a total of 483 years for the first sixty-nine weeks. The last week (7 years) seems to be chronologically separated, requiring certain events to take place before it begins.

It is fairly easy to recognize the threefold arrangement; figuring out why the weeks are separated thus is perhaps not as obvious. I think verse 25 explains why the first sixty-nine weeks are segmented. Although the arrival of Messiah the Prince is the ultimate focus, marking the end of the sixty-nine weeks, the text also issues the promise that the streets and walls of Jerusalem would be rebuilt. Remember that when Daniel received this vision, Jerusalem lay in ruins. It was part of God's promise for the city to be restored and it eventually was. So two things were going to happen in the next 483 years: the city would be rebuilt and Messiah would come. Since the rebuilding of the city took place at the beginning of this period and the majority of waiting time for Messiah followed the restoration, the years were arranged to suggest that time disparity. At least, this is my guess as to why.

The last week is separated because the text is more concerned about what happens before the commencement of the last week than with how long it takes. Remember that for a prophetic text to abandon sequential chronology in order to highlight epoch events is quite common. Verses 26 and 27 telescope the two key events that take place between the 69th and 70th week: Messiah will die and the people of the prince will destroy Jerusalem. We detect no hint as to how much time lies between those two events. The 70th week commences when that prince, the "Anti-Christ," enters into a covenant with the nation, ultimately leading to the infamous abomination of desolation.

Our concern is not now what the text says the Anti-Christ will do, but what it says Christ would do and has done. Daniel gives a direct statement of the vicarious sacrifice: "the Messiah (shall) be cut off, but not for himself." Being cut off obviously alludes to death, and "not for himself" clearly denotes the atoning significance of that death. It is regrettable that in interpreting the Seventy Weeks, people spend more time trying to figure out the identity of Anti-Christ than they do highlighting the person and work of Christ. Read verse 24 that declares the sixfold purpose of the Seventy Weeks and you will find that it is all the work of Christ: finishing transgression, abolishing sin, atoning for iniquity, ushering in everlasting righteousness, validating or confirming every prophecy, and anointing the Most Holy.

The Timing

The third issue concerns the beginning and end of the weeks. Verse 25 marks the "going forth of the commandment to restore and to build Jerusalem" as the beginning of the 483-year period before the coming of Messiah. If we can figure out when that commandment was issued, we are in business. Four possibilities have presented themselves: (1) the initial decree of Cyrus in 538 BC (Ezra 1:1-4); (2) the renewal of Cyrus's decree by Darius in 520 BC (Ezra 6:6-12); (3) the decree of Artaxerxes concerning Ezra in 458 BC (Ezra 7:11-26); (4) the decree of Artaxerxes to Nehemiah in 445 BC (Nehemiah 2:1-4).

Without going into all the arguments now, I prefer the fourth suggestion—the decree to Nehemiah—with its special focus on the streets and walls. Therefore, if we take into account some of the inherent difficulties with ancient calendar systems and that a prophetic year seemed to consist of only three hundred sixty days, the 69th week would have ended between AD 26 and 32. The prophetic precision is remarkable. Remember that the prophecy concerns Messiah's atoning death, not

His birth. According to most chronologies, we would date the crucifixion of Christ at about AD 30, well within the prophetic projection. His birth would have been before the end of the sixty-nine weeks (4 BC), His death immediately after. Just as Daniel prayed in anticipation of Jeremiah's prophecy, I would not be surprised if Simeon and Anna were counting Daniel's seventy weeks as they waited for the consolation and redemption of Israel to come. When the 70th week will begin, only God knows.

The Birthplace of Christ

Micah 5:2 is the famous text that identifies Bethlehem as the birthplace of Christ. In Chapter 5 we noted that this outstanding text does more than put Bethlehem on the map. In fact, it is what else the verse says that removes any doubt about its messianic significance. Remember that Micah described the One who would be born in Bethlehem as a Ruler who eternally existed prior to His real birth. In other words, Micah identified this King as the God/Man. That's a key clue that marks this as a messianic prophecy: eternity transcends any reference to mere man.

Nevertheless, although this verse does do more than put Bethlehem on the map, it nonetheless highlights the significance of Bethlehem, geographically linking the coming King to David. This shows the continuity to the Davidic covenant that promised the Ideal King through David's line. Significantly, Jesus Christ was the only descendant of David who shared his birthplace as well as the status of being the rightful heir to the throne. That fact alone precluded identifying any lesser son as the fulfillment of Davidic covenant. Only David and his Ideal Son would share an unroyal birth in an unroyal city. That was a messianic uniqueness that allowed the chief priests and scribes to tell Herod immediately that Christ had to be born in Bethlehem according to the word of the prophet (Matthew 2:4-6).

Recognizing Bethlehem's subtle connection to the Seed promise helps us to see that Micah's purpose was more than providing a text for a Christmas carol. His prediction of Messiah's birthplace contributed to the messianic hope and gospel message that he preached to his contemporaries. Micah preached during the days of Jotham, Ahaz, and Hezekiah. These were days of religious darkness and national uncertainty. The Assyrians threatened the independence of the nation, and

Micah warned even of the Babylonian captivity (Micah 4:10). The continuation of David's line that was so necessary for the coming of Messiah seemed to be in desperate jeopardy. But God's promise to David was inviolable, and notwithstanding the threatening circumstances, nothing would or could frustrate God's promise of Christ. The promised King was coming to Bethlehem, David's town, and all would be well. Regardless of the circumstance, Christ is always the answer to man's need. That was true then, and it is true now. The fact that Christ indeed was born in Bethlehem stands as testimony that every word of prophecy and promise will be fulfilled, regardless of how unlikely circumstances appear. Note how each of the three "C's" identifies this prophecy as messianic: (1) there are clues that transcend mere human fulfillment; (2) there is New Testament confirmation; (3) there is a contextual need for messianic hope.

The Virgin Birth of Christ

Isaiah 7:14 is the famous text that predicts the virgin birth of Immanuel. We have already considered the significance of the title "God with us" that provides a most obvious clue demanding application to the Messiah. The New Testament confirms the application to Christ. In his narrative of the birth of Jesus, Matthew, having marked the virginity of Mary, concluded, "Now all this was done, that it might be fulfilled which was spoken of the Lord by the prophet"; and he then quoted Isaiah 7:14 (Matthew 1:22-23). Although Luke does not quote Isaiah, he nonetheless confirms the prophet's prediction of the birth of Jesus, our Immanuel, by underscoring that Mary was a virgin when she conceived Christ (Luke 1:27).

The context of this prophecy is also crucial to the Old Testament's continuing development of messianic theology and hope. The house of David (the southern kingdom) was under threat from a coalition of Syria and Israel (the northern kingdom). The Lord sent Isaiah to give a word of comfort and assurance to Ahaz to encourage him to trust the Lord and not rely on help from elsewhere. He even offered to Ahaz personally the opportunity to ask from the Lord a sign of his own choosing to confirm the word of promise (Isaiah 7:11). Ahaz, in falsely pious disbelief, refused to ask the Lord for a sign (Isaiah 7:12). Isaiah then removed the opportunity for Ahaz to receive a personal sign and directed the sign of the virgin birth of Immanuel to the nation as a whole. This may appear a subtle shift, but it is one that I think crucial to a proper understanding of the prophecy. Note that in verse 11 the Authorized Version uses the second person singular pronoun "thee" when the first sign is offered to Ahaz. Modern English no longer uses that form, but it is a clear way of expressing when "you" is singular. In verse 14 Isaiah said, "Therefore the Lord himself shall give you a sign." The pronoun "you" is plural, indicating the sign is no longer for the personal benefit of Ahaz.

Ahaz's folly and disbelief threatened the continuation of David's throne and thereby seemed to jeopardize the messianic hope so intricately associated with the perpetuation of that throne. The virgin birth of Immanuel was God's answer to that folly. It was not the time of the birth but the certain fact of the birth that was crucial in this context. Neither Syria nor Israel nor Assyria nor Ahaz could frustrate or alter God's purpose in sending Christ. The prophecy of the virgin birth was a message of hope in an otherwise hopeless situation. Christ is always the answer.

Without dispute, the birth of Jesus Christ fulfilled this prophecy. Yet I need to address briefly a couple of interpretation problems. The first concerns the word "virgin" and the second concerns the word "sign." Many critics contend that Isaiah's word refers only to a young girl of marriageable age, and this notion is reflected in various modern versions. They argue that there is another word that Isaiah could have used if he really intended to convey the idea of virginity. I will say unequivocally that the word for virgin that Isaiah uses ('almah) is the only word in the Old Testament that without further definition or qualification refers to a virgin in the strictest sense of that term. The word the critics suggest should have been used is translated by the Authorized Version as "virgin" (betulah), but it does not seem to be as rigid a word as Isaiah's. For instance, this word is sometimes followed by the defining statement "neither had any man known her" (Genesis 24:16) in order to insure the idea of sexual virginity. Sometimes the word even designates a widow, whose virginity would be unlikely (Joel 1:8). Had Isaiah used this word, there would have been just reason to suspect the virgin conception. But the word he used, while it may refer to a young girl of marriageable age, always assumes the sexual purity of the girl. Granted, the sexual morality of the girl is not always the focus of a given context, but in no text is the purity ever suspect. Here are the places the word occurs if you want to check them out for yourself: Genesis 24:43-44; Exodus 2:8; Psalm 46 (superscription); Psalm 68:25; Proverbs 30:18-19; Song of Solomon 1:3 and 6:8; and I Chronicles 15:20. In addition, the Greek word used by the Septuagint and Matthew to translate Isaiah's word indisputably and unequivocally designates a virgin in the strictest sense of the word. The Septuagint reflects the "pre-Christian" understanding of the word's meaning and Matthew records the Holy Spirit's direct intent. Recognizing the rigidity of the word precludes any secondary or double fulfillment of this prophecy. There is but one virgin birth and that is the birth of Jesus Christ.

The second issue concerns the meaning of the word "sign." The problem is that if this prophecy refers uniquely to Jesus Christ how could it be a sign to Ahaz? Keep in mind here a couple of things. Remember that the virgin birth sign was not directed to Ahaz personally; he rejected the sign offer. Remember that Isaiah did not say the virgin would conceive in seven hundred plus years; he said, "Behold a virgin is about to conceive and bear a son." He used the typical prophetic language of imminency. The issue was the certain *fact* of the virgin conception, not the *when* of it. We need to understand as well that the word "sign" is used essentially in two ways: as a present persuader or as an after-the-fact confirmation. God's call of Moses illustrates nicely this dual idea. To convince Moses of his call, God gave him two signs (Exodus 4:9): the rod-to-a-snake-to-a-rod sign and the leprous hand sign. Those were present persuaders. To assure Moses of the constant divine presence, God told him that when he returned with the nation to "this mountain" and worshipped, that would be a token or sign that God had sent him on this mission. That was an after-the-fact confirmation: a divine "I told you so." I suggest that in the context of Isaiah 7 we can see both aspects of the sign. On the one hand, Ahaz was offered the present persuader; he rejected it. On the other hand, God gave the sign of the virgin birth as an after-the-fact confirmation that the Syrian-Israeli threat was nothing to worry about after all. In fact, in the time it would take for the child to grow to the age of discernment, the land that they abhorred would be "forsaken of both her kings" (Isaiah 7:16). That time period had immediate application; the particular child, Immanuel, would be the future confirmation, the divine "I told you so" that every word of promise was true.

CHRIST IN WORD PROPHECY

The Ministry of Christ

Isaiah 61:1-3 is a prophetic first-person declaration of the Messiah that encapsulates the essence of His ministry. That this is a prophecy of Christ's ministry is clear both from the familiar messianic clues (such as the anointing) and from New Testament confirmation. The Lord Jesus marked the prophetic significance of Isaiah 61 by using it to identify Himself as the Messiah at the beginning of His public ministry in His home town of Nazareth (Luke 4:16-21). Three strands of thought define the ministry of the Messiah.

First is *the authority or might of the Christ*. This might is based on the divine commission. That Jehovah anointed Him draws attention specifically to His mediatorial consecration. It implies, then, the effective operation of each of the mediatorial offices: prophet, priest, and king. As the elect of God (Isaiah 42:1), He was set apart by God to fulfill the eternal purpose of salvation and redemption. This might was effected by divine power. The Spirit's coming upon Christ without measure was a common prophetic theme (cf. Isaiah 11:2) and one of the earmarks of His ministry that unmistakably identified Him as God's Christ (John 3:34). That enabling and empowering by the Holy Spirit assured the success of every aspect of Christ's ministry: no obstacle could stand in His way or hinder Him (see Zechariah 4:6).

The second strand of thought is *the message of the Christ*: He had the words of life. Four words can summarize His message: evangelism (to preach good tidings), consolation (to bind up the brokenhearted), liberation (to proclaim liberty to captives), and admonition (to proclaim the acceptable time and the day of vengeance).

The third strand is the *mission of the Christ*. The last lines of both verse 2 and verse 3 state a threefold objective of Christ's mission relating both to the Lord and to those who mourn in Zion. (1) His mission is to justify sinners. This is suggested by the statement that the mourners are called or declared to be "trees of righteousness, the planting of the Lord." The imagery parallels Christ's warning to the Pharisees: "Every plant, which my heavenly Father hath not planted, shall be rooted up" (Matthew 15:13). But those that are planted by the Lord on the firm ground of the righteousness of Christ are secure indeed; they cannot be uprooted. (2) His mission is to transform lives. Life is different for Zion's mourners. He gives a crown in the place of ashes.

He gives the oil of gladness in the place of mourning. He replaces the spirit of heaviness with the garment of praise. The obvious point is that grace does not leave sinners where it finds them. (3) His mission is to glorify God. All that He does, He does so that "he (the Lord) might be glorified." Salvation is good for sinners, but it is ultimately to the praise of the glory of His grace (see Ephesians 1). The Lord Jesus professed to His Father the success of this part of His mission: "I have glorified thee on the earth: I have finished the work which thou gavest me to do" (John 17:4). It should not surprise us that when Jesus applied all this to Himself, "all bare him witness, and wondered at the gracious words which proceeded out of his mouth" (Luke 4:22).

The Galilean Ministry of Christ

Isaiah 9 is in the middle of the "Immanuel trilogy," and it reaches its famous climax in verse 6 with the four key titles of Messiah (see Chapter 6). Although the opening verses are often overshadowed by verse 6, they make their own contribution to the messianic promise, yet they cannot be understood apart from the climactic declaration, "for unto us a child is born, unto us a son is given." The chapter begins by describing a reversal of fortune that will take place in the northern districts of the nation, in the regions around the Sea of Chinnereth or Galilee, the region of Galilee referred to as the districts of the nations. Light and joy will replace darkness and oppression because of the promised Son. John extracted and declared the theological truth of this when he said concerning the Eternal Word, "In him was life; and the life was the light of men. And the light shineth in darkness" (John 1:4-5). Matthew, however, confirmed the specific application of this prophecy to the first stage of Christ's public ministry. Immediately after His temptation, Christ learned that John had been imprisoned and departed into Galilee, leaving Nazareth and taking up residence in Capernaum (Matthew 4:12-13). Matthew declared that this move fulfilled Isaiah's prophecy, and then he quoted Isaiah 9:1-2. The early Galilean ministry of Christ precisely fulfilled the prophecy. The territory around Gennesaret was the historic allotment of the tribes of Zebulon and Naphtali. Even Nazareth, Christ's childhood home where He made His great messianic claim (Luke 4), was part of Zebulon's territory. Christ's first miracle occurred in Cana of Galilee (John 2). Capernaum, on the shore of Galilee in the territory of Naphtali, became the city of Jesus, the headquarters for

His mission of miracles and preaching. Ironically, the region that seemed to be so despised by the elite was so honored by Christ.

The Triumphal Entry of Christ

Zechariah 9:9 is one of the most famous messianic prophecies in this book that is so rich in messianic promise and theology. The prophet commands Zion to rejoice because of the coming of the Ideal King. Both Zechariah and the New Testament place this coming during the time of Messiah's first advent. Zechariah sets the prophecy against the backdrop of a prophecy concerning Greece's world conquests and God's defeat of Greece. Significantly, it is in this prophetic revelation about Greece that Zechariah announces the coming King. The contribution that Greece made culturally and linguistically to the "fullness of time" has received much deserved attention. Although the details of those contributions are not enumerated in this text, it is nonetheless impressive that Zechariah places Messiah's coming within this general time frame. The New Testament specifically identifies the fulfillment of Zechariah 9:9 as the Triumphal Entry of Christ into Jerusalem at the beginning of what became the week of His passion (Matthew 21:5; John 12:15).

In this well-known text Zechariah makes four key statements about the coming King. Unfortunately, the implications of these statements are frequently overlooked because of the remarkable precision of the New Testament's application of the verse to Christ's riding a borrowed donkey into Jerusalem. We certainly do not want to ignore the obvious, specific fulfillment, but neither do we want to ignore the whole message, all of which applies to Christ.

First, *He is the promised King*. Zechariah's announcement, "Behold, thy King cometh unto thee," went to the heart of the Davidic covenant promise. When Zechariah preached, David's throne was vacant. But the prophet aimed the eye of faith beyond the empty throne to the sure promise. That the prophet referred to "thy" king, using the second person singular pronoun, individualized the promise. Christ's coming would indeed have national and even worldwide relevance, but it had personal application to each believer. This was the long-awaited King of promise. The prospect of seeing that King warranted the admonition to rejoice: "Rejoice greatly, O daughter of Zion; shout, O daughter of Jerusalem." Although both of the imperatives carry the idea of shrieking loudly, one with joy and the other with triumph, they express the inner celebration as well as any outward evidence of it. Nothing can bring greater joy to a saint's heart than the personal Christ. Whether then or now, it is a believing sight of Christ that satisfies the heart.

Second, *He is the righteous King*. Zechariah marked as one of the perfections of the promised king that "he is just." We have seen this over and over again as one of the essential features of the Messiah. Not only is Christ eternally and perfectly righteous by virtue of His deity, but He was animated with righteousness throughout His earthly mission and He will forever execute righteousness in His royal authority. It was part of the messianic ideal that the Davidic king would judge His people with righteousness and that righteousness would flourish in His days (Psalm 72:2, 7; see especially II Samuel 23:3). Righteousness will burgeon during the kingdom reign of Christ; however, since this verse refers specifically to Christ's first advent, this righteousness most likely designates the positive and active obedience that the Lord performed during His earthly life. In every way the Lord Jesus satisfied the expectations and demands of the ideal King.

Third, *He is the victorious King*. This coming King is "having salvation." The meaning of this statement is disputed. The Hebrew text has a form of the verb "to save" which can convey either a passive sense of "being saved or delivered" or a stative sense of "being victorious." The Septuagint, the Greek translation of the Old Testament, and other ancient versions suggest the active sense of "one who saves," a Savior. Although either the active or the passive sense would accurately apply to the Messiah, the Hebrew text is preferable. That God's Messiah King is the object of divine help and deliverance is a recurring theme both in messianic prophecy (see Psalms 18:50; 20:6; 21:1, 4-5; 22:8) and in the earthly experience of Jesus recorded in the Gospels. From His deliverance as an infant from the plot of Herod to His preservation in Gethsemane from Satan's last attempt to prevent the crucifixion, God saved the King from premature death. The greatest deliverance of all was His deliverance from the grave by the power of God in approval and vindication of His perfect life and atoning death. His deliverance marked His victory over every enemy and His ability and right to subdue every foe. His deliverance guarantees the salvation of all His people. Because He has been delivered, He is victorious and He delivers and saves His people.

Fourth, *He is the humble King*. Finally, Zechariah describes the coming King as being "lowly." This word refers to more than the Messiah's poverty and meekness of spirit; it has the idea of being afflicted or oppressed and encompasses the whole suffering life of Christ. Zechariah's use of this word for the King closely parallels Isaiah's earlier description of the Servant as being void of majesty, despised, and rejected (Isaiah 53:2-5). Although Jesus was King, in His first incarnate appearance only the eye of faith could discern His royalty. That unbelief failed to see His kingship condemns the blindness of the heart; it does not alter the truth that Christ came as the King of kings. Messiah's riding "upon an ass, *even* upon the colt the foal of an ass," further defines His humble obedience. Note, by the way, my translation of "even" rather than "and." This explicative or explanatory use of the conjunction is common and here is necessary to avoid the notion that Christ was riding two animals. The specific idea is that He was riding a young donkey, and this is the specific element of the prophecy that was fulfilled at the Triumphal Entry. The significance is not that the donkey was a lowly creature in contrast to the stately horse. Indeed, both the Old Testament and documents from the ancient Near East demonstrate that donkeys were often mounts for royalty and rulers (see Judges 5:10; 10:4; 12:14; and II Samuel 16:1-2). The people's response when they saw Christ riding into Jerusalem on the donkey was not surprise as to why a king would be on a donkey. Rather, when they saw Him they immediately cried, "Blessed is the King of Israel that cometh in the name of the Lord" (John 12:13). For a king to ride a donkey was not contrary to expectation. The significance rests, rather, in the fact that the Old Testament associated horses, war machines, with self-reliance and distrust of God (see Psalms 20:7; 33:16-17; and Isaiah 33:1). If anything characterized Messiah's first coming, it was His faithful, unwavering dependence on God. Furthermore, God's initial instructions concerning kings prohibited their multiplying horses (Deuteronomy 17:16). It would be aberrant for the ideal King, who was righteous in every other way, to associate Himself with that which marked kingly disobedience. Even in the detail of the donkey, Christ fulfilled all righteousness.

The Death of Christ

Selecting an example of a prophecy of the atoning death of the Messiah is difficult for the simple reason that there are so many. The Old Testament points to many of the specific details that the New Testament associates with the cross and its attendant events and circumstances: His betrayal, His silence before His accusers, His scourging, the plucking of His beard, the piercing of His hands, feet, and side, the division of His garments, the mockery of onlookers, and the preservation of His bones from being broken. So precise and specific are some of these prophecies that it seems the only missing details are the names of the betrayer and accusers and the designation of Roman crucifixion as the means of execution.

Zechariah 13:7 and its context will serve as a good example of a prophecy of the death of Messiah. This text is important both because of its identification of the Messiah and because of its statement of His sacrificial death. Christ's own words fix the application of this verse to the events of His crucifixion (Matthew 26:31). This verse makes two great statements that highlight the deity of Messiah. These are important clues that point beyond a mere mortal who will die. First, the Lord addresses the Messiah as "my shepherd." As we learned in the last chapter, this title often designates sovereigns, whether good or bad. We considered the development of this title from Ezekiel 34. Remember that the chapter began with God's condemnation of bad shepherds who had abused their office and failed their duty. The Lord then identified Himself as the shepherd who would do for His people all that was necessary for their welfare. Having described those gracious dealings, the Lord declared that He would appoint "one shepherd over them, and he shall feed them, even my servant David" (Ezekiel 34:23; note Zechariah's similar development in chapter 11). The Shepherd is the Lord, yet the Shepherd is distinct from the Lord. He is the perfect representation of God. This dual identification again points us to that mysterious Trinitarian relationship between God the Father and God the Son. Zechariah's brief statement "my shepherd" must be understood in the light of Ezekiel theology. The pronoun "my" suggests both the divine appointment and the special relationship that exists between the Shepherd and Jehovah.

Second, the Lord identifies the Shepherd as "the man that is my fellow." The word "man" often designates man in his strength and comes from the same root as the word "hero" that Isaiah used to name the son "Immanuel" in Isaiah 9:6 (the mighty God). Most important is the word "fellow." This word occurs only here and in Leviticus. Usually translated "neighbor" in Leviticus, it refers to those who have things in common, such as laws and privileges. It would be inappropriate for God in the Zechariah text to apply this term to mere mortal man. This one, God's associate or nearest one, stands not only in proximity to God but equal with God. He participates and shares in the divine nature; He is God. This statement conforms to Trinitarian theology that Christ and the Father are distinct in person yet one in essence. Zechariah hints elsewhere that he understood this unique relationship between Messiah and God. In 11:4-14 the rejected shepherd is Jehovah. In 12:10 Jehovah says, "They shall look upon **me** whom they have pierced, and they shall mourn for **him**." The shift in pronouns from the first to the third person testifies to the distinctive association. That God would send His perfect representative, His Son, was the great message of hope. Perhaps Zechariah 13:7 was in Christ's mind when in the New Testament chapter on the Good Shepherd He declared, "I and my Father are one" (John 10:30).

In that same passage, Christ said, "I am the good shepherd: the good shepherd giveth his life for the sheep" (John 10:11). This declaration of Christ marks another parallel to Zechariah's prophecy. God's way of salvation required the sacrifice of the shepherd, the "fellow" of God. Although Zechariah 12:10 indicates that unbelievers were responsible for piercing the Messiah, 13:7 squelches any notion that Messiah's death was anything other than the eternal purpose of God. Zechariah advances Isaiah's announcement that it was God's pleasure or purpose to bruise the Servant (Isaiah 53:10) by revealing that Christ's execution was God's command. The verse begins with Jehovah of hosts commanding the sword to awake and smite the shepherd. That God demanded the death of His "fellow" speaks volumes concerning the seriousness of sin and the immutability of divine justice. In New Testament terms it is only by and because of the death of Christ that God is both just and justifier. In Zechariah's terms it is only because God bade the sword awake against His Shepherd that a cleansing fountain could be opened "for sin and for uncleanness" (13:1).*

The Burial of Christ

The bodily burial of Christ was conclusive proof of the reality of His death. He did not faint or swoon; He died and His body was placed in a cold, dark tomb. Although the prophecies of Christ's resurrection assume His burial, one text in particular predicts the actual burial of Christ with astounding precision and amazing detail. Isaiah 53:9, part of that climactic Servant Song so explicit in its revelation of the vicarious death of the Messiah, says, "He made his grave with the wicked, and with the rich in his death." There are several things to note about this statement. The first concerns the meaning and the subject of the verb "made." The verb literally means "to give" and can have the idea of appointing or assigning. The "he" does not refer to the Messiah; rather, it is impersonal or indefinite. It could be translated "one assigned his grave with the wicked." We would normally express this idea with a passive statement: his grave was assigned with the wicked. The second issue concerns the contrast between the wicked and the rich. In Hebrew the word "wicked" is plural and the word "rich" is singular. To underscore this contrast, we should translate the "and" as "but." The final matter concerns the word "death." It is a plural word that in Hebrew would intensify the idea. By using the plural, the prophet subtly yet clearly draws attention to the uniqueness of the Messiah's death. Putting all this together, I would suggest this translation: "His grave was assigned to be with wicked men, but He was with a rich man in His uniquely significant death."

Because we now know the historic details of Christ's burial, this prophecy appears explicitly clear. Having been executed as a criminal as far as Rome was concerned, Christ would have most likely been assigned burial with the rest of the criminals had it not been for the intervention of "a rich man of Arimathæa, named Joseph," who successfully begged Pilate for Christ's body and buried Him in his own family tomb (Matthew 27:57-60). I don't know how Isaiah could have been any more precise without actually naming Pilate and Joseph.

The Resurrection of Christ

The New Testament defines the gospel specifically in terms of the death and the resurrection of Christ, both of which occurred according to the Scripture (I Corinthians 15:3, 4). The Old Testament does not omit any part of the gospel message. Indeed, that Paul defines these two essential elements as occurring according to the Scriptures indicates that the Old Testament foretold both events. One of the most direct prophecies of Christ's resurrection is Psalm 16:10. This text deserves consideration not only because of its clarity, but also because of the special way the apostles used it in their early proclamations of the resurrection of the Lord Jesus. Both Peter (Acts 2:25-28) and Paul (Acts 13:35) appealed to this text as principal Old Testament evidence of the purposed resurrection of the Savior. In appealing to this text, both apostles pointed to David's death as evidence that Christ was the single fulfillment of the prophecy. Peter makes it clear that he was not just reading Christ's resurrection back into this Davidic song; rather, he declares that Christ's resurrection was the uniquely intended subject of David's prophecy. He also makes the far-reaching statement that David, as a prophet of God, knew exactly what and who he was writing about: "He seeing this before spake of the resurrection of Christ" (Acts 2:30-31). So much for that notion that the Old Testament prophets wrote better than they knew! It is also interesting that Peter quotes verses 7-11, indicating that more than just verse 10 has messianic application. In fact, I would suggest that the entirety of the Psalm refers solely to Christ.

Keeping the resurrection prophecy in its messianic environment enriches our understanding of Christ's own perspective of messianic mission. It also illustrates again how "advanced" messianic theology was in the Old Testament dispensation. In this mysterious revelation of a prayerful soliloquy, the Messiah acknowledges His submission to the Lord, His resolute determination to do the will of the Lord, and His absolute assurance that He would succeed in His mission, knowing that He would receive a people, rise from the grave, and achieve His honored place at God's right hand. In the final chapter on finding Christ in worship, I will deal specifically with the messianic Psalms and how to recognize them as messianic. So if at this point you are not convinced that all of Psalm 16 applies to Messiah, suspend your judgment until we consider those issues. In this context I must focus our thoughts on the one verse that without dispute is messianic. But remember that we must pay attention to the entire context. Even New Testament confirmation does not justify extracting a verse from its context and dealing with it in isolation. The New Testament did not, nor should we.

That verse 10 applies to the bodily resurrection of Christ is beyond doubt, thanks to the New Testament confirmation. We have to keep this in mind as we consider the text itself. I say this because on the surface the translation in the Authorized Version, particularly of the first line, seems to refer to something other than a bodily resurrection from the grave. A proper interpretation of the verse requires defining the crucial terms correctly and utilizing the poetic structure.

Let me address the poetic structure first. The principal feature of Hebrew poetry is the parallelism of thought between the lines. Sometimes the lines say the same thing (synonymous parallelism); sometimes the lines say opposite things (antithetic parallelism); sometimes the lines combine to form an extended analogy (emblematic parallelism); sometimes the lines build up thought from a common foundation (climactic parallelism); sometimes the lines combine to form a single thought (synthetic parallelism). The point is that identifying the relationship between the lines helps to interpret the whole. In other words, one line tends to interpret the other. Verse 10 is a classic example of synonymous parallelism. "For thou wilt not leave my soul in hell" is repeated and defined by "neither wilt thou suffer thine Holy One to see corruption." The preservation from corruption obviously refers to preventing what normally happens to bodies after they die. God would not allow the body of Messiah to experience that decay. This clear reference to the body in the second line dictates that the body is also in view in the first line, exactly what the New Testament demands.

We may have difficulty seeing this because of the words "soul" and "hell" in the first line. We need a little Hebrew lesson here. The word typically translated "soul" in the Authorized Version is *nephesh*. Whereas we tend to limit "soul" to the immaterial part of man, the word *nephesh* refers to the entirety of man, the person. As a general word for the whole man, it includes both inner and outer man. There are many instances in the Old Testament where the word refers specifically to some aspect of the inner man (intellect, emotion, or will) and the translation "soul" is appropriate. There are other times, however, where the word refers to aspects of the outer man. In fact, sometimes the word refers to a corpse, the body without any life or soul. In selecting the appropriate translation of the word, we have to pay close attention to the context to determine whether what is meant is the whole person or a special focus on the inner or outer part of the person. I believe that in this context, explained by the second line and confirmed by the New Testament, the "body" is the intended sense.

The second problem word is "hell." The Hebrew word here is *she'ol.* The Authorized Version translates *she'ol* as either "hell" or "grave" almost an equal number of times. The word has three senses in the Old Testament. (1) It designates death as an abstract in contrast to life. (2) It designates the grave–not a particular kind of tomb, but wherever the dead body decays. (3) It designates the realm of departed wicked spirits, who are under the sentence of condemnation. The translation "hell" is appropriate for the last sense but not the first two. I believe that in this text, the sense of "grave" is the only sense that is contextually, theologically, and prophetically possible.

In light of this evidence, I would translate Psalm 16:10 like this: "For you will not abandon my body in the grave/ you will not allow your Holy One to see corruption." What a clear, direct declaration of the real, bodily resurrection of Christ! There is absolutely no suggestion in this verse of Christ's spirit descending into hell as the place of torment for any reason. This is a prediction of the bodily resurrection that marked the beginning of the Messiah's earned exaltation that was followed by His earned entrance into the presence of God and His session at God's right hand (verse 11; compare Psalm 68:18 for a prophecy of the Ascension and Psalm 110:1 for the revelation of the Session). It corresponds precisely to New Testament theology.

I think these few examples illustrate how remarkably precise were the Old Testament prophecies about Christ. Even though they have been fulfilled, what they teach about Christ remains relevant for us. As we study these fulfilled prophecies, our advantage and added blessing is that we can rejoice that all the promises of God in Christ and about Christ are verifiably true. The study of the fulfilled prophecies ought to generate an ever-increasing hope and expectancy for that which is yet to come. It all will come as He says it will; Christ is coming again. Even so, come, Lord Jesus.

Let me close this chapter by giving you a few more specific examples of fulfilled Old Testament prophecies about Christ. You should study these on your own using the interpretation "C's" that I suggested to validate the messianic intent and content. I think if we can practice on the prophecies specifically referred to in the New Testament, it will hone our skills and increase our confidence in dealing with the passages that do not have the cross-references supplied.

The Prophecy	OT reference	NT reference
Christ's forerunner	Isaiah 40:3-5;	Luke 3:3-6
	Malachi 3:1	Luke 7:24, 27
	Malachi 4:5-6	Matthew 11:13-14
The slaughter of the innocents	Jeremiah 31:15	Matthew 2:16-18
Christ's teaching in parables	Psalm 78:2-4	Matthew 13:34-35
Christ as God's Prophet	Deuteronomy 18:15	Acts 3:20-23
Christ a Priest like Melchizedek	Psalm 110:4	Hebrews 5:5-6
Christ's betrayal for 30 pieces of silver	Zechariah 11:12	Matthew 26:14-15
Christ's silence at His trial	Isaiah 53:7	Mark 15:4, 5
Christ's torture	Isaiah 50:6	Matthew 26:67
Christ's being pierced	Zechariah 12:10	John 19:37
Christ's bones not broken	Psalm 34:20	John 19:36
Christ forsaken by God	Psalm 22:1	Matthew 27:46
Division of Christ's garments	Psalm 22:17-18	Matthew 27:35
Christ's Ascension to Glory	Psalm 68:18	Ephesians 4:8
Christ's Session in Glory	Psalm 110:1	Acts 2:34-35 (among others)

* What I have said about these two texts from Zechariah is part of an article I wrote, "The Revelation of Christ," in the "Focus on Zechariah" issue of *Biblical Viewpoint* (November 1990). To see how throughly this one prophet sets forth the Messiah in all His fullness, you may want to read this article some time.

CHAPTER 8

CHRIST IN PICTURE PROPHECY–EXPLAINED

A picture is worth a thousand words–so they say. I'm not sure that we can make such a precise equation, but there is no question that pictures can effectively communicate ideas and that illustrations can effectively aid our understanding. Just consider how many toys or appliances have been assembled by the owner's looking at the pictures rather than reading the instructions. Instructors often use visual aids to grasp or hold their students' attention as well as actually to impart the desired information. Sunday school teachers have for years used flannelgraph stories, object lessons, and wordless books with colored pages to teach youngsters the basic facts about the Bible and the foundational truths about the gospel. Graphs, charts, and more sophisticated analogies aid even adults, with their greater attention spans and more advanced knowledge, to learn more easily. My colleague and mentor whom I mentioned in a previous chapter is a master in using analogies to explain the most complicated of theological concepts. In fact, he has an analogy for everything; I refer to him as the "analogy king." Consequently, he is a most effective teacher.

God is the most effective teacher ever. As the Revealer of truth, His desire is that man understand what He has revealed. He certainly holds man accountable for the truth. As evidence of His desire and purpose, He has from the beginning of His revelation communicated in comprehensible ways. In an earlier discussion of the concept of progressive revelation, I stressed that what God revealed often progressed from general to specific truth. He gave more and more details to advance the knowledge of the revealed truth. I suggest that an important element of progressive revelation is the manner, not just the content, of the revelation. At least it is safe to say that in time past God communicated in diverse manners (Hebrews 1:1). The Lord did not just drop a bunch of sophisticated, technical, theological terminology ("propitiation," "expiation," "vicarious atonement," etc.) from heaven, expecting man on his own to comprehend the significance. I know the folly of that firsthand. When my older son was about three years old, I remember that one day he crawled under my desk and confessed that he was hiding from God. With orthodox precision, I explained to him that God is a Spirit, infinite, eternal, and unchangeable in His being, wisdom, power, holiness, justice, goodness, and truth. God is infinite in regard to space and knowledge: He is omnipresent and omniscient. The bottom line, I concluded, is that it is impossible to hide from God. Notwithstanding the correctness of my explanation, it quickly became evident that he did not have a clue as to what I was talking about: he cried out from under the desk that God was not there. What I said was good; how I said it was not particularly effective.

Thankfully, the Lord knows best not only what to say, but how to say it. One of His key methods to explain truth was the use of pictures–illustrations, object lessons, and analogies–to clarify the profound and vitally important revelation He was graciously giving to man, not the least of which was the revelation of the Messiah. I will define the technical terms for these pictures in just a moment, but for now let me put this in terms of "X" and "Y." If "X" is the picture and "Y" is the truth, God was saying to look at "X" in order to understand something about "Y."

Much of what we read in the Old Testament is God's using "X's" to teach ultimate truths about "Y." It is important, therefore, that we learn to distinguish between "X" and "Y." The principal thing to remember is that "X" does not equal "Y." One of the most serious mistakes made in Old Testament study is the confusion or substitution of "X" for "Y." The picture points to the reality, but it is not the reality. For example, the Ark of the Covenant was a picture of God's presence, but it was not the reality of God's presence. God never lived in a box. Animal sacrifices pictured vicarious atonement, but they were not the vicarious atonement. Nevertheless, I cannot begin to count the number of people I have encountered over the years who have assumed that in the Old Testament dispensation people were saved by animal blood, whereas now we are saved by Christ's blood. They have mistakenly substituted "X" for "Y," the picture for the reality. The same people would rightly be opposed to any interpretation of the Lord's Supper or Baptism that confused or identified the picture with the reality that it symbolized. Eating the bread and drinking the cup pictures the salvation we enjoy through Christ's atonement, but it does not effect that salvation. The water of Baptism symbolizes identification with Christ, but it does not cause or accomplish that identification. Orthodox theology recognizes that these rites Christ gave the church are beautiful pictures of spiritual truth. Recognizing that the cup pictures and points to the blood of Christ's sacrifice is no different from recognizing that the animal sacrifice pictures and points to the blood of Christ's sacrifice. The one points backward; the other points forward. They both point upward to the same thing. I find it sadly ironic that naïve surface interpretation has confused and obscured what God intended as a means of clarifying truth.

Acknowledging that God used pictures and learning how to interpret those pictures are crucial to a proper and profitable use of the Old Testament. Indeed, I suggest that if we deny or ignore this means of revelation, we will never rightly understand much of the message of the Old Testament. This is particularly true when it comes to discovering what the Old Testament reveals and teaches about Christ. The Old Testament is filled with "picture prophecies" of the person and work of Messiah. God often said in essence, "Look at this person, thing, or event to see something about who Christ is and what He will do." Although perhaps not worth a thousand words, those divinely defined picture analogies spoke volumes about Christ. Picture prophecy is a good place to discover Christ. And as you well know by this time, finding Christ in the Old Testament is our objective.

Before considering some key examples of picture prophecies in the Old Testament, I need to lay some foundation that will help you identify and interpret these prophecies in your personal Bible study.

Interpretation Guidelines for Typology

Typology is the technical term for what I have been calling "picture prophecy." Unfortunately, it is a term that suffers because of inconsistent definition and application to interpretation techniques that reflect more fanciful imagination than legitimate skill. It is the term often employed by those who take from Scripture the most obscure or seemingly theologically meaningless texts they can find and then preach or teach from them the most wonderfully profound themes of the gospel, declaring that those obscure statements are types of Christ. The rest of us who read or hear these expositions are left wondering why we have never had the insight to see that reflection of Christ in the text. I confess that that kind of message often blesses my heart greatly because it draws my mind to Christ, but it dawned on me one day that the reason I have never seen some of those "types" is that they are not there. Types do not exist just because someone thinks he discerned something in the text that reminds him about Christ when he thinks about it hard enough. I want to be very clear that *typology is not an interpretation technique that we arbitrarily impose on an Old Testament text in an effort to rescue that text for Christian relevance.*

One of the most important objectives in any study of the Scripture is to discover the author's meaning. For those of us who believe in the direct inspiration of the Scripture by the Holy Spirit, this goal is crucial because we believe that God is the ultimate Author of the words we are seeking to understand. In interpreting any text of Scripture, we must recognize that "authorial intent" is more important than "reader response." We do not honor God's Word and intended message by foisting our own notions on the text and making it say whatever we want it to, not even when what we want to say is soundly orthodox.

Reacting against those who capriciously find types in everything in the Old Testament are those who refuse to recognize types unless forced to do so by the New Testament. These readers argue that the only legitimately recognized types in the Old Testament are the ones the New Testament specifically identifies; without New Testament directive, we have no warrant for looking for any other types in the Old Testament. I believe that this attitude imposes an unnecessary limitation and potentially commits the same error as the opposite extreme: failing to understand God's intended message. Let me say again that typology is not an interpretation technique; it is a method of divine revelation.

The New Testament is of immense help not only in identifying specific types for us but also in instructing us about the proper way to identify and interpret types. Rather than assume that we are not able to do things with the Old Testament that the New Testament writers could because they were inspired, we should learn to emulate their interpretation methods precisely *because* they were inspired and, therefore, were obviously able to interpret correctly. I suggest that if we are going to interpret the Old Testament correctly, we must avoid both extreme views of typology. My position is that God purposely used types in the Old Testament to communicate truth. I do not want to see types where they do not exist, and I do not want to be blind to types where they are present. Typology is not something that I am reading into the text; it is something that God put into the text that I must read out of the text.

Key Terms

There are three key terms that we need to define and keep distinct in a discussion about typology: "symbol," "type," and "antitype." The New Testament word "shadow," although not one of these three technical hermeneutical terms, helps define the relationship between type and antitype as well.

Symbol

A *symbol* is simply an object lesson. It is a sign, something real, that points beyond itself to a moral or spiritual truth. The symbol is not the truth; it is an object lesson teaching a particular truth. Let's say a Sunday school teacher, illustrating for the children the terrible effects of sin, puts a drop of coloring into a glass of water, causing the water to change to that color. That would be a vivid object lesson, but if all the child learned was an elementary chemistry lesson, missing the key lesson about the effects of sin, we would accuse the child of not having paid attention. In the Old Testament, the Lord often used such symbols or object lessons as visual aids to reinforce or illustrate the point He wanted to make to those receiving the message.

Pick a prophet and note as you follow his ministry how often the Lord instructed that prophet to add to his message an object lesson, a symbol. For instance, Jeremiah's wearing, burying, and recovering the linen waistcloth was a symbol of the nation's sin and corruption that rendered them liable to judgment (Jeremiah 13). His breaking the jar outside the city gate graphically and grimly pictured the totality of the coming judgment (Jeremiah 19). His wearing a yoke as he preached signified the coming captivity (Jeremiah 27-28). Obviously, if all the people learned from these symbolic acts was that burying linen ruins the cloth, throwing a jar breaks it, and wearing a yoke is silly, then they totally missed the point.

Interpreting the symbol requires identifying the salient correspondence between the analogy and the primary topic. The purpose of the symbol is to clarify the moral lesson, not distract from it. God expected the contemporary audience to get the point of these symbols. As we read the Old Testament and discover these symbols, we must not be naïve or inattentive and thus ourselves miss the point intended.

Type/Antitype

"Type" and "antitype" must be defined together. A *type* is an object lesson, a symbol, that foreshadows or predicts the actual, future realization or fulfillment of the pictured truth. This is why I like to define a type simply as a "picture prophecy." An *antitype* is the future realization to which the type points; it is the fulfillment of the picture prophecy. Types are divinely inspired analogies whose salient points not only correspond to but also predict the reality, the antitype, the main topic of the revelation. This definition explains why I insist that typology is not simply an interpretation technique arbitrarily foisted on a text to give it Christian relevance; instead, it is an integral and divinely intended part of the revelation.

Interestingly, these words come into English directly from Greek and both words occur in the New Testament. The historic definition of these words illustrates well the important relationship between the type and its antitype. The verb cognate means "to strike" and the noun "type" designates the mark or the impression that results from that beating. The "antitype" can refer to the instrument that is used to make the impression. The type, then, has no existence apart from the antitype. The type is something visible, but it is the antitype that defines and determines the significance of the type. The type represents and resembles the antitype, but the antitype is the reality. This is a vital distinction to keep in mind when interpreting the messianic types in the Old Testament. Christ is the ultimate reality: He is the Ideal behind—or perhaps I should say above—all the visible impressions.

CHRIST IN PICTURE PROPHECY–EXPLAINED

Shadow

The New Testament uses another helpful analogy to describe the relationship between Christ and the picture prophecies of Him. Paul, having referred to some of the Old Testament types, calls them "shadows" and calls Christ "the body" (Colossians 2:17). This suggests a couple of things. First, a shadow exists only because there is a real substance that casts the shadow. Although the form of the shadow may be fascinating, only a fool (or maybe a groundhog) would assume that the shadow is the sum and substance of anything. The normal reaction to a shadow is to look for the object that casts it. Therefore, the only reason God gave shadows or types in the Old Testament dispensation is that Christ was the substance He wanted men to see. The normal and expected reaction to the Old Testament shadows was to look for Christ.

Second, a shadow distorts the substance. In other words, it is always an imperfect representation of the reality; the substance is always better than the shadow. The shadow at best outlines; the substance is the essence. This is certainly true when we apply the shadow/body analogy to Christ and the Old Testament types. No matter how complex or beautiful the Old Testament type, it was a limited and imperfect picture. The greater its complexity or beauty, the more it declared that what was casting the shadow was even greater. That inherent imperfection was a divinely built-in obsolescence designed to generate more and more expectation for the perfection to come. In giving types, God made sure that there was no legitimate cause to substitute the shadow for the reality.

Third, a shadow disappears when the sunlight is directly overhead. When the true Light of world came, He dispelled the shadows. Just as Christ fulfilled or will fulfill every word prophecy about Him, so He fulfilled every picture prophecy about Him. This is why the Old Testament symbols and types are no longer operative or appropriate: they are fulfilled prophecies. To continue using the types after Jesus came would compromise and make suspect His identity as the Christ of God. The cessation of the Old Testament types was confirmation of His identity and successful work. Let me put it this way. We are not looking for another virgin to conceive, nor are we looking for another lamb to be slain. Both the word and the picture prophecies were fulfilled in Jesus Christ.

Interpretation Hints

Although typology is not an arbitrary hermeneutical option that we read into Old Testament texts at will, certain rules and guidelines of hermeneutics should govern and direct the interpretation of types. Two important problems face us as we read the Old Testament knowing that God is using these predictive pictures to illustrate and point to Christ: how to recognize or identify a type, and how to determine the significance of the type once it is identified. There are some objective answers to these questions, but we must also incorporate more subjective elements such as maturity, experience, overall biblical and theological knowledge, and spiritual perception. In interpreting types, as in interpreting all of Scripture, we acknowledge a requisite degree of "spiritual art" as well as "objective science." I can make some suggestions here regarding the objective answers, but the subjective elements require personal prayer and practice.

Identifying Types

First, *keep the antitype in focus*. It is vital to remember that types do not introduce or formulate "new revelation." Rather, they are prophetic analogies of truth already revealed. To state the obvious, if a type is an inspired analogy, it must be analogous to something. I have emphasized that essential to finding Christ in the Old Testament is the knowledge of who Christ is and what He does. If we know whom we are looking for, we will know Him when we see Him, even in pictures. We should always read and study the Scripture while on "Christ alert." It is messianic theology that must limit identifying types of Christ. Something about the picture must *in its context* be a reminder of something God has previously revealed about His plan and purpose of salvation in and through the promised Seed. When you see something that bears some resemblance or congruity to what you know about Christ, pause. Remember that it is the antitype that defines the type and not the other way around. It may be that what you see is not a divinely intended type, but then again it may be. There are some other criteria that will help you to be sure.

Second, *know the kinds of things that God used as types*. Old Testament types fall into three categories: people, things, and events. I want to emphasize that all were actual, historical entities and occurrences. Types were not simply hypothetical illustrations; they were real.

CHRIST IN PICTURE PROPHECY–EXPLAINED

Certain people were types of Christ not because of their personalities or character traits, but by virtue of their office. In the earlier discussion on the meaning of "Messiah," I suggested that there were many "lesser" messiahs that pointed to and increased the expectancy for the Ideal Messiah. Every prophet, priest, and king, by virtue of the office, was a lesser messiah and therefore a type of Christ. So, for instance, Moses was a type of Christ, not because he was delivered from a sentence of death in his infancy or because he was obedient, meek, and compassionate, but because he was God's chosen prophet, authoritative leader, and priestly intercessor.

Certain things or objects were types of Christ by virtue of their function. When we observe that a thing received special attention or focus in contexts of ritual, redemption, or deliverance, we have good reason for plugging in what we know about Christ to see if there is some correspondence. For instance, even without Christ's explanation of this text to Nicodemus (John 3:14), it is pretty clear that the brazen serpent that Moses lifted up in the wilderness conveyed a message beyond itself.

Certain events were types of Christ's work by virtue of either their agent or their accomplishment. In a real and important sense, all the events recorded in the Old Testament are integral elements in the history of redemption, and therefore, in one way or another, they prepare the way for the coming of Christ, the climax of redemptive history. Yet certain epoch events stand out as particularly illustrative of the redemptive work of God through Christ. Without question, the most outstanding of these epochs was the deliverance from Egypt, the Exodus. That the national deliverance was a picture of spiritual salvation is a point made by both the Old and the New Testaments. The deliverance as a whole, as well as many of its constituent parts, predicted vividly what Christ would do.

Third, *be sensitive to contextual clues.* It is important to understand that being considerate of context means more than simply noting the verse before or the verse after. Consideration of context follows the pattern of the old ripple-ring illustration. Just as a stone thrown into a pond causes the ripples to move away from the center with increasing area, so must the context-sensitive interpreter move away from the text to its immediate context, to its book context, to its context in the particular Testament, and finally to its context in the whole of Scripture.

One of the key contextual clues in identifying a person, thing, or event as typical is determining whether it was clearly symbolic. Remember the definition and connection between symbol and type. A symbol is the object lesson which communicated a moral or spiritual lesson directly in the contemporary setting, whereas a type predicts the future actualization or reality of the truth symbolized. Many interpreters, myself included, would argue that divinely intended types were divinely used symbols. In other words, all types are also symbols, although not all symbols are necessarily types. This assumption is both a safeguard and a clue for identifying types. If God is using a particular person, thing, or event to illustrate by analogy some truth, then it ought to be clear from the context (the whole expanding context).

At this point I perhaps need to distinguish between interpreting types and identifying types. In interpreting types, I feel free–indeed obligated–to factor in every interpretation aid, including the New Testament. However, in identifying types (particularly those not explicitly identified by the New Testament), I advise that we stay within the canonical context. The question is whether the person, thing, or event was "canonically symbolic." Determining the canonical context means that we factor in all the revelation that precedes the issue in question, but not the revelation that follows. The reason for this should be clear. If I am trying to figure out whether something was an object lesson at any particular time, I should limit myself to the corpus of revelation available at that time.

Nevertheless, this can hardly be considered a limitation in the normal sense. Working this way may require significant study and may involve a large corpus of Scripture. It is, however, essential. I think that one reason some are so reluctant to recognize types is that they isolate texts from their place in the canon. Because they don't see the symbolic clue in the immediate context, they refuse to look beyond the surface of the text. A failure to recognize the organic unity of God's Word–that every part is integral to the whole–is a serious interpretation fallacy. God does not have to define or redefine the symbol or type every time He uses it. For instance, there is sufficient warrant for identifying the marriage in the Song of Solomon as a type because there is a whole corpus of antecedent revelation from Moses to David that used marriage as an analogy or object lesson of God's relationship to His people. In other words, the contextual study of the Song of Solomon includes the Pentateuch.

Interpreting Types

Interpreting types is less complex than identifying them. The goal of interpretation is to determine the resemblance or the point of correspondence between the type and the antitype. The objective is to learn about the antitype, not the mechanics of the type.

I often compare the process of interpreting types to the mental process required in interpreting metaphors or similes. Remember that these are figures of speech in which comparisons are made between things that share some resemblance. A metaphor makes a direct statement (the man is a pig); a simile makes a comparative statement (the man eats like a pig). Both figures invite and challenge thought to discover the appropriate correspondence between the objects. In the examples, we look at the pig to learn something about the man. Our thoughts swing back and forth between the man and the pig in mental gymnastics as we ask ourselves what is true about the pig that applies to the man. The man is not, in fact, a pig, so not everything that is true about a pig applies to the man. Depending on the context in which the comparison occurs, it may be the pig's living conditions, eating habits, or size that to some degree describes the man.

The same kind of thinking is required in determining the point of correspondence between the type and the antitype. Think of the type as the figure and the antitype as the principal subject. There will be something about the type that resembles and points to the antitype, but not everything will. This is a caution that I must underscore. Most of the fanciful interpretations of types result from attempts to extract as many points of correspondence between the type and antitype as possible. Keep it simple; there will usually be one main point of correspondence. Focus on the specific elements about the type that stand out in the context without tyring to factor in everything that is conceivably true about the type. Remember that not even divinely inspired analogies are perfect parallels to the principal subject; they are not supposed to be lest the analogy (the type) satisfy the function of and replace the principal subject (the antitype).

For instance, Isaiah identifies Cyrus, the Persian king, as the Lord's shepherd and anointed (Isaiah 44:28; 45:1). In fact, Isaiah, one of the richest of messianic prophecies, applies the word "messiah" only to Cyrus. Isaiah, under divine inspiration, uses Cyrus as a type of Christ. Obviously, there is much about Cyrus that would be blasphemous to apply to the Lord Jesus. Cyrus was a heathen, pagan, polytheistic idolater, none of which applies to Christ and none of which is the focal point of Isaiah's context. Isaiah's point is that God will raise up a powerful leader who will successfully accomplish His purpose in delivering the nation from bondage. In that way, the powerful Cyrus is a picture prophecy of Christ, God's Ideal Leader who will successfully accomplish His purpose in delivering more than Israel from bondage.

Final Cautions

I want to emphasize two key cautions about typology: don't ignore types and don't take them too far. Interpreting types involves thinking beyond the surface of the text but not beyond the full meaning of the text. Do not confuse literal interpretation of Scripture with surface interpretation. The "deeper" meaning is part of the "full meaning" intended in the text. Ignoring the existence of types discounts an integral element in God's Word and thereby dishonors the Word. On the other hand, control your imagination. Types are not defined by whatever you can think of; they are defined by the logic and argument of the text.

At least in theory, the formula for interpreting types is simple. There are three factors to identify and consider in this order: the antitype, the type, and the point of correspondence. Reflecting on the antitype will limit the theme of the typical message to some aspect of the Messiah's person or overall mediatorial work of redemption. Reflecting on the type narrows the focus to the particular picture and its historic significance. Determining the salient point of correspondence requires careful reflection both on the context in which the type occurs and on the body of truth about the antitype. Remember that types are predictive symbols or object lessons that illustrate rather than constitute the ultimate spiritual truth. Let the type direct your attention to the particular aspect of Christ's person and work. Even though as a prophecy it has been fulfilled, it is nonetheless profitable to study because it illustrates something about Christ. The truth it illustrates remains valid. God designed His analogies to clarify, not confuse, the truth.

New Testament Models for Interpreting Typology

The New Testament unquestionably refers to and relies on the fulfillment of the Old Testament's picture prophecies. Our understanding the full significance of many New Testament statements requires that we know also the Old Testament type. In writing to a Gentile congregation, the apostle Paul linked them to their Hebrew "fathers" and concluded that what happened to Israel in the Exodus and wilderness wanderings had relevance beyond the ancient historical occasion (I Corinthians 10:1-14). Twice in this overview of Hebrew history, the apostle said that Israel's experiences were types ("examples" and "ensamples" in the Authorized Version) for those "upon whom the ends of the world are come"(10:6, 11). The inspired apostle affirms that there is a relevant message beyond the historical surface, but it is a message well-founded in the historical record.

When John the Baptist looked on Jesus and declared, "Behold the Lamb of God" (John 1: 29, 36), he artfully and skillfully summed up the prophecy of Leviticus. When the Lord Jesus drew the analogy between Himself and the serpent in the wilderness (John 3:14), between Himself and the manna in the wilderness (John 6:32-35), and between Himself and the Temple (John 2:19-21), He identified Himself as the ultimate fulfillment of those Old Testament types. The significance of what He said did not pass over His audience. Many of them did not like what He said, but they certainly understood His import.

The whole book of Hebrews argues that Jesus Christ is the fulfillment all of the symbolic and typical ceremonies of the Old Testament dispensation. Hebrews makes it clear that as wonderful as the pictures were, they were inherently imperfect and intentionally deficient representations of Christ, the reality to whom they pointed. Hebrews makes it clear that God never intended the Old Testament ceremonial economy to be anything other than object lessons of truth and picture prophecies of Christ and His finished work. The ceremonial law was "a shadow of good things to come, and not the very image of the things" (Hebrews 10:1).

Not only does the New Testament give sufficient warrant for identifying types in the Old Testament, but it also establishes a model for interpreting types. There is no small debate and disagreement among interpreters on this point. As I noted earlier, some maintain that because the New Testament writers were inspired, they had divinely sanctioned authority and liberty to do things with the Old Testament text that we ought not to do. Others, myself included, maintain that rather than shying away from the New Testament's hermeneutic, we ought to learn from it and emulate it in our efforts to interpret the Old Testament. I firmly believe that regardless of surface appearances, the New Testament never altered the originally intended meaning of any Old Testament message. The New Testament often goes beyond the surface meaning, lifting a truth from its historic reference and applying its relevance to a new temporal setting; however, it never changes the truth.

It is not my purpose here to enter into this debate, but I want to offer briefly a couple of illustrations. I've found during my years of teaching that two texts in particular are questioned by students more often than any other in this regard: Matthew's use of Hosea 11:1 and Paul's use of Genesis 21. Rather than rejecting these inspired interpretations as exceptions to what we are justified in doing, we should learn from them what we ought to do. Admittedly, issues like this require some hard thinking, so stay with me.

Hosea 11:1 and Matthew 2:15

Matthew 2 records the search of the wise men for the newborn Christ. Having followed the special star to Jerusalem, they began asking for more specific directions. When Herod, the illegitimate usurper of the throne, heard about their search, he questioned the theologians in Jerusalem concerning the birthplace of Messiah. They knew right where to look, knowing Micah's prophecy that Bethlehem would be the birthplace of the promised King. Herod learned from the wise men when the star had first appeared, and then he sent them on to Bethlehem, imploring them to return with the Messiah's address so he, too, could go and worship. Herod, of course, had other motives, and God warned the wise men to return to their homeland another way, avoiding Herod. After the wise men left, the Lord revealed to Joseph in a dream Herod's plot to kill Jesus and instructed him to take his family and escape to Egypt for safety. Before Matthew reveals the details of Herod's treachery in slaying all the children within the district and also before he records the actual return of Joseph and his family to Israel after Herod's death, Matthew sums up the whole episode by saying that they were in Egypt until the death of Herod. It is in this summary statement before the account of the slaughter and return that Matthew refers to Hosea 11:1. He writes that all of this happened "that it might be fulfilled which was spoken of the Lord by the prophet, saying, Out of Egypt have I called my son." We will see the importance of the placement of the text in due course.

At first glance, Hosea's statement seems to be another of those "word" prophecies that were so precisely fulfilled in the Lord Jesus Christ. However, considering Hosea 11:1 in its context raises some questions about Matthew's hermeneutics. We could read this Old Testament text all day long and it would never cross our mind that it was directly prophesying Christ's infant flight to Egypt to escape Herod's murderous plot to destroy the promised Seed. Hosea is reviewing some Hebrew history and is without question alluding to God's gracious and loving Exodus deliverance of Israel at their birth as a nation. Was Matthew just using his inspired imagination in applying this to Christ or did he correctly recognize something beyond the surface in the statement that both God and Hosea intended? I suggest that Matthew correctly and astutely recognized the symbolic significance of Hosea's Exodus statement and artfully and justifiably applied it typically to Christ. In other words, Matthew is saying there is something about God's loving deliverance of Israel from Egypt that is analogous to God's loving protection of Christ from Herod. Rather than being guilty of taking Hosea's statement out of context and changing its intent, Matthew evidences a profound knowledge of the theology of the Old Testament generally and Hosea's theology specifically.

Matthew's Interpretation of Hosea
Matthew illustrates the importance of full context analysis, which includes attention to previously defined messianic clues. Without ignoring or violating the immediate context, he extends the analysis to the larger context of the book and ultimately to the larger context of the Testament. This is not the place to develop an extensive theological analysis of Hosea, but I will suggest a few things that Matthew

apparently saw in Hosea's statement that warranted its application to this particular episode in the early life of Jesus.

First, he recognized the messianic significance of the Exodus. This actual historic event marked the birth of Israel as a nation. However, the monumental deliverance from Egypt was more than a Fourth-of-July occasion. It was a necessary progression in God's fulfilling His covenant promise to Abraham, at the heart of which was the promise of the Seed. God had told Abraham that his seed line of promise would be for four hundred years, not in the land of promise but in a land that would afflict them and put them in servitude (Genesis 15:13-14). At the end of that predetermined period, "God remembered his covenant with Abraham, with Isaac, and with Jacob" and then set in motion through Moses the promised judgment on Egypt and the liberation of the promised seed (Exodus 2:24). Although all this had obvious significance to those historical people, the ultimate significance of the Exodus involved the preservation of the seed of promise with a divinely unrelenting view to the coming of the Seed of promise. As there had to be an Isaac before there could be the Christ, so there had to be a nation through whom Christ according to the flesh could come (Romans 9:4-5). It is imperative to see the link between the seed and the Seed. The historical event of bringing Israel out of Egyptian bondage was a giant step toward the fullness of time.

Second, Matthew recognized the specific messianic significance of God's designation of Israel as "my son" (see also Exodus 4:22–"Israel is my son, even my firstborn"). The title "son," like "seed," is one of those important clue words that point to Christ. Not only does it speak of the unique relationship between God and those to whom the promise is given, but it also speaks of the ideal greater Son who is both the Seed and the Son of promise. By the time Hosea wrote, the expression "my son" had assumed even more explicit messianic significance in terms of God's covenant promise to David (II Samuel 7:14–"I will be his father, and he shall be my son"). It is imperative to see the link between *my son* and *my Son*. God's safeguarding his son Israel was an essential step toward the time when God would send and give His only begotten Son.

Third, Matthew recognized the symbolic significance of Egypt and the Exodus. What God did in delivering a visible Israel from a visible

Egypt provided many specific object lessons illustrating what God always does for His people both spiritually and physically. Throughout the Old Testament, the inspired writers, from Moses to Malachi, used the Exodus as a picture of God's gracious redemption, care, protection, and preservation of His people. The spiritual analogies are far too many to discuss at this point, but let me suggest a key point that is particularly relevant to Hosea's contextual argument and Matthew's perception. Because of Egypt's cruel oppression of Israel, Egypt became a vivid picture of bondage, persecution, and affliction in general. The objective of the Egyptian oppression is also theologically significant, and it therefore defined Egypt as more than merely a picture of indiscriminate oppression: the Egyptians attempted to destroy the promised Seed. Had Pharaoh's plan to kill all the sons of Israel succeeded, there would have been no Christ. The God-fearing midwives were the humble means by which God spared the male children and thereby vouchsafed the covenant promise. Consequently, Egypt was more than a place on the map. It was a picture of bondage and a symbol of that which was anti-God, anti-people of God, and ultimately anti-Christ. The Exodus deliverance, accordingly, was a vivid picture of God's preserving His people and His promised Seed. Interestingly, Hosea illustrates this symbolic significance. Although Hosea 11:1 is a direct reference to geographical Egypt and the actual historical event of the Exodus, the prophet elsewhere employed the term "Egypt" symbolically. For instance, in 9:3 he identifies Egypt with Assyria. Obviously, Assyria was not literally or geographically Egypt; it was acting like Egypt in that it was to become a place of oppression and bondage for the nation.

Matthew's Application of Hosea

I think we can at least begin to see why Matthew said that Joseph's flight into Egypt with Jesus fulfilled Hosea's statement that God called his son out of Egypt. Rather than taking Hosea's statement out of context and infusing a new meaning into it, he demonstrates a careful and thoughtful use of the text. He interpreted Hosea's statement not as the fulfillment of a singular word prediction but as the fulfillment of a picture prophecy, a type. He recognized an apparent point of correspondence between the historic Exodus and Christ's protection from Herod.

Very much on the surface is the similarity in these incidents of divine intervention to deliver the designated "son" or "Son" from a life-threatening environment. Perhaps not as much on the surface, but nonetheless indisputable, is the integral continuity between preserving Israel and preserving the child Jesus. Both were necessary if the mediatorial work of the Man, Christ Jesus, was to be fulfilled. In a very real sense Pharaoh and Herod had the same agenda: to eliminate the promised Seed. Pharaoh attempted to kill Christ's ancestors, which would have prevented His birth. Herod attempted to kill Christ after His birth, which would have prevented His saving work. I would dare say that Satan inspired them both in his vain efforts to devour the child not only as soon as He was born (Revelation 12:4) but even long before He was born. Nothing, however, can frustrate or alter God's eternal purpose and promise concerning Christ: He delivered His Son both from Pharaoh's and from Herod's Egypt.

I believe that Matthew's placement of his quotation of Hosea 11:1 immediately after the proleptic statement of Herod's death (prolepsis is a statement in anticipation of the reality it states) and before the recording of the actual events was a calculated irony and another evidence of his thorough knowledge of the type. As far as Matthew was concerned, "Egypt" did not refer to geographical Egypt but to Herod's domain. Interpreting the type consistently required that Egypt be the place of oppression, not the place of refuge. The type is exhibited not in the geographical direction taken but in God's preservation of His Son. Calling His Son out of Egypt was delivering His Son out of harm's way in Herod's Judea. John confirms that this is not a groundless analogy. He identified the place where the two eschatological witnesses would be slain because of opposition to the gospel as Sodom and Egypt, "where also our Lord was crucified" (Revelation 11:8). That was Jerusalem.

Notwithstanding the fact that he was inspired by the Holy Spirit, Matthew illustrates some key principles required for us all when recognizing and interpreting types. First, it is vital to know the Scriptures and how its parts integrate and work together. I think that one reason so many don't see in Hosea 11:1 what Matthew saw is that they don't think past Hosea 11:2. Second, it is important to stick to the main message that links the type and the antitype. Matthew did not attempt to make a tit-for-tat correspondence; some things about the historic type did not apply to the future antitype, not the least of which was the direction traveled. Again, don't take types too far.

Genesis 21 and Galatians 4:22-31

Admittedly, Paul's use of the Abraham/Sarah/Hagar triangle, particularly the climax recorded in Genesis 21, is a difficult passage that has suffered from multiple interpretations. Although it is a *crux interpretum* (what scholars call a text when they can't figure it out), it is frequently appealed to as a key text in some theological controversies, particularly the debate between Covenant and Dispensational theology. It is not part of my agenda in this forum to enter that controversy, but I do want to look at the passage to demonstrate a lesson from Paul's hermeneutic, and I will touch on some practical and theological lessons along the way. This is indeed a most important passage with distinct and far-reaching implications about the gospel. It is a good example of typology.

I refer to it as typology even though Paul called it allegory. In modern hermeneutics we distinguish materially between a type and an allegory, but it is not legitimate to impose on Paul's use of the word "allegory" any modern technical definitions. The main difference is that types involve real historical entities or events, whereas allegories, apart from any historical foundation, are figurative narratives with a higher message beyond the facts of the story. An allegory is a literary genre in which the narrative of non-factual events serves as a means of conveying the moral or spiritual truth. The apostle is certainly not denying that Abraham, Sarah, and Hagar were real people living at a real time in history. Paul was simply saying that the historical episode contained some elements that pointed beyond the surface facts. Had he been using our hermeneutical jargon, Paul would have called it a type, just as I am doing. Understanding what Paul is doing with Genesis 21 requires discovering three things: (1) Paul's contextual purpose (identifying the antitype), (2) Moses's contextual purpose (identifying the type), and (3) the common spiritual truth that unites the type with the antitype. Remember that Paul was not seeing something that wasn't there. All this may sound simple, but be forewarned: this issue, too, requires from you some focused critical thinking.

Paul's Purpose

First let's consider the context of Paul's message to the Galatians. The great theme of this book determines the tone and substance of the preaching of the apostle: free and gracious justification by faith alone apart from the works of law. There is good reason to regard Galatians as the first of Paul's letters. It is significant that from the beginning of both his preaching and his writing ministry, he (if I can turn a phrase) nailed his theses to the door.

That message of free grace and justification by faith alone in the finished work of Christ, however, met opposition almost everywhere Paul preached it. One group in particular became Paul's bitter enemy in the gospel, attempting to subvert his ministry and message at every opportunity. We refer to this group as the Judaizers. These were unconverted Jews who had become part of the visible church. They did not deny the facts of Christ's death and resurrection, but they contended that salvation depended on keeping all the laws of Judaism as well as "believing" Christ. For Gentiles to be saved required their conversion and adherence to Judaism as well as faith in Christ. Christ was not sufficient; salvation was Christ plus the keeping of the law. Paul made it unmistakably clear that salvation was Christ plus nothing. The battle lines were drawn. The Judaizers falsely charged Paul with antinomianism (being against the law). Paul sentenced them under the curse of God for preaching a gospel that was not the gospel at all (Galatians 1:6-9).

Galatians is a penetrating explanation, exposition, and defense of the one true gospel of free justification. Because the Judaizers claimed support from the Old Testament, Paul in boldface declared that they misunderstood and misapplied the Old Testament, and he proved the essential unity in what he preached and what Moses preached. Appealing to the example of Abraham's faith as the pattern for justification, he argued that "the scripture, foreseeing that God would justify the heathen through faith, preached before the gospel unto Abraham" (Galatians 3:6-8). Rather than being against the law, Paul was very much in favor of the law when kept in its proper place and limited to its proper function. He declared that the law was not against God's promises (Galatians 3:21) and explained the evangelical function of the law in leading men to Christ in order that they might be justified by faith (Galatians 3:24). His exposé of the misuse of the law by these Judaizers reached its climax in chapter 4 when he accused those desiring to be under the law of not really hearing what the law says (Galatians 4:21). His clinching argument appealed to the gospel promise given to Abraham and how that promise was to be received. Was the promise to be received through Hagar or through Sarah? Was the promise to be received through works or through faith? Paul saw something more profound in the Genesis narrative that went below the intriguing surface story of a love triangle and the consequent jealousy between Abraham's two families.

Moses's Purpose

Before we can see what Paul saw, we have to know what Moses said and meant. A proper understanding of the lesson of the type is prerequisite to a proper application of the lesson to the antitype. I think we all know the details of the story. Genesis 16 and 21 are the relevant passages in the Abrahamic narrative if you need to review. God had given Abraham the promise that he would have a seed. In the earlier chapter dealing with Christ in the covenants, we developed all the vital messianic implications of that covenant promise. At the heart of the promise of a seed was the promise of the Seed: the essence of the Abrahamic covenant was the gospel of Christ. Abraham believed the gospel and was justified through faith: there is no doubt about that. Although he never staggered at the promise of God through unbelief (Romans 4:20), the delay in the arrival of the first installment of the seed promise was a great test of faith. While Abraham was consciously rejoicing in Christ's day (John 8:56), he also knew, if I can put it this way, that there had to be an Isaac before there could be the Christ.

With a view to the ultimate promise, Abraham and Sarah took matters into their own hands. Sarah, who received the promise along with Abraham, offered Hagar, her servant girl, to become the surrogate to give birth in her place. Seemingly without argument, Abraham agreed. Although this arrangement in many ways shocks us, it was rather commonplace in Abraham's world. In fact, such arrangements were often part of pre-nuptial contracts. This in no way justifies the action; indeed, it heightens the transgression. Not only did the union between Abraham and Hagar constitute polygamy, but it also reflected Abraham's following the way of the world, his walking by sight rather than by faith.

Immediately after Hagar conceived and gave birth to Ishmael, conflict ensued between her and Sarah. Sarah and Hagar apparently got along fine when Hagar served as handmaid, but when she was elevated to a status that she assumed was equal to or practically superior to Sarah's, the discord and friction began. In God's timing, which underscored man's inability to achieve the promise on his own, Sarah conceived and gave birth to Isaac, the seed of promise. The birth of Isaac increased the strife. Now agitation broke out not only between Hagar and Sarah, but also between Ishmael, the son of the flesh, and Isaac, the son of the promise. To put it simply, Ishmael was mean to his little half-brother, and his motives for meanness most likely went beyond big-brother antics. Ishmael was getting the picture that he and Isaac could not live together; his future was in jeopardy. Sarah finally had enough and implored Abraham to "cast out this bondwoman and her son: for the son of this bondwoman shall not be heir with my son, even with Isaac" (Genesis 21:10). God confirmed. This is the part of the narrative that Paul uses and quotes in Galatians 4:30.

However, before we start making the comparisons between the facts of Genesis and Paul's interpretation, we need to identify the lessons that Moses intended in the narrative. I submit that there is more here than the obvious history and legitimate surface lessons about the folly of polygamy and its unhappy consequences. It is vital to remember who the first readers of this narrative were. An essential element in all Bible interpretation is to identify the canonical context, where a given book fits in relationship to the rest of Scripture based on when the book was written and who the original audience was. Although the narrative of Genesis begins at creation and ends no later than the first few years of the 18th century BC, Moses, inspired by the Holy Spirit, wrote the book in the middle of the 15th century. About four hundred years separated the events of Genesis 50 from the events of Exodus 1, but the books of Genesis and Exodus were intended for the same people. The same people who stood under the glory and awe of Sinai, receiving in written form the Ten Commandments and the detailed instructions for the ritualistic ceremonies, were the same people who read Genesis for the first time.

Genesis—with its emphasis on God's gracious initiation and faithful development of the covenant promise of the Seed and with its examples of faith from Eve to Joseph—was a divinely inspired safeguard against misunderstanding and misapplying the commands and instructions from Sinai. Moses made sure that the newly formed nation understood that what God was doing for them was a continuation of what God started in Eden and advanced through the entire Patriarchal period. As Paul could say that Israel's history is an example, a type, for us, so Moses was saying that the pre-Israel history of Genesis was an example, a type, for Israel itself. Therefore, without denying or ignoring the spiritual lessons for Abraham and his contemporaries, Moses directed the lessons to his contemporaries, intending them to get the message. The Abraham/Sarah/Hagar triangle with its consequent Isaac/Ishmael duel was a vivid lesson in how to receive the covenant promise and enter into the joy of the promised Seed.

In this theologically pregnant narrative, Hagar was a distinct symbol of the efforts to **achieve** the promise through the works of the flesh. Sarah was a distinct symbol of the resting and hope of faith to **receive** the promise through the grace and power of God. There was and there will always be a difference between trying to achieve salvation by works and receiving salvation by grace through faith. The one never works; the other never fails. Sarah was Abraham's first and legitimate wife. Hagar, as Sarah's handmaid, served well in her subservient role. There was nothing inherently wrong with Hagar. As noted earlier, it was only when Hagar was elevated to the position of wife and made to do that which was not intended for her to do that all the trouble began. That which is meant to serve cannot replace that which is meant to save.

I maintain that it did not require a great deal of spiritual insight or acumen for Israel to see what Moses wanted them to see. They had recently been delivered from bondage by the grace and power of God and by the blood of the lamb. They now stood at Sinai to receive all the commandments, the rules and regulations for their worship and service to the Lord. Sinai was secondary to the gracious Exodus. The laws of Sinai followed grace and were designed to be servants of that grace. The contrast between Sarah and Hagar warned them not to elevate the law to a position not intended. For them to interpret the laws of Sinai as the means whereby they could achieve the promise of salvation was to assume that law could do something God did not intend for it to do. Moses purposefully recorded the story of Sarah and

Hagar in order to warn Israel not to replace grace with the works of the law. As the intended roles of Sarah and Hagar were important but mutually exclusive, so grace and law were both important but mutually exclusive. The works of the law follow and remain subservient to grace. That is what Moses meant and that is exactly what Paul saw in the text.

The Points of Correspondence

Moses used Sarah and Hagar as a safeguard against misunderstanding the law; Paul used Sarah and Hagar to expose and condemn those who had misunderstood, misapplied, and elevated the law to a position that God never intended. To reduce what Paul did in this text to a defense of or an argument against either Covenant Theology or Dispensationalism is to miss the whole point of his message. *Paul's concern was not different dispensations but different gospels, one of which was not a gospel at all.* The Judaizers, and indeed, all Christ-rejecting Jews were guilty of the very thing Moses warned against. The attitude about the Old Testament law that Paul is refuting did not become the wrong attitude after the coming of Christ; it was the wrong attitude about the law before the coming of Christ. Follow Paul's argument and interpretation and see how it follows the same line of application that Moses intended. The only difference is that Paul directs it to the circumstances of his day; the setting is different, but the truth is the same.

After introducing the Old Testament narrative, Paul identifies Hagar and Sarah in terms of two covenants (verse 24). It is essential to note that in the Greek text, no definite article governs "two covenants." It is inappropriate, as some interpreters do, to link this statement to the two covenants that God revealed, the covenant of grace and the covenant of works. Regardless of conventional notions about those two covenants, the text is not making a contrast between them. Hagar and Sarah represent two covenants, for sure: two ways to get the promise. The contrast is between God's way and man's way. Rejecting grace and replacing it with works, even the works of God's law, is to enter a covenant with death and remain in sin's bondage.

It is in this sense that Paul links Hagar to Sinai. Both Hagar and Sinai in their divinely intended places served well; but when they were elevated to positions whereby they were used to achieve the promise, they could only fail. By drawing the analogy between Hagar and Sinai, Paul makes it clear that God **never** intended the law to be the means of attaining salvation for ancient Israel. To define God's purpose for the law in terms of how unbelievers used the law is most assuredly wrong. When the law is kept in the place that God intended, it serves grace well, both by leading men to Christ and by showing believers how to live in grace. For Israel in either the Old or the New Testament dispensation (in Moses's day or in Paul's day) to so misuse the law was to put themselves in bondage and their souls in eternal jeopardy.

In contrast to the current earthly Jerusalem as representative of grace rejecters, Paul saw a higher Jerusalem, representing the grace that generates the true, spiritual children of promise. Paul knew firsthand that the children of the earthly Jerusalem oppose and persecute the children of the higher Jerusalem, just as Ishmael, the son of the bondwoman-made-wife, persecuted Isaac, the son of the freewoman. It was that opposition that occasioned the writing of Galatians. The Judaizers had followed Paul and subverted his message of free grace and free justification through faith with their admixture of law and adulterated gospel.

Genesis 21:10 was Paul's authority for demanding separation from the Judaizers: "Cast out the bondwoman and her son: for the son of the bondwoman shall not be heir with the son of the freewoman." This was tantamount to saying that receiving salvation by grace and seeking to achieve salvation by works are mutually exclusive. Those who attempt to keep the law to earn salvation can never inherit the salvation enjoyed by those who lay hold of the promise by faith. That was true in Moses's day and Paul's day, and it is equally true in our day. Just in case his readers missed the point of the picture, he stated outright in the next chapter that "Christ is become of no effect unto you, whosoever of you are justified by the law; ye are fallen from grace" (Galatians 5:4).

Although the specific forms of legalism (working for salvation) are different in our day from those in Moses's or Paul's, the essence of the perversion is as prevalent now as ever. Understanding the symbolic, typical, spiritual message of Sarah and Hagar is essential to understanding the gospel. Justification by faith apart from the works of the law must be the message of every preacher of the gospel. If that is not the message, then there is no other gospel message to preach. Salvation is received; it is not achieved. God's way of saving sinners has always been by grace through faith in Christ. Always! I am sorely tempted myself to start preaching a little here, but this self-imposed outline I'm following has generated its own bondage. I certainly desire that you grasp the theological truth of what Paul says in Galatians 4, but my contextual concern is that you see the mechanics of his interpretation method and learn to think through other types the same way.

Recognizing and understanding types is a vital part of Old Testament interpretation. It is fundamentally important to explore the subject fully, but this chapter is getting a bit long. Consequently, I will break up our discussion a little for you and illustrate some key Old Testament types in the next chapter.

CHAPTER 9

CHRIST IN PICTURE PROPHECY–ILLUSTRATED

Having defined what types are and having considered some New Testament patterns, we are ready to look at some Old Testament examples. If we keep in mind the guidelines for identifying types, the *divinely intended* types should jump off the page as we read. Remember that types are not what we impose on the text to extract relevance and they are not encoded messages that only the imaginative elite can decode. If we are consciously reading the Old Testament with a view to Christ, from time to time we will find those prophetic analogies that God used to illustrate spiritual lessons and truths. We need to be particularly alert throughout those contexts suggestive of the redemptive and salvation themes that are associated with Messiah's work. But let me give this word of exhortation and encouragement as well. Interpreting types may take some practice and always requires prayer. And if you overlook one now and again, don't worry that you are going to miss out on some essential truth. Remember that types do not formulate truth; they illustrate truth.

Although types occur throughout the Old Testament, in no place are they more prevalent than in the books of Moses. The Mosaic era was a time of theological explanation. Genesis detailed the initiation and development of the messianic covenant promise, focusing on the Seed's person and identity. After that covenant was reaffirmed with Israel after their Exodus, the focus was on the work of the Seed. In explaining what the Messiah would do in reversing the curse of sin, God graciously gave a body of object lessons that illustrated the truths of the gospel. These symbols and types formed the basis of what we generally refer to as the ceremonial law. All the ceremonial laws of the Mosaic economy or dispensation were picture prophecies of some aspect of the work of Christ. Volumes could be written on Mosaic typology. I will, however, select just a few types and discuss them in general terms to illustrate the application of the interpretation principles you can use on your own. I will give at least one example in each of the categories containing symbolic and typical significance: people, things, and events.

People

I would suggest that persons in the Old Testament are types of Christ not by virtue of their character traits but rather by virtue of their office. Many Old Testament figures exemplified advanced sanctified lives and evidenced great Christ-likeness. For a believer, whether in the Old or the New Testament dispensations, to be conformed to the image of Christ was to fulfill the purpose of predestination (Romans 8:29). I agree that such a Christ-like life is exemplary and that it can be an effective means of evangelism in pointing sinners to Christ, but I would not say that such a life is necessarily a picture prophecy pointing to Christ. That's my opinion, and I am aware that some disagree. Nonetheless, there are many people who were types. As lesser messiahs, every prophet, priest, and king was prophetic of Christ, the Ideal Prophet, Priest, and King. Jonah was a prophet, but Christ is greater than Jonah (Luke 11:32). Solomon was a king, but Christ is greater than Solomon (Luke 11:31). Aaron was a priest, but Christ is greater than Aaron (Hebrews 7:11). Let's see if we can discover some of the salient points of correspondence between Aaron, the type, and Christ, the antitype.

The Picture of Aaron

In the first chapter I have already addressed many key elements of the mediatorial priesthood exemplified by Aaron and his descendants that the Lord Jesus Christ ideally fulfilled. Remember that the basic definition of a priest is one chosen and ordained by God to be the mediatorial representative of men before God. The three primary functions of the priest were to offer sacrifices to God, to make reconciliation for the sins of the people, and to offer intercession before the Lord in behalf of the people. The great lesson of the priesthood was that men could approach God only through His chosen priest. You might want to review that section to help you get the full picture of how the Old Testament priest, particularly the high priest, was a picture prophecy of Christ, who is indeed the only true way to the only true God (John 14:6).

Rather than discussing again those general truths, I want to focus on one particular aspect to illustrate what we can learn about Christ from the Old Testament type. Exodus 28 is a key chapter on the priesthood because it details the "holy garments" that Aaron was to wear "for glory and for beauty" (Exodus 28:2). What he wore was what the people saw, and the Lord gave specific instructions about these garments, each one of which was a symbolic object lesson. When the people looked at Aaron all dressed up, they were to reflect on the visible message and learn the spiritual truth that corresponded and pointed to the Ideal High Priest. Seven specific items are detailed, but three stand out for special attention because each includes a direct statement of purpose and function: the ephod, the breastplate, and the crown. Note the verb "bear" that links these three pieces together (Exodus 28:12, 29, 38). Briefly, I will suggest three truths that we learn about Christ from these garments.

The Ephod

The ephod teaches that *Christ has the might to uphold His people*. When wearing the ephod, "Aaron shall bear their names before the Lord upon his two shoulders for a memorial" (Exodus 28:12). First, let's get the picture. The ephod was a short garment extending from the shoulders to the waist. It consisted of two pieces of fine linen joined at the shoulders. The rich colors of gold, blue, purple, and scarlet, if nothing else, magnified the glory and beauty of the office. Most significant were the two onyx stones set in gold sockets on the shoulders, inscribed with the names of the tribes of Israel. As Aaron would stand before the Lord, he carried on his shoulders the names of those he represented as a memorial for the Lord to set His mind and will on the people. In his office, Aaron took the people into God's presence. That's what the people saw.

Second, let's get the message. The shoulders represent strength and power, the place where loads are carried. As Aaron, the type, symbolically bore the names of the people before the Lord, even more so Christ, the antitype, in spiritual reality bears the names of His people in the very presence of God. We have no power, ability, or right to stand before the Lord, but Christ our great High Priest has infinitely sufficient strength to uphold us and all our concerns before God. On His great shoulders, He carries us and upholds us in the Holy Place. When Christ passed through the heavens, He triumphantly carried with Him all that He represents. We have the right to approach God because Christ upholds us there and He will not let us down. God cannot look at Christ without seeing us in inseparable union with Him. Christ fulfills the ephod prophecy.

The Breastplate

The breastplate teaches that *Christ has the mercy to plead for us*. When wearing the breastplate, "Aaron shall bear the names of the children of Israel ...upon his heart" (Exodus 28:29-30). First, let's get the picture. The breastplate was made of fine linen folded over to make a pouch that was held in position by gold chains and blue lace over the ephod. Arranged in four rows were twelve precious stones, each stone inscribed with the name of one of the tribes. This was another obvious picture that wherever the high priest went the people went as well. The location of the stones over the heart testified to the compassion and sympathy that the priest was to have for the people. After all, the heart was the symbol of love, mercy, and pity.

Second, let's get the message. Any compassion and love that Aaron may have had for Israel pale into insignificance in comparison to the sympathy, compassion, and love Christ has for His people. The Ideal High Priest is touched with the feeling of the infirmities of all His people at all times (Hebrews 4:15). Forever on His heart, those He represents and presents before the throne of grace are precious to Him, and with tender thoughts toward them He intercedes in their behalf. Does Jesus care? O yes, He cares. Christ fulfills the breastplate prophecy.

The Holy Crown

The holy crown teaches that *Christ has the merit to present us*. Aaron was to wear the holy crown that he might "bear the iniquity of the holy things" so that the people could "be accepted before the Lord" (Exodus 28:38). First, let's get the picture. A plate of pure gold was to be placed on a background of blue lace and fixed to the miter, the turban or headpiece, of the high priest. Inscribed on the gold plate were the bold words, "HOLINESS TO THE LORD." As Aaron approached the Lord as the representative of the people, the Lord would see flash-ing from his brow the "password" for any entrance to the Lord's presence. The Lord is absolutely and infinitely holy, and without ho-liness none will or can see Him. The sin of the people had rendered them unfit and unable to approach God, so a holy mediator was es-sential. Aaron symbolically took the guilt incurred by the people against holiness, and they, with their names inscribed on his shoulders and over his heart, were, in spite of their own guilt, accepted before the Lord in the person of the mediator.

Second, let's get the message. As beautiful as the picture was, it was woefully imperfect because Aaron had his own sin and iniquity to deal with. Knowing what they knew about Aaron personally would prevent the people from seeing in him a sinless mediator. The Old Testament ceremonial law of necessity made "men high priests which have infir-mity" (Hebrews 7:28); that's the only kind of men there were—until Christ came. Unlike all the Old Testament priestly pictures of Him, the Lord Jesus was in person "holy, harmless, undefiled, separate from sinners" (Hebrews 7:26). What Aaron did symbolically, the Lord Jesus Christ did really. As our real High Priest, Christ bore the guilt of our sin in order that God might accept us on the merits of His holiness and righteousness. To be in union with Christ, who as our representa-tive bears our names on His shoulder and over His heart, is to enjoy full pardon and full acceptance before the Lord. God sees believers only through the flashing glory of Christ's holiness. His merit is the only firm ground on which we can stand. Christ is the only "password" into heaven. Christ fulfills the holy crown prophecy.

The Imperfect Picture of Aaron

As you study the functions of Aaron and his successors, do so with a view to the ideal fulfillment of the priestly ministry in Christ. What they imperfectly did pointed to the need for and the certain fact of the perfect, eternally chosen Mediator. That they did things so imper-fectly, having to sacrifice for their own sins before they could do anything for the people, was inherent evidence of the built-in obso-lescence of the Aaronic priesthood. Any Israelite with an ounce of spiritual sense would learn by watching the priests what was needed (the symbolic lessons) and perceive that a Priest was needed who would finally get it right (the typical prophecy). Every Israelite with faith looked beyond the type to the promised Messiah (the antitype of it all).

Significantly, Moses gave more clues that Aaron was not the ultimate Priest that God intended. He gave the first clue in Genesis when Abraham, the father of the nation, paid his tribute and tithe to Melchizedek, the king of Salem, the priest of the Most High God (Genesis 14:18-20). Keep in mind that Moses wrote Genesis for the same people for whom he wrote Exodus, and at about the same time. Overshadowing all the glory and beauty of Aaron was the realization that there was another priesthood that their and Aaron's father had recognized as superior. Years later David confirmed that this was a divinely intended overshadowing of Aaron when he wrote that the Lord had irrevocably sworn to the Messiah, "Thou art a priest for ever after the order of Melchizedek" (Psalm 110:4).

Interpreters differ as to whether Melchizedek was an actual Christophany or a type of Christ. My opinion is that Melchizedek was a real person who from the scanty details we know about him, was a fitting and necessary type of Christ and His Priesthood. Melchizedek conveyed something about the Ideal Priesthood that Aaron could never do. The Ideal Priest would also be the Ideal King, the King of righteousness and peace. Aaron's priesthood served nicely in defining priestly functions; Melchizedek's priesthood served nicely in affirming that there was only one mediator between God and men. For Christ to be a priest according to Melchizedek's order rather than Aaron's resolved the problem of one mediator's being both king and priest. My point here is not to develop all of the typical points of correspondence between Jesus and Melchizedek; the book of Hebrews does that most effectively (Hebrews 5-7). My point is simply that God included in the symbolic and typical priesthood of the ceremonial laws sufficient safeguards against confusing the object lesson with the reality.

Things

If any one thing was central to the ceremonial laws defined in the Mosaic covenant, it was the Tabernacle. It was a simple yet complex structure that foreshadowed Christ and the gospel from every angle and from every action associated with it. The Tabernacle with its constituent parts was a picture prophecy that found fulfillment not only in the person and work of Christ but also in the benefits, blessings, and obligations attendant to and flowing from Him. The Tabernacle with its rituals taught by object lesson how to worship the holy God and how to experience the covenant promise of life and fellowship with God. As we try to figure out all the points of correspondence between Christ, the gospel, and the Tabernacle, it is easy for us to get lost, bogged down, overly imaginative, or discouraged in all the details (there are a lot of them). Notwithstanding the details, there are some surface lessons that are most instructive. Indeed, if all we are able to discern are the surface lessons, we will still have a good, clear picture of gospel truths, all of which ultimately point to Christ. Volumes have been written and long series of sermons have been preached on the Tabernacle, so obviously I can only touch on the surface lessons here. My objective is more to get you started on your own analysis than to provide a full exposition that would keep you from the task.

The Purpose of the Tabernacle

The divine intent of the Tabernacle as an object lesson of truth is clear from all the specific instructions that God gave to guide its erection (Exodus 25-31) and from the detailed record of those instructions being carried out (Exodus 35-40). The Tabernacle section begins with God's command to Moses to follow the pattern that was revealed to him on the mount (Exodus 25:9, 40). The book ends with frequent testimony that Israel had followed the divinely given blueprints: they made it "according to all that the Lord commanded Moses" (Exodus 39:42; note that at least eight times in Exodus 40 Moses did as the Lord commanded). This makes for considerable repetition throughout the text of Exodus, but it underscores the important truth that God orders the way of worship and man cannot and must not alter that way. It is important not only that we worship the right God but that we worship the right God in the right way. God commands both (look at the first four commandments). The Tabernacle stood as constant visible witness that salvation was God's way or no way.

Before we start interpreting the types, it is important that we identify the antitypes. This will keep us on track as we seek to discover the points of correspondence between type and antitype in this remarkable analogy. We have the New Testament, so we might as well take advantage of its interpretation. This is a benefit that we have over the wandering Israelites: we know what we should be looking for from the start. The New Testament links the Tabernacle/Temple to four different antitypes. Note that the only essential difference between the Tabernacle and Temple was that the first was a portable structure whereas the second was fixed; the theology communicated is the same. I think that Exodus 25:8 provides the main clue for ascertaining the primary message of the Tabernacle in God's statement of His intent: "Let them make me a sanctuary that I may dwell among them." God's dwelling with His people is the key thought and what the New Testament emphasizes.

First, the Tabernacle typified the *Incarnation of Christ*. John unquestionably plays on Tabernacle prophecy when he declares, "The Word was made flesh, and dwelt among us" (John 1:14). The word "dwell" could well be translated "tabernacled."

Second, the Tabernacle typified *heaven*, the principal dwelling place and throne of God. Hebrews settles this. "It was therefore necessary that the patterns of things in the heavens should be purified...for Christ is not entered into the holy places made with hands, which are the figures of the true; but into heaven itself, now to appear in the presence of God for us" (Hebrews 9:23-24). Not only does the Tabernacle proclaim that God is present with His people on earth, but it also pictures the final destination of His people who will dwell with Him in heaven. That would have been good news for a people wandering in a wilderness; it's not bad news for us.

Third, the Tabernacle typified the *church corporately*. Paul warned ministers to guard their ministry lest they defile the temple of God and then reminded the Corinthian church that they were indeed that temple in which the Holy Spirit dwells (I Corinthians 3:16-17). Using Tabernacle language, John identified the seven churches as golden candlesticks and declared that Christ was walking in the midst of them (Revelation 1:13, 20; 2:1).

Fourth, the Tabernacle typified *believers individually*. Paul's argument for individual purity and separation included the fact that God regarded believers as His temple: "Ye are the temple of the living God; as God hath said, I will dwell in them, and walk in them; and I will be their God, and they shall be my people" (II Corinthians 6:16). The Tabernacle declares both God's purpose to dwell with His people and His plan whereby that goal of fellowship is achieved. With this message in mind, I will only touch briefly on some of the key surface lessons.

Names of the Tabernacle

First, there are lessons derived from the names of the Tabernacle. The word translated "tabernacle" simply means "the place of dwelling" (*mishkan*). Although it is not a biblical word, we often speak of the *Shekinah* Glory to designate the manifest demonstrations of God's presence, the theophanies associated with both Tabernacle and Temple. For instance, Exodus ends with the cloud covering the tent and the "glory of the Lord" filling the Tabernacle (Exodus 40:34-38). To label that manifestation the *Shekinah* Glory is appropriate because "*shekinah*" means "dwelling." *Shekinah* and *mishkan* derive from the same verbal root that means "to dwell or to inhabit." The word "Tabernacle," then, declares that God takes up residence with His people. He does not simply drop in from time to time; He lives with them. The Tabernacle pictured the constant abiding presence of God with His people. Certainly God, being omnipresent, fills all space immediately, but He dwells with His people in a most special and intimate way. That truth has never changed and it never will change. Remember not to confuse the object lesson with the reality. God's presence with His people was not literally confined to the Tabernacle; it was a visible reminder and declaration that God was with them. What the name "Immanuel" declares, the Tabernacle illustrated and Christ fulfilled.

Sometimes the Tabernacle is called the Tent (*'ohel*). As a portable structure, it testified to the Lord's identification with His people in their circumstances. They were living in tents; He dwelt in a tent. Again, it would be theologically ludicrous to conclude that the tent localized or limited His presence and ministry to the people. The tent illustrated what Isaiah later said concerning the Lord during Israel's wanderings: "In all their affliction he was afflicted, and the angel of his presence saved them" (Isaiah 63:9). Christ most vividly fulfilled the Tent prophecy as He came in the very likeness of sinful flesh (Romans 8:3); He is able, therefore, because of His personal experience, to be touched with the feeling of all our infirmities (Hebrews 4:15). That the Temple ultimately replaced the Tent testifies to the same truth. The people were living in houses; He dwelt in a house.

Two other names of the Tabernacle build on the Tent idea: the Tent of Testimony (*'ohel ha'eduth*) and the Tent of Meeting (*'ohel mo'ed*). These underscore particular benefits and blessings that derive from God's dwelling so intimately with them. The Tent of Testimony identifies the Tabernacle as a place of revelation. God would communicate, explain, and reveal Himself at this designated place. All of the rituals that occurred at the Tabernacle were points that the Lord made in this visible sermon. It prophesies Christ who dwelled among men as the perfect and Ideal Prophet, revealing God in person. The Tent of Meeting certainly suggests meeting together in communion and fellowship, but it also includes the important idea of meeting by appointment. Meeting with God is not haphazard, casual, or accidental. God sets the terms of meeting; He makes the appointment and guarantees His presence at those meetings. Follow the statements in Exodus 25-30 where the Lord says, "There I will meet with thee" (25:22; 29:42; 30:6) and you will learn three important truths concerning where God meets His people. At the ark, God meets His people at the place of propitiation. At the altar of burnt offering, God meets His people at the place of consecration. At the altar of incense, God meets His people at the place of prayer. Each of these places finds ultimate significance in Christ, the only place sinners can ever meet God in peace.

The final common designation of the Tabernacle is Sanctuary (*miqdash*), literally "the place of holiness." The core component of holiness is separateness or otherness. Although including the notion of separation from sin, the concept of holiness goes far beyond that. Interestingly, the antonym to holiness in the Old Testament is not that which is sinful, but that which is common, mundane, or ordinary. The Tabernacle was no ordinary tent; it announced its distinction from every other place. The Sanctuary declared that being in God's presence is special and that it therefore requires reverent caution. There is no barging into God's presence. The Sanctuary stood as witness to the truth that although He was near, access to Him was restricted. Approaching God requires clean hands and pure heart (Psalm 24:3-4). The Sanctuary declared loudly the need for an absolutely clean and pure Mediator who could approach the most holy God, taking those He represented with Him. That is exactly what Christ did and does.

Structure of the Tabernacle

Second, there are lessons derived from the structure and floor plan of the Tabernacle. The Tabernacle was divided into three distinct sections: the outer court, the holy place, and the most holy place. The outer court was under the open sky and accessible to the covenant community. The holy place was veiled but lighted, and accessible only to the priests. The Holy of Holies (a superlative statement meaning "the most holy place") was completely veiled, dark, and accessible only to the high priest, only once a year, and never without blood. Vividly, the floor plan declared that the closer to God one approaches, the greater the restrictions or requirements for holiness. The greater the awareness of God's holiness, the greater will be the consciousness of personal unholiness and of the need for a perfect Mediator.

But perhaps the most important lesson conveyed by the floor plan was the safeguard it provided against confusing the object lesson with the reality above and beyond it. Hebrews says that by these increasing restrictions, the Holy Spirit was "signifying that the way into the holiest of all was not yet made manifest, while as the first tabernacle was yet standing: which was a figure for the time then present..." (Hebrews 9:8, 9). Any Israelite with the slightest spiritual perception would conclude that the Tabernacle economy was not working if it was meant to bring people personally into the presence of God. But it was not supposed to. This was the built-in obsolescence that demanded and increased the hope for Christ who by His own blood would enter in once into the holy place, having obtained eternal redemption (Hebrews 9:12).

Furniture of the Tabernacle

Third, there are lessons derived from the furniture in the Tabernacle. Each of these items, rich with spiritual symbolism, deserves much more attention that I can give here. But let's note some of the obvious lessons.

The Altar

Just inside the outer court was the *altar*. Right up front the Lord made it clear that the only way to get to Him was through the blood of the sacrifice. The altar, the foundation of which was constructed of the raw materials of earth and unhewn stones, testified to the inability of

279

man to contribute any part or effort toward the work of salvation (Exodus 20:24-25). Thinking of the altar makes me recall Bonar's great hymn: "Not what these hands have done, can save this guilty soul...Thy work alone, my Savior, can ease this weight of sin; Thy blood alone, O Lamb of God, can give me peace within." The altar itself, made of shittim wood (acacia) overlaid with brass, suggests that it was the place of righteous judgment. That, in a nutshell, was the message of the altar. It points to the place of sacrifice and shedding of blood, without which there can be no forgiveness of sin. At the place of sacrifice, justice was served and pardon was won.

The Laver
Also in the outer court just past the altar was the *laver*, the wash basin. Its position was a vital part of the message. On the other side of the altar, the laver symbolized the purity and cleanness required for fellowship with and service of God and the means whereby the sanctifying cleansing was achieved. The sinner did not clean himself up before approaching the altar; he came to the place of sacrifice with his sins. Then, as the sinner's representative, the priest ritually washed. That the laver was made from donated mirrors (Exodus 38:8) helps to identify the antitype. The New Testament more than once compares the Word of God to a glass that reveals the blemishes and guides in the cleansing process (II Corinthians 3:18; James 1:23-25). The Lord Jesus, the Word of God, declared, "Ye are clean through the word which I have spoken unto you" (John 15:3). Paul seemed undoubtedly to have laver theology in mind when he said that Christ gave Himself for His church "that He might sanctify and cleanse it with the washing of water by the word, that He might present it to Himself a glorious church ...holy and without blemish" (Ephesians 5:26-27). Similarly, Titus 3:5 speaks of "the washing of regeneration." The laver represents an essential means of grace.

The Shewbread
There were three items inside the holy place. On one side was a table with the *shewbread*, literally, the "bread of faces" or "presentation." Leviticus 24:8 indicates that Israel presented this as a pledge of the covenant. The bread was something they had made from the grain that God had supplied. The regular presentation of the bread was an acknowledgment that they owed everything to the goodness of the

Lord. It stood as testimony to their pledged consecration and dedication to the Lord and taught that praise and thanksgiving were an essential part of worship. Presenting oneself to the Lord for His praise and purpose is always the necessary corollary to and consequence of having been saved by the blood (see Romans 12:1). It certainly points to Christ who in every way dedicated Himself completely to the glory of the Father, presenting His work as a perfect fulfillment of the covenant.

The Lampstand

On the other side was the *lampstand*. The lampstand was constructed of a single piece of gold with a predominant center shaft having six branches, three on each side. A regular supply of oil fueled the lamps. The light represents the spiritual enlightenment that God gives His people through His revelation. David later noted the link between light and life: "For with thee is the fountain of life: in thy light shall we see light" (Psalm 36:9). The New Testament suggests the same when it speaks of the light of the gospel (II Corinthians 4:4). If the light represents the gospel, the lampstand is a prophecy of both Christ and the church, corporately and individually. The Lord Jesus identified Himself and believers as the light of the world (Matthew 5:14; John 8:12). That the seven churches in the book of the Revelation are designated as seven lampstands confirms the corporate relevance.

All of this is most wonderfully suggestive. I would infer from it that the predominantly higher center shaft points to Christ, who as the Ideal Prophet reveals God and truth. The branches with their lamps directing light to the center shaft picture the function of the church to bear witness to Christ, "the true Light, which lighteth every man that cometh into the world" (John 1:9). Indeed, every believer ought to emulate the Baptist, who was "to bear witness of the Light, that all men through him might believe" (John 1:7). Because the lampstand was a single piece of gold, the branches could not be separated from the center shaft. Just so are believers inseparably united to Christ. As the oil was the energy source for the lamps, so the Holy Spirit empowered Christ and continues to empower and enable believers for their service. Christ had the Spirit without measure; we have the Spirit not only dwelling within us, but enabling us every time we ask for His gracious power (Luke 11:13). The light cannot shine without the oil.

The Altar of Incense

The last item in the holy place was the *altar of incense*, right up against the veil separating the holy place from the most holy. Significantly, this altar was fueled by coals from the altar of sacrifice in the outer court, and the priests would offer incense every morning and evening. As the smoke ascended from the altar, its fragrance would waft over the veil into the most holy place. The offering of incense was a symbol of prayer. David obviously alluded to this altar when he prayed, "Let my prayer be set forth before thee as incense; and the lifting up of my hands as the evening sacrifice" (Psalm 141:2). Two significant truths stand out: (1) prayer takes us as close as possible to the holy presence of God without our actually being there in person; and (2) prayer works only because of the blood of Christ's sacrifice, which opened up the way to God.

The Ark of the Covenant

The Holy of Holies had one item: the *ark of the covenant*. Without question, the ark was the climactic and central piece of all the Tabernacle furniture. The ark was simply a box that symbolized the presence of the Lord with His people. Although the ark was just an object lesson, the restrictions guiding its construction, content, location, and transportation were rigid and inflexible. By the box, God was declaring that there is something wonderfully fearful about His presence; man cannot trifle with the Most Holy God. Although there are manifold spiritual lessons taught by the ark, I want to isolate five key lessons that I think are very much on the surface of the ark symbolism.

(1) Its being overlaid with gold declares the sovereign majesty of God. To be in the presence of God is to be in presence of the King, and consequently it requires humble submission to His authority. This element of ark theology was prominent in later inspired writers who referred to the ark as the throne and footstool of God (Jeremiah 3:16-17; I Chronicles 28:2; Psalms 99:1-5; 132:7-8).

(2) Its being overshadowed by the cherubim declares the holiness of God. Of the entire angelic host, the cherubim seem to be the guardians and heralds of divine holiness and glory. Their first appear-

ance was at the gate of Eden, where the angels stood wielding swords to prevent fallen man from entering paradise and reaching the tree of life (Genesis 3:24). Years later, Ezekiel identified the four living creatures which attended the majestic and holy throne of God in his mysterious vision as the cherubim (Ezekiel 1, 10). Stationed over the ark, they silently proclaimed to unholy sinners that approach to the holy God was prohibited so long as they were unholy. Those who approach God must do so with clean hands and pure heart (Psalm 24:3-4). Worship and fellowship with God demand purity. At first sight, the cherubim do not extend much hope.

(3) Its containing a pot of manna (Exodus 16:33-34) and Aaron's rod (Numbers 17:10) testifies to God's gracious provision for His people. The manna was evidence of the Lord's faithfulness in sustaining His people and a reminder that man does not live by bread alone but by every word that proceeds from the mouth of the Lord. As they trusted God's promise for a new supply of the daily bread, so God's people of every generation can and should trust His every promise. He is faithful. Aaron's rod that budded confirmed that man could approach God only through mediation and only through the mediator of His choice. God set the terms: the way to His presence is His way or no way. But the grace of it is that there is a way.

(4) Its containing the tablets of the law, the Decalogue, speaks of God's righteousness and His inflexible demand for righteousness ("For the righteous Lord loveth righteousness"–Psalm 11:7). The law testified to God's covenant will toward His people yet stood as witness against them. To be righteous in terms of the law required absolute obedience both to the letter and to the spirit. From the open box, the laws cried for righteousness and demanded condemnation for unrighteousness. If the box were left open, man had no hope.

(5) Its being covered with the mercy seat proclaims hope. The mercy seat symbolized the essence of the gospel: there is a way into the presence of the sovereign, holy, and righteous God. The mercy seat is simply the "atoning lid." If the open box demanded the sinner's condemnation, the closed box declared the sinner's salvation. The mercy seat was God's visible pledge that He will be satisfied with the atonement and will by virtue of that atonement dwell with men. When the blood was sprinkled on the atoning lid, the impediments to fellowship

with God were removed. The blood was a propitiation or satisfaction of God's just wrath against the sinner. The blood was placed over the demands of the law and all was well. As clear a picture of the gospel that the ark was, it was only a picture. All that the ancient box pictured, Jesus Christ is.

I think that Jeremiah evidenced his understanding of the messianic reality conveyed by the ark when he prophesied that the day would come when no ark of the covenant of the Lord would be necessary (Jeremiah 3:16). There would be no need for the shadow when the reality was present. The apostle Paul in one of his great expositions on justification explained that we are "justified freely by his grace through the redemption that is in Christ Jesus: whom God hath set forth to be a propitiation through faith in his blood" (Romans 3:24-25). Significantly, the word translated "propitiation" is the same word the Septuagint, the Greek translation of the Old Testament, used to translate the "mercy seat." I submit that Paul knew that and made an intentional link between Christ and the ark, between antitype and type. Although the prophecy of the ark has been fulfilled, its message is still the glorious gospel and the only hope for sinners. The old hymn says it well: "There is a place where mercy sheds the oil of gladness on our heads, a place than all beside more sweet—it is the blood stained mercy seat."

Rituals at the Tabernacle

Pre-eminently, the Tabernacle was the place where the rituals and ceremonies of worship occurred. The sacrificial system that was so specifically defined under the Mosaic administration was a graphic but intentionally imperfect picture of the work of Christ. In part the sacrifices were typical events, but they were such an integral part of the Tabernacle economy that any consideration of Tabernacle theology necessitates an explication of them. In every way these sacrifices were types prophesying of Christ, "the Lamb slain from the foundation of the world" (Revelation 13:8). Since these sacrifices had no independent significance apart from what they pictured about Christ, to obey the ritual, in faith looking beyond the visible, was tantamount to obeying the gospel. The sacrifices were picture sermons of the gospel. The general and regular sacrifices fell into two broad categories: sweet savor offerings and guilt offerings. Leviticus 1-7 records the most detailed instructions about the sacrifices.

Burnt Offering

The *burnt offering*, the most general of the sacrifices, was a sweet savor offering. It shared some common features with the other sacrifices and taught key lessons about the atonement. (1) The animal selected for this offering had to be a "male without blemish" (Leviticus 1:3, 10). Symbolically, this taught that the only acceptable sacrifice had to be pure, perfect, and blameless. Since the offerer was guilty of sin, this strict requirement made it clear that atonement had to come from a source outside the self. Typically, this pure victim was a picture of Christ, the "lamb without blemish and without spot" (I Peter 1:19). The lamb without blemish points to the whole active obedience of Christ, which offered to God a perfect righteousness and demonstrated to the world His absolute perfection and sinlessness.

(2) The offerer leaned on the animal (Leviticus 1:4). The forcible laying on of hands symbolically represented the transfer of guilt from the sinner to the perfect animal, the otherwise innocent animal becoming the substitute for the guilty party. Leaning one's weight on the sacrifice suggested something as well of the nature of faith that rests on the object of sacrifice. The result of this transfer and substitution was that "it shall be accepted for him to make atonement for him" (Leviticus 1:4). Peace with God was the goal, and propitiation (atonement) of God's wrath was the means to achieve that goal. This detail proclaimed vividly the gospel truth of vicarious atonement. Typically, it declares that Christ, who knew no sin, was made sin for us "that we might be made the righteousness of God in him"(II Corinthians 5:21).

(3) The offerer had to kill the animal (Leviticus 1:5). The death of the substitutionary sacrifice symbolically taught the terrible penalty of sin. The demand of God's holy law was absolute and its penalty was severe. God's gracious mercy provided a substitute, but His holy justice could not overlook the broken law. Wages were earned, and wages had to be received (Romans 6:23). That the offerer slew the animal impressed on him the solemn reality that it was his sin that required the penalty; he was personally responsible for the death of the sacrifice. Typically, the slaying points to Christ, "who was delivered for our offenses" and who "died for the ungodly" (Romans 4:25; 5:6). Christ's

dying as the perfect sacrifice was the only way that God could be both just and the justifier (Romans 3:26).

(4) The priests sprinkled the blood of the victim on the altar (Leviticus 1:5). This use of the blood shed through death did something positive. Whereas death was the necessary penalty of sin, the blood shed through death was the specific means of propitiation, satisfying the wrath of God. Sprinkling the blood on the altar, the first piece of Tabernacle furniture, symbolically showed that there is no approach to God apart from blood. Typically, it pictures Christ's presentation of the blood of His atonement (Hebrews 9:12) whereby the believer has access into the holy place (Hebrews 10:19). This is the gospel: approach to God is only through the blood of Jesus Christ.

(5) The priests burned the entire sacrifice on the altar (Leviticus 1:9). Whereas each of the bloody sacrifices parallels the first four steps, the burning of the whole victim is unique to the burnt offering. It is this burning that is a "sweet savor" to the Lord (Leviticus 1:9). This "smell that placates" represents that which is pleasing and acceptable to God; it puts His wrath to rest. Atonement having been accomplished by the death and application of blood, the burning is a sign of reconciliation, satisfaction, and consecration. It is a clear prophecy of Christ, who gave "himself for us an offering and a sacrifice to God for a sweet-smelling savour" (Ephesians 5:2).

Cereal Offering
The *meat offering* was a non-bloody cereal offering that was presented to the Lord in association with one of the bloody sacrifices, usually the burnt offering. This offering of grain could be in the form of whole grains roasted in fire, fine flour, or baked loaves. Oil, incense, and salt were required for every offering, but honey and leaven could never be used. The materials for these offerings were produced by man's labor. By presenting the fruit of his labor, the offerer demonstrated his devotion of life, possessions, and occupation to the Lord. Of the all the details specified for the cereal offering (Leviticus 2), the prohibition of honey and leaven and the requirement of salt are the most significant for the symbolic and typical truths about the gospel. Whereas the leaven and honey would cause the offering to spoil, the salt would preserve it. It is specifically called "the salt of the covenant of thy God" (Leviticus 2:13). The association of this preservative with the

covenant symbolically declared that God's contract with the people was eternal and inviolable. God would not refuse any who came in faith by way of the sacrifice that He had prescribed. Typically, the cereal offering points to Christ, the surety of the covenant, who was completely devoted and consecrated to God and His divine commission.

Peace Offering

The *peace offering* was the last of the sweet savor offerings, and its restrictions were not as rigid as those of the other offerings (Leviticus 3:1-17; 7:11-34). The animal could be a male or a female of any age. The ritual was like the other sacrifices except that it was offered at the entrance to the outer court. The choice inward parts were burned, and the breast and the shoulder were given to the priest. The priest could share them with his family, something he could not do with the other sacrifices. The rest of the animal was returned to the offerer for a communal meal with his family, his friends, and the Levites. This was a time of fellowship between God and man. The peace offering was an object lesson showing that man was reconciled to God; there was peace between them because of the atonement. Typically, it points to Christ, who reconciled believers to God, having made peace through His blood (Romans 5:1, 10). Christ's blood satisfied all the parties concerned: the offended God, the mediating Christ, and the offending sinner.

Guilt Offerings

The *sin offering* (Leviticus 4-5:13; 6:24-30) and the *trespass offering* (Leviticus 5:14-6:7) were the guilt offerings that pictured both the satisfaction of God's wrath against sin (propitiation) and the removal of sin's guilt (expiation). Both of these sacrifices were for specific sins to teach that every sin was intolerable to God and that confession should be as specific as the sins. Although the initial steps of these sacrifices parallel those of the burnt offering and declare the same general lessons, there are some specific emphases that are important. The main objective was to put an end to the separation between God and man caused by sin. Sin pollutes and prevents fellowship with God. In each of these sacrifices blood was shed, a reminder that blood was the only means whereby God would forgive sin. These sacrifices particularly picture expiation, the effect of the atonement manward, made possible because of propitiation, the effect of the atonement Godward. Because divine wrath is satisfied, a sinner can be cleansed from the defilement that offends God. This aspect is a vivid object lesson of I John 1:7, 9 and 2:1-2, which state explicitly the importance of confessing sin and the relationship of the blood of Christ to receiving forgiveness.

Perhaps the most distinctive feature of the guilt offerings was the disposal of the sacrificial victims; they were burned outside the camp. This feature finds ultimate significance in Christ's suffering "without the gate" (Hebrews 13:12), the place of shame and uncleanness. In addition, the trespass offering required compensation to the offended party as an evidence of genuine repentance. This act of compensation points directly to Christ, who positively rendered to God everything that the law required and then paid the penalty of the broken law in behalf of His people. The trespass offering combined both the active and the passive obedience of Christ. Significantly, Isaiah refers to the suffering servant as the trespass offering (Isaiah 53:10), who offered to God everything necessary for the salvation of the promised seed. That Isaiah rightly saw Christ as the reality and the fulfillment of this picture prophecy demonstrates how every Old Testament saint saw the sacrifices.

Events

Throughout the Old Testament, events occurred that were significant for the spiritual truths they symbolized and typified. We have already learned that Abraham's casting out Hagar and Ishmael conveyed an important gospel message. Paul's exposition certainly helps to guide our thinking, but thinking through the passage ourselves confirms, in a sense, Paul's hermeneutic. Even novice application of the principles for recognizing and interpreting types reveals in the Abraham-Isaac story a vivid prophecy of God's sacrifice of His Son: as God commanded Abraham to sacrifice Isaac, the seed of promise, on Mt. Moriah but instead provided a substitute, so He Himself offered His only begotten Son, the Seed of promise, on Mt. Calvary. Many events from the Exodus to the Conquest, in addition to their historical significance in forming the covenant nation, include spiritual truths that transcend application to national Israel. The Exodus itself with its demonstration of sovereign grace, divine power, and substitutionary sacrifice is overflowing with gospel lessons and messianic picture prophecies. In addition to the regular sacrifices, the ceremonial prophecies included special days and celebrations that focused on various aspects of gospel truth. We need to pay careful attention to the feast and fast days that God set aside and defined for Israel. They were more than just holidays providing a day off from work and routine: they were special occasions that God ordered to make the Old Testament people think about certain spiritual truths. Although we New Testament people do not take those same days off, we are likewise encouraged to think about the same truths.

One of the most important events in the Old Testament calendar was the Day of Atonement. Hebrews 9:7-8, refers to this yearly epoch and tells us that the Holy Spirit was signifying some important precepts. It is important for us to discern the Holy Spirit's intent. I want to highlight three essential gospel truths that God was most obviously teaching His "before Christ" people that are just as true for us. The message is the same; the mechanics of the message are wonderfully and thankfully outmoded. I think that the overriding theme of the Day of Atonement is that sinners cannot come to God in their own way or on their own terms. God sets the terms and defines the way to Him. True religion is extremely narrow and intolerant of any other way to God than through the Lord Jesus Christ.

Although the Old Testament refers to the Day of Atonement in various places, only Leviticus 16 details the order and events. It paints a beautiful picture of the gospel and the work of Christ.

The Need for a Mediator

The first truth is that *sinners can approach God only through the mediation of a sinless Priest.* Significantly, Leviticus 16 follows several chapters which detail the laws of cleanness and uncleanness and warn the people that they are sinners living in a world defiled by sin (Leviticus 11-15). Sin defiles and precludes fellowship with the Holy God. The scene appears hopeless, but Leviticus 16 points the way to hope. God had appointed a way whereby the most sinful and defiled could approach Him, but only through the ordained mediator, the priest. The work of the lesser high priest prophesying the work of the Ideal High Priest was most vivid on this Day of Atonement. Of the many details, in overview two things stand out.

First, dealing with sin was a work of humiliation. This is most obvious in the dress of the high priest on this solemn occasion. On every other day, the high priest was adorned with special garments designating beauty and glory (we noted some of the significance of these garments above). In that rich and splendid attire, the high priest appeared in royal dignity. We need to be careful not to confuse what Aaron wore daily as he ministered in the holy place (Exodus 28:35) with what he was commanded to wear as he ministered in the most holy place. On the Day of Atonement, God instructed Aaron to remove the royal garments and don simple linen clothes, symbolizing the humility required to do the work of atonement (Leviticus 16:4). As the representative of sinful men, and as the obedient servant, the high priest was stripped of every vestige of honor as he dealt with sin in the immediate presence of God. What a clear prophecy of the Incarnation of the eternal Son of God! What Aaron graphically pictured, Christ explicitly fulfilled as He divested Himself of visible and manifest glory in order to put on the frail garment of our humanity, qualifying Him to be our perfect representative before God.

Second, dealing with sin was a work requiring purity. This was transparently evident from the fact that Aaron had to take care of his own sins before he could even symbolically deal with the sins of the people (Leviticus 16:6, 11, 17, 24). Aaron's offering sacrifices first for himself testified both to the need for a sinless priest and to the fact that he was not the sinless priest needed. Incorporated into the message was the built-in obsolescence to prevent the people from confusing the object lesson with the reality. Every time a high priest offered a sacrifice for himself, the desire for and anticipation of the perfect priest increased. If not Aaron, who? The one and only answer to that question is Jesus Christ, "who needeth not daily, as those high priests, to offer up sacrifice, first for his own sins, and then for the people's" (Hebrews 7:27). Only our Christ could on His own merit approach the God of holiness to attain mercy for us. As Aaron, the imperfect type, did the work alone (Leviticus 16:17), so Christ, the perfect antitype, is the only one who could do the necessary work of atonement.

The Need for Sacrifice

The second great truth is that *sinners can approach God only on the grounds of a vicarious sacrifice.* Although several sacrifices were offered on the Day of Atonement, one event, in two parts, constituted the principal message of the Day: the goat for the sin offering and the scapegoat. These two goats together paint a beautiful picture of the full atonement accomplished by Christ, both propitiation and expiation. The first goat declared the necessity of death and bloodshed for propitiation. All the daily sacrifices declared this same message, but what made this a special sacrifice was what the high priest did with the blood. With the blood of the slain goat, the high priest made his way behind the veil into that most restricted area of the Tabernacle, the Holy of Holies. Inside the veil, he sprinkled the blood directly on the mercy seat, that atoning lid that covered the ark of the covenant. The placement of the blood symbolized the stilling of the law's demand and the appeasement of God's righteous wrath and typified Christ's entering heaven with His own blood to accomplish that for real (Hebrews 9:8-28). There is an outstanding difference between Aaron's entering behind the veil and Christ's. Aaron's goat blood secured his personal entrance into the symbolic presence alone; the people could not follow him. Christ's own blood secured an entrance for all His people to follow; He was the forerunner for us (Hebrews 6:19-20).

The second goat illustrated expiation, the consequence of propitiation. The scapegoat was a clear picture of the removal of sin and guilt, the saving benefit of the atonement for man. Which goat was for sacrifice and which was to be the scapegoat was determined by lot (Leviticus 16:7-8). After the blood of the slain goat was offered on the mercy seat, the attention was on the scapegoat. The high priest leaned his hands on the animal, confessing the sins of the nation and thereby symbolizing the transfer of guilt (Leviticus 16:21). Then the goat, symbolically carrying the sin of the people, was led off into the wilderness (a land cut off, uninhabited), never to be seen again. It was sent to a place of no return. Interpreters have differed over the exact meaning of the term "scapegoat," literally "a goat for Azazel" (Leviticus 16:8, 10, 26). Some have identified this as a reference to the Tempter himself, suggesting that sins were sent back to their author. I don't particularly like that interpretation. Others define the word as "complete destruction" or a "rocky precipice." Regardless of the etymology of "Azazel," the message of the goat was transparent. Sin and guilt were removed from the people for whom the sacrifice had been made. The theology of the scapegoat is as simple and as wonderful as the little song I learned as a kid: "Gone, gone, gone, gone, yes, my sins are gone." Exactly where the scapegoat went may be in doubt, but one thing is beautifully certain: it never showed up in camp again. Once the blood was shed and sprinkled on the mercy seat, the scapegoat had to go. That's the message of the gospel. Propitiation guarantees expiation. We do not preach a "maybe" gospel. We declare the certainty of forgiveness whenever and wherever the blood is applied.

A Sure Salvation

The third great truth is that *sinners can be sure of salvation because of the resurrection of Christ*. Remember Paul's classic definition of the gospel, which links two vital and inseparable facts: Christ died according to the Scripture and He was raised according to the Scripture (I Corinthians 15:3-4). The Day of Atonement provides a picture prophecy of both the death and the resurrection. If wearing the simple linen and entering behind the veil to present the blood picture the humiliation and death of Christ, exiting from behind the veil and exchanging the simple linen garments for the royal garments picture the resurrection of Christ, the beginning of His earned exaltation (Leviticus 16:23-24). That Aaron came out testified to the acceptance of the sacrifice. That Christ was raised from the dead testified to the success of His atoning sacrifice. Had there been no resurrection, there would have been no atonement. I am confident in asserting that there is no way a high priest could die behind the veil. For a high priest to die behind the veil would sabotage the prophecy and jeopardize the very message. It would charge God with caprice and eliminate any hope for reconciliation with Him. Remember that the Day of Atonement was not about the personal merit or virtue of the earthly priest; it was a prophecy about the merit and work of the Ideal Priest. On the authority of the Scripture I affirm that the gospel of Jesus Christ always works!

Although the Day of Atonement and all the other Old Testament types have long passed away, never to be repeated or reinstituted (not even in the millennial kingdom), the eternal truths that they proclaimed are relevant still. I have devoted much attention to this particular means of Old Testament revelation because of its frequency, its importance, and unfortunately its confusion and misuse. I do believe that if you avoid confusing the object lesson/analogy with the reality and focus on the main points of correspondence between type and antitype, you will find in these picture prophecies of the old dispensation glorious truths about Christ. They are there. Don't worry about how much of the message you think people in the old dispensation understood. That's not the issue and it will only distract you from your own mission of finding Christ. You must read and study the Scripture to discover what you yourself must understand, believe, and do.

CHAPTER 10

CHRIST IN SONG

There is something about singing that comes naturally to believers. Throughout the Scripture, those who are the beneficiaries of God's goodness and grace break out in song. After Moses led the children of Israel through the Red Sea, he became the first choir director as he led the nation in singing unto the Lord, "The Lord is my strength and song, and he is become my salvation" (Exodus 15:2). After Deborah delivered the nation from oppression, she broke out in song: "I, even I, will sing unto the Lord; I will sing praise to the Lord God of Israel" (Judges 5:3). After David testified of God's bringing him up from the miry clay and setting his feet on a rock, he declared, "And he hath put a new song in my mouth, even praise unto our God" (Psalm 40:3). Paul marked singing as one of the evidences of being filled with the Holy Spirit: "Speaking to yourselves in psalms and hymns and spiritual songs, singing and making melody in your heart to the Lord; Giving thanks always for all things unto God and the Father in the name of our Lord Jesus Christ" (Ephesians 5:19-20). On more than one occasion in his vision of things to come, John recorded the singing of the redeemed in heaven (Revelation 5:9; 15:3). Whether in the Old or the New Testament dispensations or in eternity, God's people express their worship in song. Singing is an effective means of stirring the heart and actively fixing the emotions and passions on the Lord. It is always service rendered to the Lord; it is never entertainment for man. Singing is a key element in worship.

Since the Scripture identifies the "how" as well as the "who" of worship, it is not surprising that the Bible is so concerned with the importance of singing. In fact, the Lord inspired a hymnbook, the Book of Psalms. Although the melodies were neither inspired nor preserved, the inspired words of the Psalter transcend any tune and serve a vital function for both public and private mediation and prayer, even if not sung at all. The Psalms constitute a blueprint to follow for worship. They identify the themes for worship as well as address the obstacles and hindrances to spiritual praise. They teach us to pray whether in confessing our sins, praying our way out of trouble or depression, or praising the Lord for all His perfections and works. The Psalms set a divinely inspired standard for spiritual songs and prayers of worship. Although they deal with the issues of personal experience and testimony, predominantly they set forth essential objective truths of doctrine and the gospel. If there is any surface lesson from the Psalms, it is that worship is all about God and not about man. The Psalms reveal a theology of worship. I love the Psalms.

Resisting the temptation to discuss that theology of worship, I will direct my attention specifically to the revelations of Christ. It is not surprising that the Psalms demand attention to the Messiah. The testimony of Scripture is clear and consistent that man cannot approach God in worship, prayer, or, indeed, in any capacity apart from the one and only Mediator. What the Tabernacle taught in type, the Psalms teach in verse and song. The Psalms were an effective means of keeping Christ before the people and intensifying the desire for Him by making Him the theme of song, prayer, and worship. There is hardly a doctrine about Christ that in one way or another is not part of the Psalms' messianic theology. His humanity and deity, His death and resurrection, His mediatorial offices (prophet, priest, and king), His first and Second Advents are all part of the message of Psalms. Psalms, the book of song and worship, is a good place to find Christ.

Identification of Messianic Psalms

That Christ is a prevalent topic of the Psalms stands without question. How to identify the messianic Psalms is the question. Hopefully, at this stage of our study it is not as big a problem as it may have been at the beginning. Essentially, identifying the messianic passages in the Psalms is no different from identifying them anywhere else in the Old Testament. I suppose what makes it a little more complicated is the fact that sometimes whole Psalms are uniquely messianic and sometimes only a part of a Psalm is. Recognizing the uniqueness of the former and the transitions in the latter are key elements in the interpretative process. It is paramount to stay on Christ-alert as you read the Psalms. Let me suggest some specific guidelines and reminders that should help you to spot the messianic texts.

Analogy of Scripture

First, *be alert to messianic clues*. As I have consistently reminded you throughout this study, if you know whom and what you are looking for, you will know it when you see it. This approach involves our old analogy of Scripture principle. When you see a clue word or activity or attribute that other Scriptures have used or defined in terms of Messiah, you are certainly warranted in linking it to the Messiah in the Psalms. For instance, when you notice Psalm 89's referring to the "seed" that will endure forever (89:29, 36), you should immediately identify that as messianic. Remember that "Seed" is a messianic word, a clue word that runs throughout the entire Old Testament.

Uniqueness Principle

Second, *be alert to the "ideality" principle*. By this I simply mean that there are going to be statements that transcend any possible reference to mere men and must find their sole application in Christ. For instance, when Psalm 72 talks about a King whose dominion is universal (72:8) and whose name is eternal (72:17), you can be sure that David is not referring to himself, Solomon, or any other merely human sovereign. That is an ideal and unique reference to Christ. The same would be true in Psalm 45 when the King whose throne is forever and whose kingdom is righteousness is addressed specifically as God (45:6).

Type-Antitype

Third, *be alert to the type-antitype connection*. Keep in mind the proper definitions of type and antitype. A type is a real, historical person, thing, or event that conveys some key point of analogy to the future reality, the antitype. By definition, a Psalm that is typical of Christ must have a direct reference to a real historical person or phenomenon. This will be most common in what are often called the Royal Psalms, those that deal with the theme of kingship (2, 18, 20, 21, 45, 72, 89, 101, 110, 132, 144). All have their theological foundation in the Davidic Covenant (II Samuel 7:11-16). Although not all messianic Psalms are Royal Psalms, I think it is safe to say that all Royal Psalms are in some way messianic, some ideally and uniquely, some typically. For instance, Psalm 18 reviews God's faithfulness in delivering David from the dangers that threatened his rule. That was certainly David's testimony, but it found even greater fulfillment in David's greater Son, who experienced the preserving and protecting hand of the Lord throughout His earthly ministry. The Psalm ends with its own suggestion to take this reference beyond David: "Great deliverance giveth he to his king; and sheweth mercy to his anointed, to David, and to his seed for evermore" (18:50). The three clue words, "king," "anointed," and "seed," ought to start you thinking about the points of correspondence between David and Christ.

New Testament Authority

Fourth, *be alert to New Testament confirmations.* The cross-references in your Bible should help direct you to most of the New Testament parallels or fulfillments. It always helps to have an inspired commentary. Here are some of the messianic Psalms referred to in the New Testament. I will discuss some of these in the next section, but go ahead and read the New Testament texts to see how they use the respective Psalms. It should be instructive. That the New Testament tends to focus on a particular part of the Psalm does not necessarily mean that that part is the only messianic statement in the Psalm. Maybe it is and maybe it isn't. At least let the New Testament start or confirm your thinking that something in the Psalm refers to Christ. Study the whole context to see if or how the rest relates to Messiah:

Psalm	New Testament	Topic
Psalm 2	Acts 4:25-28	Plot to kill Christ
	Acts 13:33	Resurrection
	Hebrews 1:5	Superiority to angels
	Hebrews 5:5	Superiority to Aaron
	Revelation 12:5	Rule of iron
Psalm 8	Matthew 21:16	Children's praise
	I Corinthians 15:25;	Dominion
	Ephesians 1:22;	
	Hebrews 2:5-10	

Psalm 16	Acts 2:24-31; 13:35-37	Resurrection
Psalm 22	Matthew 27:35-46; John 19:23-25	Crucifixion
	Hebrews 2:12	Real Humanity
Psalm 40	Hebrews 10:5-10	Incarnation
Psalm 45	Hebrews 1:8-9	Deity
Psalm 69	Acts 1:16-20	Judas
Psalm 102	Hebrews 1:10-12	Deity
Psalm 109	Acts 1:16-20	Judas
Psalm 110	Matthew 22:43-45	Superiority to David
	Acts 2:33-35	Ascension
	Hebrews 1:13	Deity
	Hebrews 5:6-10	Superior priesthood
	(And others)	

There are other general rules for interpreting poetry which can help the overall process as well. Hebrew poetry is characterized by a parallelism of thought between the lines. Sometimes the lines are synonymous (saying the same thing), sometimes antithetical (saying the opposite thing), sometimes comparative. Pay attention to see if one line helps to interpret the other, as is frequently the case. For instance, as we have seen, in Psalm 16:10 the second line claiming that the Holy One will not see corruption demands that the first line about the soul's not being left in hell must refer to the bodily resurrection of Christ. This is how the New Testament interpreted it also. Further, be sensitive to subtle shifts between first, second, and third person references. For instance, in Psalm 2 the shift of speakers identifies four different perspectives about Christ, one from Christ Himself. This may be a particularly helpful clue in those Psalms that are admixtures of historical and messianic references. You may want to review figures of speech as well; poetry tends to use them frequently. For instance, whereas Psalm 40:6 says, "Mine ears hast thou opened," Hebrews 10:5 quotes it as saying, "A body hast thou prepared me." This is no contradiction. Rather, the New Testament has rightly interpreted "ear" as a synecdoche for "body." *Synecdoche*, as you recall, is a common figure of speech in which a part of something designates the whole. All of this is important, but obviously beyond our specific orbit for now.

Synopsis of Selected Messianic Psalms

Although I would love at this point to start at the beginning of the Psalter and expound every messianic text, that would, like every other "not-in-the-outline" impulse I have had in this project, take us way beyond our defined scope and purpose. My primary concern for now is to illustrate from a few selected Psalms how Israel's official hymnbook was full of messianic theology. The Israelites knew what it meant to sing of their Redeemer. As I summarize these selected Psalms, I will not always quote the verse, so it may be helpful for you to have your Bible handy to follow along.

Christ: The Object of Saving Faith

Psalm 2 is the first explicitly and uniquely messianic Psalm. It is a Royal Psalm that shows the ideal and inviolable fulfillment of the Davidic Covenant. The Psalm progresses in four distinct movements or stanzas marked by four different speakers: rebels, the Lord, the Messiah, and the Narrator (ultimately, the Holy Spirit). Each stanza expresses a particular attitude about the Messiah with a climactic warning that our attitude toward the Messiah determines our eternal destiny.

Stanza 1: Rebels

In the first three verses the rebels speak and *oppose Christ's authority*. Although the rebels include every race and every class from every age who are naturally alienated from God, the raging, plotting, and general hostility against Christ found its most grievous demonstration in the strange alliances between Jews and Gentiles and between Pilate and Herod in the trial and execution of Christ. The object of all the scheming hatred was the Lord and His Messiah. Desiring freedom from divine restraint, the rebels combined their hatred in a futile attempt to sever the "bands" and "cords" of Christ's authority by putting Him to death (see Acts 4:27-28). We know that God used their plot as the means of effecting His eternal plan for our redemption in Christ. "Him, being delivered by the determinate counsel and foreknowledge of God, ye have taken, and by wicked hands have crucified and slain" (Acts 2:23). That's what Peter said right to the face of some of the conspirators.

Stanza 2: God

In verses 4-6 God speaks and *confirms Christ's authority*, thus highlighting the futility of any attempt to thwart God's purpose in Christ. The contrast between the scheming agitation of world leaders and the serene, supreme sovereignty of the Lord (*Adonai*, the real King) who sits laughing at their efforts would be comical if it were not so tragic. His sitting in heaven testifies to His absolute authority to actually accomplish whatever He pleases (Psalm 115:3). God is not just a passive witness to what takes place in the world. He sits on a throne to rule, not "in the stands" to watch. His laughing at those who conspire against His purpose is a bold statement emphasizing the absurdity of their futile efforts. His holding them in derision is literally "to stammer disrespectfully in their face." What a vivid image of God's "getting in the sinner's face" to ridicule him and establish His infinite superiority and power to consume the rebel in a moment were it not for His longsuffering. After He mocks, He speaks. Notwithstanding the rejection of Christ's authority by sinners, the Lord declared that He had set His king on the holy hill of Zion. The word "set" literally means "to pour out" and refers to God's consecrating and exalting Christ to the position of authority. That is His resolute purpose and nothing could or ever can alter it. The Kingdom of God and His Christ is not a democracy. Whether men submit or not, Christ is the King.

Stanza 3: Messiah

In verses 7-9 Christ Himself speaks and *affirms His own authority*. This indeed is holy ground as the Messiah reveals what the Father, in the privacy of eternity, had promised Him. Three truths stand out in Christ's speech. First, Messiahship is based on God's certain decree ("I will declare the decree"). The word "declare" includes the idea of detailing, listing, or enumerating. He is going to detail some of the elements of the decree, the obligations and rules that defined the covenant agreement between Himself and the Father concerning the whole mediatorial work of redemption. This is language of certitude, and it should generate confidence and joy that God's decree concerning Christ and, consequently, concerning salvation is irreversible, irrefutable, and unfrustratable.

Second, Christ stood in a unique relationship with God the Father ("Thou art my Son; this day have I begotten thee"). This was not a prophecy to Christ that He would become the Son at the Incarnation; it was the eternal declaration of the existing Sonship. Although this statement has direct bearing on "official" messianic Sonship, I believe that the language demands that this be viewed as a direct statement of the essential Trinitarian Sonship of the Second Person of the Trinity, the eternal Son of God and chosen Mediator.

The statement "this day have I begotten thee" has caused some confusion, but it is a key statement for proper understanding of the Psalm's intent. The problem is that we tend to think of something begotten as having had a beginning. That Christ is the eternal Son of God and begotten at the same time seem to be mutually exclusive. How can both be true? The problem is more apparent than real. Although the word "begotten" can be used metaphorically, it usually refers to a familial rather than official relationship. This is why I say that the focus here is on the eternal Trinitarian relationship. Again, the word usually—though not consistently—takes a distinct form depending on the subject of the verb (whether the mother, father, or midwife). In this text, the form used usually refers to the mother's giving birth. It would be ludicrous and blasphemous even to hint that God the Father was the mother of Christ. The point is that the word is used not to suggest in any way a beginning of existence, but rather to underscore the existence of a Father-Son relationship.

Happily, the New Testament uses this verse in such a way as to confirm this interpretation—that the word speaks of the existence and not the inception of a relationship. In his sermon at Antioch in Pisidia, Paul specifically alluded to the second Psalm and appealed to the statement "Thou art my Son, this day have I begotten thee" as biblical proof that God had raised up Jesus from the dead (Acts 13:33). The fact that the Father had already spoken from heaven declaring Christ to be His Son at the baptism and transfiguration precludes interpreting the resurrection as the beginning of Sonship. Romans 1:4 explains why Paul used Psalm 2 in connection with the Lord's resurrection: by the resurrection God declared in power that Christ was His Son. The resurrection was the conclusive, irrefutable evidence of who Christ was. It vindicated and confirmed His every claim, not the least of which was that God was His Father (see, for instance, John 8:16-29).

The third truth in Christ's speech concerns His universal inheritance and unwavering authority. One of the details of that eternal agreement was that the Father would give a people to His Son. Remember that we saw this same promise in Isaiah 53:10. If the Servant would offer Himself for sin, He would see His seed. So according to the passage here, the heathen throughout the world would be Christ's for the asking. This divine offer of a people throughout the world evoked David's acknowledgement that the Seed promised through his family line was a revelation of truth for all mankind (II Samuel 7:19; see the earlier discussion on the Davidic covenant). Remember that I have emphasized that the promise of Messiah in the Old Testament was never a uniquely Jewish promise. Knowing what the Father promised the Son heightens the significance of the Great Commission that Christ gave His church to evangelize the world. Evangelism is the divinely intended means of claiming all that belongs to Christ. That ought to increase zeal and boldness in every evangelistic effort. All will in one way or another submit to Christ's authority. He conquers either by grace or by the rod of iron. Sooner or later, one way or another, every knee will bow and every tongue will confess that Jesus is the Lord, the only Christ of God.

Stanza 4: The Holy Spirit

That threat is a fitting transition to the climactic final stanza in which the narrator *recommends submission to Christ's authority* (verses 10-12). If anything is clear from the last stanza of this song, it is that eternal destiny is linked to relationship with the Son. Since it is impossible to frustrate God's eternal purpose in Christ, the best thing to do is to submit to it. With a series of five imperatives, the narrator appeals to men to submit to Christ. Being wise means to act wisely, setting aside the foolishness of rejecting Christ. Being instructed means to become teachable, setting aside the arrogance and obstinacy of self-will. Serving the Lord with fear means to surrender humbly to His authority, recognizing that He is the Lord, the Sovereign. Rejoicing with trembling means to find contentment and true happiness in the awareness and fear of the Lord. Kissing the Son means to embrace Him in homage and worship. The consequences of obeying or disobeying this gracious invitation were and are fixed. Irresistible wrath is on those who do not submit, and indescribable blessing is on those who do. Those who refuse Christ will perish. Those who seek refuge in Christ as the only place of safety are saved. In the truest sense, it is Christ who rescues the perishing. Note that these commands to trust Christ or else suffer the consequences are not prophecies of how men would be saved after the Incarnation. Christ was the only object of saving faith in the Old Testament dispensation just as He is the only object of saving faith now.

Christ: The Ideal Man

The messianic content and intent of Psalm 8 are confirmed four times in the New Testament. In answer to His enemies and would-be conspirators who protested the children's praise of Him on Palm Sunday, Jesus asked them if they had never read, "Out of the mouth of babes and sucklings thou hast perfected praise" (Matthew 21:16, quoting Psalm 8:2 and reflecting the interpretation of the Septuagint). Twice Paul explains Christ's resurrection, exaltation, and dominion in terms of Psalm 8 (I Corinthians 15; Ephesians 1). Most significantly, Hebrews 2 interprets Psalm 8 as a description of the Incarnation and earned exaltation of Christ. The whole Psalm is a song highlighting the greatness and grace of God that points to the Lord Jesus as the only means by which fallen man can come to the enjoyment and experience of the privileged rank God assigned to man in creation.

Although verses 5 and 6 are the principal messianic statements, thus having independent significance, they are an integral part of the argument of the whole Psalm. I want to focus my comments on these two verses, but I must first set them in the overall context. That the Psalm begins and ends with the same statement marks this as a hymn of praise: "O LORD, our Lord, how excellent is thy name in all the earth." This refrain says three things about God which reveal His glory and establish the topic for thanksgiving. (1) The name "LORD" is *Jehovah* and identifies God as the covenant Savior of His people. Although this name reveals much about God's eternal self-sufficiency and absolute independence (I AM that I AM), it is uniquely the salvation name that He revealed in covenant promise. (2) The title "Lord" is *Adonai*: it identifies God as the absolute Sovereign over everything. He is the Owner, the Master, the King of kings and Lord of lords. (3) That His name is excellent declares that His entire Being, with every infinite, eternal, and unchangeable perfection, is majestically glorious throughout the earth. The Lord, our Savior, has fixed His glory indelibly over all creation.

Having established the fact of God's glory, the psalmist David testifies to God's greatness and expresses his amazement that such greatness could be so gracious and condescending (verses 2-4). The praising babes and sucklings testify to God's ironic use of weak things to confound the mighty. His using such frail and defenseless beings to silence His enemies demonstrates His great power. This is a particular group of children who evidence far greater spiritual perception than religious leaders and professionals when they sing their hosannas to the Lord Jesus. Along with the infant chorus, the immense creation of the universe declares the same great glory. Notwithstanding the incomprehensible vastness of the universe, its existence is but the intricate fingerwork of God. If such an immense universe with all its complexities is but fingerwork, how infinitely great must be the "fingers" that created! From the beginning of creation until the end of time, the heavens have constantly declared and will unceasingly declare the glory of God (see Psalm 19:1). If the heavens are preaching and singing anything, it is "My God, how great thou art."

Considering the vastness of creation with its unfailing testimony to God's greatness raised the question in David's mind as to why God would give such special attention to man. He used two designations that contrasted man's puniness with creation's vastness. "What is man, that thou art mindful of him? And the son of man, that thou visitest him?" The first word, "man," underscores man's frailty, mortality, and impotence. The second expression, "the son of man (*adam*)," also represents man's inherent weakness and insignificance as earthy. Could this part of the Psalm have been in Paul's mind when he said of Adam, "The first man is of the earth, earthy" (I Corinthians 15:47)? I think so. Sadly, man did not live up to what God made him to be. Made upright, he fell into sin (Ecclesiastes 7:29). Yet notwithstanding the failure and frailty, God with divine purpose set His mind and special attention on man. The Lord intervened in the affairs of man. The thought of that condescending grace amazed David. This statement of the grace God designed to bestow is the transition to the messianic text.

Verses 5 and 6 attest to man's creation in the image of God and his subsequent dominion over everything else created. The Genesis account clearly sets Adam apart from the rest of creation as the only being created in God's image and the only created being requiring the breath of God to live. Although there are several significant implications of man's having been created in God's image, the main reflection of it in Genesis was Adam's being commissioned with dominion over everything else God had made. It was not long before Adam fell, plunging his entire race into sin, making dominion a struggle, and severely marring, though not losing, the image of God. Psalm 8:5-6, however, speaks of a man who honorably and unfailingly fulfilled the high station God intended for man. It points to the "last Adam," "the second man." Whereas the first man was of the earth, the second man is "the Lord from heaven" (I Corinthians 15:45-47). Everything the first Adam lost, the second Adam regained. This points to Christ, who, being the eternal Son of God, became the Ideal Man. In absolute perfection Jesus Christ was the "image of the invisible God" and the "brightness of his glory and the express image of his person" (Colossians 1:15; Hebrews 1:3). I would suggest that Psalm 8 provided the foundation theology for Paul's analogy between Adam and Christ.

The New Testament helpfully confirms the messianic intent of this text, but it does not create it. Messianic clues and the ideality/uniqueness principle contextually point to Christ. The first clue comes from the opening statement, "Thou hast made him a little lower than the angels." The word "made" is not a word of creation that we would expect if the reference were to the first Adam. Rather, it literally means "to diminish," "to take away from," or "to deprive." The very meaning of the word requires the existence of the object or person that is being diminished. Adam, obviously, had no existence prior to his creation, but Christ eternally existed prior to his birth. It is a most vivid term to describe the humiliation of the Incarnation. It parallels closely Paul's great Incarnation passage that declares that Christ, being in the form of God, "made himself of no reputation" (Philippians 2:6-7). The word translated "a little lower" can be a temporal as well as a spatial word. The idea is that for a little while God positioned His Son beneath the status of angels. The humiliation element of the Incarnation was not forever. It lasted only long enough for Christ to perform the necessary obedience to merit and restore life to the race of which He was the Head, the second Adam. In this temporary humiliation He, "by the grace of God," tasted "death for every man" (Hebrews 2:9).

Unlike the first Adam who had the glory and lost it, the second Adam started in humiliation and regained the honor and glory. The logic and order of verse 5 parallel Paul's in Philippians 2. After Christ humbled Himself, becoming obedient unto death, God highly exalted Him. Similarly, Peter saw in the resurrection, Ascension, and Session of Christ at God's right hand that Christ and the angels were again both in their right place (I Peter 3:21-22). That all things are put under His feet pictures triumphant victory: all power and authority belong to Christ. He earned it and He deserves it. Paul applied this merited exaltation both to Christ's mediatorial kingship over His church (Ephesians 1) and to the end of time when the last enemy, death itself, is destroyed (I Corinthians 15). While the specific details may not be as obvious in Psalm 8 as in the New Testament, the essential theology is the same. The Messiah as the Ideal Man was and is something to sing about: Joy to the world! The Lord is come.

Christic: *The Resolute Servant*

The New Testament confirms the messianic significance of Psalm 16. On the day of Pentecost, Peter appealed to Psalm 16:8-11 as his proof text for the resurrection of Jesus Christ. In so doing, he made it clear that David was a prophet who knew full well that he was writing about Christ (Acts 2:25-31). Similarly, Paul appealed to Psalm 16:10 as proof of Christ's resurrection, making it clear that the statement had no reference at all to David, whose dead body stayed buried and saw corruption (Acts 13:35-36). In the light of that inspired authority and confirmation, there can be no doubt that at least verses 8-11 have direct and unique reference to Jesus Christ. The question is whether the first seven verses are also messianic or whether there is a jump from David to his greater Son between verse 7 and 8.

We need to be aware that such jumps do occur (see Psalm 40), but I would suggest that the entirety of Psalm 16 refers to Christ. I do not see anything in the Psalm that requires a transition from David to Christ or that does not have legitimate messianic relevance. I am happy to admit that there are statements in the Psalm that can in some circumstances apply to all believers. That should not surprise us in view of the fact that Christ's humanity was a real humanity and that He endured and experienced the stuff of life. It is always good for us to see our union with Christ and His identification with us. But the purpose of our study is to find Christ, not ourselves. So I want to highlight some of the salient lessons about the Savior throughout the Psalm.

Although the term "Servant" does not occur in the song, the thing that impresses me most about the song as a whole is the absolute resolve and determination of Christ to fulfill His mission in submission to the Lord. Although it was the prophet David who wrote down the words, this Psalm records for us the mind of Christ Himself: how He viewed His God, His people, and His mission.

Christ and His God

The first lesson concerns Christ's view of God. As the Messiah, He trusted the Lord, depending on Him and delighting in His will. The opening petition for preservation was a prayer that God might watch over Him, guarding and keeping Him as a shepherd would his sheep (verse 1). How often from the manger to Gethsemane did the Father answer that prayer as the Lord Jesus was delivered over and over again from the plots of rulers, anger of crowds, and onslaughts from the devil himself? The analogy of Scripture not only parallels this theme of divine preservation of the Messiah but also warrants our seeing Christ in this Psalm as God's Servant. According to Isaiah, the Lord said to the Servant, "In an acceptable time have I heard thee, and in a day of salvation have I helped thee: and I will preserve thee, and give thee for a covenant of the people, to establish the earth, to cause to inherit the desolate heritages" (Isaiah 49:8; see also 42:6). That Christ regarded the Lord as His portion and the One who maintained or held firmly His lot in life also expressed His conscious sense of dependence on God (verse 5). This language links Christ with the priesthood, whose only inheritance was the Lord (Deuteronomy 18:2). What the Levites imperfectly typified, Christ fulfilled perfectly. Ironically, He who created the world, while in the world, had no place even to lay His head. But daily He knew the fellowship and communion of His Father.

Most outstanding is Christ's determination to do the will of God. The emphasis parallels other clear messianic statements. In another place Christ testified, "In the volume of the book it is written of me, I delight to do thy will, O my God: yea, thy law is within my heart" (Psalm

40:7-8). Although somewhat difficult to translate, the closing line of Psalm 16:2 is a synopsis testimony of Christ's total commitment to God. Let me offer this translation: "You are the Lord, my happiness is not in addition to you." The sense is simply that Christ found His contentment in and directed His goodness to the Lord only. With unrelenting resolve, Christ set Himself to accomplish the purpose for which He came into the world. As the Ideal Prophet, daily He received His instructions from the Lord: "I will bless the Lord, who hath given me counsel: my reins also instruct me in the night seasons" (Psalm 16:7). Compare this verse with another of Isaiah's Servant Songs for this same focus: "The Lord God hath given me the tongue of the learned…he wakeneth morning by morning, he wakeneth mine ear to hear as the learned. The Lord God hath opened mine ear, and I was not rebellious, neither turned away back" (Isaiah 50:4, 5). Just as God's instruction to the Servant was followed with perfect and resolute obedience, so in this Psalm the counsel is followed with the inflexible determination to keep the Lord's presence and purpose foremost (verse 8). I think you can see that once we factor in the messianic theology we know and plug in the parallel passages, it is not difficult to see the messianic relevance.

Christ and His People

The second lesson concerns Christ's view of His people. Two statements in particular stand out: verse 3 and verse 6. From verse 3 we learn that what Christ did in fulfilling the will of God (verse 2), He did with *respect* to or in *reference* to His people: "To the saints that are in the earth, and to the excellent, in whom is all my delight." The saints are the holy ones, those who are set apart as the beneficiaries of the mediatorial work of Christ: those who are saved. The term "excellent" further defines the saints as those who enjoy special rank and privilege of position. The point is very simply that Christ's people are special to Him. I suggest that at least in part it was the sight of His people that constituted "the joy that was set before him" as He endured the shame and suffering of the cross (Hebrews 12:2).

From verse 6 we learn that Christ was confident that a people had been given to him and that therefore His mission would not be in vain: "The lines are fallen unto me in pleasant places; yea, I have a goodly heritage." Notwithstanding the frequent use of this verse in testimony meetings expressing thanks to God for station in life, the messianic significance of this verse takes us right back to the eternal promise to Christ that He would see His seed (Isaiah 53:10) and have His own house, "whose house are we" (Hebrews 3:6). The word "line" designates a rope or a cord and refers to an allotment that would be marked off by the measuring cord. According to Deuteronomy 32:9, "the Lord's portion is his people; Jacob is the lot of his inheritance." Similarly, in Psalm 2 the Lord offered the heathen and the uttermost part of the earth to Messiah as His inheritance and possession. That is precisely the idea in this context. His saints and excellent ones are His inheritance who will populate His glorious kingdom. Believers have a part in verse 6 after all: we are the goodly heritage. That is a blessing that far exceeds any temporal placement in this life.

Christ and His Mission

The third lesson concerns Christ's view of His mission. This brings us specifically to the portions used in the New Testament. Christ knew from before His Incarnation the direction and the end of His mission. He knew that glory would certainly follow His obedient humiliation and atoning death. According to verse 9, He rejoiced and confidently rested in that certain hope. Verses 10 and 11 fix on two essential elements in Christ's exaltation: the resurrection and the Session at God's right hand. Although this Psalm does not explicitly refer to Messiah's death, the simple fact that Christ expresses His confidence in a sure resurrection presupposes His knowledge of an antecedent death. In Chapter 7, dealing with word prophecy, I explained verse 10 in some detail so I will not repeat that analysis. Remember that the proper definition of "soul" and "hell," the poetic structure, and the New Testament all require this verse to be an explicit declaration of the bodily resurrection of the Messiah from the grave. It has unique reference to Jesus. Verse 11 ends this prophetic prayer of Christ with His glorious presence at the right hand of God. We refer to this as the Session of Christ. This is the place of the present mediatorial work of Christ as He represents His people, having guarnateed for them an entrance to where He is. The reference to the path of life that the Lord showed Him from death to glory is the way that will be followed by all His believing people. As the Firstfruit of the resurrection, He is the surety of our resurrection. He is the Way, the Truth, and the Life.

Every believer will share in the earned pleasures and glory of Christ, the Savior. But sorrow awaits those who reject Christ for some other god. With sobering words, Christ declares that He will provide neither a sacrifice nor a prayer for those who reject Him (verse 4). This is not a happy note in this song, but it is one that must be sounded loudly by every believer. We must issue the warning and offer the invitation to sinners to come to our wonderful Savior.

Christ: The Suffering and Successful Savior

Psalm 22 is one of the places in Scripture that demand the removal of our shoes because we are on holy ground. This has been appropriately labeled the Crucifixion Psalm or the Psalm of the Cross. It is hard to imagine that any Christian, regardless of the degree of spiritual acumen, could come to this Song without being confronted in some way or to some extent with thoughts of the suffering Savior. As a preacher and teacher, I confess that this is one of those places that on the surface seem so easy to preach or teach yet defy every effort to scale their height or plumb their depth. In this venue, I cannot begin to give a full exposition of the Psalm, but I can suggest some things to consider and meditate on as you read and study this Song. I would recommend that you just take your time and let the wonder of it all sink in.

This Psalm is messianic from beginning to end. It divides into two main parts, marked by a significant transition statement in verse 21. The first division concerns the Suffering Savior (1-21); the second division concerns the Successful Savior (22-31). Perhaps because the details of the suffering are so explicit and because they parallel so closely the Gospel narratives of the crucifixion, the first division is better known. But the second division finishes the gospel theology by moving to the resurrection and beyond. Its focus is not so much on the events of the exaltation but rather on its saving implications.

Between the suffering and the success is a one-word transition: "You answered me." It's one word in Hebrew, anyway. I would translate verse 21 like this: "Deliver me from the mouth of the lion and from the horns of the wild oxen. You have answered me." Admittedly, this translation ignores the parallelism in the verse itself, but it highlights the shift from the series of imperatives to the indicative verb. A contrast occurs. I believe that logically, as well as grammatically, the last word is set off from the preceding petitions that begin in verse 19. The

311

Lord expresses His confidence that His prayers have been heard and then in the next section begins to detail the answer to those prayers. It becomes clear in the second division that all the suffering of the first division was not in vain. As you meditate your way through this Psalm, do so with what should become an overwhelming impression that you are reading what the blessed Savior said, thought, and prayed while He was suffering vicariously for His people on the cross. The New Testament reveals that the initial lament was audible: "My God, my God, why hast thou forsaken me?" (see Matthew 27:46; Mark 15:34). There is no indication that men could hear the rest of the prayer, but God heard. In this Psalm, we are allowed into the mind and soul of the Savior. You can see why I say that this is holy ground.

The Suffering Savior

The first division highlights three spheres of suffering endured by the Savior. He suffered before the holy God (1-5), by cruel men (6-11), and in His whole person, body and soul (12-18). The opening stanza brings us to the heart of the atonement. The simple answer to Christ's agonizing question "Why hast thou forsaken me?" is that God forsook His Son in order that He might forgive us. With our sin and guilt imputed to Him, He who knew no sin, having become sin for us, took the full force of God's just and necessary wrath against our sin. While Christ was suffering on the cross, God dealt with Him in terms of us. I confess a total inability to explain the utter dereliction of Christ that is expressed by this statement. It boggles the mind. It declares how absolutely offensive sin is to the holiness of God and how absolutely gracious God is in giving His dear Son to be the only Savior. How dare any man say that there is any other way to God!

The second stanza testifies to the cruelty of spiritually blind men who can look directly at the cross and reject the Savior. Note how closely Isaiah 53 echoes the language of verse 6 that describes the natural perception of Christ by unbelievers. He was despised and rejected, a man of sorrows indeed. Note how closely Matthew 27 and Luke 23 reflect the actual taunts of verses 7 and 8 made by the spectators, religious leaders, and soldiers surrounding the cross. He, who had heard the praise of pure angels, on the cross endured the mockery of puny men. Whether then or now, it is impossible to look at the cross of Christ without some reaction. Better to kiss the Son as Psalm 2 recommended than to join the mockery and unbelief that doom the soul to destruction.

The final stanza vividly describes the immense agony Christ experienced on the cross. Part of the agony was in His innermost being as the bestial crowd hurled their hatred toward Him. Described as strong bulls (12), roaring lions (13), starving, mangy, wild dogs (16), and wild oxen (21), the crowd inflicted pain that whips and nails could not. Part of the agony was physical torture that defies comprehension. He was exhausted with burning anguish (14); His bones were disjointed (14) and his body stretched (17); He endured intolerable thirst (15); His hands and feet were pierced (16). Adding insult to all the immense injury was the fact that He was totally naked in public shame. They took His garments and cast lots for the meager robe, His last material possession (18). When Adam and Eve brought the curse, plunging the race into sin, God in His grace provided garments to cover the shame of their nakedness. On the cross, the Lord Jesus in reversing the curse was void of even that token of God's grace. He paid the price of sin in complete shame. Yet I see a twofold irony in His nakedness. On the one hand, while He was naked He wove for us a garment of salvation, clothing us with a robe of righteousness (Isaiah 61:10). On the other hand, what appeared to be an evidence of defeat was in reality the ultimate victory. It was normal procedure for soldiers to cast lots to divide the spoils of those they had conquered. But this booty was so paltry that sharing it would give them nothing. So they cast lots to see who would take the whole prize. It seemed as though wicked men had won the day against Christ. The irony is that in His death Christ won the day. The cross crushed the serpent's head, and in just three days the victory over death and Satan would be declared by the resurrection of Christ from the grave.

The Successful Savior

The second division reveals a most obvious shift from suffering agony to joyous celebration. Even as He suffered and died, the Savior was confident of the success of His mission. The joy was always before Him. His success is the subject of praise (22-24). It is significant that the first statement of the Savior's activity is that He declared God's name. Declaring God's name is prophet work. Remember that the Lord Jesus had staked His entire reputation and Messiahship on His prophecy that God would raise Him from the dead. The resurrection sealed and confirmed Jesus Christ as the Ideal Prophet. His life after death was the ultimate answer to all His prayers and petitions for deliverance (Hebrews 5:7). What a message this was to proclaim to His brethren (see Hebrews 2:12 for the unmistakable reference to Christ). The entire congregation of those who feared the Lord joined in praising God for the answered prayer in delivering the Suffering Savior from His affliction, from death to life.

His success is also the surety of life for His people (25-29). In a most remarkable statement, the Savior pledges to fulfill His vows to those who fear the Lord. Verses 26 and 27 define the vow: He promises life and satisfaction to all throughout the world who will seek and turn to the Lord. Eating is a common image in both Testaments to picture the personal appropriation of faith. Just as eating sustains life and brings physical satisfaction, so faith in Christ brings life and spiritual satisfaction. Christ said that those who eat and drink of Him will never hunger or thirst again. Finding satisfaction and life in Christ is vital because "none can keep alive his own soul" (verse 29).

The climactic statement of His success is that there is a guaranteed seed (30-31). The seed that the Father had promised Him (Isaiah 53:10) will in fact serve Him. Although the seed is fixed by promise, the means of claiming that seed for Christ is equally fixed. God's plan for claiming the seed revealed here parallels God's plan explained by Paul in Romans 10. Faith comes by hearing the Word of God, and the normal way of hearing the Word of God comes via evangelists. These are not necessarily professional preachers or evangelists, but rather all those who themselves have heard and believed and consequently have the life-giving message for others. So according to this passage, the message concerning the Lord will be recounted (repeatedly told) to the generation. The word "generation" designates contemporaries of any particular span of life. The declaring of His righteousness to a people not yet born (this refers to us, you know) suggests that every generation has the duty and privilege to pass on the gospel truth to the next. The message for the future people was simply "he hath done." That says it all. Whatever had to be done for the salvation of guilty sinners, the Suffering and Successful Savior did. On the cross, He declared, "It is finished," and it was. Nothing else need be or can be done to add to the work of Christ. To realize that we are part of that unborn people in the mind and heart of Christ on the cross and destined to hear the message of Christ is an overwhelmingly thrilling thought. Ought it not compel us to tell our generation the good news that Jesus saves?

Christ: The King and Priest

If Psalm 22 is holy ground, Psalm 110 is the Grand Canyon. Spurgeon called his commentary on the Psalms *The Treasury of David*. That title could stand well over this one Psalm. Applying virtually every one of our interpretation principles for identifying messianic Psalms points our attention in this Psalm directly to Jesus Christ. The New Testament quotes Psalm 110 more than any other single text in the Old Testament, fourteen times. In each instance, it applies the Psalm to Christ. This Psalm is a compendium of theological truths concerning the person and mediatorial operation of Christ, from His place in the Trinity to His Royal Priesthood to His final triumph over every enemy. The argument of this Psalm flows from the two propositions in verses 1 and 4, the verses most frequently quoted in the New Testament.

Kingship

The first proposition is that *Christ is king*. Three issues about Christ and His kingship stand out in this section: who He is, where He is, and what He does. The opening words identify Christ: "The oracle of Jehovah to my Sovereign." This literal translation highlights some important truths. The word "oracle" is more common to the prophets than poets, but here David speaks with prophetic authority as he records the communication between Jehovah and His Son, David's superior Seed. The particular form "my Lord," which I translated "my Sovereign," is key to the argument and an essential point in some of the New Testament quotations. There is a subtle, yet significant difference between this form and the form that invariably refers to deity. The word *Adonai* always refers to God, including Christ specifically. In other words, when Messiah is identified as *Adonai*, it is always evidence of His deity. The word here is *Adoni*, not a big difference. Even though this form does not necessarily designate deity, it does designate one who is the superior owner and master. For David, the king and the highest superior on earth, to acknowledge One to be his Superior and Master and Sovereign was an expression of his faith in the covenant promise that the Ideal King coming through his family line was indeed the Messiah. Note that this form (*Adoni*) does not preclude the deity of David's confessed Sovereign. That is just not the point he is making here. Instead, here is the point that Christ focused on in one of His contests with the Jewish religious leaders to prove His Messiahship and to prove that David knew it. His logic was irrefutable (Matthew 22:41-46). Who is Christ? He is David's King, the one, true Mediatorial King.

Jehovah's word to Christ answers the question of where He is: He is sitting at the right hand of God. God's right hand is a unique position of honor, exaltation, and majesty. Theologically, this refers to Christ's Session. It is a position that He earned by His mediatorial obedience (parallel this to Philippians 2:6-11). The New Testament often links this to the fact that Christ successfully dealt with sin by His vicarious, finished, and accepted sacrifice, as well as to His current and effective intercession for His people. Having been raised from the dead and having ascended on high, He sat down at the right hand of God. That He sat down suggests that the work of redemption was done. That He sat down at the right hand suggests that the work was well done.

What Christ does is rule. This is what kings do. His Session is not passive. Although there is an eschatological aspect to His kingship, the focus in this first section seems to be on His present rule. His ruling from His place of honor will continue until every enemy becomes His footstool. The Psalmist is presenting the relatively common contemporary image of a conqueror with his foot resting on the neck of a defeated enemy as a gesture of victory. That He is ruling with His royal scepter (the rod of thy strength) in the midst of His enemies indicates that all the enemies are not yet subdued, but that they most certainly will be (see I Corinthians 15:24). Although I believe the day will come when Christ will rule personally from earthly Zion, the reference to Zion in this context seems to identify the place of His current throne, the heavenly city (see Hebrews 12:22).

Proverbs 14:28 says that "in the multitude of people is the king's honour." The Psalmist, therefore, fittingly draws special attention to those who are ruled by the messianic King. The contrast between His subjects is significant: they are either enemies or a willing people. He rules and conquers either by grace or in wrath, but He certainly rules and conquers. Again we see that His kingdom is not a democracy. Even if all the specific images used to describe the willing people are not immediately clear, the overall message is transparent. Grace transforms enemies of Christ into soldiers of Christ. Every believer can well sing, "What a wonderful change in my life has been wrought, since Jesus came into my heart." Having Christ ruling from the heart is eternally better than having His foot on the neck.

Priesthood

The second proposition is that *Christ is priest*. If nothing else does, this confirms the unique messianic identification in this Psalm. One of the most conclusive of our messianic clues is the uniting of the kingly and priestly offices. After the establishment of the official Aaronic priesthood and official Davidic kingship, the offices of king and priest were distinct. Only in the Ideal King and Ideal Priest would these two mediatorial operations be united in a single person. Therefore, whenever and wherever we see the King/Priest, we can be sure that in some way we are looking at Christ.

Psalm 110:4 is a theological benchmark in Old Testament revelation. It resolves the paradox of how one person could fulfill these two offices that up to this point were represented by two distinct tribes and families. How could Messiah be from the tribes of Levi and Judah at the same time? Obviously, He could not. In the discussion of typology, I suggested that from the beginning of Aaron's priesthood the Lord had built in some factors that pointed to the obsolescence of Aaron's temporary priesthood. Remember that Genesis with its record of Abraham's encounter with Melchizedek was written to the same people at about the same time as the details establishing and explaining the Levitical priesthood. From the beginning, God made it clear that there was a priesthood superior to Aaron's. Just in case Israel or readers of Scripture missed the subtlety of that connection, Psalm 110:4 flat out says it. David, at least, under inspiration, understood and declared that the Messiah's priesthood was not after Aaron's order, but after Melchizedek's. All you have to do to see the importance of this benchmark declaration is to read the book of Hebrews.

Three important elements of Christ's priesthood are presented in verse 4. First, Christ is a priest on the authority of God's irrevocable decree. What God says without oath is both sure and steadfast. For

God to swear is to heighten and intensify beyond description the certainty of what He says. The certainty of the decree is strengthened even more by the promise that He will not repent, which simply means that He will never regret His decision or change His immutable mind. This stands as a stern warning against attempts to approach God apart from this one and only Priest whom He has chosen and ordained.

Second, Christ is a priest forever. Unlike Aaron, Christ would not be the head of a dynasty of priests. None would follow Him, because His priesthood was perfect and effective. Hebrews explains the significance of this far better than I can: "But this man, because he continueth ever, hath an unchangeable priesthood [i.e., not transferable, not to be passed to another]. Wherefore he is able also to save them to the uttermost [i.e., completely and finally] that come unto God by him, seeing he ever liveth to make intercession for them" (Hebrews 7:24-25). This is something that Aaron could not do.

Third, Christ is a priest after a special order. He is like Melchizedek. Apart from the historical introduction of Melchizedek in Genesis 14, Psalm 110 is the only other Old Testament reference to him. The book of Hebrews, however, expands and explains why and how Melchizedek's priesthood was so superior to Aaron's and why it prefigured so well the priesthood of Christ. I noted in the discussion on typology that Melchizedek conveyed something about the Ideal Priesthood that Aaron could never do. The Ideal Priest would also be the Ideal King, the King of righteousness and of peace. Following the order of Melchizedek resolves the tension between kingly and priestly functions that could not be resolved outside of Jesus Christ. Not only is the union of the two offices in a single person unique to Christ, but so is the union of the two virtues. The name Melchizedek literally means "king of righteousness," and according to the Genesis record, he was the king of Salem, which means "peace."

That "just happened" to be his name and the name of his domain, but his antitype, the Lord Jesus, was the embodiment and achiever of both righteousness and peace. That is a most amazing combination of virtues when we realize that righteousness and peace have not coexisted in any man since the Fall. Man's unrighteousness renders peace with God impossible. But in the perfect Man, the perfect Priest who represents His people, "mercy and truth are met together; righteousness and peace have kissed each other" (Psalm 85:10). That beautiful statement may have other implications, but it certainly sums up the essence of Christ's "Melchizedekian" priesthood.

Perhaps to emphasize that this decreed Priest of verse 4 is the same exalted King of verse 1, the activity of the Priest delineated in the closing verses relates more to kingly operations and than to priestly functions. Whereas verses 2 and 3 seem to describe aspects of Christ's present rule, verses 5-7 seem to jump ahead to the final eschatological contests in which every last one of His enemies becomes His footstool. It reminds me of the book of Revelation, which links those final judgments with the wrath of the Lamb. These verses put in boldface His just and thorough wrath against His enemies. The language is graphic and fearfully wonderful. According to verse 5, in the day of His wrath, He with the Lord at His right hand will irreversibly beat into pieces the opposing kings. According to verse 6, He will execute justice on sinners, heaping up their dead bodies in rotting piles—not a pretty picture.

But most significantly, He will "wound the heads over many countries." Interestingly, the word "wound" is the same word translated "strike through" in verse 5. Since the word literally means to beat into pieces, this would be, to say the least, a fatal blow or wound. Also noteworthy is the fact that the word "heads" is actually the singular form "head." I don't think I am going too far in identifying this head as Satan himself, who in that last day gathers the nations in his last-ditch effort against Christ (see Revelation 20:7-10). Not only does this point ahead to that future and final victory over Satan, but it also points back to that first gospel promise that the Seed of the woman would crush or pulverize the head of the serpent (Genesis 3:15). Isn't it thrilling how everything ties together in God's Word?

Finally, verse 7 describes Christ's ultimate victory. Having crushed Satan's head, He lifts up His own head in triumph and glory. With His head held high, He rests His feet. Certainly, those who have in grace already submitted to this King/Priest can rejoice and lift up their heads with Him, knowing that their redemption draws nigh (Luke 21:28). This Psalm stands as testimony that Christ will fulfill every mediatorial duty necessary for our salvation. It also stands as a warning to sinners who have not submitted to Him to submit before His mercy gives way to wrath.

Many more Psalms either in part or in whole, in fact or in type, direct attention to Christ. No matter what your normal Bible reading and study schedule is, it would be good to include the Psalms on a daily basis. With your heart open and your messianic clues in hand or in mind, it will not be long before you find something about Christ. When you find him, remember that you have found Him in the book of worship and song. May Christ, indeed, be the theme of your song.

CONCLUSION

If you are like me, this may be the first thing in the book you are reading. We expect a conclusion to tell us something about the premise, scope, and plan of the book. Recognizing this tendency, I will, therefore, offer a brief synopsis of what I have done. After that I will make some concluding remarks that are corollary to this study.

Summary

The theme of this book is simply finding Christ in the Old Testament, and the purpose is to establish and illustrate the necessary principles of interpretation for discovering what the Old Testament reveals about Christ. Recognizing that not every student of the Bible has the same level of experience or background in theological study, the same hermeneutical skills, or any knowledge of the biblical languages (Hebrew, Aramaic, and Greek), I have tried to deal with these issues from the layman's perspective. The Bible is God's Word, a wonderful gift He has given not just to the scholar or preacher but to us all. My underlying premise for this study and indeed for my entire ministry is that the Bible is the inspired, infallible, authoritative, and powerful Word of God. It is a Book to be taken seriously and studied well; it is the only guide both for faith (what we are to believe) and for practice (how we are to behave).

If we are going to understand the Bible, it helps, as it does regarding any book, to know its central theme and primary purpose. On the authority of the words of the Lord Jesus Christ Himself (Luke 24:25-47), I suggest that Christ is the central theme and message of all Scripture, including the Old Testament. This does not mean that He is the only theme, but it does mean that in one way or another every other theme and topic addressed in Scripture relates in some way to Christ. It means that every other theme can be interpreted, understood and applied properly only in the light of Christ. That's what being a central theme means. I suggest that the overall purpose of the Scripture as God's special revelation is to reveal to men doomed by the curse of sin the only way of escape from that curse: salvation in, through, and because of Jesus Christ. There are many corollaries to this general theme and purpose, all of which declare God's glory, but we have to face it: without the Scripture, God is still glorified, but man is hopelessly lost.

321

So if Christ is the central theme of Scripture, it is imperative to find Him when reading and studying the Bible. Realistically, I have to admit that it is easier to find Christ in the New Testament than in the Old. That fact is more than obvious, seeing that the New Testament was written after the Lord Jesus had come to earth to accomplish His saving work and that the Old Testament could only look forward to His coming. Although not as apparent on the surface, Christ is the message of the Old Testament. My objective has been to show how and where the Old Testament reveals Christ, the Messiah. Finding Christ in the Old Testament is finding the life of the Old Testament; it is what gives life to what otherwise seems to be dry and outdated.

Part 1

In the first part of the book, I simply identify who Christ is. A significant part of the difficulty in finding Christ in the Old Testament is not knowing precisely whom or what we are looking for. If we have a profile of Christ that we can use as we read the Old Testament, it will help guide us and stop us at those places where Christ is in focus. In the first three chapters, I identify some key clues that will help us to find Christ. In this section, the New Testament is freely used to make the theological portrait of Christ as detailed and nearly complete as possible. If we know whom we are looking for, we will know it when we find Him. We want to use all the data available to make sure that we know as much about Him as we can. We do not want to miss Him anywhere.

Chapter 1 discusses the meaning and significance of the term "Messiah." "Messiah" is the Hebrew term for "Christ"; both words mean "anointed" and refer to a person who has been anointed. The term "Messiah" sums up the entire mediatorial work of the Lord Jesus as the God-ordained and God-anointed Prophet, Priest, and King. Knowing what prophets, priests, and kings are and what they do provides key clues in identifying the Lord Jesus as the ideal, perfect, and ultimately one and only Mediator between God and men. Even in places where the Old Testament does not actually use the word "Messiah," we can find Christ by recognizing the functions of His mediatorial offices. The purpose of this chapter is to identify the significance and functions of prophets, priests, and kings so that they become effective pointers to Christ.

Chapter 2 discusses the person of Christ. Christ is a unique Person. His uniqueness consists of the union of the divine and human natures in one person. He is the God/Man. The Second Person of the Trinity is completely God: everything God is, the eternal Son of God is. The eternal Son of God in the fullness of time became man. He took to Himself a perfect, pre-fallen humanity, and from then until forever He continues as God and Man in two distinct natures, yet one person. That God was manifested in the flesh stands wonderfully and inexplicably as the great mystery of godliness. Although the mechanics of the Incarnation defy human understanding and explanation, the fact of it makes Christ easy to spot. Only the Lord Jesus Christ is the God/Man. Therefore, when we see evidences of deity and evidences of humanity linked in a single individual, we know that that person must be Christ. In this chapter, I consider the biblical and theological data that prove that Christ is both God and Man. The purpose of this chapter is to identify the characteristics of deity and humanity so that they become effective pointers to Christ.

Chapter 3 discusses the work of Christ. My premise is that it is possible to identify people by what they do. A person's work says something about him, even if the person himself is not directly in view. Seeing the work makes us think of the person. As the eternal Son of God, Christ participates in certain works that are unique to Deity and the Godhead generally: creation, providence, and miracles. As the Son of Man, Christ shares behavior that is common to humanity. The unique works of God and the common features of humanity when applied to Christ testify to His uniqueness as the God/Man, but they do not necessarily identify Him particularly. There are certain works, however, that only Christ does. There are certain works that only Christ can do correctly. In this chapter, I consider the special works of Christ that He performed during the years of His first advent, is currently performing at His Session at God's right hand, and will perform at His Second Advent. The purpose of this chapter is to identify these special works so that they become effective pointers to Christ.

Part 2

Part 1 identifies whom we are looking for; Part 2 identifies where to look. With the messianic "profile" in mind, we have a list of clues to use in our search for Christ in the Old Testament. Using those clues, the analogy of Scripture, and sound canonical and contextual consideration should identify texts that transcend any application other than to Christ. Part 2 constitutes the principal part as I suggest the key places where we can expect to find Christ. Our chances of finding Christ increase the more we know what He looks like and where He tends to be. To our advantage also is the fact that Christ is not hiding from us. Searching for Him in the Old Testament is not a game of hide and seek. If we are paying attention, it will be as though He is standing out in the open, waving His hands at us to see. Many do not see Christ in the Old Testament for the simple reason that they are not looking for Him. Here is a summary of some of the places you can be sure to find the Lord Jesus.

Chapter 4 discusses the revelation of Christ in the covenants. A covenant is a mutually binding agreement between two parties and is at the heart of God's gracious provision of salvation for sinners. Beginning with Adam and Eve and ending with the fulfillment and continuing application of the New Covenant ratified by the blood of the Lord Jesus Christ, God has graciously bound Himself to covenant promise, thereby guaranteeing the reversal of the curse and the reclamation of repentant and believing sinners. Christ was the essence and center of every covenant institution. Each covenant renewal advanced revelation about the Messiah and narrowed the identity of the promised Seed. In many ways, the covenant promise of Christ is the theological thread that ties all the Old Testament together and links it necessarily to the New. Finding Christ in the covenants is a sure thing.

Chapter 5 discusses the revelation of Christ in His pre-incarnate personal appearances. From time to time in the Old Testament dispensation, generally at times of crisis, the eternal Son of God actually and visibly appeared on earth. These pre-incarnate appearances are called Christophanies. The most common manifestation of this special appearance was in the person of the Angel of the Lord, the Messenger who is Jehovah. It is vital to note, even in summary, that in these personal appearances it only seemed as though He was man. The Son of God did not take to Himself the human nature until the Incarnation. These mysterious and temporary appearances hinted at the inexplicable Trinity and offered remarkable aids to faith to those

Old Testament saints who did not have all the Scripture that we have. The Christophanies provided a visible token and foretaste of Christ's mediatorial work as the Ideal Prophet, Priest, and King. Finding Christ in the Christophanies is a sure thing.

Chapter 6 discusses the revelation of Christ in His names. The names or titles of God generally and of Christ specifically are important means whereby God revealed truth about Himself or Christ. The names of God and Christ are never used haphazardly or casually; they are always an integral part of the revelation. These titles always communicate some essential truth about Christ's person, work, or perfections. It is important not to treat these simply as labels of identification, but to stop, define, and factor in the definition of those labels to the overall context of the passage. Finding Christ and learning about Him in His names is always a sure thing.

Chapter 7 discusses the revelation of Christ in predictive prophecy. Although the Old Testament of necessity predicted the advents of Christ and the attendant circumstances of those advents, it never predicted that Christ would someday in the future become the object of saving faith. My point is simply that whether before or after the Incarnation, Christ has always been the only object of saving faith. The Old Testament saint believed in a Christ who was certain to come and perform the saving work; the New Testament saint believes in a Christ who has certainly come and performed the saving work. Both they and we believe in a Christ who is knowable only on the basis of God's Word. I contend that God's predictive Word is just as reliable and fixed as His historical Word. But word prophecy is different from word history and it requires certain interpretation skills and principles. After discussing the nature and purpose of predictive prophecy, I deal with some of the great predictive passages in the Old Testament that in remarkable detail preview and provide an overview of aspects of Christ's first and Second Comings as well as His current work in His heavenly Session. Finding Christ in word prophecy is a sure thing.

Chapters 8 and 9 discuss the revelation of Christ in types, what I call picture prophecies. The interpretation of types has suffered by extremes. On the one hand are those who are guided and limited only by their imaginations as they multiply types in an attempt to rescue and salvage a relevant message from some obscure Old Testament text. On the other hand are those who because of their suspicion of the others are reluctant to recognize types at all. They tend to limit meaning to the text's surface. In Chapter 8 I try to resolve some of the hermeneutical tension by explaining what types are and offering some sensible, objective guidelines for interpreting types. Basically, types are divinely appointed analogies or object lessons that point upward to spiritual truth and forward to the ultimate reality. They are beautiful but imperfect pictures of the infinitely more beautiful and perfect reality. Throughout the Old Testament and particularly in the complex ceremonies revealed to Moses, God used these predictive object lessons to point to the Messiah. The simple fact that they are picture prophecies of Jesus Christ explains immediately why the ceremonies are no longer operative: they are fulfilled prophecies. In Chapter 9 I select a few examples of types to illustrate the techniques of interpretation as well as the significant lessons they teach about Christ. The Old Testament points to Christ by typical people, things, and events. Admittedly, the process of recognizing and interpreting types requires a little more thinking and overall awareness of the revelation that precedes the type, but figuring out the points of correspondence between the picture analogy and Christ still supplies significant information about Christ and His work. The discontinuation of the type does not annul the truth it conveyed. Finding Christ in picture prophecy is a sure thing.

Chapter 10 discusses the revelation of Christ in worship. The Book of Psalms is the divinely inspired songbook of the Old Testament: it reveals the "how-to" of worship. The message of the songs transcends the ancient and forgotten tunes and defines the patterns for prayer and praise that are pleasing and acceptable before the Lord. Although the Psalms reveal much about proper worship, they make clear that attention to Christ is an essential element of worship, whether private or public. There is hardly a truth about Christ and His work that does not find some expression in the Psalms. Christ was the theme of song, and the Psalms were an effective means of keeping the messianic hope before the worshipping people. In this chapter, I suggest some principles for identifying messianic Psalms and offer a synopsis of selected Psalms that unmistakably point to Jesus Christ. Finding Christ in the Psalms is a sure thing.

CONCLUSION

Final Thoughts

How many Christians today handle the Old Testament is tragic. They either totally ignore it or read it out of a sense of guilty obligation. To many Christians, the Old Testament is often nothing more than a source for ancient biographies that may illustrate some exemplary character traits to emulate. It is often a smorgasbord of texts for special agendas: any text that proves the special interest point is taken and the rest is left. It is often lifted from its objective and intended meaning by those who mean well in their attempts to force Christian application into it. My contention is that there is a relevant message in the Old Testament that is discernible and discoverable by sound and sensible methods of interpretation that consider the full, not just the surface, meaning of the text. Although not in every line and perhaps not on every page, the message of Christ overshadows the entire Old Testament. Finding Christ is the key that both unlocks and locks in the message of the whole Word of God. Jesus Christ is God's final, perfect, incomparable Word. In the final analysis, it is safe to say that Jesus Christ is God's only Word for man. From man's first need of a Savior, God gave His word that there would be a Savior. From eternity God gave His only begotten Son, and into time that Son came to be the only Savior of sinners. The Bible is God's special revelation which directs sinners to Christ, guides believers in Christ, and warns against rejecting Christ. The Old Testament makes a vital contribution to that revelation.

Although I have taught New Testament and Greek courses over the years and have preached who knows how many messages from the New Testament, I have a special love for and interest in the Old Testament. In the good providence of God, my doctoral training was, and my principal ministry is, Old Testament study. It has been my desire and prayer over the years to generate that same interest and love for the Old Testament in my students and in all those I have had the privilege of serving in the ministry. I am convinced that a key factor in consistently reading and studying the Old Testament is the realization that it has a relevant Christian message. There is no relevant Christian message apart from Christ Himself. It has been my prayer from the beginning and throughout this project that God would use it to open eyes to see the Lord Jesus. If I can be a guide to finding Christ in the Old Testament, I give my humble thanks to the Lord.

About the Author

Michael P.V. Barrett (B.A., M.A., Ph.D.) has been a professor of Ancient Languages and Old Testament Theology and Interpretation at Bob Jones University since 1976.

He is an associate editor for the *Biblical Viewpoint*, the publication of the BJU seminary faculty.

He has also authored *Themes from the Old Testament* in the Bible Truths for Christian Schools, and co-authored *Old Testaments Poets and Prophets* for the Institute of Biblical Studies at Bob Jones University and the *Hebrew Handbook*, an elementary Hebrew grammar.

Dr. Barrett has also been the assistant minister at Faith Free Presbyterian Church since 1977.